1 YEAR UPGRADE
BUYER PROTECTION PLAN

PROGRAMMING
LEGO®
Mindstorms™
WITH Java

The ULTIMATE Tool
for Mindstorms
Maniacs!

Giulio Ferrari
Andy Gombos
Søren Hilmer
Jürgen Stuber
Mick Porter
Jamie Waldinger
Dario Laverde Technical Editor

KEY	SERIAL NUMBER
001	99K6GTTBE8
002	2WYH4RUJAZ
003	2QMJF6TVXD
004	3JHGF56YZP
005	S45TG2SP9U
006	5VGBBHWE44
007	6Y6Q4V9NFR
008	7MFGM99EFV
009	W3YHVDKPZ4
010	8GFHR5TNU8

PUBLISHED BY
Syngress Publishing, Inc.
800 Hingham Street
Rockland, MA 02370

Programming LEGO® MINDSTORMS™ with Java

Printed in the United States of America

  2 3 4 5 6 7 8 9 0

ISBN-13: 978-1-928994-55-8
ISBN-10: 1-928994-55-5

Technical Editor: Dario Laverde
Technical Reviewer: Simon Ritter
Acquisitions Editor: Catherine B. Nolan
Developmental Editor: Kate Glennon
CD Production: Michael Donovan

Cover Designer: Michael Kavish
Page Layout and Art by: Shannon Tozier
Copy Editor: Jesse Corbeil, Michael McGee
Indexer: J. Edmund Rush

Distributed by Publishers Group West in the United States and Jaguar Book Group in Canada.

Acknowledgments

We would like to acknowledge the following people for their kindness and support in making this book possible.

Karen Cross, Lance Tilford, Meaghan Cunningham, Kim Wylie, Harry Kirchner, Kevin Votel, Kent Anderson, Frida Yara, Bill Getz, Jon Mayes, John Mesjak, Peg O'Donnell, Sandra Patterson, Betty Redmond, Roy Remer, Ron Shapiro, Patricia Kelly, Andrea Tetrick, Jennifer Pascal, Doug Reil, and David Dahl of Publishers Group West for sharing their incredible marketing experience and expertise.

Jacquie Shanahan, AnnHelen Lindeholm, David Burton, Febea Marinetti, and Rosie Moss of Elsevier Science for making certain that our vision remains worldwide in scope.

Annabel Dent and Paul Barry of Elsevier Science/Harcourt Australia for all their help.

David Buckland, Wendi Wong, Marie Chieng, Lucy Chong, Leslie Lim, Audrey Gan, and Joseph Chan of Transquest Publishers for the enthusiasm with which they receive our books.

Kwon Sung June at Acorn Publishing for his support.

Ethan Atkin at Cranbury International for his help in expanding the Syngress program.

Jackie Gross, Gayle Voycey, Alexia Penny, Anik Robitaille, Craig Siddall, Darlene Morrow, Iolanda Miller, Jane Mackay, and Marie Skelly at Jackie Gross & Associates for all their help and enthusiasm representing our product in Canada.

Lois Fraser, Connie McMenemy, Shannon Russell and the rest of the great folks at Jaguar Book Group for their help with distribution of Syngress books in Canada.

Thank you to our hard-working colleagues at New England Fulfilment & Distribution who manage to get all our books sent pretty much everywhere in the world. Thank you to Debbie "DJ" Ricardo, Sally Greene, Janet Honaker, and Peter Finch.

A special thanks to Matt Gerber at Brickswest for his help and support for our books.

Contributors

Søren Hilmer (SCJP, SCJD, SCWCD) is Research and Development Manager at IT+, a company in the TietoEnator group. He currently works on security related projects involving Single Sign On. Søren holds a master's degree in computer science and a bachelor's degree in physics from the University of Århus. Søren has been giving talks on programming the RCX with Java, most notably at the JAOO conference in 2000 (www.jaoo.org). He has been programming in Java since 1996, at that time using Java for coding industrial control systems. Søren would like to dedicate his part of the book to his wonderful wife Joan and his children, Rebecca and Sebastian.

Giulio Ferrari works as a Software Developer at EDIS, a leader in publishing and finishing solution and promotional packaging. He studied engineering and economics at the University of Modena and Reggio Emilia, and in the past has developed applications, entertainment software, and Web sites for several companies. He is fond of physical and mathematical sciences, as well as of puzzles and games in general (he has a collection of 1500 dice of every kind and shape). Giulio co-authored the best-selling *Building Robots with LEGO Mindstorms* (Syngress Publishing, ISBN: 1-928994-67-9) with his brother, Mario and Ralph Hempel (technical editor), a book that has quickly become a fundamental reference and source of ideas for many LEGO robotics fans. He has been playing with LEGO bricks since he was very young, and his passion for robotics started in 1998, with the arrival of the MINDSTORMS series. From that moment on, he held an important place in the creation of the Italian LEGO community, ItLUG, now one of the largest and most important LEGO users group worldwide. He works in Modena, Italy, where he lives with his girlfriend, Marina.

Jamie Waldinger (SCJP) is a developer at Viant Corporation in Boston, where he develops Web-enabled systems for a global client base. He has coded in Java for three years, and holds a bachelor's degree in business from the University of Massachusetts. Jamie wishes to dedicate his portion of this book to his beautiful fiancée, Rory, and also both her and his loving parents for their endless support.

Jürgen Stuber is one of the administrators of the leJOS project and one of the few people who have worked on the internals of leJOS. Jürgen has made important contributions to the leJOS virtual machine, in particular fixes that made rotation sensors usable and that improved the speed of the main instruction loop. Jürgen holds a doctorate from the University of Saarbrücken, Germany. He is currently working as an INRIA postdoctoral fellow at the LORIA Research Institute for Computer Science in Nancy, France. His main research interests are theorem proving and term rewriting.

Mick Porter (SSJCP, MCP) is a Senior Technical Architect for Logica, a global systems integrator. Mick specializes in the design and implementation of wireless and mobile commerce systems. With 15 years of experience in the IT industry, Mick has worked on an enormous variety of systems and projects, and over the last few years, he has delivered a number of major e-commerce systems. Mick holds a bachelor's degree in computer science, and became a Sun Certified Java Programmer five years ago, as well as having passed eight Microsoft Certified Professional exams. Mick lives in Sydney, Australia, with his wife, Andrea and children, Holly and Anthony. Mick is glad that his children give him an excuse to play with LEGO again.

Andy Gombos is a sophomore at John Hardin High School. He has been programming in Java for four years, and started programming the RCX with TinyVM almost two years ago. He is the author of the leJOS Visual Interface and Simlink, two tools for leJOS. Andy wishes to thank his parents for their support, and Kevin Sheppard for providing him with software used.

Technical Editor

Dario Laverde is a freelance Java Software Architect. As the Vice President of System Architecture at PlayLink, Inc., a Java online games development company, he created the initial framework of the client/server architecture and graphical user interfaces. Prior to that he was a Senior Applications Developer at UGO, an online entertainment portal and InterWorld, an e-commerce software company where he developed online community software. He has programmed with Java for six years, and C++ for 10 years. Dario holds a bachelor's degree in electrical engineering from Manhattan College. He is the current Chair of C++ and Java SIG (Special Interest Group) of the NYPC Users Group.

Technical Reviewer

Simon Ritter (CNA, Certified Java Programmer) is a Technology Evangelist with Sun Microsystems, Inc. He currently assists developers in understanding the latest Java technologies being created by Sun Microsystems, both through presentations and publishing on the Web. His specialties include most areas of Java, from the Micro Edition through to the Enterprise Edition. Simon's background includes positions as a Senior Consultant at AT&T, UNIX System Labs, and Novell. He has worked for Sun since 1996 in roles covering Java development and consultancy. Simon has created and delivered presentations and demonstrations using Java and the LEGO MINDSTORMS system around the world.

Contents

Foreword   xix

Chapter 1 Introducing LEGO MINDSTORMS   1

Introduction   2
The LEGO MINDSTORMS RIS Kit   2
  A Brief History of the LEGO
    MINDSTORMS RIS   3
  What's Included with the Robot Kit   4
RCX: The Robot's Brain   7
  How It Works   7
    The Physical Structure   7
    The Logical Structure   9
  Expanding the RCX Brain   11
    Replacing the RIS Software   11
    Replacing the RCX Firmware   14
The RIS Software Environment   16
  Installing the Firmware into the RCX   16
  A Visual Programming Interface: RCX Code   18
RCX Bytecodes   20
  The LEGO Assembly Code for the RCX   20
LEGO Expansion Kits   21
  Alternative Processing Units   22
  Add-on Building Elements   24
Summary   26
Solutions Fast Track   26
Frequently Asked Questions   28

RCX: The Robot's Brain

- The RCX is a microcomputer than interfaces with input and output devices. Programs can be written on a PC and then downloaded to the unit through the IR tower.

- The RCX uses two types of memory: read-only memory (ROM) and modifiable random access memory (RAM).

- The RCX can be expanded in two ways: using a different programming software like NQC or the Java APIs, or replacing the default firmware with a new one.

**Serial Port Control and
Status Signals**

Abbreviation	Definition
RTS	Request To Send
CTS	Clear To Send
DTR	Data Terminal Ready
DSR	Data Set Ready
RI	Ring Indicate
CD	Carrier Detect
OE	Overrun Error
FE	Framing Error
PE	Parity Error
BI	Break Indicator
DA	Data Available
BE	Output Buffer Empty

Chapter 2 The Java Communications API   31

Introduction   32
Overview of the Java Communications
  Extension API (JCE API)   32
    Understanding the JCE Framework   34
      Port Discovery and Enumeration   34
      Port Ownership Management   37
      Asynchronous event-based I/O   42
      Encapsulation of Underlying
        Native Ports   43
    Java Communication API's Event Based
      Architecture   43
Installing and Configuring the
  Java Communications API   46
    Installing the Native Library   46
    Installing the Java comm.jar Library   47
      The javax.comm.properties
        Configuration File   47
    Configuring your Development
      Environment   48
Reading and Writing to Serial Ports   50
    Simple Read Example   50
    Simple Write Example   54
Debugging with Serial Ports:
  The "Black Box" Example   57
    Selected Code   62
Extending the Java Communications API   64
    Using More than Serial or Parallel Ports   65
      USB Port Access   68
Summary   76
Solutions Fast Track   77
Frequently Asked Questions   78

Chapter 3 Communicating with
the RCXPort API   81

Introduction   82
Overview of the RCXPort Java API   82

Troubleshooting Problems with RCXPort

There are several things that could potentially go wrong when trying to run RCXPort. The more common mistakes are listed below:

- Make sure your RCX is turned on and within range of the IR tower.

- Make sure the IR tower is properly connected to the correct serial port.

- Make sure that another program (possibly running in the background) isn't using the serial port.

- Make sure you have named the correct serial port (COM1, for instance) in the command line.

- If you are downloading byte code from a file, make sure that file is in the same directory as RCXPort.

- Make sure you have downloaded the Java Communications API, and that it is correctly installed.

- Make sure that your classpath references both *rcxport.jar* and

How RCXPort Works   82
  Formatting RCX Commands   82
  RCXPort Object Model   84
Limitations of RCXPort   85
  Compiling Java into Machine Code   85
  Restrictions of Using Direct Mode   85
  Reliance on Java Communications API   86
Programming the RCX Using RCXPort   86
Downloading Programs with RCXPort   91
Interfacing External Software with RCXPort   93
An Advanced Example Using RCXPort   97
Summary   106
Solutions Fast Track   106
Frequently Asked Questions   108

Chapter 4 Communicating with the RCXJava API   **111**
Introduction   112
Designing an RCX Java Communications
  Architecture   112
  The Basic Components of an RCX API   122
    Port Configuration and Error Handling   122
    Protocol Management and
      Message Parsing   122
    Tower Communications   123
    RCX Communications   123
  Reusability: Protocols and Ports   123
    Supporting Similar Protocols   123
    Using Java Interfaces to Support
      Ports Other than Serial Ports   124
Overview of the RCXJava API   124
  The RCX Package   125
    Classes   125
    Interfaces   126
    Exceptions   127

RCXLoader

Using the RCXLoader Application   129
  The User Interface   131
    Handling and Parsing Response
      and Error Messages   131
Beyond Serial Port Communications:
  The RCXApplet Example   131
    Communicating over the Network   132
      Using Sockets   135
    Building and Extending the Simple Applet   139
Direct Control Programming
  for the RCX Using Java   147
    Basic Remote Control Application   147
    Creating a Direct Control
      Framework for Java Programs   150
        Direct Control Using AI   151
Summary   164
Solutions Fast Track   165
Frequently Asked Questions   167

**Create Custom
Components**

Q: What happens if more
than ten programs are
downloaded to the
RCX at once?

A: The 11th (and further)
programs will appear
in the program list,
represented using
blanks.

Q: What if I have a LEGO
tower connected to
the USB port?

A: Set the RCXTTY
environment variable
to the value USB,
instead of to a serial
port value.

Chapter 5 The leJOS System   169
Introduction   170
Basic leJOS Usage Guidelines   170
  Using the lejosc Compiler   172
The LEGO Java Operating System   173
  The TinyVM   176
Overview of the leJOS Architecture   177
  Exploring the josx.platform.rcx Package   178
    Using the Button and ButtonListener
      Classes   179
    Using the MinLCD, LCD, Segment,
      LCDConstants, and TextLCD Classes   180
Using leJOS: A Simple Example   195
  Controlling Motors   195
  Reading Sensors   196
Summary   200
Solutions Fast Track   200
Frequently Asked Questions   202

**Debugging leJOS
Programs**

- The best way to debug a leJOS program is to use the Sound and LCD classes in unison to provide you with feedback of the robot's state.

- Normal Java exception handling applies to leJOS, allowing you to separate code for normal operation and code for error situations.

Chapter 6 Programming for the leJOS Environment   203

Introduction   204
Designing Java Programs to Run in leJOS   204
    Using Memory Wisely   205
        Using the Right Java Classes
        (and Using Them Correctly)   206
An Advanced Programming
  Example Using leJOS   210
    Controlling the Steering   222
        Restricted Steering   223
        Getting Back to the Line   225
Debugging leJOS Programs   236
    Using Sounds and the LCD   236
    Exception Handling with leJOS   237
Testing leJOS Programs   238
    Using the leJOS Simulator   238
Summary   241
Solutions Fast Track   241
Frequently Asked Questions   243

Chapter 7 leJOS Tools   245

Introduction   246
Programming Environments for leJOS   246
    The Command-Line Tools
    that Interact with the RCX   247
        Using the lejosc Compiler   247
        Using the lejos Linker   248
        Using the lejosfirmdl Downloader   250
    The Command-line leJOS Emulator   251
        Using the emu-lejos Emulator   251
        Using the emu-lejosrun Linker   251
    Using Exisiting IDEs   251
        Configuring Forte   252
Using the leJOS Visual Interface   253

**Dialog to Create a
New Simulator Run**

Encoding of Java Types in Signatures

Java Type	Encoding
void	V
boolean	Z
char	C
byte	B
short	S
int	I
long	J
float	F
double	D
package..... package.Class .../package/	Lpackage/ Class;
array	[(type of elements follows)

The leJOS Visual Interface   253
    Installing lVI   254
    Setting Up lVI   255
    Basic Usage   257
Using a leJOS Simulator: Simlink   258
    Getting Started with Simlink   258
        Installing and Configuring Simlink   260
        Running Your First Simulation   261
    Designing a Floor Plan for Simlink   262
        Non-visual Declarations   264
        Visual Declarations   264
        Navigational Declarations   268
    Creating a New Simlink Robot Body   269
        Creating a Body: Passive Components   270
        Active Body Classes: Sensors
            and Wheels   272
        Creating a Simple Robot Design   277
        Future Tools for Designing Robots   280
Additional Tips and Tools for leJOS   281
    RCXDownLoad   282
    RCXDirectMode   283
Summary   285
Solutions Fast Track   285
Frequently Asked Questions   287

Chapter 8 leJOS Internals   289
Introduction   290
Advanced Usage of leJOS   290
    Multiprogram Downloading   291
    Storing Persistent Data   292
Examining leJOS Internals   297
    From Source Code to Execution   297
    Inside the leJOS Linker   299
        The C Wrapper   299
        The Java Main Program   300
        Building the Binary   302
        The leJOS Binary Format   303

Inside the leJOS Firmware   304
  The Structure of the leJOS Virtual
    Machine   305
  Real-Time Behavior   306
  RCX Memory Layout   308
  The Emulator   310
  The leJOS Source Code   311
Extending leJOS with Native Methods   314
  Native Methods in leJOS   314
  Adding a Native Method   315
Additional Tips and Tricks with leJOS   323
  Changing Stack Sizes   324
  Determining the Amount of Free Memory   324
  Measuring Latency   324
Summary   327
Solutions Fast Track   328
Frequently Asked Questions   330

Chapter 9 Programming LEGO MINDSTORMS with Jini   333

Introduction   334
Overview of the Jini Architecture   334
  Jini as a Network Protocol   336
A Simple Jini Service Example   337
  What's Required for Installing and
    Running Services   337
  A Simple Service and Client   341
Proxies and Service Architectures   355
  Selecting the Right Architecture   356
  Using Proxies   356
A RCX Jini Proxy Service   356
  Why a Proxy?   356
  Interfacing with the RCX Java API   358
Using the RCX Jini Service:
  Example Server and Client   358
  A RCX Jini Server   359
  A RCX Jini Client   378

Overview of Jini

- Jini is a Java technology built on top of RMI, enabling clients and services to interact in a network with little administrative overhead.

- One feature of Jini is that it is vary applicable to embedded devices, including devices like the RCX.

- The Jini Technology Starter Kit (TSK) includes all of the required jar files as well as some service implementations such as reggie, an implementation of a lookup service.

Summary   394
Solutions Fast Track   394
Frequently Asked Questions   396

Appendix A Resources   399

**Appendix B Programming
LEGO MINDSTORMS with Java Fast Track   407**

Index   421

Foreword

I purchased my first LEGO MINDSTORMS Robotics kit in 1998. I felt like a child on Christmas morning as I opened up the box and found the hundreds of LEGO pieces and the RCX—the small programmable brick that was the foundation of MINDSTORMS. As I began to build my first robots and experiment with the included software, my excitement turned to disappointment; I quickly realized that the software included for programming the RCX was geared to a younger or novice audience. It only required the use of a simple drag-and-drop visual interface, and I wondered if I could program the RCX's "brain" *without* having to use the included software. Well, as it turns out, a number of programming enthusiasts had already begun to tackle that same issue, notably Kekoa Proudfoot, who in fact had become a leader in the endeavor by documenting the protocol and RCX internals. Kekoa and a few other individuals had begun to write programs. At first these programs were written in C, and then in David Baum's new, aptly-named language, NQC (Not Quite C).

As I have been an active Java programmer since 1995, it seemed natural to me to use Java to program the RCX rather than to use C or to invent a new language for my MINDSTORMS hobby. Of course, there's nothing wrong with NQC (which is quite popular for programming LEGO MINDSTORMS), but Java has outlived its initial hype and has grown steadily to become a standard object-oriented programming language. The logic that led to my decision to use Java was this: The infrared tower that communicates with the RCX robot was connected to my PC via a serial port, and the Java Communications API that supports serial ports had also been updated in 1998. My mind jumped at the possibilities and I felt compelled to create an RCX Java API in order to program my MINDSTORMS robots with Java.

Programming LEGO MINDSTORMS with Java is as much about robotics programming as it is about Java programming. This book is for all levels of MINDSTORMS users, from hobbyists to the serious MINDSTORMS aficionados. This book is also appropriate for a variety of programming levels; both those with only a modicum of Java knowledge and more advanced programmers will learn much within these pages. We cover all the basics of programming the RCX, beginning with the introduction of the Java APIs available for communicating remotely with the RCX using its default firmware, all the way through more advanced topics like embedded programming using a custom Java Virtual Machine (JVM)—Jose Solorzano's Lego Java Operating System (leJOS)—which allows us to run Java inside the RCX.

Most of the software packages and APIs we cover and use *in Programming LEGO MINDSTORMS with Java* are open source projects. The source code from each chapter is included on the companion CD-ROM, ready for use in your own creations. These projects are mostly a labor of love by those who initially designed and contributed to them, and are always open to new contributors. We'll even delve into the internals of a few. For example, we'll show how to add new native calls to leJOS, and how to add USB support to Java, because the latest LEGO MINDSTORMS release uses USB instead of the serial port.

In Chapter 1, "Introducing LEGO MINDSTORMS," Giulio Ferrari offers a thorough introduction and examination of what is included in LEGO MINDSTORMS and its related kits, and what the specifications of the RCX are. There is also an overview of all the software languages available for the RCX.

In Chapter 2, "The Java Communications API," I go into a detailed definition of the Java Communications API and how it is used to access serial and parallel ports. I begin to dig more deeply into how the Java Communications API works and how to extend the API to include support for USB ports, providing an alternate solution until a Java standard is available.

In Chapters 3 and 4 we cover two Java APIs used to program the RCX using the firmware that comes with the kit. In Chapter 3, "Communicating with the RCXPort API," Jamie Waldinger examines Scott Lewis's RCXPort API. Topics in this chapter include downloading tasks into the RCX and an advanced example using a robot to sort candy. In Chapter 4, "Communicating with the RCXJava API," I discuss the design of my RCXJava API and provide examples of how to create an applet for remote controlling a robot, as well as an introduction to simulating Artificial Intelligence with the RCX.

Søren Hilmer introduces us to leJOS in Chapter 5, "The leJOS System," and offers tips on design and debugging before presenting some advanced programming examples in Chapter 6, "Programming for the leJOS Environment." Chapter 5 covers the architecture and APIs that are currently available, and demonstrates a few of the available tools (such as the *lejosc* compiler) with simple examples. Chapter 6 covers using memory wisely, and provides an example of programming a line-following robot. Chapter 6 also offers an introduction to the subsumption architecture, exception handling, and using the *emu-lejos* and *emu-lejosrun* emulators.

In Chapter 7, "leJOS Tools," Andy Gombos covers some of the more popular available leJOS tools, including command-line tools and visual integrated development environments (both existing and custom visual IDEs) for developing leJOS programs. Andy also covers his Simlink LEGO MINDSTORMS simulator, which is a linking set of classes and interfaces for the Rossum Project and leJOS. The Rossum Project (known as Rossum's Playhouse) is a two-dimensional robotics simulator.

Chapter 8, "leJOS Internals," provides a detailed look into the internals of leJOS. Jürgen Stuber, who is currently one of the leading contributors to leJOS development project, gives us the details into how the leJOS internals operate and also how to extend leJOS using native code. He demonstrates this with his latest leJOS additions.

Chapter 9, "Programming LEGO MINDSTORMS with Jini," is an overview of the Jini distributed computing framework technology, with an example using the RCX. Mick Porter shows us how to use Jini service proxies with several robots. In his example, he has two dancing robots imitate each other's movements by communicating via Jini.

Other notable contributors to this project are Ron Gonzalez, who offered his technical editing skills to Chapters 2 and 4, and Simon Rittner, a Java technology evangelist with an avid interest in LEGO MINDSTORMS, who performed the technical review for this work.

It has been a very rewarding experience to be a part of the team that gathered all of this useful information together with the purpose of sharing it with the LEGO MINDSTORMS community. I feel confident that the material presented here, in conjunction with the companion volume, *Building Robots with LEGO MINDSTORMS* (ISBN: 1-928994-67-9) by Mario and Giulio Ferrari, will provide enthusiasts with material for many exciting hours exploring the potential of programming their own LEGO MINDSTORMS robots.

As of the current printing, this book and accompanying CD-ROM include the most up-to-date versions of the software, but be aware that, programmers being who they are, continued updates of both are guaranteed! You can find updates to this book, as well as new versions of the included software, posted by the Publisher as they become available at www.syngress.com/solutions.

Finally, I'd like to thank Catherine Nolan and Kate Glennon at Syngress for their editorial guidance, and Andrew Williams for approaching me with the idea for this book. Now go have fun!

—Dario Laverde, Technical Editor

## Chapter 1

Introducing LEGO MINDSTORMS

Solutions in this chapter:

- The LEGO MINDSTORMS RIS Kit
- RCX: The Robot's Brain
- The RIS Software Environment
- RCX Bytecodes
- LEGO Expansion Kits

☑ Summary

☑ Solutions Fast Track

☑ Frequently Asked Questions

Introduction

Soon after its release, the LEGO MINDSTORMS Robotics Invention System (RIS) quickly became popular not only with its initial intended audience of children aged 11 and up, but also within a community of adult LEGO robotics enthusiasts that developed and spread worldwide with significant help from the Internet. Before long, hackers had deciphered the communication protocol and command set, and published the operational codes (opcodes) of the RCX's interpretive operating system on the Internet for easy access by all software developers. This was a very good thing for LEGO fans and programmers, for it allowed them to create many new tools and software applications for the RIS. These applications are under continuous development, and many are based on open source or freeware programs. In the meantime, LEGO has released new versions since the first RIS, with minor updates always maintaining backward compatibility.

Not only has the RIS become very popular, but it has also renewed interest in robotics; LEGO continues to offer many additional robotics kits. This chapter will introduce the novice to these robots and explain exactly how, and perhaps why, they work the way they do. Overviews of how they function physically and how they are programmed both at high and low levels are presented, as well as their limitations and expansion possibilities.

The LEGO MINDSTORMS RIS Kit

The LEGO MINDSTORMS system is a complete series of products for the development of robots and automation applications in general. The central set of the LEGO robotics line is the RIS, a set of tools that offers you computing power, great ease of use, and versatility. With this kit, you can design your own robot, build it using ready-to-use pieces, program it with a specific programming language, and finally test it to see if it matches your expectations—and most important, to rebuild and reprogram it as you wish. The brain of the system is the *RCX microcomputer*, initially developed in collaboration with the Massachusetts Institute of Technology (MIT) Media Lab; the kit also contains many other fundamental pieces, including input and output devices (sensors and motors). From this very powerful combination you can make countless completely independent robots, which is a great way to enhance your creativity and imagination; and best of all, it's hours of great fun.

A Brief History of the LEGO MINDSTORMS RIS

The commercial version of the LEGO MINDSTORMS RIS was released in late 1998, but its origins date back many years. The product is actually the result of two separate research and innovation processes.

The first process is represented by the LEGO Company's continuous development of new products since the first appearance of a reusable brick in 1949 (the "Automatic Binding Brick"), that led also to the creation of the TECHNIC series in 1977. The TECHNIC sets opened up new ways for children and adults to create working models of increasing complexity. The second process stems from research conducted at the Epistemology and Learning Group at the MIT Media Laboratory, led by Fred Martin, Brian Silverman and Randy Sargent under the guidance of Professors Seymour Papert and Mitchel Resnick and support from the LEGO Company. This work, started in 1986, lead to the development of the so-called "*Programmable Brick*," a small unit capable of connecting to the external world through a variety of sensors and actuators, designed for the creation of robots and other applications in which a computer might interact with everyday objects.

The sum of these two efforts brought life to the RCX, a microcomputer by the LEGO Company partly based on the technology developed at Media Lab for the MIT Programmable Brick. The RCX was completed with sensors and other special parts, existing pieces taken from the LEGO TECHNIC series, and specifically designed software capable of interfacing with a standard PC. This set of tools became the MINDSTORMS Robotics Invention System 1.0.

The RIS became an instant hit and its use spread widely among robotics and LEGO enthusiasts all over the world. In the years following the initial success, two updates to the original set and many other MINDSTORMS kits were created, reaching an increasing number of people. *CyberMaster*, another programmable unit that shares some concepts with the RCX, had appeared shortly before the RIS, while in 1999 the *Robotics Discovery Set* and the *Droid Development Kit* were equipped with less powerful versions of the RCX, which displayed limited programming capabilities but improved ease-of-use. Additional sets and pieces are continually introduced to expand the possibilities of the original system. We will discuss these kits in detail later in the chapter.

What's Included with the Robot Kit

If you were to open a brand new RIS 2.0 box and analyze the contents of the kit in detail, you would find more than 700 pieces, most of which are standard TECHNIC parts, such as beams, plates, gears, axles, pulleys, wheels, cables, and connectors. However, there are also specific items included that are aimed at robotics development, and represent the heart of the system. They are:

- The RCX Programmable Microcomputer, Version 2.0
- 2 Motors (9V)
- 2 touch sensors
- 1 light sensor
- A USB infrared (IR) transmitter tower
- A fiber-optic cable
- A printed Constructopedia manual
- Software on CD-ROM

The RCX can be thought of as the kernel of the entire set. It can read external events through sensors and control movements through motors; and it can be easily programmed with the *RCX Code*, which is a specific programming language provided on the software CD-ROM (it can also be programmed with the help of third-party tools, which we will explore later on). As you can see, the kit contains both *input* devices; active (light) and passive (touch) sensors, and *output* devices (the two motors). These components are fundamental to robotics, as they provide a way for them to interact with the world. Touch and light sensors can give your robot information on its movements, positioning, and general behavior. Motors are the starting point for every movement and activity; they can control gears, wheels, axles, and other moving parts.

The black and gray tower you find in the set is the component through which your LEGO robots communicate with your PC. It is in fact an infrared (IR) transmitter that sends code and information from your computer to the programmable unit. Also, the fiber-optic cable has a very specific function: if connected to the IR tower it allows you to program the Micro Scout (the smallest member of the MINDSTORMS family) through a communication protocol called Visible Light Link (VLL). We will describe VLL at the end of this chapter.

The Constructopedia manual offers building tips and tricks, and serves as a kind of idea book, suggesting some challenges to improve one's skill. The

Constructopedia can also be used in conjunction with the CD-ROM, which contains multimedia versions of the same challenges, as well a complete visual programming environment and other tools for the RCX.

NOTE

For more ideas, check out the Syngress book *Building Robots with LEGO MINDSTORMS*, written by Mario and Giulio Ferrari, and edited by Ralph Hempel. The book contains detailed descriptions on how to get the most out of your robots at every level of difficulty, ranging from fundamental tools and building strategies up to the design and construction of the most complex creations. Visit the Syngress Web site for more information (www.syngress.com).

The MINDSTORMS RIS has evolved from its initial release in 1998. We already mentioned that three different RIS versions (1.0, 1.5 and 2.0) have been released since then. Basically, there is very good compatibility between them, but each set has its own peculiarities. At this point in time, The LEGO Company produces and sells only version 2.0, which contains a number of significant improvements and innovations, especially regarding the software, but it is not too difficult to find a used (or even unused) RIS. Table 1.1 summarizes the differences among the three releases.

Table 1.1 RIS Version Comparison

	RIS 1.0	RIS 1.5	RIS 2.0
Release date	1998	1999	2001
Pieces	727	727	717
RCX version	1.0	1.0	2.0
Firmware version	0309	0309	0328
DC/AC power adapter	Yes	In a few earlier sets only	No
IR tower	Serial	Serial	USB
Fiber-optic link cable	No	No	Yes

In terms of hardware, we can see that there haven't been any major changes in the most common pieces (specifically the TECHNIC series pieces), even if the contents have been slightly modified with every version. The RCX has changed slightly from version 1.0 to 1.5, because the DC/AC jack adapter has been removed from all but the first version 1.5 units produced (maybe for an increased security or to reduce production costs), and some electronics have changed. Recent units instead work only with six 1.5V batteries, although it's still possible for one who is familiar with electronics to connect the RCX with an external power source. For those who find the DC/AC adapter to be an important factor, RCXs with a DC/AC power adapter are still available from LEGO Dacta, which is the LEGO Company's educational branch (www.pldstore.com). No major changes have affected the hardware; so for the purposes of a wide range of projects, RCX 1.0 is nearly identical to RCX 2.0.

On the software side, however, version 2.0 saw the introduction of new firmware in conjunction with an improved RCX Code interface, which brought to the latest Kit many new advantages that were soon also available in non-LEGO development tools, such as NQC. The best news is that the new firmware can be easily installed on any RCX version, and that the USB tower has maintained a full backwards compatibility.

In the case that you have the possibility of choosing which release to buy, you may wonder which one is the best option. The AC adapter can be of some advantage in a few projects, so the best component combination is probably a RCX 1.0, a USB tower, and the RIS 2.0 programming environment.

Bricks & Chips...

Choosing between the Two Towers

There are two kinds of IR towers: *serial* and *USB*. The version you have depends on the RIS version you bought. The serial version came in RIS 1.0 and 1.5; the USB tower is currently sold with RCX 2.0. This was a technical choice, as the USB system offers some advantages in terms of ease of use and configuration. Let's look at the major drawbacks and advantages of each version.

The serial port tower...

- Requires external power (9V battery).
- Can change the baud rate to increase the speed.
- Is supported on most operating systems.

Continued

The USB tower…

- Does not require batteries.
- Uses more recent technology, and is easy to configure.
- Is not yet supported under all operating systems.

There is no problem in using the latest RCX Code (the software) version with either the USB or serial port transmitter, but there is a compatibility issue when using the new tower and the old software, because the old software wasn't designed to support the USB technology. Be sure to install the most recent software and firmware before attempting to use the USB tower.

RCX: The Robot's Brain

The Robotics Command Explorer (RCX) is the brain of any MINDSTORMS robot. It is often called the "programmable brick," or "smart brick," because it resembles a standard LEGO piece in many of its characteristics, though a great power hides within it. The RCX is actually a small computer based on the Hitachi H8 series microprocessor and fully equipped with memory, timers, and input and output devices. When you write a program on your personal computer, download it to the RCX, and execute it, the result is a completely self-sufficient entity that can behave autonomously, which is the difference between a true "intelligent" robot and an automated machine.

How It Works

Let's see how the RCX works in detail by examining the physical and logical structures. A complete analysis of the two models leads to better knowledge and the discovery of some elements that are usually hidden from the end user.

The Physical Structure

Suppose you remove the screws from your RCX and disassemble it (be careful, this could damage to the unit). On the inside, you find a main board on which are mounted and soldered many components (see Figure 1.1). The top view shows a large LCD display surrounded by four contacts for the rubber buttons and twelve clamps that connect to the six input and output ports. On one side there are two infrared (IR) LEDs and an IR receiver These provide two-way communication with the PC tower, a remote control, or another RCX. A speaker, two big capacitors and many other small elements complete this part of the board. In the bottom view, you can see that a large square chip, the microcontroller, also hides a built-in memory. As in most computers, the memory is made of two types:

- **Read Only Memory** (ROM) This type of memory is permanently written on the chip and cannot be altered in any way;

- **Random Access Memory** (RAM) This type of memory can be easily modified or accessed at any point. This kind of device needs to be constantly supplied with power to avoid erasing the content.

Figure 1.1 The RCX Board

TOP

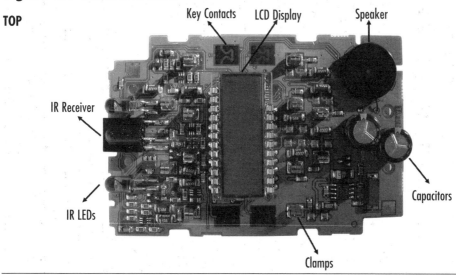

BOTTOM

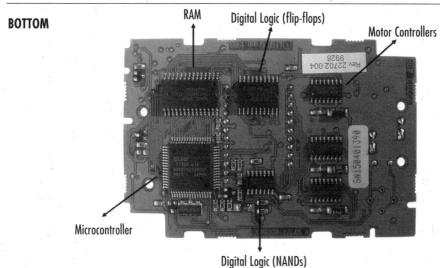

In the RCX, there are 16 Kb of ROM embedded in the microcontroller, and 32 Kb of RAM placed on an external chip. Memory provides a way to store data and the user's programs; otherwise the processor would be completely useless. Finally, you can see three controllers for the 9V motors on the right, and two chips for digital logic processing in the middle of the board.

Table 1.2 describes hardware specifications for all versions of RCX. The three versions are very similar, the only notable difference being the lack of the external power supply in units produced after 1999.

Table 1.2 RCX Hardware Specifications

Processor	8-bit Hitachi H8/3292, 16 MHz
ROM	16 Kb
SRAM, on chip	512 bytes
SRAM, external	32 Kb
Outputs	3 motor ports, 9V 500 mA
Inputs	3 sensor ports
Display	1 LCD
Sound	1 sound unit
Timers	4 system timers (8-bit)
Batteries	6x 1.5V
Power adapter (only in RIS 1.0)	9–12V, DC/AC
Communications	IR port (transmitter + receiver)

The Logical Structure

Let's outline a logical working model to better understand how the RCX hardware works. Imagine a structure made of multiple layers (see Figure 1.2). At the very bottom there is the processor, which is an Hitachi H8300 series. This processor executes the machine code instructions. Additional components have the task of converting input signals from the three sensor ports into digital data.

The next layer in the system is the ROM code. A new RCX comes with a set of instructions that provides all the basic functionalities to the unit, like port control, display, and IR communications. If you're familiar with its architecture, you can compare the ROM to the BIOS of a personal computer that boots and communicates with its peripherals. Without this low-level behavior you couldn't do anything with the RCX, because you wouldn't be able to interface it to the external world.

Figure 1.2 The Logical Structure

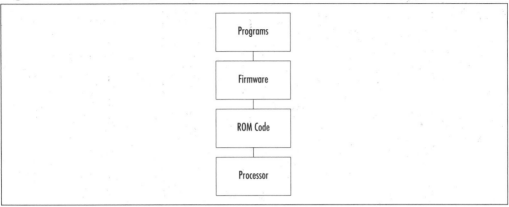

Just above the ROM code in our schematic structure is the *firmware*. This is a sort of operating system for our RCX unit, providing functionality to the entire system. The word "firmware" identifies a particular kind of software that is usually not alterable by the final user, though in this case there's an important exception, as we will see. The firmware's duty is to interpret the bytecode and convert it into machine code instructions, calling the ROM code routines to perform standard system operations. It is stored in the RAM, meaning that it is downloaded at your first installation of the MINDSTORMS system; yet it needs to be downloaded again through the IR tower every time you power down the RCX for more than a few seconds , namely by removing the batteries.

On top of the firmware there is your own code and the stored data. The RIS software on your PC converts the RCX Code into a format that is more compact and readable by the RCX processor (that is, bytecode). The RAM is logically divided into different sections: 16 Kb for the firmware, 6 Kb for storing user programs, and the rest used for interpreting the bytecode and handling data for the program's execution. Even if they are all in the same physical area, following our layer-based logical structure, we can consider the programs to be in a higher level.

Note that when you turn your RCX off, the RAM remains connected to the power supply so that it can retain its contents (both the firmware and the program data), so it will slowly consume the batteries even when switched off. To avoid this, you can remove the batteries if you plan not to use the unit for a long time, but remember that you'll have to redownload the firmware (and any program you had already stored in RAM) before attempting to use it again.

The process of programming the RCX is very simple: you prepare your code on the PC, download it to the RCX unit, and run it from there. A few steps are actually hidden from the user, so it's useful to summarize the process in a top-to-bottom scheme:

- Using RCX Code (or other software), you write a program on your PC;

- Your program's instructions are transformed into low-level instructions (bytecodes);

- You download the program (in bytecode form) to the RCX's RAM using the IR transmitter tower;

- The firmware interprets the bytecode and converts it into machine code instructions using ROM routines;

- The processor executes the machine code.

As you can see, the programming process follows the layered logical model we described, going from user-written information to low-level hardware, like ROM or the processor.

Expanding the RCX Brain

The RCX, though powerful and versatile, has its own limitations. Some of them are mechanical restrictions, and cannot be overcome in any way: as with any computer product, the RCX has specific hardware characteristics, like the speed of the processor, the memory, or the number of ports. For example, you would never be able to store more than 32K of data in the RCX's RAM area. Other limits relate to the software side, either to the firmware or to the programming language that you use. In this case, you can sometimes work out solutions that let you push the RCX beyond its original limits.

There are basically two approaches to expanding the RCX: the first being the use of an alternative programming environment to gather better performances and more flexibility; the second, more radical approach, is the replacement of the entire original firmware with a new one, taking advantage of the fact that it is stored in an area (the RAM) that can be accessed and modified.

Replacing the RIS Software

The RCX code, even though it has been deeply restructured since the first release and now enjoys much greater degrees of power and control, is a somewhat limited tool. It is quite surprising to see that the LEGO MINDSTORMS solid and powerful firmware cannot unleash its full power due to the limitations of the LEGO programming language.

A huge effort has been put into this area from the international community of LEGO robotics enthusiasts. Soon after the release of the first RIS in 1998, Kekoa Proudfoot presented the results of the reverse engineering work he did on the programmable brick with the help of other hackers, revealing many details of the RCX hardware and publishing a list of bytecodes for the interpreter. His Web site, "RCX Internals" (http://graphics.stanford.edu/~kekoa/rcx) has been one of the most important landmarks in the process of expanding the possibilities of the RCX.

From this fundamental starting point, new programming languages began to appear. Though each of these new languages has interesting features, they all share some common features:

- Their approach consists of making a new interface able to generate bytecodes;

- They work with text programming rather than graphical (visual) developing;

- Their development method is based on the syntax of a widespread programming language like C or Java.

- They often share the freeware concept at the heart of their philosophy; most programming tools for the RCX are free and usually under public licenses. The wide availability of these open source projects is often a key point to their success, and helps to ensure the tools' continuing development.

Not Quite C

Created by Dave Baum, Not Quite C (NQC) is definitely the most widespread third-party development tool for the RCX. NQC is a multi-platform program (it runs on PC, Mac and UNIX-like systems) that works on the standard firmware and takes advantage of its stability and reliability, while at the same time giving the user a lot more computational power.

A key to NQC's success is that it is based on a simplified version of the C language, which is very well known by programmers around the world. Many resources, including online documents and tutorials, offer new users the possibility to learn the language quickly and easily.

NQC is a very well supported and constantly improved development language. Baum is always adding new features and working on new releases as new important technical developments appear, such as a new programmable unit or a new firmware version (NQC currently supports RCX, Scout, CyberMaster and the latest 2.0 firmware).

NQC is a command-line executable file; not only is installation quick and easy, but you only need a text editor (like Windows' Notepad) to write the code and you're done. There are also interesting integrated development environments (IDEs) like BricxCC or Visual NQC that encapsulate the compiler inside a complete system of editors, tools, direct control and diagnostic utilities.

Java APIs

In a search for more flexibility, others have created tools based on the Java language, like the RCXJava API by Dario Laverde and RCXPort API by Scott Lewis. Both take advantage of the cross-platform features of Java systems and rely on a Java Virtual Machine (JVM).

The Java Application Programming Interfaces (APIs) are basically sets of command libraries that allow a user with a JVM-equipped computer to communicate with an RCX that is using the original firmware. You can send out requests and commands through a serial IR port and interact with your robots. Chapters 3 and 4 will cover programming with these tools in more depth.

Designing & Planning...

An Interesting Alternative: ROBOLAB

The RCX Code is not the only software available from LEGO. The company also markets the interesting tool ROBOLAB, or "MINDSTORMS for school," which is a programming environment made especially for educational and research purposes. ROBOLAB is usually sold in conjunction with LEGO Dacta products (but is also available separately). It shares a lot with the RIS software, as it also uses a graphical environment, but ROBOLAB incorporates a lot of noteworthy embedded elements and can probably be considered the best "official" release.

In addition to all the RIS features, ROBOLAB version 2.5 includes:

- Data analysis, comparison, and graphing

Continued

- Internet communication with the included "ROBOLAB Server"
- Presentation modes, like project data, can be transformed into HTML pages
- Video camera (not only LEGO's Vision Command) compatibility, with visual recognition system
- Use and calibration of non-LEGO DCP sensors (to measure pressure, voltage, sound level, etc.)

Replacing the RCX Firmware

The key to surpassing the RCX code is due to the LEGO Company's decision to store the firmware in RAM, so that it can be accessed and modified. Some languages replace the RCX's entire firmware instead of only creating bytecodes for the interpreter. There are many advantages in this approach, for example the possibility to overcome the original system's 6 Kb memory limit for user programs, and increased speed.

Remember that replacing the firmware is not a one-way street: you can always go back to the original firmware (or decide to try a different one!) simply by erasing the RCX memory and downloading it anew, with no actual risk to the hardware of your unit.

legOS

The legOS project was the first attempt to write a replacement firmware for the RCX; it was started in 1999 by Markus Noga, and has since been transformed into an open source project, which is currently managed by Paolo Masetti and Luis Villa. The main goal of legOS is to bypass all the limitations of the original RCX interpreter by running code directly on the Hitachi processor. You link a series of system routines to your C or C++ program, and legOS compiles and loads it in place of the firmware. The benefit of using this method is that you can unleash the full power of the hardware, taking advantage of a strong language like C, and controlling every device at a very low level to run your programs at an outstanding speed.

The main drawback of this method is that you need to be skilled enough in programming to use the software; with legOS, you have to deal with a standard C language, as opposed to the simplified version in NQC. The legOS installation is also a bit awkward, and you often have to deal with cross-compilers or UNIX emulators.

pbForth

FORTH is a language with a strong tradition in robotics and automated applications in general. Conceived in the sixties, it is a complete interactive environment for embedded systems rather than a simple language. Ralph Hempel's version of this tool, called *programmable brick Forth* (pbForth), lets you download a kernel to the RCX and interface with it using a command-line terminal.

pbForth has a slightly steeper learning curve than the other APIs, and you may find it a bit challenging at first; you have to start thinking of your programs in terms of a structured set of layers. Further, pbForth uses *reverse Polish notation* (RPN), which requires you to write the operator after the operands This is unusual for a developing tool. However, the result is efficient code that is very powerful and remarkable in terms of its portability.

LEGO Java Operating System

Jose Solorzano started the TinyVM Project a few years ago. Tiny VM is essentially a small JVM featuring an API with native methods that provide access to the RCX hardware resources. It supports a subset of the typical Java APIs, so it lacks many of the most complex features of a complete Java system. This comes as no surprise, as Tiny VM is designed to be as compact as possible (about 10 Kb on the RCX).

Tiny VM was the starting point for a more complex project called LEGO Java Operating System (leJOS), that features a fully functional implementation of the Java language, including pre-emptive threads, multi-dimensional arrays, recursion, floating point operations, trigonometry functions and string constants, just to name a few of the features. The main leJOS goal differs a bit from its predecessors', because it aims to be as complete and efficient as possible rather than very small (the current footprint on the RCX is 17 Kb).

LeJOS is an open source project currently available on UNIX-like and Win32 systems, and is under continuous development by a small team of developers, now managed by Paul Andrews and Jürgen Stuber; TinyVM remains only as a low-footprint alternative for the RCX.

Even though leJOS is the youngest third-party solution on the MINDSTORMS programming scene, it is certainly one of the most valuable tools, as it offers the user a complete, state-of-the-art language that is fast, efficient and extremely portable. The availability and continuous development of graphical interfaces like *leJOS Visual Interface* and *RCXDownload/RCXDirectMode* make this system even more attractive to first-time users.

In Chapter 5, we will cover leJOS programming in depth and analyze the development process with this amazing little tool.

The RIS Software Environment

The graphical programming environment that is included on the LEGO MIND-STORMS CD-ROM is targeted mainly at kids and non-programmers. Even after major updates and improvements it still lacks in power if compared to the third-party languages; however, it is worth analyzing because it certainly has some benefits, especially in terms of ease-of-use. In addition, exploring the entire RIS software environment help you to understand and appreciate other languages and firmware alternatives.

Installing the Firmware into the RCX

When you unpack your RCX for the first time, it only has the code that is stored in its ROM area; there isn't even an active firmware on-board. Why doesn't the firmware come pre-loaded on the unit? Well, as we mentioned earlier, it has to be stored in the RAM, and this type of memory doesn't work without power. As a consequence, firmware can be loaded in the RCX only if there are batteries correctly installed and charged.

When you install and set up the RCX Software on your computer, it launches the user interface, configures the basic connection system (namely the IR tower), and immediately asks you to bring your RCX close to it (the unit needs to be close to the IR transmitter) and turn it on to start the firmware download. This process takes a few moments; once the firmware is successfully downloaded, the RCX emits a tone to confirm that it's now alive. If, for some reason, you have to download the firmware from the CD-ROM again, simply repeat the process.

If your turn on the RCX without installing a firmware on it, the RCX display will be quite empty, showing only the selected program slot (which can be changed with the **Prgm** button) and the outline of a figure standing still. Once the firmware has been installed, the screen shows a four-digit clock starting from zero.

With firmware only, the RCX is still totally powerless because there are no programs stored in its memory. If you press the **Run** or the **View** buttons (normally used to display sensor readings), nothing will happen. However, once the RCX is working and ready to be programmed, it is able to perform motor control, sensor readings, IR port use, and so on.

RCX 2.0 Firmware

The latest firmware release (specifically the one coded "firm0328.lgo"), introduces a bunch of interesting new features to the old functions. A lot of these characteristics improve the efficiency of the user-written programs; pushing the RCX limits a bit further, and giving the programmer more space to invent and create powerful new robots. The main characteristics, starting from most important, are:

- Arrays
- Events monitoring
- Access control mechanism
- Global motor and sound control
- 32 local and 16 global variables
- Variables display on the LCD panel
- Direct IR output control
- High resolution timers
- Counters
- Re-seedable random numbers
- Possibility to start a program from another
- Sound mute and un-mute, clearing
- Battery level check
- Firmware revision number check

This firmware can be found in the latest MINDSTORMS products: the RIS 2.0 kit; the RIS 2.0 upgrade CD; the Visual Command camera; and the MINDSTORMS Software Development Kit (SDK) 2.0 package.

The MINDSTORMS SDK 2.0 is a set of free tools designed to program the RCX with low-level instructions. It also comes with a lot of information and help files that are very useful in understanding the unit's behavior. You can download the file from the LEGO Web site at http://mindstorms.lego.com/sdk2.

Note that RCX Code versions 1.0 and 1.5 work with any firmware release, but they lack the capability to use the new features just described, while the version 2.0 needs instead to be used in combination with the most recent release. NQC supports either.

A Visual Programming Interface: RCX Code

We have mentioned that the LEGO Company supplies a programming tool to program RCX robots, called RCX Code. Everything in the RCX Code has been designed for ease of use: it is a fully graphical, event-driven programming environment, loosely based on Logo-type languages (Logo is a programming language that was developed as a tool for educational purposes in the 60s at MIT). In RCX Code, you don't actually have to write any code at all, instead using the visual programming interface to set the behavior of your robots. This means that you drag, drop and stack commands, which are shown as *code blocks*, to connect them and then set variables and parameters. It's a bit like building a program with LEGO bricks, using different code blocks for various functions (motor actions, sensors, delays, and sounds), and to control instructions to direct the flow of your code according to the state of sensors, timers, and counters. You can also use *big blocks* (sets of multiple commands) like subroutines that can be reused to write more functional software.

This no-code approach is a clear advantage for inexperienced users, but has major drawbacks: its set of instructions is very limited and doesn't take advantage of all the RCX's power, nor is it suitable for writing large programs. For example, if you have hundreds of instructions, your program may slow down and suffer from a lack of readability. For these reasons, if you want to develop robots with any complexity, you'll soon discover that RCX Code is an obstacle rather than a useful tool.

Figure 1.3 shows a simple program written in the RCX Code environment. The code refers to the steering line follower described in the companion Syngress book *Building Robots with LEGO MINDSTORMS* (ISBN 1-928994-67-9), a robot built basically to go along a black line located on a white floor (specifically, it follows the black–white border of the line, turning rapidly to correct its direction).

The main task calls a calibration procedure that makes a 3-second light reading and calculates the black/white threshold, powers motor B (which will be running continuously), and starts a repeat statement that changes the front motor's direction according to the light reading in order to set its direction. As you can see, a very simple program like this requires a lot of effort compared to other programming methods.

With a few mouse clicks you can download the program to the robot and run it to see if it meets your expectations. In Figure 1.4 you see the robot in action, following a line on the RIS Test Pad.

Figure 1.3 An Example of RCX Code

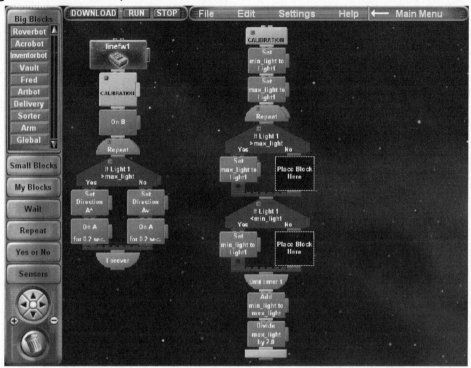

Figure 1.4 The Programmed Robot on the Test Pad

RCX Bytecodes

When you push the **Run** button on your RCX, it starts interpreting instructions. To *interpret* means that the unit's processor reads and executes every single command, statement by statement. As a result, you have to provide the RCX with low-level instructions (or *bytecodes*) that are usually generated by the graphical programming environment.

The LEGO Assembly Code for the RCX

The working model of the RCX is a *virtual machine* (see Figure 1.5, modeled out of Kekoa Proudfoot's original scheme). Note that the byte code interpreter executes commands from two different sources, namely the programs and the PC link system. The main feature of these instructions (or opcodes) is that they can be used both as a part of the serial protocol to communicate with an IR emitting device (a PC, another RCX or a remote control), and internally to run any user-created programs that are stored in memory. To interpret the bytecodes and correctly run the programs, the processor needs to store its data in a structured memory location called the *register file*. This is a hidden part of the system that is not accessible by the end-user. Your RCX can contain up to five programs in five slots, each with a maximum of 10 tasks and 8 subroutines, with their locations kept in a memory map so the interpreter can access them quickly. This method allows you to rely on multitasking and subroutines to increase the efficiency of your programs.

Figure 1.5 The RCX Virtual Machine

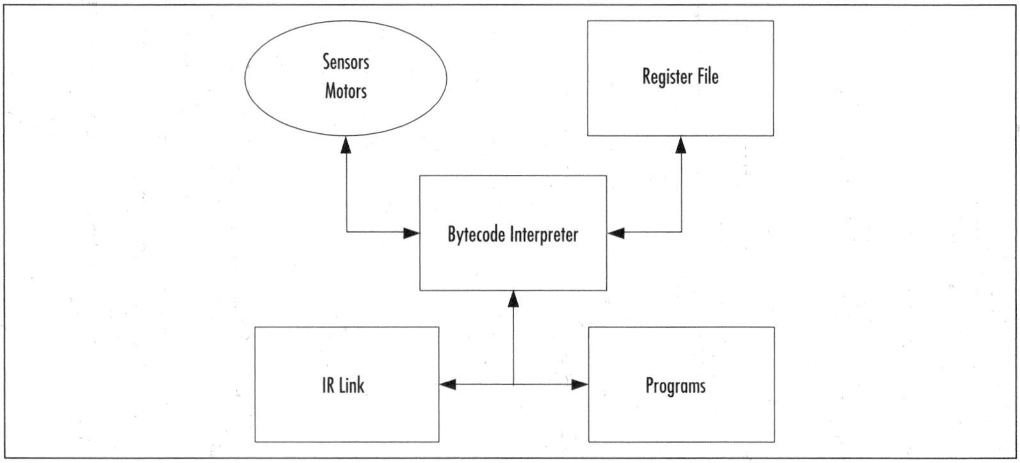

The RCX opcodes handle a number of different functions: commanding motors, sensors, arithmetic operations, flow control, downloading and uploading, registers, data logging, sound and timers. They can basically be divided into three groups, as described below (note that the opcodes given are only some small examples to explain their structure and functionalities; the complete reference is included in the MINDSTORMS SDK 2.0 documentation).

Direct control commands These provide interactive behaviors to a unit that is connected to the PC tower or another IR-emitting device, and cannot be used to program the RCX in a user-written program. For example, the *UploadRam* command uploads raw data from the RCX, with a maximum length of 150 bytes (because of an automatic shut-down of the IR tower):

```
0x63 | RAM address (LO) | RAM address (HI) | Byte count
```

Program commands These commands can be used only inside a piece of software code: *Wait*, for example, stops the current execution of a task for an amount of hundredths of seconds as specified by the parameters:

```
0x43 | WaitSource | WaitValue (LO) | WaitValue (HI)
```

Multifunctional commands These can be used in either fashion, but they sometimes behave differently depending on whether they're executed from the RCX or a remote unit. *SelectProgram* stops all tasks in the current program, then sets the current slot with the given parameter. Note that if it is executed from a downloaded software, *SelectProgram* also starts *task 0* in the new program:

```
0x91 | Program Number (0-4)
```

LEGO Expansion Kits

Aside from the RIS, there are other robotics kits that belong to the LEGO robotic family, based on different types of central units instead of the RCX. These expansion kits share some common characteristics, but they generally only offer a subset of the RIS' functionalities.

If you want to get more from your RCX-based robots, there are many kits or spare parts available that can help. Sometimes, a few additional components allow you to push the system's limit a bit further, giving you the possibility to build and program robots with more complex structures or behaviors.

Alternative Processing Units

The MINDSTORMS series offers three kinds of processing units: RCX, Scout, and Micro Scout; in addition to these, there are a couple of LEGO sets that don't belong to the family: CyberMaster is a less powerful RIS-like system, and there is also an unusual programmable robot called the *Code Pilot*. They have different features and target different user categories. We've already described the RIS set in detail, now let's take a look at the others:

- **CyberMaster** CyberMaster appeared shortly before the RIS. The main unit incorporates two motors with embedded rotation sensors, three inputs (only for passive sensors) and one output port. It can be programmed from a PC, but in this case the communication is based on radio frequency instead of infrared light. CyberMaster has limited functionality, because its main unit lacks the power and flexibility of an RCX computer. Moreover, at 412 bytes of RAM, CyberMaster has much less memory than does the RCX so it cannot host more than a very short program. Nor can the system be upgraded , as the firmware is stored in ROM instead of RAM.

- **Scout** Younger brother of the RCX, the Scout is included in the Robotics Discovery Set (RDS), which is a kit targeted mostly at children or adults with little to no programming experience. It can be programmed through the same RIS infrared tower (not included),thought the usual method is through the included large display and a set of buttons that allow you to choose from among predefined behaviors. Basically, you can set up a default action and responses to external events, that sensed through two passive input ports and an embedded light sensor. Like in CyberMaster, Scout's firmware is stored in ROM. LEGO recently discontinued the RDS, although some sets can still be found, mainly in online shops. This kit is no longer supported.

- **Micro Scout** This is an even simpler microcomputer, with many limitations; the Micro Scout comes with seven pre-programmed behaviors. You can select the current program slot with the help of a very small single-digit display; an embedded light sensor and a built-in motor complete the unit's offerings; a PC is not required. The Micro Scout has been included in two different sets: 9748 Droid Development Kit (DDK) and 9754 Dark Side Developer Kit (DSDK). The eighth program slot, the "P" mode, can be used to control the Micro Scout with the VLL communication protocol, through the Scout's built-in LED or the RIS 2.0 USB tower link.

- **Code Pilot** For the sake of completeness we'll also mention the first robotics kit set to appear on the scene, the 8479 Barcode Multi-set. It is based on an atypical programming method that uses bar codes and a special light reading unit (the Code Pilot) to set the model's behavior. Software to create barcodes is available online (http://eaton.dhs.org/lego), and the unit also supports the VLL protocol. It's not a very interesting robotics application in comparison to that of even the Micro Scout.

Table 1.3 summarizes the differences between the RIS and the alternatives just described; the comparison is based mainly on embedded components, number and types of sensors, output ports, and programming methods.

Table 1.3 LEGO Robotics Kits

	RDS	DSD/ DSDK	CM	Barcode	RIS
Unit	Scout	Micro Scout	CyberMaster	Code Pilot	RCX
PC required	No	No	Yes	No	Yes
Programming	Direct / PC	7 built-in +P	PC	Bar codes	PC
Input ports	2, passive	-	2, passive	1, passive	3, active/ passive
Embedded sensors	1 light	1 light	2 rotation	-	-
Output ports	2	-	1	1	3
Embedded motors	-	1 motor	2 motors	-	-
Updateable firmware	No	No	No	No	Yes
Communications	IR, VLL	VLL	Radio	VLL	IR

Add-on Building Elements

If you discover that you like robotics, you'll soon feel the need to try out more complex projects. This will probably create a need for more resources, be it on the software or the hardware side. Regarding the former, this means you will need to use an alternative software development environment, while the latter signifies that you basically need more parts. Luckily, LEGO provides a lot of ways to do either. On the hardware side, the simplest option is to buy sets from the TECHNIC series; you can get bulk pieces that are perfectly compatible with the MINDSTORMS components, just remember to carefully choose which set you will take parts—you can search for motors, gears, TECHNIC beams, or focus on pneumatics.

This covers the low-level building elements, but if you want to make the most out of your RCX, you have to look for more complex components, like sensors. These components can be bought directly from the LEGO Company, as well as through many other channels. A few additional sensors can really change your (LEGO) life, especially if they're not included in the RIS kit. For example, with a rotation sensor you can give your robots the capability to control their movements and position with increased accuracy. Moreover, third-party sensors can be bought online or even be home-made if you're skilled enough in electronics. They can be designed to reproduce a standard behavior or add new functionalities to your creations. For example, a IR proximity detector can locate objects and walls without having to touch them. You can check out Michael Gasperi's site for a lot of useful information on this subject (see www.plazaearth.com/usr/gasperi/lego.htm).

Furthermore, the LEGO Company produces special add-on kits that include pieces and special parts. Getting one of those kits is often more convenient than searching for spare parts:

- **Ultimate Accessory Set** This kit contains a remote control, a touch sensor, a rotation sensor, and a small LEGO lamp. This kit makes a good first-time expansion to a RIS set, mostly because you get a number of very useful tools, many of which are not included in the basic assortment.

- **Ultimate Builders Set** This is the latest of the expansion kits; it contains a 9V TECHNIC motor, transparent parts from the pneumatics series, a CD-ROM with new projects, and some special elements (gears, wheels, a turntable). This is a good choice if you want to start using pneumatics and if you need additional motors. Three motors are essential if you want your robots to do complex tasks.

- **Visual Command** This is a fully functioning PC video camera based on the Logitech QuickCam. It can record up to 30 frames per second and comes with a built-in microphone. It can be used as a standard stand-alone camera, or to work in conjunction with your RCX and take advantage of the Command Center vision recognition software. It can detect changes in light, motion, or color. It is available only in USB version, so unfortunately your robot must always be connected to the PC via a 5 meter cable, soyou can't build a fully autonomous and independent robot if you decide to use the camera.

There are also some other, older kits in the MINDSTORMS line, including Exploration Mars, RoboSport, and Extreme Creatures. These are assortments of pieces for particular tasks,which are usually quite expensive for the real value of the contents, so get them only if you are looking for specific parts that you know are included. For example, Exploration Mars has two very long electric cables, RoboSport one 9V motor, and Extreme Creatures has a fiber-optic system (FOS).

Finally, you can always expand your RIS with another RIS. It might sound a bit strange, but the second RIS brings with it a lot of pieces, sensors, motors, and a second RCX unit, all of which can be very useful for building bigger and more complex robots. The large number of pieces and second RCX unit can make the high cost of a second RIS a worthwhile purchase.

Summary

The Robotic Invention System (RIS) is the central set of the LEGO MIND-STORMS series, a robotics line designed both for kids and adults. The system is based on the RCX, a microcomputer that controls devices, reads sensors, runs motors, and communicates with other computers via an IR protocol. The unit is programmed from the end-user's PC.

RCX Code is the standard development environment provided by LEGO. RCX Code is limited in functionality, but many third-party tools have been created to overcome its limitations. NQC is an alternative text-based language that is easy and powerful; JavaAPIs are cross-platform programming interfaces; legOS, pbForth and leJOS are firmware replacements that allow the user to go even further.

Other kits and spare parts are available to extend the building options for your robots. Additionally, most TECHNIC pieces are fully compatible with LEGO MINDSTORMS kits. There are also other members of the LEGO robotics family, which are easier to use than the RCX-based RIS but more limited in building and programming possibilities.

Solutions Fast Track

The LEGO MINDSTORMS RIS Kit

☑ The MINDSTORMS series comes from a collaboration between the LEGO Company and the Massachusetts Institute of Technology (MIT) Media Lab that led to the creation of a "programmable brick."

☑ The Robotic Invention System (RIS) is the basic kit, and the starting point for every MINDSTORMS robot of more than basic complexity.

☑ The RIS includes everything you need to build and program robots: the RCX unit, three sensors, two motors, an infrared (IR) tower, manuals, more than 700 TECHNIC pieces and a software CD-ROM.

RCX: The Robot's Brain

☑ The RCX is a microcomputer than interfaces with input and output devices. Programs can be written on a PC and then downloaded to the unit through the IR tower.

☑ The RCX uses two types of memory: read-only memory (ROM) and modifiable random access memory (RAM). The latter stores both user-written programs and the system firmware, which is the RCX's operating system.

☑ The RCX can be expanded in two ways: using a different programming software like NQC or the Java APIs, or replacing the default firmware with a new one (legOS, pbForth, and leJOS solutions).

The RIS Software Environment

☑ The RIS kit contains RCX Code, which is the standard programming language from LEGO. It contains tools for downloading firmware and a visual programming interface that makes writing code a very easy task.

☑ RCX Code is targeted at kids and beginners; its capabilities are too limited for the development of more complex robots.

RCX Bytecodes

☑ The RCX architecture uses an interpreter-based virtual machine to execute commands statement by statement.

☑ Opcodes, the assembly commands, are used both by the RCX's stored programs and the IR emitting devices, like a PC with an IR tower or a remote control.

LEGO Expansion Kits

☑ There are other robotics kits besides the RCX-based system: CyberMaster, Scout, Micro Scout, and Code Pilot. Each of these kits features only a subset of the full RIS' capabilities.

☑ Standard LEGO TECHNIC pieces can be used to expand building possibilities, as can sensors and other spare pieces that are available separately.

☑ MINDSTORMS can be expanded with kits that contain sensors, motors, and special pieces. Further, Vision Command (VC) is a LEGO video camera with an advanced visual recognition system that can be used to add more functionalities to your LEGO MINDSTORMS robots.

Frequently Asked Questions

The following Frequently Asked Questions, answered by the authors of this book, are designed to both measure your understanding of the concepts presented   in this chapter and to assist you with real-life implementation of these concepts. To have your questions about this chapter answered by the author, browse to **www.syngress.com/solutions** and click on the **"Ask the Author"** form.

Q: How much memory do I have available for my programs?

A: With the default firmware you can store about 6 Kb of data.

Q: Can I get more memory?

A: Yes, but only if you install a new firmware, like legOS, pbForth, or leJOS.

Q: How can I use the new firmware features (version 0328)?

A: Use the RIS Software 2.0 or a recent version of NQC. Remember that the same features, and a lot more, can be found on alternative systems (like legOS and leJOS).

Q: I have an RIS 1.0 and want to use the new firmware. Is that possible?

A: You need only to get the file called "firm0328.lgo" and install it on your RCX. The easiest way is to get the MINDSTORMS SDK from the LEGO Web site, which also provides a utility to download the new firmware to your unit.

Q: Can I use a USB tower with an RIS 1.0?

A: The RCX has no problem with that, but be sure to upgrade to RIS software 2.0, as older versions don't support the new tower.

Q: I want to use MINDSTORMS on my Mac. Which of the two towers is the most compatible with different operating systems?

A: At the moment, the serial tower is very well supported under most OSs, including Mac and UNIX-based computer systems, because it was the first to appear on the robotics scene. LEGO and third-party software are slowly updating their applications to add the USB support, but it's still not available for every tool.

Q: I just bought an RIS as my first MINDSTORMS set. What's the best expansion for it?

A: The first parts you need are a third motor and a rotation sensor. You can get them individually, or included in add-on sets, the best of which are probably the Ultimate Accessory Set and the Ultimate Builders Set.

## Chapter 2

The Java Communications API

Solutions in this chapter:

- Overview of the Java Communications Extension API (JCE API)

- Installing and Configuring the Java Communications API

- Reading and Writing to Serial Ports

- Debugging with Serial Ports: The "Black Box" Example

- Extending the Java Communications API

☑ Summary

☑ Solutions Fast Track

☑ Frequently Asked Questions

Introduction

The Java Communications API is a standard Java Extension API that provides communications capabilities to serial and parallel ports. These capabilities are not present in the core Java runtime environment, but can be added to various versions of the environment as a Java *extension* API. This provides applications with these capabilities by redistributing the extension API along with the deliverable application. This chapter will provide an introduction to the use of the Java Communications API as well as an overview of its design and architecture. Simple and advanced example applications are presented with source code to illustrate the use of the Java Communications API and how to extend its functionality—specifically in relation to communicating with the LEGO MINDSTORMS RCX. This will also be examined in detail in later chapters.

Overview of the Java Communications Extension API (JCE API)

The Java Communications API 2.0 was released in 1998 as the standard communication mechanism for serial (RS232/434) and parallel (IEEE 1284) ports using pure Java. That is, standard Java code will run across all compliant platforms, using the official interface.

The current implementations are found in the following locations:

- **Windows and Solaris** http://java.sun.com/products/javacomm
- **Linux** www.vorlesungen.uni-osnabrueck.de/informatik/robot00/ftp/ javacomm.html
- **Mac OS** http://homepage.mac.com/pcbeard/javax.comm.MRJ

For the most part, communication is performed through standard input and output streams in Java. These streams are provided from the underlying ports through a common interface. All the ports extend a common abstract class (called *CommPort*) that provides the basic representation of a given port. This allows for standard mechanisms to open, read/write, and close ports. This is one of the two primary functions provided by the Java Communications Extension (JCE) API. The other is port management and ownership, which is described below.

Similar to other Java APIs, the JCE API makes use of the observer pattern; event notifications are triggered upon a change of port ownership, as are specific data notifications (as with the case of serial ports).

The Java Communications Extension library primarily consists of one package: *javax.comm.**. This library contains the classes, interfaces and exceptions listed in Table 2.1.

Table 2.1 Components of the *javax.comm* Package

Classes	Interfaces	Exceptions
CommPort	CommDriver	NoSuchPortException
CommPortIdentifier	CommPortOwnershipListener	PortInUseException
ParallelPort	ParallelPortEventListner	UnsupportedComm OperationException
ParallelPortEvent	SerialPortEventListner	
SerialPort		
SerialPortEvent		

We will go into the architecture of the Java Communications API in greater detail later; but what stands out from the list at first glance are the event classes and event listener classes. This allows the framework to handle asynchronous notifications of not just specific serial port and parallel port events, but also of port ownership changes and updates. Hence one would know when a specific port is available, or one could wait until it is available or closed. The classes of note above (other than the encapsulation of serial and parallel objects of course) are the *CommPort* and *CommPortIdentifier* classes.

The *CommPort* is an abstract class that serves as the base class for all ports, enabling you to manage and handle all the ports in the same way. It contains the minimal and basic common methods that one would expect from all communication ports, except for one: *open()* is handled by the *CommPortIdentifier*. The *CommPort's* notable methods are *getOutputStream()*, *getInputStream()*, and *close()*.

This leads us to the *CommPortIdentifier* class through which we will create, manage and identify all ports. Think of this class as a port factory that allows you to discover and enumerate all the ports in the system and handle the ownership of those ports.

The *CommDriver* Java interface gives the developers of new communication port drivers the ability to add to the Java Communications API in a consistent manner. We will also examine how one would use this to add a new custom port.

Lastly, as listed in Table 2.1, there are custom Java exceptions in this API that allows for notification of errors specific to this framework that might occur: if a given port is already in use, if a requested port does not exist, and if a specific operation on a given port is not supported. One would think that all of *CommPort's* abstract methods should be implemented by all ports, as they are a general list. This exception allows for any future type of port to be added easily, as the *CommPort* contract is not too rigid. For example, a future port XYZ, might not be expected to implement the abstract *enableReceiveTimeout()* method in the *CommPort* class if the underlying hardware cannot support this kind of behavior. Basically one would first test to see if a function is supported before trying to use it. If the unsupported exception is thrown, it can then be caught and handled gracefully.

Understanding the JCE Framework

As stated, the Java Communications API provides a clean and simple framework for allowing access to both serial and parallel ports from 100 percent Java code. This permits you to write applications ranging from modem software to custom printer drivers, or provide access from Java to a multitude of devices that interface with serial and parallel ports. These include devices ranging from mp3 players or video capture devices to home automation devices (such as X10 devices). Table 2.2 shows some of the features and limitations of the Java Communications API that will be addressed in the following sections.

Table 2.2 Features and Limitations of the Java Communications API

Features	Limitations
Port Discovery and Enumeration	Limited to serial and parallel ports.
Port Ownership Management	Difficult for third party implementations of new device protocols to be added to the core API.
Asynchronous event based I/O easier.	Initial configuration could be made
Clean encapsulation of underlying native ports for several platforms including Windows, Solaris, Linux and Macintosh	

Port Discovery and Enumeration

In this section we will illustrate how to enumerate all ports available on a system. This is the first step with all applications that use the Java Communications API. The following classes and methods highlight the enumeration process:

- *CommPort* Provides input and output streams to the ports and is the base class to SerialPort and ParallelPort.

- *SerialPort* Extends CommPort to represent a RS232 serial port

- *CommPortIdentifier* Provides control of ports in a system. Serves as both a port identifier object and a port ID. Note this distinction which at first glance can be confusing. A port identifier object is not a port object but identifies and interfaces with an associated port object.

- *public static Enumeration getPortIdentifiers()* This static method will provide a complete identifier list of all ports (serial and parallel) on a system.

- *public String getName()* The name of this port identifier

- *public int getPortType()* The type of port this port identifier represents, namely one of the following:

  - *CommPortIdentifier.PORT_SERIAL*

  - *CommPortIdentifier.PORT_PARALLEL*

The code shown in Figure 2.1 illustrates how the API is used to list all the available serial ports for the entire system (computer). This code can be found on the companion CD with this book.

Figure 2.1 TestEnumeration.java

```
import javax.comm.CommPortIdentifier;

import javax.comm.SerialPort;

import javax.comm.PortInUseException;

import java.util.Enumeration;

import java.util.Vector;


public class TestEnumeration {

    public static void main(String args[]) {
        Vector portslist = TestEnumeration.getAvailableSerialPorts();
        System.out.println("found "+portslist.size()+" open ports");
    }
    public static Vector getAvailableSerialPorts() {
        CommPortIdentifier pId=null;
        SerialPort sPort=null;
        Enumeration pList=null;
```

Continued

Figure 2.1 Continued

```
boolean foundport=false;
pList = CommPortIdentifier.getPortIdentifiers();
String port=null;
Vector ports=new Vector();

if(!pList.hasMoreElements()) {
    System.err.print("warning: no ports found - ");
    System.err.println("make sure javax.comm.properties file is found");
    return ports;
}
while (pList.hasMoreElements()) {
    pId = (CommPortIdentifier) pList.nextElement();
    if (pId.getPortType() == CommPortIdentifier.PORT_SERIAL) {
        foundport=true;
        try {
            sPort = (SerialPort)pId.open("serialport", 1000);
        } catch (PortInUseException e) {
            foundport=false;
            System.out.println(pId.getName()+ " is closed");
        } finally {
            if(sPort!=null) {
                try { sPort.close(); } catch(Exception e) {}
            }
            if(foundport) {
                ports.add(pId.getName());
                System.out.println(pId.getName()+ " is open");
            }
        }
    }
}
return ports;
}
}
```

Sample output:

```
>java TestEnumeration
 COM1 is open
 COM2 is open
 COM3 is closed
 COM4 is closed
 found 2 open ports
```

Starting with *main()*, the call to the *getAvailableSerialPorts()* method will return a vector of strings of the available serial ports' names. In this simple example, we get the vector and print its length, telling us how many serial ports there are.

As we step into the *getAvailableSerialPorts()* method, we find the usual first step for enumerating all the ports: *CommPortIdentifier.getPortIdentifiers()* is called.

If no ports are found, a warning message is displayed; this is unusual and usually indicates a configuration problem, namely that the javax.comm.properties file is in the wrong place.

We then loop through the enumeration, checking the port type with each iteration. If it's a serial port type, we open the port to see if it is available.

Now, why does *CommPortIdentifier* use the *open()* method in one step instead of first retrieving the port and then having *CommPort* invoke the *open()* method? This clarifies the concept that port discovery and control (ownership) must be done in only one central point: the *CommPortIdentifier*. Perhaps *CommPortIdentifier* should have been renamed to "CommPortManager" or "CommPortFactory," but then it would require breaking out the ID portion to a separate class; or perhaps the factory could have implemented it as an interface. A factory implementing an interface? Well okay, perhaps not, but nonetheless this chapter will mention *CommPortIdentifier* more than any other class, due to its many responsibilities.

Port Ownership Management

Port ownership allows one to wait for an available port while respecting requests from other applications that seek access to the port. Ownership contention usually occurs after enumeration. The following classes and interfaces are used for port ownership contention:

- **CommPort** Provides input and output streams to the ports, and is the base class of *SerialPort* and *ParallelPort*.

- **SerialPort** Extends *CommPort* to represent a RS232 serial port.

- *CommPortIdentifier* Provides control of ports in a system. Serves as both a port identifier object and a port ID.

- *public String getCurrentOwner()* This method obtains the owner of the underlying port to which the port identifier wants to connect, or already owns. This is not the owner of the identifier itself but rather of the actual port at that specific time.

- *public boolean isCurrentlyOwned()* This method tells you if the port is currently owned. Again there is no ownership of the identifiers.

- *public void addPortOwnershipListener(CommPortOwnershipListener listener)* This method allows you to add a callback listener to the following ownership events:

  ```
  CommPortOwnershipListener.PORT_OWNED

  CommPortOwnershipListener.PORT_UNOWNED

  CommPortOwnershipListener.PORT_OWNERSHIP_REQUESTED
  ```

- *CommPortOwnershipListener* This interface has only one method, the *public void ownershipChange(int event)* callback, which indicates a change in ownership for any of the above events. The integer parameter is one of the ownership events listed above, and is usually processed with a switch statement.

Figure 2.2 (also provided on the CD that accompanies this book) illustrates the monitoring of port ownership as well as port contention.

Figure 2.2 TestOwnership.java

```java
import javax.comm.CommPortIdentifier;

import javax.comm.CommPortOwnershipListener;

import javax.comm.SerialPort;

import javax.comm.NoSuchPortException;

import javax.comm.PortInUseException;

import java.io.IOException;


public class TestOwnership implements CommPortOwnershipListener {


    public static void main(String args[]) {

        TestOwnership test = new TestOwnership(args[0]);

        test.loop();
```

Continued

Figure 2.2 Continued

```
    }

    private CommPortIdentifier portID1,portID2;
    private SerialPort sPort1,sPort2;

    public TestOwnership(String port) {
        try {
            portID1 = CommPortIdentifier.getPortIdentifier(port);
            portID2 = CommPortIdentifier.getPortIdentifier(port);
        } catch (NoSuchPortException e) {
            System.err.println(e);
            return;
        }
        portID1.addPortOwnershipListener(this);
    }

    public void ownershipChange(int type) {
      switch (type) {
        case CommPortOwnershipListener.PORT_UNOWNED:
            System.out.println(portID1.getCurrentOwner()+": PORT_UNOWNED");
            break;
        case CommPortOwnershipListener.PORT_OWNED:
            System.out.println(portID1.getCurrentOwner() + ": PORT_OWNED");
            break;
        case CommPortOwnershipListener.PORT_OWNERSHIP_REQUESTED:
            System.out.println(portID1.getCurrentOwner()
                                          + ": PORT_OWNERSHIP_REQUESTED");
      }
    }

    public void loop() {
      while(true) {
        switch((int)(Math.random()*5)+1) {
          case 1:
            try {
```

Continued

Figure 2.2 Continued

```
                     sPort1=(SerialPort)portID1.open("portID1",1000);
            } catch(PortInUseException e) {
                System.err.println(portID1.getCurrentOwner()
                      +" failed to open "+portID1.getName()
                      +" because it's owned by "+e.currentOwner);
            }
            break;
         case 2:
            try {
               sPort2=(SerialPort)portID2.open("portID2",1000);
            } catch(PortInUseException e) {
                System.err.println(portID1.getCurrentOwner()
                      +" failed to open "+portID1.getName()
                      +" because it's owned by "+e.currentOwner);
            }
            break;
         case 3:
            try {
               if(portID1.isCurrentlyOwned())
                    sPort1.close();
            } catch(Exception e) { }
            break;
         case 4:
            try {
               if(portID2.isCurrentlyOwned())
                    sPort2.close();
            } catch(Exception e) { }
         }
        try {Thread.sleep(1500);}catch(Exception e) { }
      }
    }
}
```

Sample output:

```
>java TestOwnership COM1
 portID1: PORT_OWNED
```

```
portID1:  PORT_OWNERSHIP_REQUESTED
portID1 failed to open COM1 because it's owned by portID1
Port currently not owned:  PORT_UNOWNED
portID1:  PORT_OWNED
portID1:  PORT_OWNERSHIP_REQUESTED
portID1 failed to open COM1 because it's owned by portID1
Port currently not owned:  PORT_UNOWNED
portID2:  PORT_OWNED
portID2:  PORT_OWNERSHIP_REQUESTED
portID2 failed to open COM1 because it's owned by portID2
Port currently not owned:  PORT_UNOWNED
portID1:  PORT_OWNED
portID1:  PORT_OWNERSHIP_REQUESTED
portID1 failed to open COM1 because it's owned by portID1
```

In this example, we pass a parameter from the command line to indicate the port with which we want to test ownership. For simplicity's sake, there's no parameter checking so you have to supply a parameter. We then enter a continuous loop. As the result output shows, we will see a random request to open or close the port from two different identifiers with errors displaying the current owner of the port. As a variation of this example, one could try passing in more than one port. I used only one in this example because that way it's more likely that ownership contention will occur when two identifiers try to own the same port.

In the constructor, we will see the creation of two port identifiers for the same port that we passed in. We also see that the first port identifier registers itself as a listener to ownership events using the *addPortOwnershipListener(this)* method. We will implement the *CommPortOwnershipListener* interface and also the *ownershipChange(int type)* method to receive the events.

We cannot add more than one listener. If we do, the *TooManyListenersException* error will be thrown. This could be considered a limitation of the Java Communications API, but normally one doesn't add more than one listener to a specific port anyway; one would add a listener for each port. In this case we only need one of each to show us all the events for the port in question.

If we get an error when we try to open a port, we can use the *PortInUseException* to tell us what caused it (who the current owner of the port is, for example). In this example, when we try to close the port, we first check to see if it's already owned by someone else, using the *isCurrentlyOwned()* method.

It is important to realize that if one tries to open or close a port, the callback *ownershipChange(int type)* will not generate a new event. This is to prevent the deadlock that would ensue if new events were created every time these actions were executed.

The most interesting aspect of ownership contention (and perhaps of the entire Java Communications API) is the fact that you can run the above example in two different Java virtual machines and still be able to send and receive ownership events across the VMs. This can seem a bit startling at first, but it turns out to be very useful for testing and debugging purposes. The owner names will also be propagated, with external native applications that own a given port being labeled "Unknown Windows Application."

Asynchronous event-based I/O

Event based I/O is usually the most efficient means of communication, allowing for near real-time responsiveness. This is demonstrated quite well when adjusting reception parameters, a concept that applies to all types of ports.

The five properties shared by all ports, as defined by the abstract *CommPort* class, are as follows:

- **Receive Timeout** This is the number of milliseconds before the read method returns.

- **Receive Threshold** This is the number of bytes present before the read method returns.

- **Input Buffersize** This is the number of bytes the port's input buffer will hold before the read method returns.

Table 2.3 summarizes the effect these first three properties have on blocking the input stream.

Table 2.3 Input Stream Blocking Parameters

ReceiveThreshold	ReceiveTimeout	InputBuffer	Behavior
Disabled	Disabled	n bytes	Block until any data is available
Enabled, m bytes	Disabled	n bytes	Block until min(m,n) bytes received
Disabled	Enabled, x ms	n bytes	Block for x ms or until any data is available

Continued

Table 2.3 Continued

ReceiveThreshold	ReceiveTimeout	InputBuffer	Behavior
Enabled, *m* bytes	Enabled, *x* ms	*n* bytes	Block for *x* ms or until min(*m,n*) bytes received

- **Receive Framing** This forces the read method to return immediately, overriding all other values.
- **Output Buffersize** This must be large enough to prevent a buffer overrun in the event that the software runs faster than the hardware can handle.

Not all five methods need to be implemented by all subclasses of *CommPort*. Enabling timeout, framing and threshold all have the option of throwing the *UnsupportedCommOperationException*. One should check for this exception to determine if these properties are supported.

Encapsulation of Underlying Native Ports

Access to the native ports on different platforms (specifically Windows and Solaris) are currently provided by the Java Communication API. The *CommPortIdentifier* hides the process of selecting the native driver and provides the instance of *CommPort* (the abstract base class for serial and parallel ports). We will see this process in more detail in a later section.

Java Communication API's Event Based Architecture

As we've examined so far, there is an event-based mechanism for handling port ownership. Similarly, there are data events for the serial and parallel ports that are used for efficient communications. Both of these are major parts of the Java Communications API, and rely on an event-based architecture. The classes and interfaces are defined to support this.

Figure 2.3 shows the UML diagram for the Java Communications API.

There are a few non-public helper classes for *CommPortIdentifier* that help it manage the list of port owners that aren't shown; these classes simply provide ID owner list management. The relationships in Figure 2.3 are pretty straightforward, and we've already covered some of the relationships (for example, *CommPort* is the base abstract class for all ports). The relationship that *CommPortIdentifier* has with *CommDriver* will be covered later in the section called "Extending the Java Communications API." What you should notice in Figure 2.3 is that both serial and parallel ports have associated event and listener classes, such as *SerialPortEvent* and *SerialPortEventListener*. Just as we saw with the *CommPortOwnershipListener*, the callback mechanism works by having the listener register with the port in order to receive events in its callback method; *SerialEvent(SerialPortEvent evt)*. This differs from the ownership event notification in that we can choose which events will notify the listener by calling the appropriate *notifyOn[name of event]()* method on the port itself.

Figure 2.3 The javax.comm Package

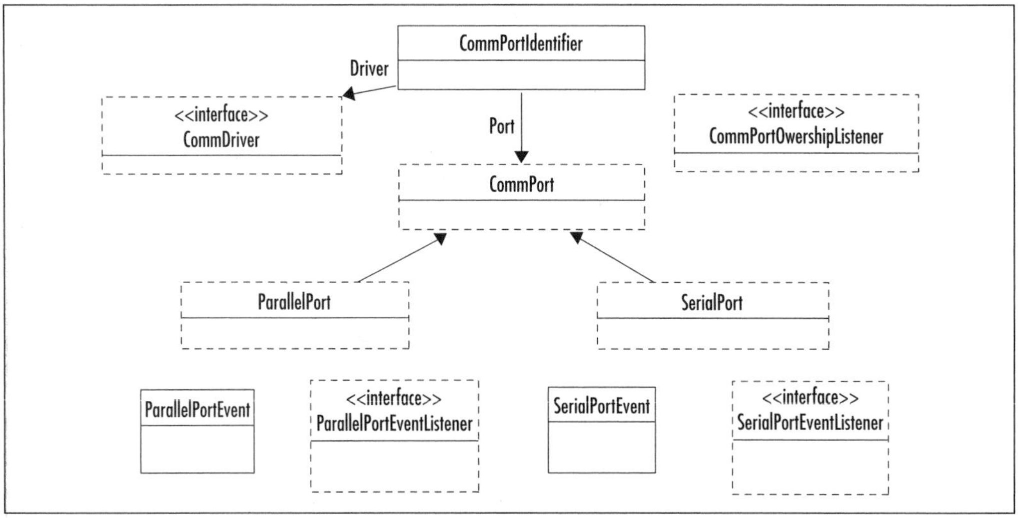

We will look specifically at the *SerialPort* class and the event signals that are available for all serial port implementations.

Table 2.4 shows the serial port's control and status event signals.

Table 2.4 Serial Port Control and Status Signals

Abbreviation	Definition
RTS	Request To Send
CTS	Clear To Send
DTR	Data Terminal Ready
DSR	Data Set Ready
RI	Ring Indicate

Continued

Table 2.4 Continued

Abbreviation	Definition
CD	Carrier Detect
OE	Overrun Error
FE	Framing Error
PE	Parity Error
BI	Break Indicator
DA	Data Available
BE	Output Buffer Empty

An example of a method for requesting notification is *notifyOnDataAvailable (boolean enable)*.

The signals shown in Table 2.4 are mainly for the physical control lines of the serial port and some error notifications. There are also two other serial port properties that one can set but that are not event driven. The first is *serial port data control functions*:

- **Baud Rate** The rate of change of the data state (not necessarily bits per second).

- **Data Bits** The number of bits in each communication packet.

- **Parity** Even, Odd or none. An extra bit per packet set for data integrity.

- **Stop Bits** Also for data integrity and error checking; the number of extra bits added to signal the end of a packet.

The second is serial port flow control functions:

- **RTS/CTL** Hardware shaking using control lines.
- **XON/XOFF** Software based control using special characters.

These properties are generic to all serial ports. They have corresponding abstract methods in the *SerialPort* class that are implemented by the native classes. In turn, the native classes extend the abstract methods for each platform such as *Win32SerialPort.*for the Windows platform.

Installing and Configuring the Java Communications API

The Java Communications API download includes installation documentation, as well as the documentation for the packages and many sample programs that use the API. However, many of the installations still have configuration problems that arise from a failure to understand exactly how the *CommPortIdentifier* finds and loads the native shared libraries. There are also general Java classpath issues that arise when installing the *comm.jar* file; we'll look at two options.

One option, as noted in the API documentation, is to add the comm.jar file to your classpath and drop the native shared library somewhere in your runtime path, then add the properties file to your Java SDK (or JRE) library folder. What the documentation fails to say is that, as of Java 2, there's no need to have a classpath environment variable. A Java 2 variation of this option is to put .jar files (especially since *comm.jar* is a standard extension) in the */lib/ext* folder (located under the *jre* folder for either the SDK or JRE installations). The safest bet for the properties file, *javax.comm.properties* is the */lib* folder, where all the system properties are kept anyway.

However, if you do drop the comm.jar file into the extensions folder, be aware of whether you are adding it to the JRE or the JDK installation, since they could reside in different folders altogether. In fact, in some releases, the java.exe executable for the JRE installation is placed in the system path. Place it in the folder that corresponds to your Java executables.

The second, easier option (though not necessarily the most convenient) is to place all the files into your application's current runtime folder (assuming you include the current folder in your classpath—this isn't necessarily always the case).

Installing the Native Library

On Windows, the native library is the win32com.dll file. On Solaris, it's *libSolarisSerialParallel.so*. For other applications check the redistributables for the shared library.

On all platforms the library must reside where your application can find it. Whether it is included in the runtime path or in the current path from which the application is run.

For example, on Solaris you would have to specify the following (where *pwd* is your present working directory):

```
setenv LD_LIBRARY_PATH `pwd`:$LD_LIBRARY_PATH
```

Alternatively, you can add it to your /usr/lib path (assuming you have privileges).

Likewise on Windows platforms you can add it to your path, as follows:

```
set PATH=%PATH;\pwd
```

or copy it to your \windows directory (assuming you have the appropriate privileges).

Installing the Java comm.jar Library

As mentioned earlier, you can add this to your classpath by moving it to the extension folder or keeping it in the current working folder. Make sure that the current working folder is part of the classpath. You could also set the system variable *CLASSPATH* to explicitly include both the current working folder and the path to *comm.jar*.

When running an application like *RCXTest.java*, for example, you would generally do the following:

```
java RCXTest
```

which won't work if the application needs the *comm.jar* (unless it is specified in the CLASSPATH variable). You can add the jar file as follows:

```
java -cp comm.jar RCXTest
```

You would also need to add the current path (unless the current path is already in the classpath or you are not using the *-cp* flag)

```
java -cp .;comm.jar RCXTest
```

It's generally a good idea to place the current directory first in your classpath to give it precedence.

The javax.comm.properties Configuration File

This file is what tells the Java Communications API where to find your native library. It basically lists the Java files (strictly speaking, Java "classes" might be a better term since only classes are actually loaded) that need to be loaded at run-time to provide platform-specific interfaces. The entries on the Windows and Solaris platforms respectively look like this:

```
# Windows Serial Driver
Driver=com.sun.comm.Win32Driver
```

```
# Solaris Serial Driver
Driver=com.sun.comm.SolarisDriver
```

Of course the two entries above are not in the same file, but you could have multiple entries per file for a platform as follows:

```
# Windows Serial Driver
Driver=com.sun.comm.Win32Driver
# Windows USB Driver for Lego Mindstorms
Driver=rcx.comm.Win32USBDriver
```

I said you "could" because this isn't a recommended practice unless you are extending the Java Communications API itself (which we will attempt later in this chapter). The current *Driver* entry is used by the *CommPortIdentifier* to select which *CommDriver* implementation is to be used (Win32Driver above implements *CommDriver*). We'll go into more detail when we discuss adding USB ports to the Java Communications API.

Configuring your Development Environment

There are several different approaches to installing Java extension libraries or packages. First there's the approach that promotes ease-of-use for the developer. The second approach makes the end user's environment a staging/development environment.

In the first scenario, we can follow the convention of placing the Java extension jar file where all the extensions should go: The extension folder in the Java Runtime Environment's library folder. In the case of a Java Development Kit (JDK) on a Windows platform, this would mostly likely be found as follows:

```
c:\j2sdk1.4.0\jre\lib\ext
```

Notice that it is the \jre folder. This is where we should look, as opposed to the root folder when looking for the ext folder. This may not seem intuitive since there is also a c:\ j2sdk1.4.0\lib folder, but the Java executable will use the \jre folder when looking for extension libraries and property files, such as the javax.comm.properties file.

The following Java Communications *threesome* has caused great frustration for thoseusing and installing JCE (Java Communications Extension):

- **comm.jar** This should go in the ..\jre\lib\ext folder or added to the global classpath (which is not recommended).

- **javax.comm.properties** This would go in the ..\jre\lib folder. It tells JCE which native library to use.

- **win32comm.dll** This is the Windows-native shared library for JCE. This library should go somewhere in the global path (for example, c:\windows).

The result is the convenience of compiling and testing as follows (the test example uses JCE):

```
javac Test.java
java Test
```

No mention of jar files or fiddling with *CLASSPATH* environment variables. One can even traverse all the sample folders that come with JCE without worrying about what the current path is.

NOTE

When compiling with your own package you must use the *-d* option to allow the creation of package folders. It's safer to use *javac –d . Test.java* when compiling, for instance. Otherwise you may run into the *NoClassDefFoundError* exception.

Of course, the other scenario is to develop and test under release conditions. Under release conditions, you will most likely not install your application by installing all the necessary files in all these separate folders. In fact, since the JCE is redistributable, you will find it more convenient for installation and deinstallation purposes to package all your files in the same folder. JCE will also look for the properties file in the classpath where comm.jar resides if it fails to find it in the lib folder of the current Java runtime environment:

```
java -cp .;comm.jar Test
```

This can be safely hidden in a run.bat file, or if you are ambitious you can wrap an executable to hide the command line and provide extra features, such as determining which Java Runtime is installed—and maybe even installing and downloading one if there isn't already one present. Keep in mind that on Windows platforms, one can avoid the additional download of a Java runtime by using Microsoft's Java runtime. (*jview*). Yes, the Java Communications Extension API will work with jview.

Note above that the current directory is included in the added classpath entry on the command line. Also residing in the current path would be the native dll file, which does not need to be specified in the global path.

Keep in mind that using script files (bat files) is also convenient for the developer because it allows one to switch and test several versions of Java runtime environments.

Since JCE has been tested and is available for most platforms (for example, Linux, Mac OS, and Solaris), the same applies to those platforms with the exception of the native shared libraries names .

One more tip is to specify the output directory when using the command line compiler:

```
javac -classpath .;comm.jar -d . Test.java
```

Note in the above line that the *−d* directive specifies the current directory as your output directory. Normally this is the default, but with Java runtimes on some platforms, if you have a package that creates output folders, it will fail to do so unless you specify where to create them.

Reading and Writing to Serial Ports

The Java Communications API comes with several simple examples that illustrate the usage of both parallel and serial ports. In this section we will walk through examples that cover the previously discussed concepts. This will tie in both basic port creation and access, as well as event notifications and, where necessary, the use of threads.

Simple Read Example

In the following example we will illustrate the implementation of the *Runnable* and *SerialPortEventListener* interfaces. This means that we will register to receive serial port events using the *SerialEvent()* event handler callback as well as illustrating the use of a thread for continuous reading from the port.

```
public class SimpleRead implements Runnable, SerialPortEventListener
{
    static CommPortIdentifier portId;
    static Enumeration portList;
    InputStream inputStream;
    SerialPort serialPort;
```

```
    Thread readThread;

public static void main(String[] args)
{
  boolean portFound = false;
  String defaultPort = "COM"; "COM1";

  if (args.length > 0) {
      defaultPort = args[0];
  }

  portList = CommPortIdentifier.getPortIdentifiers();

  while (portList.hasMoreElements()) {
      portId = (CommPortIdentifier) portList.nextElement();
      if (portId.getPortType() == CommPortIdentifier.PORT_SERIAL) {
        if (portId.getName().equals(defaultPort)) {
          System.out.println("Found port: "+defaultPort);
          portFound = true;
          SimpleRead reader = new SimpleRead();
        }
      }
  }
  if (!portFound) {
      System.out.println("port " + defaultPort + " not found.");
  }

}

public SimpleRead() {
  try {
      serialPort = (SerialPort) portId.open("SimpleReadApp", 2000);
  } catch (PortInUseException e) {}

  try {
      inputStream = serialPort.getInputStream();
  } catch (IOException e) {}
```

```java
    try {
        serialPort.addEventListener(this);
    } catch (TooManyListenersException e) {}

    serialPort.notifyOnDataAvailable(true);

    try {
        serialPort.setSerialPortParams(2400, SerialPort.DATABITS_8,
                        SerialPort.STOPBITS_1,
                        SerialPort.PARITY_NONE);
    } catch (UnsupportedCommOperationException e) {}

    readThread = new Thread(this);

    readThread.start();
}

public void run() {
    try {
        Thread.sleep(20000);
    } catch (InterruptedException e) {}
}

public void serialEvent(SerialPortEvent event) {
    switch (event.getEventType()) {

    case SerialPortEvent.BI:
    case SerialPortEvent.OE:
    case SerialPortEvent.FE:
    case SerialPortEvent.PE:
    case SerialPortEvent.CD:
    case SerialPortEvent.CTS:
    case SerialPortEvent.DSR:
    case SerialPortEvent.RI:

    case SerialPortEvent.OUTPUT_BUFFER_EMPTY:
```

```
        break;


    case SerialPortEvent.DATA_AVAILABLE:
        byte[] readBuffer = new byte[20];


        try {
        while (inputStream.available() > 0) {
            int numBytes = inputStream.read(readBuffer);
        }


        System.out.print(new String(readBuffer));
        } catch (IOException e) {}


        break;

    }

  }

}
```

From *main()* we either specify a port on the command line, or if not, COM1 will be used by default. We then find the port using *CommPortIdentifier* as before and create an instance of this *SimpleRead* class. We then proceed to open the port, get an input stream, and register our *SimpleRead* instance as a serial port event listener. At this point, we tell the port what event (or events) we're interested in and in this case we call on *notifyOnDataAvailable()*. Also, there are a slew of *notify* type methods that you can read from the documentation for the other events of which you might be interested in being notified. This could have been called before registering as a listener but we don't want to miss any events. Finally, we create a new thread passing the *SimpleRead* instance as the runnable object to the thread, and start that thread.

Upon receiving the event we proceed to read in a loop while there is data available. This is a pretty standard reading technique that uses the input stream's *available()* method.

This thread will eventually end because in our *run()* method we simply decide to sleep for 20 seconds. We could also have timed out the connection and closed gracefully after a certain period of time from when the last *DATA_AVAILABLE* event was sent.

Simple Write Example

The following example illustrates the other half of the equation by writing to a port. Additionally, we will use event handling to check for when the buffer is empty.

```java
public class SimpleWrite implements SerialPortEventListener
{
  static Enumeration portList;
  static CommPortIdentifier portId;
  static String messageString = "Hello, world!";
  static SerialPort serialPort;
  static OutputStream outputStream;
  static boolean outputBufferEmptyFlag = false;

  public static void main(String[] args) {
    boolean portFound = false;
    String  defaultPort = "COM1";

    if (args.length > 0) {
        defaultPort = args[0];
    }

    portList = CommPortIdentifier.getPortIdentifiers();

    while (portList.hasMoreElements()) {
      portId = (CommPortIdentifier) portList.nextElement();

      if (portId.getPortType() == CommPortIdentifier.PORT_SERIAL) {

        if (portId.getName().equals(defaultPort)) {
            System.out.println("Found port " + defaultPort);

            portFound = true;

            try {
              serialPort = (SerialPort) portId.open("SimpleWrite", 2000);
            } catch (PortInUseException e) {
```

```
         System.out.println("Port in use.");
           continue;
         }

         try {
           outputStream = serialPort.getOutputStream();
         } catch (IOException e) {}

         try {
           serialPort.setSerialPortParams(2400,
                           SerialPort.DATABITS_8,
                           SerialPort.STOPBITS_1,
                           SerialPort.PARITY_ODD);
         } catch (UnsupportedCommOperationException e) {}

         try {
             serialPort.notifyOnOutputEmpty(true);
         } catch (Exception e) {
           System.out.println("Error setting event notification");
           System.out.println(e.toString());
           System.exit(-1);
         }

         System.out.println("Writing \""+messageString+"\" to "
                                           +serialPort.getName());
         try {
           outputStream.write(messageString.getBytes());
         } catch (IOException e) {}

         try {
             Thread.sleep(2000);
         } catch (Exception e) {}
         serialPort.close();
         System.exit(1);
       }
     }
   }
```

```
        if (!portFound) {
            System.out.println("port " + defaultPort + " not found.");
        }
    }

    public void serialEvent(SerialPortEvent event) {
      switch (event.getEventType()) {

      case SerialPortEvent.BI:
      case SerialPortEvent.OE:
      case SerialPortEvent.FE:
      case SerialPortEvent.PE:
      case SerialPortEvent.CD:
      case SerialPortEvent.CTS:
      case SerialPortEvent.DSR:
      case SerialPortEvent.RI:
      case SerialPortEvent.DATA_AVAILABLE:
          break;

      case SerialPortEvent.OUTPUT_BUFFER_EMPTY:
          serialPort.close();
          System.exit(0);
          break;

        }
      }
    }
```

Once again, the port identifier list is traversed until we find an available serial port. This time, after we register the *SimpleWrite* instance as an event listener, and tell the serial port that we are interested in the output buffer empty signal with *notifyOnOutputEmpty()*, we don't need to start any threads because we're simply going to send one message to the port, sleep for two seconds and then close gracefully. We can also choose to close as soon as we know that we have success-fully written out the message, thanks to the *OUTPUT_BUFFER_EMPTY* event. We also output the appropriate error code upon exiting. If two seconds pass before we get signaled, then it's possible that the write may have failed.

Debugging with Serial Ports: The "Black Box" Example

One of the sample programs included with the Java Communications API goes beyond the call of duty. Written by Tom Corso for Sun Microsystems, it's a fully featured serial port analyzer. As one of its features, it provides line monitoring where the application will use two serial ports, acting as a "black box" between them. This is useful for monitoring and analyzing data and protocols, similar to the methods by which the RCX opcodes were originally discovered and documented outside of the LEGO Company. See the "Reverse Engineering" sidebar for a full explanation of the "black box" concept.

Here's how it's run:

```
java -cp BlackBox.jar BlackBox [-h] | [-f] [-l] [-m] [-n] [-s] [-d
receive_delay] [-p ports]
```

The command line options are:

```
-h      help message

-f      friendly mode - will relinquish control of the port to others
        that request ownership.

-l      run as a line monitor - connects to serial ports together

-m      modem mode - converts newlines to \n\r.

-n      do not use receiver threads - used to check flow control

-s      silent mode.  - doesn't display received data.

-d      sleep for receive_delay milliseconds after each read -  used to check
        flow control.

-p      open only the ports specified (separated by spaces).  If not
        specified, all ports will be opened. Note: This must be the last
        argument given.
```

Figure 2.4 shows a frame window containing one panel that represents a serial port. For each available serial port (only one is shown in the Figure) another identical panel (a *SerialPortDisplay*) is displayed and added to the frame, following a simple top-down layout.

One can toggle the port open and closed by clicking on the port name. Its status is displayed with the following label colors:

- **Green** Port is open.

- **Yellow** Port is in use.
- **Red** Port is closed.

Figure 2.4 BlackBox Sample Program

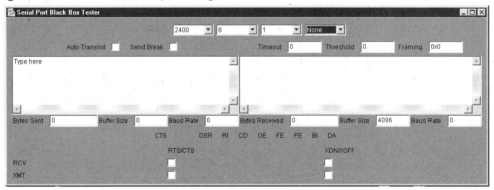

There are a set of controls whose values can be manipulated the values in real time for:

- Baud rate
- Data bits
- Stop bits
- Parity

Also all the standard serial port indicators (some of which can be toggled by clicking) are: RTS, CTS, DTR, DSR, RI, CD, OE, FE, PE, BI, DA, and EE.

There is also a set of checkboxes for setting flow control, either RTS/CTS or XON/XOFF, and an **Auto Transmit** feature that sends a continuous test pattern. **Send Break** sends a 1000-millisecond break signal.

There's also a text area for sending data and a display of the buffer in use, number of bytes sent and the actual calculated baud rate. By clicking on the **Bytes Transmitted/Received**, **Baud Rate** and **Buffer Size** labels you can reset the value. Text shown in the **receive** window will have nonprintable characters converted.

Figure 2.5 shows all the classes, each of which has a corresponding Java source file. Most of the objects are GUI components, starting with *BlackBox* (which is the frame window). The class that does most of the work is *SerialPortDisplay*. Following that would be the *Transmitter* and *Receiver* classes.

- *SerialPortDisplay* manages all the aspects of a connection, signalling and receiving input from all the other components.

- *Transmitter* and *Receiver* handle the input and output streams using dedicated threads and handle the display of the message traffic.

Figure 2.5 BlackBox UML Diagram

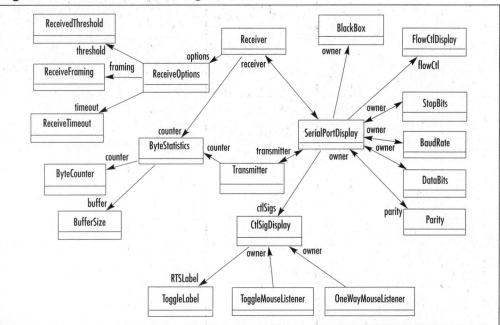

Debugging...

Reverse Engineering

When the LEGO MINDSTORMS Kit was first released in 1998, the programmable RCX brick's many possibilities were immediately evident to a group of enthusiasts who quickly took it apart and began to reverse engineer it to discover how it works—for example, what the communication protocol was and ultimately how to improve upon it. Since there was initially no official documentation, a few individuals took it upon themselves to document the RCX protocol online. Kekoa Proudfoot was one of the first to do so.

Continued

How was it done? One basically interposes oneself in the middle of the communications pipeline to see exactly what messages are being sent between the computer and the device—in this case, the infrared tower and the computer, via a serial cable. Imagine placing a "black box" (so to speak) between the computer and the device, severing the physical connection to place the "box" in between. One has the messages sent first from the computer to the black box, and then after the box looks at the message traffic (perhaps processing and logging it), it passes the message to the device as if nothing had happened. Each side of the communication would not know any better. This is what's known as *sniffing*.

Sniffers are a standard tool used by hackers to reverse engineer communications, although *hacking* may conjure up a negative image in some minds (I won't address that issue here). Suffice it to say that one should be alert to any legal repercussions to reverse engineering in general, as they may vary from state to state and depending on the software license used. Technically, we aren't reverse engineering software, but a protocol. Also, LEGO had no problem with what the MINDSTORMS enthusiasts were doing and have been quite supportive since.

An alternate name for *sniffer* is a *serial proxy*. Proxies are intermediaries that can allow (selectively or not) traffic to travel between two end points as if they were connected together.

There was a need to understand the underlying protocol in order to communicate with the RCX and that the only way was to use a tool like the BlackBox example from the Java Communications API. The black box setup is shown in Figure 2.6. First we connect the serial cable from the computer that is running the LEGO MINDSTORMS software, to the second computer's first serial port. For the sake of the example, let's say we have two PCs and the first computer uses its COM1 serial port, which is connected to the COM1 port of the second computer (the one that will run the BlackBox or serial proxy).

Figure 2.6 Reverse Engineering Setup

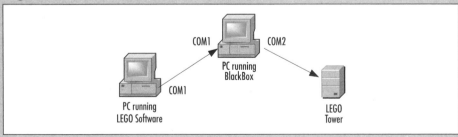

Continued

We then connect the MINDSTORMS infrared tower to the second computer's second serial port (COM2). The BlackBox program will run as a software line monitor by forwarding all traffic back and forth between the two serial ports.

First, we determine the proper serial port settings that we must use to successfully connect. We can monitor the data in real time to determine which settings are correct, and experiment with buffer sizes. We could also go by trial and error to determine the correct settings, trying out the many permutations until we successfully communicate to the tower using the original controlling software.

At this point we are able to communicate as if the serial cable were directly connecting the first computer and the tower and we can monitor the data traffic. We'll try sending all the different commands to determine patterns in the data. At this point we would see the following bytes for example, going to the RCX:

```
55 ff 0 10 ef 10 ef 55 ff 0 51 ae 5 fa 56 a9 . . .
```

After going through the many sent messages, we can discern repeated patterns such as this one from in the line above:

```
55 ff 0
```

As it turns out, this is the message header for every message that is sent to the RCX (we're just looking at messages sent—there is also a reply to each message, sent back from the RCX).

It would be very tedious to retrace each step of the process to find patterns and determine how the data differs on a message-by-message basis. Let's just jump ahead to what our reverse engineers discovered these messages to be. From the line above, we have two messages:

```
55 ff 0 10 ef 10 ef

55 ff 0 51 ae 5 fa 56 a9
```

It was discovered that each byte sent has a corresponding byte that is simply a bit-wise complement of the first command byte (this was apparently designed as such so that ambient light doesn't affect the infrared messages as much). So pairing up the bytes and dropping the headers, we have:

```
10ef 10ef

51ae 5fa 56a9
```

Continued

As the reverse engineering progressed, it was discovered that there was a checksum byte pair ending each message; dropping the checksum and the second complimentary byte of each pair we have:

- 10 A ping command
- 51 5 A beep command with a parameter of value 5 which is one of the several default beeps.

As it turns out the two sent commands were an "alive" message, which is basically just a ping message used initially to establish communications (basically to get a reply; remember that all messages have corresponding replies) and the second message is a command to sound a specific beep in the RCX. All messages have unique values known as opcodes, and in this case one of the messages also has a parameter following the opcode. It's a little more complicated in that each opcode can be represented differently depending on whether the command was sent twice in a row or not (a bit is toggled such that the command will indeed be interpreted as an intentional request to send the command again and not a retry).

The following chapters will address additional APIs that will manage and hide the underlying raw protocol used by the RCX, such that one would only need to know the opcodes and parameters to send. These are all documented at the RCX Internals site, as well as in the SDK available from the LEGO Company, which has finally documented all the opcodes.

This reverse engineering approach is basically the same for tackling new undocumented message protocols for the various devices that connect to serial or parallel ports, such that one can use the Java Communications API. In summary, the basic process is to use a serial proxy, format the data to look for patterns and for correlation to other messages, and to exercise the original software by sending each possible command. Oh, and hope that it isn't encrypted!

Selected Code

The following sample code snippet is from *SerialPortDisplay.java* of the BlackBox sample application included with the Java Communications API. In this snippet we will examine the code that interchanges the streams between two ports to allow the monitoring of messages.

```
public void setLineMonitor(SerialPortDisplay other, boolean value)
{
```

```
/*
 *  To make a line monitor, we simply take two ports
 *  and interchange their output streams!
 */

this.lineMonitor = value;
other.lineMonitor = value;

if (this.lineMonitor)
{
    this.setOutputStream(other.getOutputStream());
    other.setOutputStream(this.outSave);
}

else
{
    other.setOutputStream(this.getOutputStream());
    this.setOutputStream(this.outSave);
}
}
```

Developing & Deploying...

Let's Not Forget Parallel Ports

For the sake of completeness, here are the aspects of parallel ports, specifically the *ParallelPort* class, that everyone should know:

- **Parallel Port Modes** These are accessed with *getMode()* and changed *setMode(int mode)*. Among the modes are values for specific type of printers such as *ParallelPort.LPT_MODE_ECP* (enhanced capabilities port)

- **Parallel Port States** These are states that include *isPrinterBusy()*, *isPaperOut()*, and *isPrinterError()*.

- **Parallel Port Events** Just like with serial ports, we can request specific events and register listeners that implement

Continued

> the *ParallelPortEventListener*. An example would be *notifyOnBuffer()* which would send a *ParallelPortEvent* to indicate when the output buffer is empty. The registered listener would then be notified through its *parallelEvent()* method.

Essentially what this does is swap the output streams such that whatever gets received by one port gets sent to the other and vice versa. This function is called when the −*l* command line parameter is set and the Boolean parameter value simply marks the ports as line monitors.

The output streams will be swapped or swapped back depending on whether you are setting or resetting the line monitoring feature.

You can reuse this for writing a simpler line command monitor, or embed this diagnostic feature in your applications for diagnostics and debugging. This concept isn't limited to serial ports; it can be used by any I/O protocol.

Extending the Java Communications API

This section will discuss how to extend the use of the Java Communication API by adding custom software (in both native and Java code) to support a new type of port. We will go through the process of adding support for a customized USB port to access version 2.0 of the LEGO MINDSTORMS infrared tower (previous to version 2.0 of the IR tower, connections were made via the serial port rather than the USB port).

Since the installed user base for the 1.0 and 1.5 version is a considerable, the need to support serial ports and add USB support to a framework API will be necessary for some time. The ideal would be to continue to use the Java Communications API and simply add USB to it. This sounds simple in theory, but it doesn't seem as if generic support for USB will be available any time soon (see the sidebar titled "Why won't USB be officially part of the Java Communications API?").

USB support can be developed by referring to the supporting documentation from LEGO MINDSTORMS 2.0 SDK, which is available online. It documents the new USB tower and makes references to how the USB driver for the tower may be accessed and controlled.

Basically, it states that the USB Tower driver (on Windows only) has an interface available for access by programmers. It mentions the specific Win32 APIs that are available for developers; and that the standard I/O Win32 calls, such as *CreateFile*, *ReadFile* and *WriteFile* can be used on the USB driver to communicate with the tower. This alleviates the task of not only writing native USB driver code but, but also specific code to access and control the tower itself. These are two different implementations that are being addressed by the LEGO developer community for the Linux platform. As for the Macintosh platform, there isn't a specific implementation as of this printing but the Linux implementation should be similar enough to be easily ported to Mac OS X.

Once I looked at a way to access the LEGO USB driver with a simple port I/O interface, it became apparent that it would make a good candidate for a wrapper "driver" interface similar to serial port native drivers.

The general drawbacks and limitations will be addressed in the following section, as will extending the Java Communications API to include support for USB ports.

Using More than Serial or Parallel Ports

The basic mechanism for providing alternate "driver" code for new ports is discovered by looking at how the serial port was implemented for a specific platform. Figure 2.7 shows a UML diagram of the *com.sun.comm.* * package and its classes.

Figure 2.7 com.sun.comm UML Diagram

```
                        ┌─────────────────────────┐
                        │     Win32SerialPort      │
                        ├─────────────────────────┤
                        │                         │
                        └─────────────────────────┘
                           ↙ port  ↑ port  ↖ port
                                              notification Thread
┌──────────────────────┐ ┌──────────────────────┐ ┌──────────────────────┐
│ Win32SerialOutputStream│ │ Win32SerialInputStream │ │   NotificationThread   │
├──────────────────────┤ ├──────────────────────┤ ├──────────────────────┤
│                      │ │                      │ │                      │
└──────────────────────┘ └──────────────────────┘ └──────────────────────┘

   ┌──────────────────────┐ ┌──────────────────────┐
   │    Win32ParallelPort   │ │      Win32Driver       │
   ├──────────────────────┤ ├──────────────────────┤
   │                      │ │                      │
   └──────────────────────┘ └──────────────────────┘
```

The process starts by parsing the properties file and dynamically loading the *CommDriver* instance. This is followed by calling the *initialize* method (the only method of the *CommDriver* Java interface) on the instance of the driver. On the

Windows platform, Win32Driver (as specified in the properties file) is the implementation of *CommDriver*.

We'll follow the Java Comm engineers' lead and create our own package. Let's call it *rcx.comm*.* to contain three Java classes that are equivalent to their serial port counterparts, namely *Win32USBPort.java, Win32USBOutputStream.java and Win32USBInputStream.java*.

The input and output stream classes simply extend the standard Java *InputStream* and *OutputStream* classes as a convenience and to allow for method synchronization. A reference from the port class is used to get the actual streams.

It is the *Win32USBPort.java* class that extends *CommPort* class and provides us with the interface to the native code. This is accomplished using the standard Java Native Interface (JNI). Basically, the process of writing JNI code is as follows:

1. Write the Java code that will call the *native* methods (the methods use the *native* keyword).

2. Run the *javah* command line tool to create a native C header file, populated with the method prototypes using proper JNI-type nomenclature. This file should not be edited.

3. Write the native code that will implement the methods in the generated header file.

4. Create the shared runtime library. In this case it'll be *win32usb.dll* and should be placed alongside the one from the Java Comm API, *win32com.dll*.

We will focus on the Java code that will allow us to use this native dll in the same fashion in which *win32com.dll* supplies us with access to serial and parallel ports on the Windows platform.

Bricks & Chips...

Why won't USB be officially part of the Java Communications API?

The Java Communications API was originally designed to be extensible such that it would provide more than just support for serial and parallel ports. In fact, the included FAQ refers to possible future inclusion of USB and Bluetooth technologies.

Continued

The necessary hooks into the Java Communications API are in place (to a degree) for third party implementers to provide access to new communications devices using native code. The idea was to provide a drop-in mechanism to enable developers to expand the API without having to change the core library. This would require access to the core library's source code, most of which was not made available.

What has happened since 1998 (the last major release of JCE)? Where is the USB addition to the Java Communications API?

The answer is simple: the existing API worked well for serial and parallel I/O devices but became cumbersome to adapt as a generic communications API for all future I/O protocols. The USB and Bluetooth protocols, and their related technologies have themselves evolved to become quite complex and accommodating them would require significant modifications to the core JCE API.

In fact, there has since been a new proposal for a standard USB-specific Java API. The Java Specification Request (JSR) #80 introduced the *javax.usb* extension API for USB devices. It is nearing completion and there is even a reference implementation for Linux made available by IBM, one of the committee members for that JSR.

USB differs from the serial and parallel interfaces in major areas. USB not only provides more than 100 times faster I/O than serial ports, but it allows for up to 127 devices to connect to a USB bus by using the concept of USB hubs. Some of the issues that would not have been addressed by JCE without changing the core include:

1. Dynamic plug-and-play attaching to and detaching from the USB bus.

2. The ability for a USB device to serve as a USB hub to allow additional devices to be connected to one port.

3. The definition of endpoints for devices. Each device can define source and target endpoints as well as interfaces.

4. Several types of data transfer mechanisms, such as bulk, interrupt and control data transfers; as well as what is called *isochronous* data transfers, which allows for bandwidth negotiation.

As you can see, as newer technologies and protocols become more complex, they will require their own APIs. In fact there is already a JSR (#82) for a Bluetooth Java API. This seems to leave the Java Communications API limited to just serial and parallel I/O ports. Unless significant changes are made to the Java Communications API to allow

Continued

it to be much more abstract and extensible, the API will have run its course, as newer computers will move away from serial and parallel ports towards better and faster technologies such as USB, Bluetooth, and Firewire.

USB Port Access

Inside the Java Communications API samples folder is a folder called *porting*. The Readme file claims this is what is needed to implement custom ports to new platforms. There is no example of how this is done, though—in fact the only file present is the source code to *CommPortIdentifier* (with selected portions omitted). There is no documentation or examples to explain how the process works so that we can add our own code.

However, having the source to *CommPortIdentifier* is a still helpful enough to for us to understand how the Java Communications framework loads and uses the native interfaces.

We do know from JavaDocs that there is an interface, called *CommDriver*, used by the *CommPortIdentifier* to actually obtain access to the ports.

Looking at the process which starts with reading the javax.comm.properties file, then loads each *CommDriver* class listed and obtains the port identifiers from *CommPortIdentifier. getPortIdentifiers();* we come up with the flowchart shown in Figure 2.8.

Figure 2.8 The Native Comm Port Loading Process

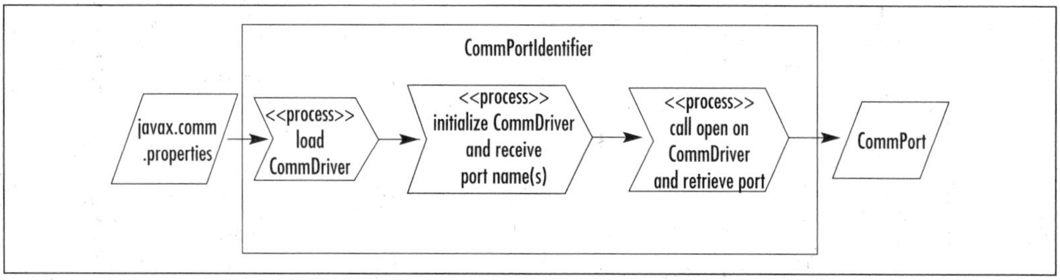

The process starts with the parsing of the *javax.comm.properties* file where each entry is dynamically loaded by *CommPortIdentifiers* upon creating its class instance. It's the loading and instantiating of the *CommDriver* instances that gives Java Comm its native dependencies—at the cost of a configuration file.

The next thing that happens is that *CommDriver's initialize()* method is called. This is where the driver adds its port names to *CommPortIdentifier* using the following:

```
CommPortIdentifier.addPortName(String portName, int portType, CommDriver);
```

This is exactly where the reference to the class driver is passed back to *CommPortIdentifier* such that when it goes through the port name list (or IDs list), it knows which *CommDriver* to call when opening a port. The method that it calls is *getCommPort()* which will create the port and open it, returning a *CommPort* object (which is why the native ports, such as. *Win32USBPort* have to be an instance of *CommPort*).

One should also note that the *portType* parameter is usually one of the *PORT_SERIAL* or *PORT_PARALLEL* type, which are types 1 and 2 respectively. New port types should start with 3 or above.

We return to our mirror implementation of the serial classes in the *sun.com.comm* package.

The following code snippet shows how one would go about encapsulating the Win32 USB port for use with the Java Communications API. It closely follows the serial port example.

```
package rcx.comm;


public class Win32USBPort extends CommPort
{
    static boolean LibLoaded;
    public long nativeHandle = -1;
    boolean closed;
    private InputStream ins;
    private OutputStream outs;
    int receiveTimeout= 0;


    private native int _open(String port);
    private native int _read();
    private native int _read(byte[] byteArray, int offset, int len);
    private native int _write(int b);
    private native int _write(byte[] byteArray, int offset, int len);
    private native int _close();
    private native int _setReceiveTimeout(int timeout);
```

```
    private native int _available();

    public int open(String portname) throws IOException{

        if(!(portname.startsWith("COM")||portname.startsWith("LPT")))
            name = "\\\\.\\"+portname;
        else
            return -1;

        if(_open(name)<0)
            return -1;

        closed=false;

        outs = new Win32USBOutputStream(this);
        ins = new Win32USBInputStream(this);

        return 0;
    }


    public Win32USBPort() {
        closed=true;

        if(!LibLoaded) {
            try {
                System.loadLibrary("win32usb");
            } catch (SecurityException se) {
                System.err.println("Security Exception loading win32usb
.dll: " + se);
                return;
            } catch (UnsatisfiedLinkError ule) {
                System.err.println("Error loading win32usb.dll: " + ule);
                return;
            } catch (Exception e) {
                System.err.println("Exception with win32usb.dll: " + e);
                return;
            }
        }
```

```
        LibLoaded=true;
    }
}


    protected void finalize() throws Throwable {
        close();
    }
```

. . .

```
}
```

Since it extends *CommPort*, all the abstract methods we've seen in *SerialPort* before (such as setting timeouts etc.) are also implemented above, but not shown for the sake of brevity. One note is that the close method should call *super.close()*.

Let's take a look at the section that gives us access to our native code.

The native methods declared include more than just the expected *open*, *close*, *read*, and *write*; I added *setReceiveTimeout()* for setting the read timeout and *available()* for use with streams.

Let's look at the constructor. This is where the native shared library is loaded using *System.loadLibrary()*. We avoid loading this more than once by using the class static flag *LibLoaded*.

The *open* method in this class will actually open the port. The passed-in port name is prepended with \\.\ because this is how Windows identifies its ports (even serial ports). The reason I check whether this is a serial or printer port by name is in case the port owner tries to open those ports using the wrong associated driver in the port ID. It should not open; otherwise access to the ports with the wrong driver could occur.

The input and output streams are created and the port is now open. One thing to watch for is if this object gets destroyed before *close()* is called. To prevent this, we implement the *finalize()* method and have that call the close.

The *CommDriver* will create a specific *CommPort* instance, which is the interface we implement with *Win32USBDriver*.

```
public class Win32USBDriver implements CommDriver
{
    public void initialize() {
        CommPortIdentifier.addPortName("LEGOTOWER1", 3, this);
        CommPortIdentifier.addPortName("LEGOTOWER2", 3, this);
```

```
    }

    public CommPort getCommPort(String portName, int portType) {

        Win32USBPort port = new Win32USBPort();

        try {
            if(port.open(portName)<0)
                port=null;
        } catch (java.io.IOException ioexception) {
            port=null;
        }

        return port;

    }
}
```

In *initialize()* above, one can populate the port list IDs. Its counterpart, *Win32Driver,* added the lists for both serial and parallel ports to *CommPortIdentifier.* Here I added the possibility of having two towers. It's a meager attempt because we don't have access to a native method that will enumerate all the towers present. Again this is not a full-fledged USB driver; we're wrapping some access to the LEGO Company's native USB driver. The specific port names listed above were as provided by LEGO's SDK documentation.

In theory we have all the parts in place and we add an entry to the properties file:

```
# Windows Serial Driver
Driver=com.sun.comm.Win32Driver
# Windows USB Driver for Lego Mindstorms
Driver=rcx.comm.Win32USBDriver
```

This should work, but it doesn't. In fact, *Win32USBPort* won't compile. Why? It's because *CommPort*'s initializer is package private: all of its subclasses must reside inside the *javax.comm* package. This is a serious limitation because we can't just drop in a new type of port without breaking package rules. You can't deliver *javax.comm.** classes outside of the *comm.jar* because the extension would then cease to be standard.

What did *com.sun.comm.Win32SerialPort* do to get around this limitation? Technically the way around it was to have an additional abstraction between it and

CommPort. In that case it was able to extend *javax.comm.SerialPort* without a problem. That's because Java Comm supports serial and parallel ports out of the box. We would still run into the problem of having to create a *javax.comm.USBPort*; we weren't intending to introduce generic USB port support, we just want to add our customized USB port into the mix. Adding generic USB support would require changing the core API to add new port types, and currently the only way to extend it is to add new serial or parallel port implementations. The existing implementation should be able to handle all standard generic devices over serial or parallel ports. Any protocol differences could be handled by the application using the Java Comm API without having to write additional native code, unless you plan to improve on the existing native implementation.

The only alternative we have is to instantiate the *Win32USBPort* and not use *CommPortIdentifier* to create the port. We can keep the same class and just not have it extend *CommPort*. This of course eliminates the ability for *CommPortIdentifier* to "discover" us. However, in all likelihood, the end application may find it more efficient to just ask which version they are running (serial or USB). The discovery process could be time consuming because the application would need to find, then communicate on, each port. Even LEGO's MINDSTORMS 2.0 software gives the user the option to install for USB or serial port, and choose a target serial port or whether to search for serial ports. Even when we use the Java Comm API to search for the first available serial port there is a noticeable delay, compared to when we specify a particular port. As long as the application can save this information on disk so that it won't have to keep asking, this shouldn't be an insurmountable problem; the application can search only once and save the information, only searching again when it fails.

By using an interface similar to that of *SerialPort,* we can still share common code between both types of ports. As it stands, reading and writing through the streams are identical. The only difference lies in creating the port, and even this can be accomplished by having both implement a common Java interface (which is what *CommPort* should have been). The next chapter will introduce an RCX library that allows us to exactly that.

Figure 2.9 presents sample code directly instantiating *Win32USBPort*.

Figure 2.9 TestUSB.java

```java
import java.io.*;
import rcx.comm.*;


public class TestUSB {
```

Continued

Figure 2.9 Continued

```java
public static void main(String args[]) {

    Win32USBPort usbPort = new Win32USBPort();

    try {
        if(usbPort.open("LEGOTOWER1")<0) {
            System.err.println("Error opening USB port: is tower
                plugged in?");
            return;
        }
        OutputStream os = usbPort.getOutputStream();
        InputStream is  = usbPort.getInputStream();

        os.write(testArray);

        os.close();

    } catch(IOException e) {
        e.printStackTrace();
    }
}
}
```

And that's all there is to it. In fact, the tower's infrared LED should light up
when you send it the byte "42."

We should still provide a platform-independent solution for providing USB
ports, and this would require a factory design pattern. We can obtain the port
from *USBPortFactory* in a standard way by having all the platform encapsulations
implement a common interface (*USBPort*). We then get the package hierarchy as
shown in Figure 2.10.

The line that would change in the example shown in Figure 2.10 would be
as follows:

```java
Win32USBPort usbPort = new Win32USBPort();
```

changing to the more platform neutral:

```
USBPort usbPort = USBPortFactory.getUSBPort();
```

Figure 2.10 The Revised USB Support rcx.comm Package

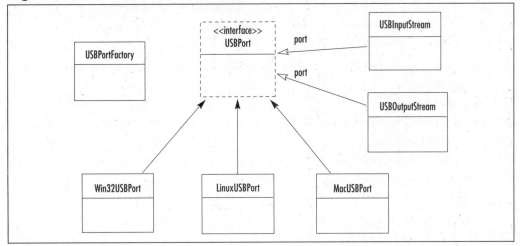

The rest remains the same and the same code should work across platforms.

NOTE

Please see the associated files on the CD to build the native code. The source code for win32usb.dll is found in the **win32usb** folder. The **linuxusb** and **macusb** folders contain the JNI header files and references to information on how to develop and build the native shared libraries.

Summary

When the LEGO MINDSTORMS Robotics kit was introduced in 1998, Sun had just released the Java Communications API 2.0. Since the RCX communicated with the PC via a standard I/O port (the serial port), there was an opportunity for many programmers to develop for the RCX. The Java Communications API is a standard Java extension API, meaning that, though it's not part of the core Java runtime environment, it is a standard when redistributed with an application. The multi-platform support is comprehensive and the API stable and widely-used.

The Java Communications API provides not just an encapsulation of serial and parallel ports, but also a comprehensive port management system. Through the *CommPortIdentifier* class we are able to discover and enumerate all the ports of a system, whether or not they are available. Port ownership is also provided with the ability to detect requests and receive ownership notifications across applications and even Java virtual machines. The I/O can be made synchronous or asynchronous by following Java-style event notifications. A port can be enabled to generate events and send them to listeners who register as event listeners. Serial and parallel ports have specific events. For instance, the serial port can listen on control lines.

Java Comm API configuration involves a properties file, a native shared library that should be present in the execution path, and a jar file that should be accessible from the Java classpath. This is the mechanism that allows the core classes to be separate from the native implementation of the ports. Several examples of reading and writing to ports were presented, as was an interesting serial port analyzer that allows one to monitor a line of communications using two ports.

We examined extending the API as it was designed to be extended, with an eye towardsadding a custom USB implementation for communicating with RCX 2.0. The process for doing so was discovered by studying how the *CommPortIdentifier* loaded the serial port driver for Windows. It seems that the caveat for adding ports is that the port type must be either serial or parallel. Nonetheless, we were able to encapsulate access to the USB port in a fashion similar to the serial port by using JNI to access the native code that accesses the port. Although the Java Communications Extension API may not be expanded in the future, its architecture is robust and vital for accessing serial and parallel ports from 100% Java code. The JCE API is freely distributable with Java applications and is the foundation block from which we'll communicate with the RCX 1.0 and 1.5 in the following chapters.

Solutions Fast Track

Overview of the Java Communications Extension API

☑ The Java Comm API provides the mechanism for port enumeration and ownership as well as event driven notification of change of ownership.

☑ Asynchronous and synchronous I/O is possible due to the standard Java-style event-driven architecture.

☑ The *SerialPort* and *ParallelPort* classes provide a clean encapsulation for supporting the many platforms for which the JCE API is available.

Installing and Configuring the Java Communications API

☑ There are three deliverables: a jar file, a properties file, and a native shared runtime library.

☑ Several options are available depending on ease-of-use versus ease-of-configuration. The simplest is to keep the three deliverable files together in the same folder so long as it is the application's working folder.

☑ There are possible version control caveats, but fortunately the API has stabilized enough such that it's not a big issue.

Reading and Writing to Serial Ports

☑ The Java Communications API comes with several simple examples that illustrate the usage of both parallel and serial ports.

☑ Adding event-driven notifications is straightforward using *EventListeners.*

☑ Working with the parallel ports is similar to working with any port that extends the *CommPort* abstract class.

Debugging with Serial Ports: The Black Box Example

☑ A close look at a specific advanced Java sample program that comes with the JCE illustrates all functionality of the serial port by serving as a serial port analyzer and line monitor.

☑ The BlackBox sample program can be used as is as a serial proxy or sniffer tool without modifications.

☑ The way that the output and input streams were used in the BlackBox example can be used as the basis of custom applications that provide similar functionality.

Extending the Java Communications API

☑ The mechanism for adding new functionality exists via the *CommDriver*, *CommPort* and *CommPortIdentifier* classes.

☑ A step-by-step process of how a customized USB driver was implemented for use with the RCX 2.0 USB tower.

☑ The limitations shown include the inability to add external packages as the source for new port drivers. This would break the package naming convention of not adding to or changing the classes in the *javax.comm* hierarchy.

Frequently Asked Questions

The following Frequently Asked Questions, answered by the authors of this book, are designed to both measure your understanding of the concepts presented   in this chapter and to assist you with real-life implementation of these concepts. To have your questions about this chapter answered by the author, browse to **www.syngress.com/solutions** and click on the **"Ask the Author"** form.

Q: What exactly is *receive threshold* and what does it do? I thought receive timeout was all I needed.

A: *Receive threshold* is the minimum number of bytes that need to be present for a call to read returns. Setting a timeout also determines when to return from *read*. Usually both are used together with the first one to complete causing the read to return. Using timeout is generally good enough for timing out reads, but when used in conjunction with threshold you can be more precise and more efficient. For instance, if you know the smallest size of the packet of bytes you expect, you can use that value as a threshold.

Q: Does Sun have any plans to update the Java Communications API?

A: As of this printing the latest version is 2.0.2, which dates to 10/19/2000. This comprises of only minor bug fixes available only to the Solaris platform, with the other platforms supposedly forthcoming.

Q: Can the BlackBox serial port example program be used to analyze protocols used by different devices such as my mp3 player?

A: Yes; if they interface through a serial port, you can set up a serial proxy on a separate computer to analyze the protocol as indicated in the RCX reverse engineering example.

Q: What is the future of the Java Communications API if there are wholly new Java APIs for newer standards like USB and Bluetooth?

A: The Java Communications API has been available for over four years now and has been used extensively by Java applications to interface with serial and parallel ports. It is a proven API that is available on a wide variety of platforms. As long as there are still serial and parallel ports in use, the future looks good for JCE.

## Chapter 3

Communicating with the RCXPort API

Solutions in this chapter:

- Overview of the RCXPort Java API

- Programming the RCX Using RCXPort

- Downloading Programs with RCXPort

- Interfacing External Software with RCXPort.

- An Advanced Example Using RCXPort

☑ Summary

☑ Solutions Fast Track

☑ Frequently Asked Questions

Introduction

RCXPort is one of two pure-Java interfaces to the RCX that are currently available to the public. The RCXPort API was written by Scott Lewis in 1999, and made available to RCX users over the Internet by an open source license. You can find the source code at www.slewis.com/rcxport. He originally wrote the RCXPort interface to allow another project of his (ROAPI) to interact with the LEGO RCX. ROAPI is a replicated object system that allows you to build a wide variety of collaborative applications, such as multiplayer games or distance learning environments. More information can be found at Scott Lewis' Web site.

In this chapter we will introduce the RCXPort API and show you some example code, along with a discussion of RCXPort's limitations and future directions. You will learn how to use features such as downloading programs that are written in the popular language Not Quite C (NQC). Finally, we will show you an advanced example program written in Java using the RCXPort API.

Overview of the RCXPort Java API

Similar to the RCXJava API, which came out in 1998 and described in the next chapter, RCXPort relies on the Java Communications package to send data to the RCX via your computer's serial port. The Java Communications package is incompatible with USB ports, so users of the RIS 2.0 should refer to Chapter 2 for using Java with USB ports. I will discuss this limitation further in the section entitled "Limitations of RCXPort."

How RCXPort Works

In this section you will learn about the RCX object model, why it was built the way it was, and how it communicates with the RCX. The RCX understands a very basic set of commands called *opcodes,* which are simple machine-level instructions made up of individual bytes. For more on the history of these commands, refer to the sidebar later in this chapter called "Reverse Engineering the RCX Opcodes."

Formatting RCX Commands

As we've mentioned, programs and commands are sent to the RCX in opcodes, which are organized into a simple set of commands that the RCX firmware can understand. These commands comprise all of the most basic functions of the RCX; playing tones, getting readings from input sensors, turning motors on and off, and keeping time with its four internal timers. The commands can also instruct the RCX to store a given program, shut itself down, or make a computation on one of its 32 internally-stored variables.

The RCXPort API provides a means of sending these commands to the RCX independently of the LEGO MINDSTORMS software and RCX code. By itself, RCXPort can download programs written in byte code to the RCX or send individual commands one at a time, allowing a programmer to directly control the RCX from the Java Runtime Environment (JRE) on a personal computer. Since the RCX is programmed to respond to these opcodes, all a Java program needs to do in order to control the RCX is to transmit opcodes in a format that the RCX recognizes.

Bricks & Chips...

Reverse Engineering the RCX Opcodes

When the first LEGO MINDSTORMS sets were released in 1998, they created a lot of buzz in the academic computer programming and robotics worlds. Many enthusiasts wanted the ability to do more with their RCX-powered robots, as well as to better understand how they worked. Kekoa Proudfoot, then a graduate student at Stanford University's computer graphics department, is widely credited with being the first to publish a complete set of the opcodes that control the RCX's every move. He did this by a process known as *packet sniffing*, where a hardware or software listening device is placed somewhere between the RCX software on a PC and the RCX itself. By knowing what types of commands are being sent to the RCX, and intercepting the byte codes traveling to the RCX at that time, one can extrapolate patterns and eventually come to identify the opcodes themselves and their use. This list of commands can be found at: http://graphics.stanford.edu/~kekoa/rcx/opcodes.html.

Every command that goes to the RCX via the infrared tower is of a format that ensures the correct transmission and reception of messages, and that no part of any command is lost. The message format consists of three parts: the header, the body, and a checksum byte. The header prepares the RCX for the command it is about to receive; the body of the message contains the actual commands; and the checksum byte tells the RCX how many total bytes of information are contained in the message. This serves as a check to make sure that no part of the message was lost.

One other failsafe technique is used in the message formatting: each byte in the message body, as well as the checksum byte, is followed by its bitwise complement. Since the header is fixed and contains an equal number of '0' and '1' bits, this guarantees that the entire message has an equal number of 0s and 1s. Thus the RCX knows to expect a message that has an average value of .5 and can make adjustments if the infrared signal is affected by ambient light.

RCXPort Object Model

The RCXPort API includes an *RCXPacket* object, which represents each individual message that is sent to the RCX. It contains a *getBytes()* message, which packages a set of RCX opcodes into a format that the RCX understands. Because this class constructs every message that gets sent to the RCX, it is an integral part of the RCXPort API.

The *RCXPort* object itself is the class that is responsible for opening and maintaining a connection with the infrared tower. When running RCXPort, you indicate in the command line the serial port on your computer to which the tower is connected, and the *RCXPort* creates a connection to the tower through the specified port.

Note that RCXPort relies on the Java Communications API to make this connection, and that this API is not compatible with USB ports. If you are using the USB infrared tower that comes with the Robotics Invention System 2.0, you will need to refer to Chapter 2 for instructions on how to make this connection.

Whenever a command is sent to the RCX, it echoes the same command back to the tower (except for the RCX 2.0 USB tower version) This value can then be checked to ensure that the correct message was received. After echoing the message, the RCX then sends a reply command, which may or may not contain data as well. The reply command always begins with the bitwise complement of the sent command. In such cases where data is needed from the RCX, it will include this data in the reply message. For instance, if you wanted to get a reading from the light sensor, the RCX would return the current value from the light sensor in its reply message. These messages follow the same formatting rules as messages that are sent to the RCX. Each reply returned by the RCX is represented by an *RCXResult* object.

The *RCXCmd* class stores constants for all the opcodes that are known to the RCX. This is a convenient way of representing each command destined for the

RCX. In this way, you need not remember every opcode; you instead need only refer to a command by name when building an RCX command.

The RCX is capable of storing and running five programs, each with 10 tasks and eight subroutines, and it is around this framework that the rest of the *RCXPort* object model is based. The remaining three classes, *RCXProgram*, *RCXTask*, and *RCXSub* represent these programs, tasks, and subroutines, respectively.

Limitations of RCXPort

Any early release of software is bound to have limitations and shortcomings as it grows and evolves. While the RCXJava and RCXPort APIs offer all sorts of new opportunities for Java programmers who wish to write code for LEGO MIND-STORMS, they are no exception to this rule. Part of their shortcomings are due to the fact that the average Java programmer does not have the ability to code control statements around their RCX commands in byte code that is understandable to the RCX firmware. Also, these packages are very reliant on the Java Communications API, which has its own limitations that in turn limit the functionality in RCXPort. In the following sections we discuss these drawbacks.

Compiling Java into Machine Code

RCXPort offers an excellent interface for communicating with the RCX. It greatly simplifies the task of creating a message packet, sending it to the RCX, and retrieving reply data. It allows you to easily download a program to the RCX. However, since the standard RCX firmware does not understand Java code, these programs must be sent to the RCX in a format that the firmware can understand. It is no simple task to translate the structured language of a high-level Java program into the low-level machine code that can run on an RCX. LeJOS (introduced in Chapter 5) overcomes this problem by replacing the standard RCX firmware with one that can run Java code. NQC, the popular language written by Dave Baum, includes this functionality in its compiler; code that is written in NQC's high-level C-like syntax gets compiled into low-level code that is understood by the RCX's firmware. Scott Lewis, author of RCXPort, created the API with the eventual goal of including a high-level compiler similar to that of NQC, but this is not yet available.

Restrictions of Using *Direct Mode*

Earlier in the chapter we discussed the *direct mode* technique, in which controlling the RCX is done via commands sent directly from a Java program. A program is run in the Java Runtime Environment on your personal computer, and sends commands to the RCX via the infrared tower. In this way, a Java program can have complete control of the RCX, taking full advantage of the Java language's advanced structure without downloading any programs to the RCX. This allows you to write powerful programs in Java, although this technique is severely limited by the reliability of the infrared signal between the RCX and the IR tower. Because the tower was designed primarily for downloading and uploading, it does not lend itself well to communication with an RCX that is moving—it may transmit a command that sends the RCX further away from the tower, and ensuing commands may get lost, especially if the RCX goes beyond the tower's signal range. For this reason, it is best to use direct mode only when your RCX will be stationary and within close range of the IR tower. Also, the amount of time that it takes for a command to be sent and a reply returned via the tower can slow down your program significantly.

Reliance on Java Communications API

We have already mentioned that RCXPort relies on the Java Communications API to interface with your computer's serial ports. Because the Java Comm API is not compatible with USB ports, this prevents users of the RIS 2.0 from using RCXPort as-is. This is a difficult problem, since the greatest advantage of Java is its platform independence. This platform independence allows RCXPort to be run on Windows, Linux or MacOS; However, USB port implementation in Java code is highly platform-specific. There is currently no published API that allows communication with a USB port on every platform, but Dario Laverde has written some code that allows RCXPort to work with USB on Windows or Linux operating systems. You can find his code in the Chapter 2 directory on the CD included with this book. This is a re-architecture of the existing published RCXPort code, and therefore comes with the caveat that it has not been thoroughly tested. We include it with the book as an example for advanced users who wish to take advantage of USB's faster communication speeds.

Programming the RCX Using RCXPort

We'll start with a basic example that demonstrates how to write a Java program using the RCXPort API. First, we'll need to create a basic class, *MyRCX* and import *RCXPort* and *RCXCmd*. We'll need these to establish a connection to the IR tower and to create each individual command that we send to the RCX. We need not include *RCXPacket*; RCXPort will make the method calls to build our packets for us.

NOTE

The blocks of code in this section belong to Figure 3.1, the MyRCX.java file. Explanations are inserted in between the blocks of code. The entire source file can be found on the CD that accompanies this book.

Figure 3.1 MyRCX.java

```
import rcxport.RCXPort;
import rcxport.RCXCmd;


public class MyRCX
{
```

We'll declare an RCXPort object *rcxp* because our class will always need a connection to the IR tower. Then we'll add a constructor method so that instantiating *MyRCX* will also instantiate our RCXPort object *rcxp*. The constructor will take an argument, *port*, to indicate to which serial port the IR tower is connected (COM1, for instance). Since instantiating a new RCXPort may throw an I/O error exception, we'll need to handle or throw an exception here also. We'll just throw one:

```
RCXPort rcxp;


public MyRCX (String port) throws Exception
{
    rcxp = new RCXPort(port);
}
```

We should now have a connection to the IR tower, so we're ready to give the RCX some commands. Let's start with some simple commands that will make the RCX beep and do a little dance. In the *beep()* method, we'll need to choose what kind of sound we want the RCX to play. The RCX knows six different beeps, each represented by a number from 0 to 5. We'll choose the double beep that the RCX makes when it's turned on. The index for this sound is 1, so we'll pass the argument *1* to RCXPort's *playSound()* method. Be sure to cast the number into a byte first.

```
public void beep()
{
    byte sound = (byte) 1;
    rcxp.playSound(sound);
}
```

Next we'll add a method to make the RCX wiggle back and forth. Our example assumes that you have set up the RCX with four wheels and two motors; one motor connected to output A and powering the left two wheels, and the other connected to output B and powering the right set of wheels. For our purposes we are going to use the Simple Steering Drive Robot created by Mario and Giulio Ferrari. Figure 3.2 shows a picture of the Roverbot.

Figure 3.2 A Simple Steering Drive Robot

The *RCXPort.sendData()* method takes in a byte array argument containing the commands to be sent. We will therefore need a byte array to hold each command or opcode before we send it to the RCX:

```
public void wiggle()
{
    //a byte array to hold each command
    byte [] commands;
```

We'll create some constants in this method to represent the motors we wish to control, and the directions we want them to move in. In the RCX opcodes, output A is always represented by the 2^0 bit, which is "0x01" in hex. Output C is represented by the 2^2 bit, or 0x04. To indicate that we want to instruct both outputs to do something, we combine the two bytes using the bitwise *or* operator: **0x01 | 0x04 = 0x05**, where "|" represents the operator.

```
//bytes representing motors and on/off states
byte MOTOR_A = (byte) 0x01;
byte MOTOR_C = (byte) 0x04;
byte BOTH_MOTORS = (byte) MOTOR_A | MOTOR_C;
byte TURN_OFF = (byte) 0x40;
byte TURN_ON = (byte) 0x80;
byte FLIP_DIR = (byte) 0x40;
```

To make the RCX wiggle, we'll instruct it to turn the left motor on, then the right, then reverse the direction of both motors. Repeating this four times will make the RCX wiggle back and forth.

The *RCXCmd.set()* method takes up to six bytes as arguments, and returns these bytes in a byte array, which is just the format we need for the *sendData()* method. By using the bitwise *or* operator to combine the *MOTOR_A* and *TURN_ON* bytes, we create one byte that, when preceded by the *RCXCmd.OutputMode* opcode, will instruct the RCX to turn on output A.

```
//repeat this four times
for (int i=0; i<4; i++)
{
    //turn left motor on then off
    commands = RCXCmd.set(RCXCmd.OutputMode,(byte) MOTOR_A |
        TURN_ON);
    rcxp.sendData(commands);
    commands = RCXCmd.set(RCXCmd.OutputMode,(byte) MOTOR_A |
        TURN_OFF);
    rcxp.sendData(commands);
```

In this example, we immediately follow the *turn on* command with a *turn off* command, without telling the program to wait for any period of time. Under other circumstances, this might happen in the blink of an eye given the speed at which our Java program can run. However, because we are limited by the slow connection between our computer, the IR tower, and the RCX, there is a slight delay between commands.

```
//turn right motor on then off
commands = RCXCmd.set(RCXCmd.OutputMode,(byte) MOTOR_C |
    TURN_ON);
rcxp.sendData(commands);
commands = RCXCmd.set(RCXCmd.OutputMode,(byte) MOTOR_C |
    TURN_OFF);
rcxp.sendData(commands);
//reverse both motors
commands = RCXCmd.set(RCXCmd.OutputDir,(byte) BOTH_MOTORS |
    FLIP_DIR);
rcxp.sendData(commands);
    }

}
```

Developing & Deploying…

Abstracting the Byte Code Layer

Although the examples we've used thus far are simple, they give you an idea of all that is possible with Java and the RCX. In the above example, we did little more than automate the grouping of bytes and opcodes into commands and deliver them to the RCX. By declaring constants to represent opcodes, we are able to remove ourselves somewhat from dealing with the lowest level of programming the RCX—the opcodes. With more coding, we can abstract the opcodes even further so that we are dealing only with the Java language and higher-level methods that might be called *getLightSensorReading()* or *reverseDirection()*. Later sections in the chapter will demonstrate how to further abstract these byte codes, bringing us towards Scott Lewis' eventual goal: to abstract the byte code layer so that programming can be done exclusively in Java. leJOS (introduced in Chapter 5) accomplishes this abstraction via a different technique: replacing the standard RCX firmware with a small VM, or virtual machine, that can run Java code.

Now we'll need a static *main()* method to call these two functions and spring our RCX into action. As you remember, our constructor method calls for a port name, so we'll provide it with the "COM1" port name. This is for our example, you may be using a different port for your IR tower; or to make your code more flexible, you could input the port name from the command line.

```
public static void main(String [] args)
{
    MyRCX rcx = new MyRCX("COM1");
    rcx.beep();
    rcx.wiggle();
    rcx.beep();
}
```

If you run this program with your RCX turned on, your RCX should beep twice, wiggle back and forth, then beep twice again. Congratulations, you've just written your first program using the RCXPort API!

Downloading Programs with RCXPort

The RCXPort class offers the *downloadProgram()* method, which stores a series of commands in one of the RCX's five stored program slots. RCXPort's main method offers an easy interface with which we can download these commands from a file that is stored locally on our personal computer. For now, we'll create this file manually. Later we will demonstrate how to produce more complex byte code programs that can be stored on your RCX, and finally, how to update your RCX's firmware using RCXPort.

Following are the byte codes that were sent to your RCX in the previous section (in hex):

```
51,01,          (play 'beep beep')
21,81,          (turn on output A)
21,41,          (turn off output A)
21,84,          (turn on output C)
21,44,          (turn off output C)
e1,45,          (reverse outputs A and C)
(the preceding 5 lines are repeated three more times)
51,01           (play 'beep beep')
```

Save these codes (without my remarks) in a text file on your PC, in the same directory as your *rcxport.jar* file. We'll call it "dance.lis," since it is a list of commands that will make the RCX dance. Notice how I have separated each byte with a comma; this is because RCXPort recognizes three types of delimiters when reading bytes from files: spaces, commas and tabs. I've chosen commas because they are the easiest to see.

Now go to the directory where your *rcxport.jar* file is located and run RCXPort as follows (try **java rcxport.RCXPort –usage** for an explanation of command line options):

```
java rcxport.RCXPort -p COM1 -n 1 -f dance.lis
```

If you named your file "dance.lis" and are using the COM1 port, then your standard output should show the following:

```
Opening port COM1...done.
Reading byte codes from file: dance.lis...Done.
Downloading program 1 to RCX...done.
```

You now have the program stored on the RCX as "program 1." However, when you press the **Run** button a curious thing happens—the RCX plays two double beeps, but doesn't move at all! This is because when we were running the same commands in direct mode, we were relying on some delay time between commands due to the slow speed of the data transfer when using the serial port and infrared tower. This time, however, all the commands are stored internally to the RCX, so there is no longer any delay. The commands come so quickly that the RCX doesn't even have time to respond. To correct that, insert this string of bytes: *43,02,0a,00,* in between the commands that turn the motors on and off. Your file should now look like this:

```
51,01,
21,81,
43,02,0a,00,
21,41,
21,84,
43,02,0a,00,
21,44,
e1,45,
etc...
```

This will cause the RCX to wait for one-tenth of a second between turning a motor on and turning it off again. If you return to the command line and download the file again, you should see your RCX wiggle once again.

Now that we've seen at a very low-level how the RCX works, it may become more apparent why it is not so simple to have your Java code run as-is directly from the RCX; The RCX firmware doesn't understand Java code. In order to run more complex programs on the RCX, we must overcome this problem in one of two ways: we can teach the RCX to understand Java, or we can transform our code into a format that the RCX can understand. Chapter 5 will introduce you to leJOS, an implementation of Java that can run on the RCX when its firmware is replaced by a small Java Virtual Machine (JVM). In the following section, I will demonstrate how to use a non-Java language to introduce more complex control structures to your existing RCX's original firmware.

Interfacing External Software with RCXPort

Dave Baum's Not Quite C (NQC) provides a simple way for one to compile a higher-level programming language into the low-level byte code that the RCX understands. NQC syntax is based on C, and is therefore quite similar to Java syntax. The NQC language is very intricate; you can refer to www.enteract.com/~dbaum/nqc for more detailed information. In this section I will introduce a program written in NQC, then demonstrate how to run this program on the RCX using the RCXPort interface. If you are familiar with NQC, then the following program should be pretty straightforward. Since some readers may be new to the language, I have done my best to indicate what is going on with in-line comments.

To run this program, you should set up your Roverbot with a single front bumper as shown in the Constructopedia and in Figure 3.2. The motors will be attached to outputs A and C, and the bumper's touch sensor should be attached to sensor 1. This example also uses a light sensor, which is attached to sensor 3 and mounted anywhere on the Roverbot.

The following program, LightRover.nqc (Figure 3.3), will cause your RCX to explore a room, reversing direction whenever the front bumper strikes an object. This particular Roverbot is programmed to seek out darkness. It will continue to explore the room until it finds a location that is below a certain darkness threshold, as defined in the program. Once it finds such a location, it will stop and rest until such time as increased light wakes it up again. You may find that you need to adjust these light thresholds depending on the amount of ambient light in the area where the RCX is running.

The program defines an event that will be fired when the light sensor reads a value lower than a predefined threshold of 30. It will run a loop wherein the RCX will continue to explore until such an event occurs. It will turn around whenever it runs into another object. The following code can be found in the Chapter 3 directory on the CD that accompanies this book.

Figure 3.3 Program your RCX To Be Afraid of Light (LightRover.nqc)

```
//predefined constants for use in the program
#define BUTTON               SENSOR_1
#define LIGHT_SENSOR         SENSOR_3
#define MOTOR_A              OUT_A
#define MOTOR_C              OUT_C
//predefined light thresholds
#define LOW_LIGHT_LEVEL      30
#define WAKE_UP_LEVEL        35


//this task will run when the program is started
task main()
{
        // tell RCX what kind of sensors are used
        SetSensor(BUTTON, SENSOR_TOUCH);
        SetSensor(LIGHT_SENSOR, SENSOR_LIGHT);

        //continue to loop as long as program is running
        while(true)
        {
                //create an event that will be fired whenever the
                //light falls below the threshold
                SetEvent(1, LIGHT_SENSOR, EVENT_TYPE_LOW);
                SetLowerLimit(1, LOW_LIGHT_LEVEL);

                //loop until low light event is fired
                monitor(EVENT_MASK(1))
                {
```

Continued

Figure 3.3 Continued

```
                            //both motors on
                            OnFwd(MOTOR_A + MOTOR_C);

                            //Continue until touch sensor is pressed
                            until(BUTTON == 1);

                            turnAround();
                    }
                    //will run if low light event is fired
                    catch
                    {
                            PlaySound(SOUND_DOWN);
                            //rest until light value reaches WAKE_UP_LEVEL
                            Off(MOTOR_A + MOTOR_C);
                            until(SensorValue(2) > WAKE_UP_LEVEL);
                            PlaySound(SOUND_FAST_UP);
                    }
            }
    }


void turnAround()
{
        //we have hit something so turn around
        PlaySound(SOUND_DOUBLE_BEEP);
        Off(MOTOR_A + MOTOR_C);
        OnRev(MOTOR_A + MOTOR_C);
        Wait(50);
        Off(MOTOR_A + MOTOR_C);
        Wait(10);
        OnRev(MOTOR_A);
        OnFwd(MOTOR_C);
        Wait(200);
        Off(MOTOR_A + MOTOR_C);
}
```

To run this program, you must first download the NQC compiler, which is available at: www.enteract.com/~dbaum/nqc. Then copy Figure 3.3, which can be found on your CD as "LightRover.nqc," to your NQC directory. To compile the program, enter the following command while in your NQC directory:

```
nqc -TRCX2 LightRover.nqc
```

This will compile the NQC code into a byte code file with an *.rcx* extension in the same directory. We will soon download this file (which contains all the byte code for our program) to the RCX, but first we must format it correctly. In the previous section we downloaded a byte code file to the RCX using *RCXPort.downloadProgram()*. Now, we will do the same thing with *LightRover*. First, we must save it as a text file and format it the way we did before—with comma delimiters for clarity.

Once you have done this, copy the file to your *rcxport* directory and run the following command:

```
java rcxport.RCXPort -p COM1 -n 2 -f LightRover.txt
```

This should successfully download the application to program slot number 2 on the RCX. If your RCX is set up as directed, you are now ready to run your program.

The NQC compiler takes advantage of the more complex RCX opcodes to translate NQC program structures into similar structures in byte code. This is how the NQC compiler can create loops, events, functions and other more advanced structures.

Debugging...

Troubleshooting Problems with RCXPort

There are several things that could potentially go wrong when trying to run RCXPort. The more common mistakes are listed below. Run through this list to rule out these more frequent problems.

- Make sure your RCX is turned on and within range of the IR tower.
- Make sure the IR tower is properly connected to the correct serial port.

Continued

- Make sure that another program (possibly running in the background) isn't using the serial port.
- Make sure you have named the correct serial port (COM1, for instance) in the command line.
- If you are downloading byte code from a file, make sure that file is in the same directory as RCXPort.
- Make sure you have downloaded the Java Communications API, and that it is correctly installed.
- Make sure that your classpath references both *rcxport.jar* and *comm.jar*.

An Advanced Example Using RCXPort

In this section we will be programming a candy sorting robot (as shown in Figure 3.4). Refer to the Pro Challenges in your LEGO MINDSTORMS software for detailed instructions on building this type of robot. The robot consists of a base on which the RCX is mounted, a silo where the multi-colored candy is stored, and a rotating platform with a conveyor belt that is used to detect the candy's color and to dispense the candy into bins.

When built and programmed properly, the candy sorter will first determine the color of the candy in the chamber using the light sensor. Based on the result, it will position itself over the appropriate bin, dispense the candy into the bin, return to its starting point, and repeat.

The robot has four basic functions that we must program in our code: turning; getting a reading from the light sensor; pushing the candy out of the chute; and advancing the conveyor belt to drop off the candy. Three of these are functions of the motor, but one, getting a light reading, is of course done with the light sensor. The motor built into the base will be connected to output C, and it will rotate the upper platform to the left and right. The upper motor will connect to output A, powering two functions; the conveyor belt and the pushrod that will push the candy out of the chamber. A differential combined with one-way gearing allows us to accomplish these two tasks with one motor. The light sensor is attached to sensor 1, and is aimed at the base of the candy chamber. When the time comes to take a reading, our program will retrieve the value from the RCX and use that value to determine the color of the candy. Then we will rotate the platform into position in order to put the candy into the appropriate bin.

Figure 3.4 The Candy Sorting Robot

A touch sensor tells when the pushrod has backed out of the chamber, indicating that a new piece of candy has moved into position and that we are ready for another light reading. Because of the limitations of the IR communication speed that we discussed earlier in the chapter, we will deploy some of the code directly on the RCX. This will prevent the timing of the pushrod from being too far off, and also illustrate how direct mode can be combined with programs stored on the RCX itself. To set this up, we will write a very simple NQC program (Dispense.nqc) that will drive the pushrod to dispense a candy, stopping as soon as the touch sensor has been toggled. Dispense.nqc (Figure 3.5) shows what we will download to the RCX's program slot number 1. You can also find this code on the CD that accompanies this book.

Figure 3.5 A Short Candy-dispensing Task To Be Stored on the RCX (Dispense.nqc)

```
task main()
{
        SetSensor(SENSOR_3, SENSOR_TOUCH);
        On(OUT_A);
        until(SENSOR_3 == 1);
        until(SENSOR_3 == 0);
        Off(OUT_A);

}
```

This simple program will push the candy onto the conveyor belt and leave the candy-pushing rod in position for the next iteration. This short task will then be called by the Java program that we are about to write. If you wish to run this without using NQC, here is the sequence of bytes that you should download into program slot number 1:

```
52 43 58 49 02 01 01 00 01 00 00 00 00 00 20 00
13 07 02 07 E1 87 32 02 01 42 02 20 21 81 95 82
09 01 00 02 FA FF 95 82 09 00 00 02 FA FF 21 41
00 00 05 00 6D 61 69 6E 00
```

Our *CandySorter.java* class (whose source code can be seen in Figure 3.6 and on the CD) will call this task using the program number and the appropriate opcodes. The rest of the functions will be performed by the Java code, sending opcodes to the RCX in individual commands as we did earlier in the chapter. Our class will have a *main* method, which will instantiate our class and run it through the process of sorting the candy. We will use some helper methods to build the opcodes and use *RCXPort.sendData()* to send them to the RCX. The rest of the class will consist of very basic methods that will perform the main operations needed by the candy sorter. For rotating the upper platform, we have *turnLeft()* and *turnRight()* methods; and for dropping off the candy, we have a *dropOffCandy()* method. These methods take a *howLong* argument, which is then used to determine how long to rotate left, right, or to advance the conveyor belt. Due to the inaccuracies of running a program in direct mode, we suggest that you allow for some larger drop zones for the candy to allow your candy sorter room for error: perhaps a bowl instead of a cup.

Figure 3.6 A Program To Bring Your Candy-sorting Robot to Action
(CandySorter.java)

```java
package rcxport;

public class CandySorter
{
        RCXPort rcxp;
        //byte constants used for opcodes
        public final byte OutputA = (byte)          0x01;
        public final byte OutputB = (byte)          0x02;
        public final byte OutputC = (byte)          0x04;
        public final byte AllOutputs = (byte)       0x07;

        public CandySorter(String port) throws Exception
        {
                rcxp = new RCXPort(port);
        }

        public static void main(String [] args) throws Exception
        {
                String portName = getPortName(args);

                CandySorter rcx = new CandySorter(portName);

                rcx.forwardMotors();
                // 10 pieces of candy will be sorted
                for(int i=0; i<10; i++)
                {
                        int value = rcx.getLightReading();
                        //check if light reading is greater than 37%
                        if (value > 37)
                        {
                                rcx.turnLeft(100);
                                rcx.dispenseCandy();
                                rcx.dropOffCandy(500);
                                rcx.turnRight(100);
```

Continued

Figure 3.6 Continued

```
                }
                else
                {
                        rcx.turnRight(100);
                        rcx.dispenseCandy();
                        rcx.dropOffCandy(500);
                        rcx.turnLeft(100);
                }


        }


    }

private int getLightReading() throws Exception
{
        RCXResult res = sendData
            ( RCXCmd.set(RCXCmd.Read,(byte)0x09,(byte)0x0) );
        int value = -1;
        if (res != null)
        {
                byte [] codes = res.getResult();
                value = codes[1];
        }
        return value;
}

private void dispenseCandy() throws Exception
{
        //these opcodes will call program #1,
        //which has been stored on the RCX ahead of time
        sendData(RCXCmd.set((byte)0x91,(byte)0x0));
        sendData(RCXCmd.set((byte)0x71,(byte)0x0));
        //allow time for dispensing
        Thread.sleep(500);
}
```

Continued

Figure 3.6 Continued

```
private void dropOffCandy(int howLong) throws Exception
{
        reverseMotor('a');
        //advance conveyor belt
        onMotor('a', howLong);
}


private void turnLeft(int howLong) throws Exception
{
        reverseMotor('c');
        onMotor('c',howLong);
}


private void turnRight(int howLong) throws Exception
{
        forwardMotor('c');
        onMotor('c',howLong);
}


//get correct byte code for motor - each output is
//represented by a different byte
public byte getCodeForMotor(char whichMotor)
{
        byte code;

        switch(whichMotor)
        {
                case 'a':
                case 'A':
                        code = (byte)OutputA;
                        break;
                case 'b':
                case 'B':
                        code = (byte)OutputB;
```

Continued

Figure 3.6 Continued

```
                                      break;
                          case 'c':
                          case 'C':
                                      code = (byte)OutputC;
                                      break;
                          //if other char is passed,
                          //return byte for all motors
                          default:
                                      code = (byte)AllOutputs;
                                      break;
                }

                return code;
        }


        public void forwardMotor(char whichMotor) throws Exception
        {
                byte code = getCodeForMotor(whichMotor);
                RCXResult res = sendData( RCXCmd.set( (byte)RCXCmd
.OutputDir,(byte)(code | (byte)0x80) ) );
        }


        public void forwardMotors() throws Exception
        {
                forwardMotor('z');
        }


        public void reverseMotor(char whichMotor) throws Exception
        {
                byte code = getCodeForMotor(whichMotor);

                RCXResult res = sendData( RCXCmd.set( (byte)RCXCmd
.OutputDir,(byte)(code | (byte)0x40) ) );
                return;
        }
```

Continued

Figure 3.6 Continued

```
public RCXResult sendData(byte [] codes)
{
        RCXResult res = null;
        try
        {
                res = rcxp.sendData(codes);
        }
        catch (Exception e)
        {


        }
        return res;
}


public void onMotor(char whichMotor, int forHowLong) throws
Exception
        {
                byte code = getCodeForMotor(whichMotor);

                RCXResult res = sendData( RCXCmd.set( (byte)RCXCmd
.OutputMode,(byte)(code | (byte)0x80) ) );
                Thread.sleep(forHowLong);
                res = sendData( RCXCmd.set( (byte)RCXCmd.OutputMode,
                (byte)(code | (byte)0x40) ) );

                return;
        }

        private static String getPortName(String [] args)
        {
                String portName = "COM1";
                if (args.length > 0)
                {
                        portName = args[0];
```

Continued

Figure 3.6 Continued

```
                }
            return portName;

        }


}
```

As you can see in Figure 3.6, we have hard-coded a value of "37" as the threshold between two different colors of candy. Any candy generating a light reading of greater than 37 will be dispensed to the left, all others will be dispensed to the right. You may have to adjust this value for your specific candy, or have your program set the value dynamically based on the first two candies to pass through.

The *getCodeForMotor()* method is a means of abstracting the byte code from our more conceptual methods. The three methods that directly control the motors on the RCX are: *forwardMotor(), reverseMotor(), and onMotor()*. Each of these methods uses *getCodeForMotor()* to determine what byte code should indicate the method call's target motor. Within the *getCodeForMotor* method we have hard-coded bytes to represent each possible RCX output. The byte 0x01 represents output A, 0x02 indicates output B, and 0x04 indicates output C. These bytes can be combined using the bit wise *or* operator to indicate that you want a command to affect more than one motor.

The *sendData()* method simply calls the same method of the *RCXPort* class. We do this simply to allow the exceptions to be caught in one location, and also so that each *CandySorter* method calling *sendData()* need not refer to the *RCXPort* instance directly.

Summary

The default RCX firmware understands a limited set of commands called opcodes. Using the RCXPort API, you can send these commands to the RCX from your Java Runtime Environment (JRE). RCXPort makes a connection with your machine's communications port using classes from the Java Communications API. In direct mode, commands are sent one-by-one to the RCX, which then executes the commands as they are received. The RCX responds with corresponding reply bytecodes, which can be either interpreted or ignored by your Java program.

Alternatively, you can use the *RCXPort.downloadProgram()* feature to store programs in the RCX's memory. This frees you from having to operate the RCX in constant communication with the infrared tower. Currently, programming the RCX in this fashion requires writing the code in NQC or having a solid understanding of the RCX opcodes.

Hopefully you have found this introduction to RCXPort helpful. It is a technology in its infancy; it has great potential but is limited in its current implementation. Most likely you are intrigued by the potential of programming the RCX with Java. Perhaps you feel limited by the functionality that's available to you with direct mode. You will be pleased to know that more options are out there; in Chapter 5, you will learn about leJOS, a fully-functional adaptation of the Java programming language that can be run on the RCX using a small JVM that replaces the RCX firmware.

Solutions Fast Track

Overview of the RCXPort Java API

☑ The code in the RCXPort Java API establishes a connection with your infrared (IR) tower through the appropriate serial port. It relies on the Java Communications package to control the port. USB support is not included.

☑ The *RCXPacket* class wraps commands into a format that the RCX can understand before they are sent to the tower.

☑ *RCXCmd* includes all of the standard opcodes that are used to control the RCX. These bytes are declared as static in the *RCXCmd* class so that they may be called from other classes without instantiating an *RCXCmd* object.

☑ Existing RCXPort functionality does not allow for the running of Java code directly on the RCX or for high-level Java code to be compiled into byte code for downloading to the RCX. This functionality is forthcoming.

Programming the RCX Using RCXPort

☑ By inserting RCX commands into a Java program that runs on your PC, you can control the RCX in direct mode, provided your RCX remains within range of the IR tower for the duration of the program's execution.

☑ When running programs in direct mode, there is a slight delay between commands as the data is sent from the computer's serial port to the IR tower, then on to the RCX.

☑ Programming in direct mode allows for the increased power and flexibility of the Java programming language, yet limits you to keeping the RCX within range of the tower.

Downloading Programs with RCXPort

☑ RCXPort also provides functionality to download byte code files to the RCX, where they are stored in random access memory (RAM) and can be run by pressing the **Run** button.

☑ Storing programs on the RCX frees you from having to stay near the tower when running a program.

☑ Programs can be written manually in byte code, or written in a high-level language, such as 'Not Quite C' (NQC), then compiled into byte code.

Interfacing External Software with RCXPort

☑ NQC, a high-level language based on C syntax, can be compiled into byte code that is understood by RCX's firmware. This allows you to take advantage of more advanced control structures such as loops, events and functions.

☑ RCXPort is capable of downloading compiled NQC byte code to the RCX.

☑ These programs, once stored on the RCX, can be run by themselves or called from an RCXPort-based program that is running on your personal computer.

An Advanced Example Using RCXPort

☑ Our example uses a hard-coded value to represent the light threshold between two colors. This value could vary widely due to different amounts of light and different colored candies used in your experiment. This simple branch in the code could also be used to sort the "darks" and "lights" from a bag of multicolored candies. Alternatively, you could assign ranges to your different colors and check for read values that are within these ranges.

☑ Programs stored on the RCX can be called from Java code when controlling the RCX in direct mode. This allows you to better control the timing of RCX operations that would otherwise be thrown off by variance in the infrared communications.

Frequently Asked Questions

The following Frequently Asked Questions, answered by the authors of this book, are designed to both measure your understanding of the concepts presented in this chapter and to assist you with real-life implementation of these concepts. To have your questions about this chapter answered by the author, browse to **www.syngress.com/solutions** and click on the **"Ask the Author"** form.

Q: Why can't I create an *RCXResult* instance from my own code?

A: *RCXResult* is a protected class with a protected constructor. This was done so that the object would only be instantiated from within the *RCXPort* class. However, you can have an *RCXResult* object get returned from RCXPort's *sendData()* method, as I did in the Candy Sorter example.

Q: Can I run NQC code on the RCX without using RCXPort?

A: Certainly. We used RCXPort only to illustrate how to use the two together. NQC comes with its own compiler that will perform the download as well. The compiler is available at www.enteract.com/~dbaum.

Q: Will RCXPort soon be upgraded with the ability to compile into byte code?

A: Not likely. The author is a very busy guy.

Q: What does *forwardMotor('z')* do? There is no such output named *'z'*.

A: I wrote a switch statement in the *getCodeForMotor* method that, when it receives an argument other than 'a,' 'b,' or 'c,' will automatically return the byte representing all motors/outputs. I begin the program by calling *forwardMotors()*, which sets the direction of both motors to "forward." This was just a habitual check in case a motor had been left in the wrong direction by a previous program.

Q: Is there RCX functionality that was not covered in this chapter?

A: Yes. We have taken a look at many of the more common commands that the RCX can perform. There are several more, and for more information you should see the opcodes list at http://graphics.stanford.edu/~kekoa/rcx/opcodes.html.

## Chapter 4

Communicating with the RCXJava API

Solutions in this chapter:

- Designing an RCX Java Communications Architecture

- Overview of the RCXJava API

- Using the RCXLoader Application

- Beyond Serial Port Communications: The RCXApplet Example

- Direct Control Programming for the RCX Using Java

☑ Summary

☑ Solutions Fast Track

☑ Frequently Asked Questions

Introduction

Shortly after the initial information on the protocol and opcodes used for communicating with the RCX was made available, many developers began writing software to interface with the LEGO MINDSTORMS robot. Since communication with the host PC occurred through the serial port, the use of the Java Communication API was the logical choice for interfacing with the RCX. (As you learned in Chapter 2, the Java Communications API is a standard Java Extension library that allows you to interface to serial ports using 100 percent Java code. You also learned from that chapter, however, that the API does not support USB ports, so a custom interface using custom code is required.) Managing and hiding the protocol and message details would be accomplished with a reusable Java library, using a public RCX-to-Java interface to allow for direct control of the RCX from Java applications running on a host PC. Using this library, it is possible to send messages and program files to run inside the RCX itself.

Designing an RCX Java Communications Architecture

In this section we will examine the design of an architecture that allows Java to communicate with the RCX. This includes managing the RCX protocol, parsing messages and encapsulating the physical port that connects the PC to the infrared (IR) tower, which will in turn communicate with the RCX. A design that includes a high-level API to control the RCX's motors, sensors and sounds will also increase the API's ease-of-use.

First, let's take a look at how we would communicate with the RCX (serial or USB port) using the Java Communications API in its simplest form by using the raw byte opcodes as documented by either the LEGO MINDSTORMS SDK or Kekoa Proudfoot's "RCX Internals" documentation (http://graphics.stanford.edu/~kekoa/rcx/#Opcodes). The code example shown in Figure 4.1 (available on this book's companion CD as SimpleWriteRead.java) tests basic communication with the RCX by sending a command to trigger one of the default sounds. It's the simplest form of communications with the RCX, consisting of writing two messages: the alive (or ping) message, and a sound request message. Reading a corresponding message reply from the RCX follows each write.

Note that in Figure 4.1 the classpath was set to include both comm.jar and rcx.jar. In addition, the javax.comm.properties and native shared libraries are in the current path. For Windows platforms, the native libraries are win32com.dll for Java Communications API and win32usb.dll for USB support (for other platforms, please refer to the Java Communications API implementation for that platform for serial port access). For USB, please see the accompanying CD for Linux and Macintosh implementation details; the equivalent shared libraries would be linuxusb.so and macusb.shlib, respectively.

 Figure 4.1 Basic RCX Communication (SimpleWriteRead.java)

```java
import java.io.*;

import java.util.*;

import javax.comm.*;

import rcx.comm.*;


/**
 * Simple Java Communications API Test Program:
 *
 * This is a simple example of writing and reading from a comm port.
 *
 * Additionally it will illustrate the following:
 *   - Discovering all available serial ports and using the first one
 *     (unless one is specified on the command line)
 *   - How to use the USB port add-on to the Java Communications API
 *     using the rcx.comm package.
 *   (requires a specific port name on the command line e.g. LEGOTOWER1 )
 */
public class SimpleWriteRead {

    // statics to allow use in main() which is static
    static Enumeration portList;

    static CommPortIdentifier portId;

    static boolean useUSB;

    static SerialPort serialPort;

    static USBPort usbPort;

    static OutputStream outputStream;

    static InputStream inputStream;


    // alive msg
```

Continued

Figure 4.1 Continued

```
static byte[] testArray1={(byte)0x55,(byte)0xff,(byte)0x0,
                (byte)0x10,(byte)0xef,(byte)0x10,(byte)0xef};
// beep msg
static byte[] testArray2={(byte)0x55,(byte)0xff,(byte)0x00,
    (byte)0x51,(byte)0xae,(byte)0x05,(byte)0xfa,(byte)0x56,(byte)0xa9};


public static void main(String[] args) {

    useUSB = false;
    String portName = "";
    int numBytes;
    int numread;

    // first, are we using usb or serial?

    if(args.length > 0) {
        portName = args[0];
        if(portName.startsWith("LEGO"))
            useUSB = true;
    }

    if(!useUSB)
    {
                        // FIND SERIAL PORT (unless specified):
        if(portName.length()<1) {

            // get all avail serial ports -see this method at bottom
            Vector ports = getAvailableSerialPorts();

            if(ports.size()==0) {
        System.out.print("no available serial ports found - ");
        System.out.println("check for conflict with another app");
                return;
            } else {
```

Continued

Figure 4.1 Continued

```
System.out.println("found "+ports.size()+ " avail serial ports");
        }

        portName  = (String)ports.firstElement();
    System.out.println("using first available port: "+portName );
    }
    try {
        portId = CommPortIdentifier.getPortIdentifier(portName);
    } catch (NoSuchPortException e) {
        System.err.println("Error: no such port "+portName);
        return;
    }


            // SETUP SERIAL PORT:
    try {
       serialPort =
         (SerialPort) portId.open("SimpleWriteRead", 1000);
    } catch (PortInUseException e) {
        System.out.println("port already in use");
        return;
    }

    try {
        serialPort.setSerialPortParams(2400,
              SerialPort.DATABITS_8,
              SerialPort.STOPBITS_1,
              SerialPort.PARITY_ODD);
        serialPort.enableReceiveTimeout(30);
        serialPort.enableReceiveThreshold(14);
    } catch (UnsupportedCommOperationException e) {
        e.printStackTrace();
    }

    try {
```

Continued

Figure 4.1 Continued

```
            outputStream = serialPort.getOutputStream();
            inputStream = serialPort.getInputStream();
        } catch (IOException e) {
            e.printStackTrace();
        }


    }


    else                    // SETUP USB PORT:
    {
        usbPort = USBPortFactory.getUSBPort();

        try {
            if(usbPort.open(portName)<0) {
            System.err.println("USB port error: is tower plugged in?");
                return;
            }
            outputStream = usbPort.getOutputStream();
            inputStream  = usbPort.getInputStream();

        } catch(IOException e) {
            e.printStackTrace();
        }
    }

    // now write and read (same way for both types of ports)

    try {

        // write a message out:
        System.out.println("sending 'alive' message... ("
            +testArray1.length+" bytes) "
                +ArrayToString(testArray1,testArray1.length));
```

Continued

Figure 4.1 Continued

```
outputStream.write(testArray1); //alive msg

byte[] readBuffer = new byte[30];
numBytes=1; numread=0;

// read a message in:
while (numBytes>0) {
    numBytes = inputStream.read(readBuffer,0,30);
    if(numBytes>0)
  System.out.println("read response to 'alive' message... ("
                +numBytes+" bytes)"
                    +ArrayToString(readBuffer,numBytes));
    numread+=numBytes;
}


if(!useUSB) {
    // note: serial port tower echoes commands
    if(numread<14) {
        System.err.println("Error: is the RCX on?");
        return;
    } else if(numread<1) {
System.err.println("serial port error: is tower plugged in?");
        return;
    }
} else {
    if(numread<1) {
        System.err.println("Error: is the RCX on?");
        return;
    }
}

System.out.println("sending 'beep' message... ("
    +testArray2.length+" bytes) "
        +ArrayToString(testArray2,testArray2.length));
```

Continued

Figure 4.1 Continued

```
              outputStream.write(testArray2); //beep msg


              numBytes=1; numread=0;
              while (numBytes>0) {
                  //msg response
                  numBytes = inputStream.read(readBuffer,0,30);
                  if(numBytes>0)
                System.out.println("read response to 'beep' message... ("
                          +numBytes+" bytes) "
                          +ArrayToString(readBuffer,numBytes));
                  numread+=numBytes;
              }


              // the following could be one call using an interface
              if(!useUSB)
                  serialPort.close();
              else
                  usbPort.close();


          } catch (Exception e) {
              e.printStackTrace();
          }
      }


  public static Vector getAvailableSerialPorts() {
      CommPortIdentifier pId=null;
      SerialPort sPort=null;
      Enumeration pList=null;
      boolean foundport=false;
      pList = CommPortIdentifier.getPortIdentifiers();
      String port=null;
      Vector ports=new Vector();


      if(!pList.hasMoreElements()) {
          System.err.print("warning: no ports found - ");
```

Continued

Figure 4.1 Continued

```
     System.err.println("make sure javax.comm.properties file is found");
          return ports;
     }
     while (pList.hasMoreElements()) {
          pId = (CommPortIdentifier) pList.nextElement();
          if (pId.getPortType() == CommPortIdentifier.PORT_SERIAL) {
               foundport=true;
               try {
                    sPort = (SerialPort)pId.open("serialport", 1000);
               } catch (PortInUseException e) {
                    foundport=false;
               } finally {
                    if(sPort!=null) {
                         try { sPort.close(); } catch(Exception e) {}
                    }
                    if(foundport) {
                         ports.add(pId.getName());
                    }
               }
          }
     }
     return ports;
}


public static String ArrayToString(byte[] message, int length) {
     StringBuffer strbuffer = new StringBuffer();
     int abyte = 0;
     for(int loop = 0; loop < length; loop++) {
          abyte = (int) message[loop];
          if (abyte < 0) abyte += 256;
          strbuffer.append(Integer.toHexString(abyte) + " ");
     }
     return strbuffer.toString();
}
}
```

The following is sample output for the SimpleWriteRead program. Please note that the current path and the rcx.jar are specified on the command line. The alternative is to add the .jar file to the global *CLASSPATH* environment variable to avoid specifying it on the command line.

```
>java -cp .;rcx.jar SimpleWriteRead LEGOTOWER1


  sending 'alive' message... (7 bytes) 55 ff 0 10 ef 10 ef
  read response to 'alive' message... (7 bytes) 55 ff 0 ef 10 ef 10


  sending 'beep' message... (9 bytes) 55 ff 0 51 ae 5 fa 56 a9
  read response to 'beep' message... (7 bytes) 55 ff 0 ae 51 ae 51



>java -cp .;rcx.jar SimpleWriteRead COM1


 sending 'alive' message... (7 bytes) 55 ff 0 10 ef 10 ef
 read response to 'alive' message... (14 bytes) 55 ff 0 10 ef 10 ef 55
   ff 0 ef 10 ef 10


 sending 'beep' message... (9 bytes) 55 ff 0 51 ae 5 fa 56 a9
 read response to 'beep' message... (16 bytes) 55 ff 0 51 ae 5 fa 56 a9
   55 ff 0 ae 51 ae 51
```

Let's start by looking at the *imports* package; rcx.comm.* contains the USB port support (as presented in Chapter 2). This add-on does not actually work within the Java Communications API but works alongside it.

We use the command line to optionally pass in the name of the port. If none is specified, the Java Comm API finds the first available serial port . The list of available serial ports is compiled using the method called *getAvailableSerialPorts()* as shown in Figure 4.1 (Chapter 2 explains how this method works). If there is a port name starting with "LEGO" on the command line, we can determine that it is using the USB tower (RCX 2.0 set) On the Windows platform it will be LEGOTOWER1 (for the first USB tower) as opposed to COM1, which would specify a serial port. Also note under Windows, the USB port assumes you have the USB driver installed as provided by the LEGO Company.

For the serial port, whether we specify a port name or use the first one available, we follow the Java Comm convention of obtaining a port identifier with *CommPortIdentifier.getPortIdentifier(portName),* and we open the port identifier to obtain the serial port. We then set the appropriate baud rate, stop bits, parity, receive timeout, and receive threshold settings on the port that will communicate with the tower, and obtain standard input and output streams from the serial port.

For the USB port, we use a *USBPortFactory.getUSBPort()* to provide us an instance of a USB port where we then get the input and output streams.

Developing & Deploying…

RCX Internals

We'd like to present here a subset of the LEGO Opcodes as referenced in this chapter, with details of the source arguments (for complete opcode and usage information please refer to the LEGO MINDSTORMS SDK documentation or the aforementioned "RCX Internals" Web site by Kekoa Proudfoot) http://graphics.stanford.edu/~kekoa/rcx/. As a quick overview of the protocol, note the following important points:

- Each message (to and from RCX) has a message header of **55 ff 00**

- Next is the opcode, followed by any parameters that are needed by that opcode and ending with a checksum byte. Each byte (including the opcode and checksum bytes) has a complementary byte, creating byte pairs. Here's an example (omitting message headers):

```
51 ae 5 fa 56 a9
```

  where 51 is the opcode, 5 is the parameter and 56 is the checksum.

- In addition, there is a bit that needs to be flipped when sending the same command twice in a row (otherwise the RCX will ignore it). To send the same message again, we use the following (note how checksums are affected):

```
59 a6 5 fa 5e a1
```

  Ignoring header, complements and checksum, the response from the RCX will be **ae** (from the first message) or **a6** (from the message sent twice).

We write and read from the I/O streams in the exact same way on either port. We send hard-coded byte arrays that are already pre-formatted for the "alive" and "play sound 5" (fast upward tones) messages, and read byte arrays back after each write. The arrays are large enough to allow for possible message lengths. We use the *ArrayToString(byte[] array)* method to convert the array for display purposes. For more information on the actual format of the message bytes, see the "RCX Internals" sidebar in this section.

And finally, we close the port depending whether it's the serial or USB port. It would be nice to reference the port just once, and not continue to check to see if it's a serial or USB port. The best way would be to encapsulate the specific port type inside a generic *rcx port* object.

This is where the RCXJava API comes in. Rather than worry about the actual RCX protocol and physical port details, we encapsulate these details in a library.

The Basic Components of an RCX API

The RCXJava API holds a library consisting of a Java jar file (rcx.jar) that, in conjunction with the Java Communications API, will provide serial port support and a programming interface to the RCX.

There are also shared native libraries for physical access to the ports. For example, on Windows platforms, the Java Communications API requires the javax.comm.properties file and win32com.dll shared library in addition to the comm.jar file. rcx.jar requires win32usb.dll (on Windows) for USB support.

The RCXJava API addresses serial port configuration, protocol management and communications with the tower and the RCX.

Port Configuration and Error Handling

An RCX API must configure the port name and handle low level communication errors gracefully. As we'll see, the RCXJava API handles this in a standard manner, currently allowing one to specify either serial or USB port names (handling the LEGO MINDSTORMS RCX 1.0, 1.5 and 2.0 sets) and using error message callbacks for optional error notifications.

Protocol Management and Message Parsing

Constructing messages manually with the RCX protocol can be tedious. Tasks handled by the RCX API include the managing of repeated messages (the repeated message must differ every time to allow for infrared message retries), as well as calculating checksums and parsing the multi-byte messages sent and received. The construction of byte arrays should be considered as low-level details that should be hidden inside the API library.

Tower Communications

The way the tower handles messages is slightly different depending on whether or not you are using the USB port. With the serial port, the tower echoes messages and their replies from the RCX back to the PC. This allows you to distinguish between errors received from the tower and from the RCX itself. The API should also allow for this difference. Note the additional bytes in the serial port (COM1) output compared to the USB port response in the sample output for the SimpleWriteRead example.

RCX Communications

The RCX replies to every command message received, regardless of whether the reply contains response values or not. Thus, with every write to the RCX a read is required and the reply code should be checked to see if it corresponds to the sent command opcode. Again, an RCX API should hide these error checks and provide a mechanism for retries should they be necessary (for example, the robot could be temporarily out of range).

Reusability: Protocols and Ports

The RCX API should allow for extensibility and customization for both different protocols and port types. By encapsulating these details using well-known Java design patterns, it should be possible to introduce new ports that implement the same interface to the API at a lower level. As for protocols, there should be some room to change or upgrade the implementation by providing the opcode lookup table in its own class.

Supporting Similar Protocols

Although this book covers the LEGO MINDSTORMS RCX, there also exist the related CyberMaster and Scout robot sets, which provide slightly different functionality but essentially use the same protocol as the RCX.

The CyberMaster uses basically the same opcode set as the RCX. However, the protocol differs in the following way:

- The message header it uses is different: instead of *55 ff 0*, it uses *fe 00 00 ff* as the message header for commands going out to the RCX.
- Instead of using the same header for sending and receiving messages, it uses *ff* as the message header for receiving messages from the RCX.

Using Java Interfaces to Support Ports Other than Serial Ports

Java Comm takes care of serial and parallel ports. But what if we need support for new types of ports? The best solution is to encapsulate the different port types in their own classes within the RCX API and allow all of them to implement a common interface so that we can refer to all the ports in one way.

USB

The USB port was designed to be almost identical to the serial port implementation as discussed in Chapter 2, however it does not work within the Java Communications API, instead using its own factory pattern to create the appropriate USB port, depending on the platform. This may break the 100-percent Java claim, but until the standard USB Java API is available, it's the only way to use Java for the RCX 2.0 (USB tower) sets.

TCP Sockets

To provide support for TCP Sockets as a different type of port, the RCXJava API allows us to use the same Java interface (*RCXCommPort*) across a network or the Internet, without changing the application when using the RCXJava API. The type of port used is determined by the name of the port.

Overview of the RCXJava API

The RCXJava API grew out of the need for a reusable library to manage the RCX protocol, parse messages, select, and encapsulate a physical port to communicate with the RCX via the tower. It was designed to be small and easy to use, as well as extensible. It is licensed using the LGPL license and comes with complete source code, sample code and documentation. Figure 4.2 displays the core classes and interfaces that comprise the RCXJava API:

NOTE

The rcx.comm.* subpackage (covered in Chapter 2) deals exclusively with providing USB support for not just this API, but any Java API that needs to access the LEGO USB Driver.

Figure 4.2 rcx.* package UML Diagram

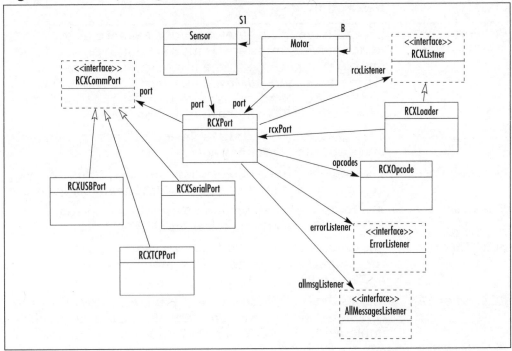

This UML diagram shows us the relationships of the different components of the rcx.* package, which we will look at in detail in the next section.

The RCX Package

This package includes support for several ports. it also handles the core responsibilities of message parsing and error handling; and provides a standard API for sending and receiving messages, both in a raw form and at a higher level. There is also an application tool included inside the rcx.* package that uses the core API to implement a GUI interface for sending and receiving messages.

Classes

Table 4.1 shows the Java classes that are the core classes of the RCXJava API. They handle the encapsulation of the physical port to which the tower connects as well as providing high level encapsulation to motors and sensors.

Table 4.1 The RCXJava Library Classes

Class	Description
RCXPort	Encapsulates and creates a specific instance of the *RCXCommPort* interface. Handles the RCX protocol and message dispatching to the listeners: *RCXListener*, *ErrorListener* and *AllMessagesListener*. Provides high-level calls for handling sensors, motors, and sounds consistent with leJOS nomenclature (Chapter 5).
RCXOpcode	Encapsulates the opcode table and utilities for handling and displaying byte messages.
RCXSerialPort	Encapsulates the *SerialPort* class provided to us by Java Comm API. This implements the *RCXCommPort* interface.
RCXServer	A proxy server that will map a remote instance of *RCXSerialPort* to the physical serial or USB port.
RCXUSBPort	Encapsulates the *USBPort* class provided to us by *rcx.comm.USBPortFactory*. This implements the *RCXCommPort* interface.
RCXSocketPort	Encapsulates a TCP socket as if it were another port for communicating with a remote PC RCX controller. This implements the *RCXCommPort* interface.
RCXLoader	Sample application that serves as a tool for sending and receiving messages via a GUI interface and for looking up opcodes. This application resides in the rcx. * package.
Motor	An encapsulation of a motor with methods for sending motor commands to RCX.
Sensor	An encapsulation of a motor with methods for sending and receiving sensor messages to and from the RCX.

Interfaces

Table 4.2 shows the Java Interfaces that are used to provide a transparent implementation of different types of RCX ports and to allow event-driven messages to be sent to listeners. Only one listener per port is allowed by the RCXJava API.

Table 4.2 The RCXJava Library Interfaces

Interface	Description
RCXCommPort	Provides a common interface for all ports, allowing for a single way of referencing the ports.

Continued

Table 4.2 Continued

Interface	Description
RCXListener	An interface used to register for all error and message callbacks This interface is the equivalent of both *ErrorListener* and *AllMessagesListener* combined.
ErrorListener	Provides an interface for receiving errors through callbacks. If not implemented, errors can still be seen on the console. This interface is useful for displaying the error messages in a GUI component or for handling errors in a certain way, for example, closing the application or prompting for a fix.
AllMessagesListener	This allows for access to all the messages coming from the RCX, including those handled in custom methods within the *RCXPort* class. This allows for further action on those messages, or the implementation of the messages that aren't handled at a higher level.

Exceptions

Error handling is done via the *ErrorListener* interface, as well as *RCXListener*, which is a superset of *ErrorListener*. Standard Java exceptions still take place and are thrown; when there are I/O exceptions, for example. At this time, however, there aren't any new custom exceptions introduced by the RCXJava API.

Figure 4.3 shows a simple use of the RCXJava API. The complete source code for Figure 4.3 appears on the companion CD for this book.

Figure 4.3 Sending and Receiving RCX Opcodes (RCXSimpleTest.java)

```
import rcx.*;

public class RCXSimpleTest implements RCXListener {

    public static void main(String[] args) {
        String cmd = null;
        if(args.length>0)
            cmd = args[0];
        new RCXSimpleTest(cmd);

    }
```

Continued

Figure 4.3 Continued

```
public RCXSimpleTest(String cmd) {

    RCXPort port = new RCXPort(cmd);
    port.addRCXListener(this);

    // set motor A direction (forwards)
    port.send("e1 81");
    // turn motor A on
    port.send("21 81");

    // play sound
    port.send("51 05");

    //delay for a sec
    try { Thread.sleep(1000); } catch(Exception e) { }

    // turn motor A off (float, 2141 is stop)
    port.send("21 41");
}

public void receivedMessage(byte[] message) {

    // simply convert to String and print the message
    StringBuffer strbuffer = new StringBuffer();
    for(int loop = 0; loop < message.length; loop++) {
        int abyte = (int) message[loop];
        if (abyte < 0) abyte += 256;
        strbuffer.append(Integer.toHexString(abyte) + " ");
    }
    System.out.println("Response: " + strbuffer.toString());
}

public void receivedError(String error) {
    System.err.println("Error: " + error);
}
}
```

The output from a sample run would look as follows:

```
>java -cp .;rcx.jar RCXSimpleTest LEGOTOWER1
  Response: 16
  Response: d6
  Response: a6
  Response: d6
```

The result is that a motor on A will run for about a second, with a sound playing at the same time. As you can see from the sample output, each command received a reply code that corresponds with the opcode sent to the RCX. All the added checksum and corresponding complement bytes are stripped out from the response because that's a hidden protocol detail.

The differences with the example in Figure 4.1 show the advantages of having an API to hide the details. Starting with the command line, we specify a port name but we don't need to code for the Java Communications API or worry about having a USB port (as indicated by having "LEGO" in the port name).

After we create an *RCXPort* object we register ourselves as a *RCXListener*, which allows us to get message responses and errors via the *receivedMessage(byte[] message)* and the *receivedError(String error)* methods.

We then proceed to set the motor direction, turn the motor on, play a sound, wait for one second and turn off the motor. Each of the messages are sent to the RCX using *RCXPort*'s *send(String msg)* method, which will handle a string representation of the message byte array (which allows for spaces between the bytes). Each of the four sent messages consisted of an opcode command and a parameter. (see the sidebar "RCX Internals" for the interpretation of each message).

Using the RCXLoader Application

We now move on to the example utility program that resides in the core rcx.* package, called RCX Loader. This program is primarily used to send and receive messages from the RCX in real-time using the opcodes, which are available as a lookup table from within the program. This example serves as a minimal interactive example for communicating with the RCX. It consists of a window frame with an input text field and an output text area component. A single button will pop open another window containing an opcode lookup table. The RCX Loader application also uses the parameters.txt configuration file, which contains one entry, for example:

```
port=COM1
```

In this specific example, the port to be opened upon start up will be the COM1 serial port. One could also specify a USB port name. Otherwise, if no ports are specified, the first available serial port will be used.

The screen shown in Figure 4.4 is what is displayed when one runs **java -cp rcx.jar rcx.RCXLoader**.

Figure 4.4 RCXLoader

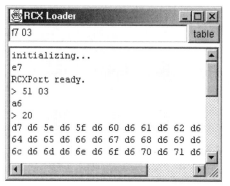

The screenshot shows status messages, entered commands and the responses from the RCX. By default, the instance of *RCXPort* will send an alive message to wake up the RCX Tower (which is needed in the case of serial towers) and a ready message will tell you that you can now enter commands. The first command entered in our example was a request to play sound 3 followed, by a request to get a memory map.

Figure 4.5 shows us the RCXLoader and its associated classes.

Figure 4.5 RCXLoader UML Diagram

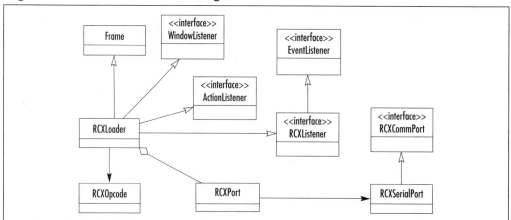

The User Interface

RCXLoader is a frame window that listens to window and button events, RCX reply messages, and error messages. The *RCXOpcode* class is used to display the opcode table window frame, which is callable from any application that needs it. This is a minimal test RCX communication program that allows you to send and receive opcodes at a low level and serves as a template for more elaborate examples.

Handling and Parsing Response and Error Messages

Since it implements *RCXListener*, the RCX responses will be handled by the *receivedError(String error)* method and *receivedMessage(byte[] array)*. The message is formatted for display in the text area and error messages are generated in the case of bad user input or port failures.

Beyond Serial Port Communications: The RCXApplet Example

The next progression of examples will have a full-fledged GUI to represent the three physical motors and three sensor inputs. In the visual interface application that we will develop in this section, we will basically have buttons to turn the motors on and off, stopping without braking (also referred to as *floating*), selecting motor direction, and displaying the sensor values as they change.

To make the program even easier to work with, why not build it as a browser-based Java applet instead of running it as a command line based application? Yes, this means controlling an RCX robot from a Web page! At first glance, one would think that it's not possible to do this with an applet because applets require access to native code, which is impossible without going through the process of *signing* applets (explicit security permissions). There are also implementation issues arising from signing with different browsers and Java virtual machines. However, the fact is that one wouldn't want to run the applet to directly access the port, but rather to have it access the RCX remotely from any browser. In this way it would not require access to native ports, instead accessing an application that would work as proxy on your behalf and control the RCX.

We'll design an applet that would allow us to remotely turn on motors and retrieve sensor values over the Internet. Figure 4.6 displays the resulting web browser page with an applet that can remotely control a RCX robot.

Figure 4.6 RCXApplet

To run this applet you need to run the server as follows:

```
java -cp rcx.jar rcx.RCXServer LEGOTOWER1 (or COM1) 174
```

where the two parameters indicate the local port to which the tower is connected and the server socket port number to which applet will connect (the default is 174). Please note that the port number is hard-coded in the applet tag and must match the port number of the server. The server's host name is also indicated in the applet tag. This will be described in more detail in the following sections.

Communicating over the Network

The applet example not only demonstrates a more visually advanced example but it also shows how we can represent the RCX port over a network connection. The *RCXCommPort* interface allows us to create arbitrary ports, such as those included in the RCXJava API. In addition to the serial and USB port, the *RCXSocketPort* encapsulates access to a TCP socket port in much the same way, since all the ports implement *RCXCommPort*. Figure 4.7 illustrates how one would create a new type of port that implements *RCXCommPort*, which RCXPort would then encapsulate as it does with the other ports. *RCXSocketPort* is included in the rcx.* package.

Figure 4.7 A Socket RCX Port (RCXSocketPort.java)

```java
public class RCXSocketPort implements RCXCommPort
{
    private Socket tcpPort;

    public boolean open(String portName) {

        if(portName==null)
            return false;

        try {
            String host = getHostName(portName);
            int portnum = getPort(portName);
            tcpPort = new Socket(host,portnum);
            tcpPort.setSoTimeout(0);
        } catch(Exception e) {
            System.err.println("Error opening socket: "+e);
            return false;

        }

        return true;
    }

    public void close() {
        if (tcpPort!= null) {
            try {
                tcpPort.close();
            } catch(IOException ioe) {
            }
        }
    }

    public OutputStream getOutputStream() {
        if(tcpPort!=null) {
            try {
                return tcpPort.getOutputStream();
```

Continued

Figure 4.7 Continued

```
            }
            catch(Exception e) {
                e.printStackTrace();
            }
        }
        return null;
    }


    public InputStream getInputStream() {
        if(tcpPort!=null) {
            try {
                return tcpPort.getInputStream();
            }
            catch(Exception e) {
                e.printStackTrace();
            }
        }
        return null;
    }


    private String getHostName(String portName) {
        String host = "localhost";
        if(portName.length()<7) return host;
        int pos = portName.lastIndexOf(':');
        if(pos<6) return portName.substring(6);
        return portName.substring(6,pos);
    }


    private int getPort(String portName) {
        int port = 174;
        if(portName.length()<7) return port;
        int pos = portName.lastIndexOf(':');
        if(pos<6) return port;
        try {
            String portnum=portName.substring(pos);
```

Continued

Figure 4.7 Continued

```
        port = Integer.parseInt(portnum);
    } catch(Exception e) {
    }
    return port;
    }
}
```

Notice that the necessary methods are those that implement the *RCXCommPort* interface, namely *open(), close(), getInputStream()* and *getOutputStream()*. For the *RCXSocketPort*, the TCP socket implements these using the standard Java Socket class.

What this now allows us to do is share the code base on both the server and client side. In fact, the code can be identical on both, except when referencing the port name. The convention, as seen in the code, takes the form of a URL:

```
rcx://[hostname]:[port]
```

As an example (these are also the default values if none are entered):

```
rcx://localhost:174
```

The result is that we can use the identical code that specifies the use of serial or USB ports by name (COM1, for example) as we can using the *rcx* "protocol" name (as shown above) which allows us to clearly distinguish this socket-based port from the other types of ports.

Using Sockets

The applet by itself won't work unless you have a server-side proxy ready to accept commands and dispatch them to the port that's controlling the RCX (Figure 4.8 illustrates this client-server communication). Fortunately, the RCXJava API includes RCXServer.java, which will create a server-side socket that will redirect its input and output streams to the input and output streams of the RCXPort controlling the RCX. If there is a failure opening the port, or the error listener on the server receives an error message, these exceptions are propagated to the client.

The one other function for which the RCXServer is responsible is closing the RCX port when the socket connection to the client is lost. RCXServer is provided as part of the rcx.* package.

Figure 4.8 RCX Network Communication

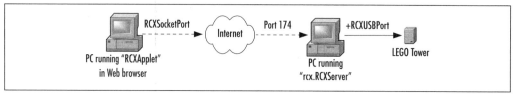

As shown in Figure 4.9, in RCXServer.java, we loop around a standard *accept()* call on a server socket to obtain a client connection. For obvious reasons, we will only handle one client at a time. We then create buffered input and output streams to interface with the *RCXPort* instance. The *setStreams(InputStream tcpin, OutputStream tcpout)* method is used for handing off the streams and instructing the port to map the input and output streams of the client socket to the output and input streams of the RCX port. We will then wait before getting the next remote client socket. This will occur when the current connection is broken.

Figure 4.9 A TCP to RCX Proxy Server (RCXServer.java)

```
public class RCXServer implements RCXErrorListener, Runnable
{
    private ServerSocket listenSocket;
    private Socket tcpPort;
    private int portNumber;
    private RCXPort rcxPort;
    private String rcxPortName;
    private boolean waitforRCX=true;
    private boolean waitforClient=true;

    public static void main(String[] args) {
        int portnum = 174; //default
        try {
            if(args.length>1) {
                portnum = Integer.parseInt(args[1]);
            }
            if(args.length>0) {
                RCXServer rcxServer = new RCXServer(args[0],portnum);
                rcxServer.run();
                rcxServer.stop();
```

Continued

Figure 4.9 Continued

```
        } else {
    System.out.println("Usage: RCXServer rcxportname [port number]");
        }
    } catch(Exception e) {
    }
}

public RCXServer(String rcxport,int portnum) {
    rcxPortName = rcxport;
    portNumber = portnum;
}

public void run() {
    RCXPort.skipalive=true;
    InputStream tcpin;
    OutputStream tcpout;
    boolean loop=true;

    try {
        listenSocket = new ServerSocket(portNumber);
    } catch (IOException ioe) {
        ioe.printStackTrace();
        return;
    }

    System.out.println("creating rcx port on "+rcxPortName);
    rcxPort = new RCXPort(rcxPortName);
    rcxPort.addRCXErrorListener(this);

    while(waitforClient) {
        waitforRCX=true;
        if(!rcxPort.isOpen()) return;
        System.out.println("Listening on port "+portNumber);
        try {
            tcpPort = listenSocket.accept();
```

Continued

Figure 4.9 Continued

```
            try { System.out.println("accepted connection to "
                    +(tcpPort.getInetAddress()).getHostName());
            } catch(Exception e) { }


        tcpin=new BufferedInputStream(tcpPort.getInputStream());
        tcpout=new BufferedOutputStream(tcpPort.getOutputStream());


        rcxPort.setStreams(tcpin,tcpout);


        while(waitforRCX) {
            try { Thread.sleep(100); } catch(Exception e) { }
        }
        try {
            System.out.println("disconnecting "
                +(tcpPort.getInetAddress()).getHostName());
            tcpPort.close();
        } catch(Exception e) { }
    } catch(IOException ioe) {
        try {
            System.out.println("Exception - disconnecting "
                +(tcpPort.getInetAddress()).getHostName());
        } catch(Exception e) { }
        try {
            tcpPort.close();
        } catch(Exception ee) { }
    }
    } //while
}

public void stop() {
    waitforClient=false;
    waitforRCX=false;
    if (tcpPort!= null) {
        try {
            tcpPort.close();
```

Continued

Figure 4.9 Continued

```
        } catch(IOException ioe) {
        }
    }
    if (listenSocket!= null) {
        try {
            listenSocket.close();
        } catch(IOException ioe) {
        }
    }
}


public void receivedError(String error) {
    System.err.println("Server got error: "+error);
    waitforRCX=false;
    if (tcpPort!= null) {
        try {
            tcpPort.close();
        } catch(IOException ioe) {
        }
    }
}
}
```

One can now easily develop both applications and applets to access a remote machine with the RCX over the Internet by specifying a URL as the port name.

Building and Extending the Simple Applet

The code listings we'll see in this section show that we're handling the communication with an *RCXPort* over the Internet identically as with a direct local connection to the tower. We also demonstrate a higher level API, using the *Motor* and *Sensor* classes, that encapsulate their functionality and access. This part of the applet code is short and concise because most of the work is done in the *RCXControl* class, shown in Figure 4.10. This class is an AWT panel that can be easily reused in applications and not just applets (the application version, RCXControlApp.java, is included on the CD).

Figure 4.10 The RCX Remote Control Applet (RCXApplet.java)

```java
import java.applet.*;
import java.awt.*;


public class RCXApplet extends Applet
{
    private RCXControl controlPanel;

    public void init() {
        setBackground(Color.yellow);

        String portName = getParameter("rcxport");

        controlPanel = new RCXControl(portName);
        add(controlPanel);
    }
}
```

Note that the only thing passed into RCXControl is the port name. With an application, the port name is passed in from the command line, but with an applet we pass the port name in as a standard parameter within the applet tag as follows:

```
<applet codebase="." code=RCXApplet.class archive=rcx.jar width=275
 height=125>
<param name=rcxport value="rcx://localhost:174">
</applet>
```

For the parameter name we indicate a hostname and port number to which the server will connect (This may have to change to correspond to the actual hostname and port number). The next listing we have is shown in Figure 4.11. It is a subclass of Java's AWT Panel, which allows us to reuse it in both applets and applications.

Figure 4.11 The Remote Control Panel (RCXControl.java, abridged)

```java
import java.awt.*;
import java.awt.event.*;
import java.io.*;
```

Continued

Figure 4.11 Continued

```java
import java.util.*;
import rcx.*;

public class RCXControl extends Panel implements ActionListener,
                                        RCXErrorListener, Runnable
{
    private String     portName;
    private RCXPort     rcxPort;
    private Thread      thisThread;
    private boolean     isRunning;
    private Panel       topPanel,bottomPanel;
    private TextField sensorField1,sensorField2,sensorField3;
    private Panel     motorPanel1,motorPanel2,motorPanel3;
    private Button    motor1fwd,motor1bwd,motor1stop,motor1float;
    private Button    motor2fwd,motor2bwd,motor2stop,motor2float;
    private Button    motor3fwd,motor3bwd,motor3stop,motor3float;
    private int s1value,s1prevalue,s2value,s2prevalue,s3value,s3prevalue;

    public RCXControl(String portname) {

        portName = portname;

        topPanel  = new Panel();
        topPanel.setLayout(new FlowLayout(FlowLayout.CENTER,4,4));
        bottomPanel = new Panel();
        bottomPanel.setLayout(new FlowLayout(FlowLayout.CENTER,5,5));
        motorPanel1 = new Panel();
        motorPanel1.setLayout(new BorderLayout(5,5));

        sensorField1 = new TextField(9);
        sensorField1.setEditable(false);
        sensorField1.setEnabled(false);

        motor1fwd = new Button("forward");
        motor1fwd.addActionListener(this);
```

Figure 4.11 Continued

```
        topPanel.add(sensorField1);

        motorPanel1.add(motor1fwd,"North");

        bottomPanel.add(motorPanel1);

        setLayout(new BorderLayout());
        add(topPanel,"North");
        add(bottomPanel,"South");
        setBackground(Color.yellow);

        thisThread = new Thread(this);
        thisThread.start();
    }

public void run() {
        rcxPort = new RCXPort(portName);
        rcxPort.addRCXErrorListener(this);

        Sensor.S1.setTypeAndMode(SensorConstants.SENSOR_TYPE_LIGHT,
                              SensorConstants.SENSOR_MODE_PCT);
        Sensor.S2.setTypeAndMode(SensorConstants.SENSOR_TYPE_LIGHT,
                              SensorConstants.SENSOR_MODE_PCT);
        Sensor.S3.setTypeAndMode(SensorConstants.SENSOR_TYPE_LIGHT,
                              SensorConstants.SENSOR_MODE_PCT);
        isRunning=true;

        sensorField1.setText("0");
        sensorField2.setText("0");
        sensorField3.setText("0");

        while(isRunning) {
            // this delay can be adjusted or eliminated
            try{Thread.sleep(1000);}catch(Exception e) { }
```

Continued

Figure 4.11 Continued

```
        s1value=Sensor.S1.readValue();
        if(s1value!=s1prevalue) {
            s1prevalue=s1value;
            sensorField1.setText(Integer.toString(s1value));
        }
        s2value=Sensor.S2.readValue();
        if(s2value!=s2prevalue) {
            s2prevalue=s2value;
            sensorField2.setText(Integer.toString(s2value));
        }
        s3value=Sensor.S3.readValue();
        if(s3value!=s3prevalue) {
            s3prevalue=s3value;
            sensorField3.setText(Integer.toString(s3value));
        }
    }
}


public void actionPerformed(ActionEvent e) {
    Object obj = e.getSource();
    if(obj==motor1fwd) {
        Motor.A.forward();
    }
    else if(obj==motor1bwd) {
        Motor.A.backward();
    }
    else if(obj==motor1stop) {
        Motor.A.stop();
    }
    else if(obj==motor1float) {
        Motor.A.flt();
    }
}


public void receivedError(String error) {
```

Continued

Figure 4.11 Continued

```
        System.err.println("Error: "+error);
        close();
    }


    public void close() {
        isRunning=false;
        if(rcxPort!=null)
            rcxPort.close();
    }
}
```

Most of the listing in Figure 4.11 deals with the visual interface (abridged as to not show all the components, such as the numerous buttons). Here we introduce the static instances of the motors and sensors in the *Motor* and *Sensor* classes. Using a method signature similar to that of leJOS (which we'll discuss in Chapter 5), we can control the motors via simple methods such as *forward()* and *stop()*. For the sensors, we use the *setTypeAndMode()* method for setting up a sensor and *readValue()* for reading the current value from the sensor (there are several read methods, depending on the value type expected).

In this case we set the sensors as light sensors and read back a percentage value. This will also work for touch sensors, displaying "0" or "100" instead of "true" or "false". In the main loop, where all we do is read sensor values (since the motors are controlled from action events fired by pressing the buttons), we have to introduce a hard-coded delay. This delay controls the polling frequency, which does not need to be too frequent when reading over the Internet. Improvements for this code would be to add controls to adjust motor power, as well as pull-down lists to select the type of sensors to use.

Another improvement would be to extend the applet as an advanced remote control that includes visual feedback, since near real-time control would be difficult without actually seeing the robot. If you use the Java Media Frameworks with your applet, you can stream a video feed from a web cam that is pointed at your robot. The alternative is to have any one of many web cam-enabling software packages to run on the same HTML page as your RCX applet. In addition, the possibilities of using a RCX remote control for your robot to assist in home automation are endless, from feeding the cat to turning on your air conditioning.

Debugging...

Emulation

The RCXJava API allows one to add a level of debugging statements by calling the *setDebug(boolean debug)* method on RCXPort.java; this shows you any byte arrays that are sent out (you use the listener interfaces to view all byte arrays that are received), as well as additional miscellaneous debugging information that was used while developing the RCXJava API.

In addition to this, there is also an emulation mode that is useful for situations when developing with an RCX Tower attached is inconvenient or impossible.

The emulation mode is initiated by simply setting "EMULATION" as the port type. In emulation mode, there are no error messages generated by not successfully writing or reading to the port or tower because what gets emulated are the higher level API calls, which are the *Motor* and *Sensor* classes. Of course, the emulation mode is not useful when sending opcode byte arrays or expecting to receive the responses via the message listener.

How one would use the emulation is to have a test program create a separate thread to randomly (or not so randomly) generate input events for the sensors as demonstrated in Figure 4.12.

This allows for controlled unit tests of code you already have or are currently developing and debugging.

Figure 4.12 Emulating Sensors (RCXSensorEmulation.java)

```
import java.awt.*;

import java.awt.event.*;

import java.io.*;

import java.util.*;

import rcx.Sensor;


public class RCXSensorEmulation implements Runnable
{
    private Thread      thisThread;
    private boolean     isRunning;
```

Continued

Figure 4.12 Continued

```
public RCXSensorEmulation() {
thisThread = new Thread(this);
    thisThread.start();
}

public void run() {
    isRunning=true;
    while(isRunning) {
        try {Thread.sleep(1000);} catch(Exception e) { }
        switch((int)(Math.random()*5)+1) {
            case 1: Sensor.S1.setPreviousValue((int)
                (Math.random()*1024)+1);
                break;
            case 2: Sensor.S2.setPreviousValue((int)
                (Math.random()*1024)+1);
                break;
            case 3: Sensor.S3.setPreviousValue((int)
                (Math.random()*1024)+1);
                break;
            case 4: try {Thread.sleep(3000);}
                catch(Exception e) { }
                break;
        }
    }
}

public void stop() {
    isRunning=false;
}
}
```

This code will simply generate sensor values in a pseudo-random fashion. This isn't a core RCX class; it is simply provided as a template for creating custom unit tests.

Continued

To use the above sensor emulation, simply stick the following line in your code (also shown in Figure 4.13):

```
if(portName.equals("EMULATION")) new RCXSensorEmulation();
```

Controlled unit tests are more reliable and efficient than using a connected RCX for testing, especially when testing a suite or framework of classes.

Direct Control Programming for the RCX Using Java

As we've just seen with the RCXApplet example, we can program for the RCX using abstractions such as *Motor* and *Sensor* on the PC to directly control the RCX. By using these abstractions we can control the RCX directly without having to download tasks into it. We can have the tasks run on the PC in near real time (albeit with a noticeable time lag), and these applications could handle entire tasks on the PC in a similar fashion to tasks running inside the RCX. In fact, the method signatures are similar to the leJOS methods (leJOS will allow us to run Java tasks inside the RCX, as we'll see in Chapter 5). With direct control programming, we are using the RCX's "brain" only to pass commands from a proxy "brain" residing on a PC.

Basic Remote Control Application

In the command-line-driven application shown in Figure 4.13, we again monitor the sensors, but we also have the application decide when to change the motor activity. This program uses the command line only to change the inputs and outputs.

Figure 4.13 Basic Remote Control of an RCX (RCXTest.java)

```
import rcx.*;

public class RCXTest implements RCXErrorListener {

    private static RCXPort port;
    private static int motor;
    private static int direction;
```

Continued

Figure 4.13 Continued

```java
private static int power;

public static void main(String[] args) {
    String portName = null;
    if(args.length>0)
        portName = args[0];
    else if(args.length==0) {
        System.out.println("Usage: RCXTest portname");
        return;
    }

    new RCXTest(portName);
}

public RCXTest(String portName) {

    port = new RCXPort(portName);
    port.addRCXErrorListener(this);

    if(portName.equals("EMULATION")) new RCXSensorEmulation();

    System.out.println("battery power left: "
                        +port.getBatteryPower()+" volts");

    Motor.A.forward();

    try { Thread.sleep(500); } catch(Exception e) { }

    Motor.A.backward();

    try { Thread.sleep(500); } catch(Exception e) { }

    Motor.A.stop();

    port.beep();
```

Continued

Figure 4.13 Continued

```
Sensor.S1.setTypeAndMode(SensorConstants.SENSOR_TYPE_TOUCH,
                             SensorConstants.SENSOR_MODE_BOOL);
Sensor.S2.setTypeAndMode(SensorConstants.SENSOR_TYPE_LIGHT,
                             SensorConstants.SENSOR_MODE_PCT);
Sensor.S3.setTypeAndMode(SensorConstants.SENSOR_TYPE_TOUCH,
                             SensorConstants.SENSOR_MODE_BOOL);

int s2light,s2prevlight=0;
boolean s1touch,s3touch,s1prevtouch=true,s3prevtouch=true;

while(true) {

    s1touch=Sensor.S1.readBooleanValue();
    if(s1touch!=s1prevtouch) {
        s1prevtouch=s1touch;
        System.out.println("reading sensor 1: "+s1touch);
    }
    s2light=Sensor.S2.readValue();
    if(s2light!=s2prevlight) {
        s2prevlight=s2light;
        System.out.println("reading sensor 2: "+s2light);
    }
    s3touch=Sensor.S3.readBooleanValue();
    if(s3touch!=s3prevtouch) {
        s3prevtouch=s3touch;
        System.out.println("reading sensor 3: "+s3touch);
    }
}
}

public void receivedError(String error) {
    System.exit(1);
}
}
```

In this example we see a call to *getBatteryPower(),* which returns the RCX's remaining battery power, in volts. This is another example of a higher-level encapsulation of RCX opcode messages. We then proceed to run motor A forward and backward for a about a half-second each before stopping, making a sound, and entering a loop that will simply monitor the sensors. In this case we set up two touch sensors and one light sensor. We simply display the values on the console indefinitely though we could have taken a specific action upon any given input event. Notice that, like the applet, we only display the values if they have indeed changed.

To improve upon the program, we could create custom applications as external tasks and even pass in settings and directions for our sensors and motors from the command line. We could design crude one-line script commands that could add the desired responses to the inputs in addition to configuring simple actions; what this would do is create mini "tasks" that we could piece together in batch files appropriate for the batch-style programming of the RCX.

Creating a Direct Control Framework for Java Programs

One could potentially make a complete clone of the LEGO MINDSTORMS visual programming interface in Java using the RCXJava API. Such a framework would give you the ability to create and store your creations or programs onto disk. Although the capability to download tasks is not available with this API, one could build that capability into a framework, as well as allow for the translation of different data formats (such as NQC files). Or one could come up with a new data format that would consist of custom Java class files. This could also be addressed by replacing the firmware altogether so as to run Java programs inside the RCX (as we'll see in Chapter 5 with leJOS). But if one were to keep the existing firmware, a framework could be built to translate leJOS Java programs into an intermediary format to download and run in the RCX with the current firmware.

Direct Control Using AI

Another possible framework would be the ability to add artificial intelligence (AI) to our RCX robots. That's the other advantage that direct control gives us, along with capabilities that far exceed the RCX brain itself. Using a PC allows us to program very large and complex AI programs. What type of AI could we use? Well, the first that comes to mind is the type that would be useful for programming something along the lines of a chess robot, one that determines moves using min-max searches. But a more interesting branch of AI, especially with regards to robotics, is neural network programming.

The following example demonstrates the use of neural networks to have our RCX "learn" the right response to stimuli all on its own. This code is based on the original Visual Basic version of the program developed by Bert Van Dam and available from his site, "Artificial Intelligence and Machine Learning" (http://home.zonnet.nl/bvandam), which uses the CyberMaster robot.

The user interface simply consists of **Start** and **Stop** buttons that will start the learning process by basically starting the RCX robot to move. There is also a **Reset** button to reset the learning process. A screen shot of the RCXNeuralTest program is shown in Figure 4.15. The ideal robot for this example would be a simple explorer such as the one from Chapter 14 in Syngress Publishing's *Building Robots with LEGO MINDSTORMS* book by Mario and Giulio Ferrari (shown in Figure 4.14). This example uses two touch sensors and two motors, which will be the inputs and outputs to the neural network. As the robot "learns," it will record the successful results based on its inputs and outputs. The neural network matrix or "brain" that represents the robot's current knowledge of solutions, based on the inputs and outputs, is displayed as a four-by-four matrix.

Figure 4.14 The Room Explorer Robot

The matrix displayed in the frame window's text area component (Figure 4.15) is a solutions matrix consisting of all possible input and output states. The current state is checked against the matrix by multiplying the current state vector with the matrix (the neural brain contents). Such a vector is described as follows:

```
+1 Input sensor 1
+1 Input sensor 3
 ? Output motor A
 ? Output motor C
```

where '+1' and '–1' indicate on and off respectively and '?' is the answer we are looking for. In this specific case we want to know what to do with the motors when both touch sensors are on. If the above vector [+1,+1,?,?] (ignoring question marks) when multiplied with the matrix yields [+1,+1,-1,-1] then we have the motors stop. This would be a solution that was found because the inputs match. If not, we haven't learned that scenario yet and have to add it to the brain—if it is the correct solution.

Figure 4.15 A Simple RCX AI Application

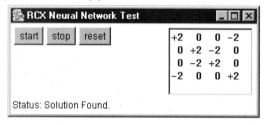

The reset button will clear the matrix to its default state and start the learning process from scratch again. There is also a text display at the bottom of the frame window, which indicates the application's current status. The following listing in Figure 4.16 is the AI test application, RCXNeuralTest. This application refers to the *RCXNeuralBrain* class, which encapsulates the matrix and its related functions. The two methods of *RCXNeuralBrain* shown in Figure 4.17, *search()* and *learn()* are the crux of the class as the remaining methods and supporting classes, namely *matrix* and *vector*, support mathematical operations.

Figure 4.16 Sample AI Test Program (RCXNeuralTest.java)

```java
import java.awt.*;
import java.awt.event.*;
import java.io.*;
import java.util.*;
import rcx.RCXPort;
```

Continued

Figure 4.16 Continued

```
import rcx.RCXErrorListener;

import rcx.Motor;

import rcx.Sensor;

import rcx.SensorConstants;


/*
 * Sample neural network test program for the RCX
 *    based on the visual basic code by Bert Van Dam:
 *        http://home.zonnet.nl/bvandam
 */
public class RCXNeuralTest extends Panel implements ActionListener,
                        Runnable, WindowListener, RCXErrorListener {
    private RCXNeuralBrain brain;

    private String   portName;

    private RCXPort rcxPort;

    private boolean isRunning;

    private Panel    buttonPanel;

    private Button   startButton, stopButton, resetButton;

    private Button   emulateSensor1, emulateSensor3;

    private int      sensor1val, sensor3val;

    private Label    textLabel;

    private boolean motorA, motorC;

    private boolean s1touch, s3touch;

    private boolean s1prevtouch=false, s3prevtouch=false;


    public RCXNeuralTest(String portname) {
        portName = portname;

        buttonPanel  = new Panel();

        buttonPanel.setLayout(new FlowLayout(FlowLayout.CENTER,4,4));

        brain = new RCXNeuralBrain();

        startButton = new Button("start");

        startButton.addActionListener(this);

        stopButton = new Button("stop");

        stopButton.addActionListener(this);
```

Continued

Figure 4.16 Continued

```
    resetButton = new Button("reset");
    resetButton.addActionListener(this);
    textLabel = new Label("Status: waiting");

    buttonPanel.add(startButton);
    buttonPanel.add(stopButton);
    buttonPanel.add(resetButton);

    setLayout(new BorderLayout());
    add(buttonPanel,"West");
    add(brain,"East");
    add(textLabel,"South");
    setBackground(Color.white);

    if(portName.equals("EMULATION")) {
        emulateSensor1 = new Button("S1");
        emulateSensor1.addActionListener(this);
        emulateSensor3 = new Button("S3");
        emulateSensor3.addActionListener(this);
        buttonPanel.add(emulateSensor1);
        buttonPanel.add(emulateSensor3);
    }
}

public static void main(String[] args) {
    RCXNeuralTest neuraltest;
    Frame appFrame = new Frame("RCX Neural Network Test");
    String portName = null;
    if(args.length>0)
        portName = args[0];
    else if(args.length==0) {
        System.out.println("Usage: RCXNeuralTest portname");
        return;
    }
    neuraltest = new RCXNeuralTest(portName);
    appFrame.add(neuraltest);
```

Continued

Figure 4.16 Continued

```
        appFrame.addWindowListener(neuraltest);
        Dimension screen = Toolkit.getDefaultToolkit().getScreenSize();
        appFrame.setBounds(screen.width/5,screen.height/5,325,140);
        appFrame.setVisible(true);
        Thread thread = new Thread(neuraltest);
        thread.start();
    }


    public void run() {
        long startTime=0L;
        isRunning = true;
        boolean solutionfound=false;

        rcxPort = new RCXPort(portName);
        rcxPort.addRCXErrorListener(this);

        Sensor.S1.setTypeAndMode(SensorConstants.SENSOR_TYPE_TOUCH,
                                SensorConstants.SENSOR_MODE_BOOL);
        Sensor.S3.setTypeAndMode(SensorConstants.SENSOR_TYPE_TOUCH,
                                SensorConstants.SENSOR_MODE_BOOL);

        if(portName.equals("EMULATION")) {
            Sensor.S1.setPreviousValue(0);
            Sensor.S3.setPreviousValue(0);
        }

        while(isRunning) {

          if(checkSensors()) { // if inputs changed

            if(brain.search(s1touch,s3touch)) { // if solution found

              setStatus("Solution Found.");
              setMotors(brain.getOutputs());

            } else {
```

Figure 4.16 Continued

```
boolean saveS1sensor = s1touch;
boolean saveS3sensor = s3touch;
solutionfound=false;

setStatus("Solution Not Found - finding new solution");

while(!solutionfound) {

  // pick a solution
  setMotors(brain.getRandomOutputs());
  startTime=System.currentTimeMillis();

  while(isRunning) { // wait 2 sec for a solution

    if(checkSensors()) {
      solutionfound = true; // new solution found
      setStatus("New Solution Found.");
      brain.learn(saveS1sensor,saveS3sensor,motorA,motorC);
      break;

    } else {

      if((System.currentTimeMillis() - startTime)>2000L) {
        setStatus("Solution Not Found - picking another");
        break;
      } // if time ran out waiting for sensor change

    } //else no change with sensors

  } //while waiting for new solution to check out

} //while picking random solution

} // else no solution found in brain - find new one
```

Continued

Figure 4.16 Continued

```
        } // if inputs changed at all

    } // main while

} // run()

public void actionPerformed(ActionEvent e) {
    Object obj = e.getSource();
    if(obj==startButton) {
        setStatus("starting robot");
        boolean[] motors = {true,true};
        setMotors(motors);
    }
    else if(obj==stopButton) {
        setStatus("stopping robot");
        Motor.A.stop();
        Motor.C.stop();
    }
    else if(obj==resetButton) {
        setStatus("brain state reset");
        brain.reset();
    }
    else if(obj==emulateSensor1) {
        sensor1val = (sensor1val==0) ? 100 : 0;
        Sensor.S1.setPreviousValue(sensor1val);
    }
    else if(obj==emulateSensor3) {
        sensor3val = (sensor3val==0) ? 100 : 0;
        Sensor.S3.setPreviousValue(sensor3val);
    }
}

public boolean checkSensors() {
    boolean check = false;
```

Continued

Figure 4.16 Continued

```
        if(portName.equals("EMULATION")) {
           try { Thread.sleep(200); } catch(Exception e) {}
        }
        s1touch=Sensor.S1.readBooleanValue();
        if(s1touch!=s1prevtouch) {
            s1prevtouch=s1touch;
            check=true;
        }
        if(portName.equals("EMULATION")) {
           try { Thread.sleep(600); } catch(Exception e) {}
        }
        s3touch=Sensor.S3.readBooleanValue();
        if(s3touch!=s3prevtouch) {
            s3prevtouch=s3touch;
            check=true;
        }
        if(check)
        System.out.println("\ncheckSensors(): sensor1 = "
                             +s1touch+" sensor3 = "+s3touch);
        return check;
    }


public void setMotors(boolean[] outputs) {
        if(outputs[0]) {
            Motor.A.forward();
            motorA=true;
        } else {
            Motor.A.stop();
            motorA=false;
        }
        if(outputs[1]) {
            Motor.C.forward();
            motorC=true;
        } else {
            Motor.C.stop();
```

Continued

Figure 4.16 Continued

```java
                motorC=false;
        }
    }

    public void setStatus(String stat) {
        textLabel.setText("Status: "+stat);
        textLabel.repaint();
        System.out.println("Status: "+stat);
    }

    public void close() {
        setStatus("shutting down");
        isRunning=false;
        if(rcxPort!=null)
            rcxPort.close();
    }

    public void receivedError(String error) {
        System.err.println("Error: "+error);
        close();
    }

    public void windowActivated(WindowEvent e) { }
    public void windowClosed(WindowEvent e) { }
    public void windowDeactivated(WindowEvent e) { }
    public void windowDeiconified(WindowEvent e) { }
    public void windowIconified(WindowEvent e) { }
    public void windowOpened(WindowEvent e) { }
    public void windowClosing(WindowEvent e) {
        close();
        System.exit(0);
    }
}
```

Figure 4.17 Code snippet from RCXNeuralBrain.java

```java
public boolean search(boolean input1, boolean input2) {
    // create inputs vector
    vector inputs = new vector(input1,input2);

    // create a question with inputs and uknown outputs
    vector question = new vector(inputs, new
vector(UNKNOWN,UNKNOWN));

    System.out.println("\nsearch(): search quesiton :\n"+question);

    // find the answer
    vector answer = brain.multiply(question);
    answer.normalize();

    // get inputs portion for verification (first part of vector)
    vector answer_inputs = answer.sub(0,2);

    boolean solutionFound = answer_inputs.equals(inputs);

    if(solutionFound) {
        System.out.println("\nsearch(): answer found :\n"+answer);

        //get outputs part of input/output answer pair vector
        outputs = answer.sub(2,2);

    } else {
        System.out.println("\nsearch(): answer not found\n");
    }
    return solutionFound;
}

public void learn(boolean input1, boolean input2,
    boolean output1, boolean output2) {

    System.out.println("\nlearn(): current brain :\n"+brain);
```

Continued

Figure 4.17 Continued

```
        // create an input and output vector
        vector newinputs = new vector(input1,input2);
        vector newoutputs = new vector(output1,output2);
        vector newsolution = new vector(newinputs,newoutputs);

        // create a new solution matrix from combined vectors
        matrix solution = new matrix(newsolution);

        System.out.println("learn(): new solution vector :\n"+newsolution);
        System.out.println("learn(): new solution matrix :\n"+solution);

        // and add it to the brain matrix (learn)
        brain = brain.add(solution);

        System.out.println(
                "learn(): current brain + new solution = new brain
:\n"+brain);

        //and show it
        display();
    }
```

The test begins by hitting the **Start** button. The only pre-learned state that the neural network or brain has is to move forward (both motors) when no input is occurring. This makes sense because it needs to do something by default. We could have an empty brain (a zeroed matrix), but at some point we have to provide rules to determine a correct solution. As shown in Figure 4.16, we are constantly checking the sensors for a change in status. We then check to see if we have a solution to the new "question," or rather the new state of the sensors. If not found in the matrix, a correct solution would be one that successfully changes our current state within two seconds, otherwise we try again. Once we find that solution, we enter it into our knowledge base and continue until we bump into another problem. Over time, we should approach an ideal solution that will provide an answer to any question without having to guess at a new solution. *RCXNeuralTest* calls on the *RCXNeuralBrain* to perform all operations on the matrix, including displaying the current state in the supplied text area. Both files are available in the source code folder for this chapter on the CD. For more information on the mathematics, again refer to the AI and Machine Learning web site: http://home.zonnet.nl/bvandam. One way to improve this program is to add the ability to save and load the matrix to disk; and to add more visual elements to the application interface, such as current status of the sensors and motors. One should also note that this example demonstrates the ability to test in emulation mode, where additional buttons are used to emulate the sensors.

Obviously this is a very simplistic problem domain. We could have just passed in the actual solution matrix as the default set of rules for this specific exploring robot. This example, however, demonstrates how you could build more elaborate robots and have them learn the new rules on their own as they encounter a more complex environment or as you add more inputs and outputs and other interaction with additional RCXs.

Bricks & Chips...

Using More than One RCX

One of the many interesting robots available in the *Building Robots with LEGO MINDSTORMS* book is a mechanical arm that can play chess (from Chapter 20 of that book, shown here in Figure 4.18).

This is one example of using more than one RCX and tower. You can obtain another RCX and tower, if you're lucky enough, by finding an older, less expensive kit (1.0 or 1.5) or if you have the older kit, by upgrading to 2.0 so that you'll have two towers, one serial and one USB. Of course, you could also use two USB towers, but make sure you name the second port "LEGOTOWER2" to avoid USB port conflicts.

With more than one port object, you would have the *Motor* and *Sensor* classes refer to one port or the other by calling the *setPort(RCXPort port)* static method and switch its static instances to refer to a new port. This of course assumes you only use the *Motor.A-C* and *Sensor.S1-S3* instances. but of course you can create your own instance of *Motor* and *Sensor* instead of using these global static objects. When creating the objects, one simply passes into the constructor the ID of the object (A to C for motors and 0 to 2 for sensors) and the port with which it will be associated.

Continued

Figure 4.18 The Broad Blue Chess Robot

```
RCXPort port1 = new RCXPort("COM1");
RCXPort port2 = new RCXPort("LEGOTOWER1");


Motor port1_motorA = new Motor('A',port1);


Sensor port2_sensor1 = new Sensor(0,port2);


port1_motorA.forward();
int p2s1value =  port2_sensor1.readValue();
```

We simply access different RCX ports by creating our own instances of the *Motor* and *Sensor* instead of using the default motors and sensors (remember that the global static instances refer only to the last created RCX port). We accomplish this by specifying the port name and the specific *RCXPort* to inform the new *Motor* or *Sensor* instance of which port we were referring. We can then refer to each of them uniquely by calling on its methods. Remember that if you listen to callbacks from the ports, then each port would need a single, separate listener.

Summary

This chapter introduced you to the RCXJava API, which allows you to control the RCX (1.0-2.0) using 100 percent Java code, except for using native shared library code to access the USB Port. The RCXJava API hides all the unnecessary details to focus on sending and receiving commands from the RCX. It encapsulates the RCX protocol itself, as well as the port type. It is an extensible API that allows for future expansion by both adding high-level abstractions to additional commands, and new types of ports.

First considering code listings that had raw byte arrays being sent without an API, we examined how the RCXJava API's would enable us to explicitly specify the serial or USB ports to reduce the size and complexity of the code. The API allows a simple callback mechanism when dealing with responses and errors, and introduces higher level methods that wrap the message creation for cleaner code that doesn't contain opcode commands. By including a basic window-based example in the core library, we have a template upon which to build, and a built-in utility for sending and receiving messages as opcode byte arrays with a convenient opcode lookup table.

We introduced abstractions to the sensors, motors and sound in a manner consistent with other Java APIs, specifically leJOS. This means that the code can be essentially reused inside and outside the RCX. Using these abstractions and the capability of remote computer access via the socket port type (also available with RCXJava API), we demonstrated an applet that can run in browsers, enabling true remote control of an RCX robot over the Internet. This effectively demonstrates the concept of directly programming the robot by using the PC as the robot's brain. Although there are serious penalties in terms of responsiveness and lag, the PC gives one much more computing power, extensibility, and remote access capabilities than does the RCX alone. Consequently, extensive computation, such as neural network programming (an example of an AI method that one can use with RCX), is feasible using the RCXJava API.

The RCXJava API lays a good groundwork for the many possibilities that exist in terms of building complex programs and systems to control RCX robots. Frameworks can be built to handle the design and programming of RCX (with both visually complex interfaces and AI frameworks), and the control of several robots, including access to multiple towers.

Solutions Fast Track

Designing an RCXJava Communications Architecture

☑ The use of the Java Communications API facilitates the automatic search for an available serial port, and use of the rcx.comm package gives us USB capability in a platform-neutral manner. Allowing the configuration of the port to be based on the port name improves ease-of-use.

☑ Management and encapsulation of RCX protocol details is hidden from the application user.

☑ The use of standard Java design patterns and Java interfaces enables us to use new and different types of ports without changing a line of code.

Overview or the RCXJava API

☑ The RCXJava API is an open source and extensible API.

☑ It supports serial, USB and new ports such as sockets.

☑ It lays the groundwork for a full-fledged programming environment for the RCX by using high level methods that follow the same method signature naming convention of other Java efforts like leJOS.

Using the RCXLoader Application

☑ The RCXLoader is an out-of-the-box utility and test tool for interfacing with the RCX.

☑ It provides a convenient lookup table of all the opcodes and their arguments.

☑ It provides the starting point or template for creating more advanced examples.

Beyond Serial Port Communications: The RCXApplet Example

☑ Control of an RCX can not only be enabled from a stand-alone application but also over the Internet using a Java-enabled Web browser, providing the same GUI as one would get with the stand-alone application.

☑ Using *RCXSocketPort*, one could control a number of RCXs over a network and the network via a proxy server.

☑ Use of the direct control API methods gives you the capability of creating complex frameworks similar to the visual-programming interface that comes with the LEGO MINDSTORMS kit.

Direct Control Programming for the RCX Using Java

☑ With direct control programming, we are using the RCX's "brain" to pass commands from a proxy "brain" residing on a PC. There are significant advantages to programming tasks to run on the PC's resources rather than running tasks inside the RCX.

☑ Tasks can run on the PC in near real time (there is a noticeable time lag).

☑ We can add Artificial Intelligence (AI) capabilities when programming our RCX robots. Neural network programming allows an RCX to "learn" the right response to stimuli all on its own.

Frequently Asked Questions

The following Frequently Asked Questions, answered by the authors of this book, are designed to both measure your understanding of the concepts presented in this chapter and to assist you with real-life implementation of these concepts. To have your questions about this chapter answered by the author, browse to **www.syngress.com/solutions** and click on the **"Ask the Author"** form.

Q: What versions of the Java Runtime Environment does the RCXJava API support? Specifically, is Microsoft's JVM supported?

A: All versions of Java 1.1 through 1.4 are supported. Microsoft's Java VM is also supported, as long as one doesn't use Java Swing for the GUI. You may also want to make sure you're using the latest version that supports Sun's JNI interface.

Q: How can I add to *RCXPort's* higher level methods for handling messages that it doesn't already handle? For example, as with the *motor* and *sensor* classes, I want to add methods for handling the RCX's display.

A: You can either submit the proposed changes for a later release or you can add a helper class that handles messages outside of *RCXPort*. Having your class implement either the *AllMessagesListener* or the *RCXListener* interfaces does this.

Q: Can I trigger tasks to run inside the RCX and receive messages from other tasks running inside the RCX?

A: Yes, you can send the opcodes that run specific tasks inside the RCX at any given time, as well as monitoring sensors and values inside the RCX by sending the appropriate opcodes and requesting the values.

Q: What's the difference between RCXJava API (described in this chapter) and the RCXPort API (described in Chapter 3)? I noticed they both have an *RCXPort* class.

A: Both are Java APIs designed for accessing the RCX through Java. The RCXJava API was the first Java API to address RCX communication using the Java Communications API. It originally had the *RCXPort* class as one of its core classes. The RCXPort API followed afterwards and addressed the limitations of the RCXJava API, namely the ability to download tasks into the RCX. However, this can also be implemented by an application that uses the RCXJava API, and may be added to the core classes in the future.

Chapter 5

The leJOS System

Solutions in this chapter:

- **Basic leJOS Usage Guidelines**
- **The LEGO Java Operating System**
- **Overview of the leJOS Architecture**
- **Using leJOS: A Simple Example**

☑ **Summary**

☑ **Solutions Fast Track**

☑ **Frequently Asked Questions**

169

Introduction

The LEGO Java Operating System (leJOS) allows you to run Java code inside the RCX, letting you program in a familiar language as opposed to using the default LEGO interpreter. It includes an API that gives you direct access to the inputs and outputs from Java itself, as well as a subset of the standard Java API. Since this is not a fully-featured Java OS, an alternate compiler is provided for compiling and generating classes for the leJOS; if you happen to be familiar with JavaCard or Java 2 Micro Edition (J2ME) this is the same approach used in those environments. The Java programs and standard Java API are a subset of standard Java so they can easily evolve to a fully-featured OS in the future, given that RCX memory constraints allow that.

LeJOS was originally developed solely by Jose Solorzano, but is now maintained by Paul Andrews and Jürgen Stuber. Great effort has been taken in making a Java environment for the RCX, given the inherent constraints of the RCX. So, knowing about Java will give you a head start in creating programs for your RCX. The fact that leJOS is a new firmware for the RCX, and thus does not leverage the LEGO firmware, will allow you to make programs which are more advanced than what is possible using either the LEGO programming environment or NQC (Not Quite C).

Since the RCX has a lot of features you would want to use—motors, sensors, buttons and so on—a very comprehensive Java package for accessing these features is provided with leJOS: the *josx.platform.rcx* package. The various classes contained in this package will be explained in detail in this chapter. Information on how to set up your environment for use with leJOS, so you can start making your own Java programs for the RCX will also be provided.

This chapter also explains the necessary environmental setup for compiling your Java programs and transmitting them to the RCX for execution.

Basic leJOS Usage Guidelines

The very first thing to do is to get a copy of leJOS. It comes in a version for Windows and one for Linux; you can download them from http://lejos.source-forge.net (select **Download**, then under **Download Area at Sourceforge**, select **Download area**). The Linux version is a .tar.gz file and the Windows is a .zip—the ones used for this book are the 1.0.4alpha for Linux and the 1.0.4alpha2 for Windows. Do not forget to download the documentation files, as you will not have the JavaDoc for the base classes, which is a must when programming for leJOS (of course you can build the JavaDoc yourself, but you might find that a bit irritating). After the download, unpack the files.

NOTE

After unpacking the downloaded lejos_1_4_0.tar.gz file for Linux, you need to issue a make command from within the LEJOS_HOME directory.

To use the leJOS system, you must have a standard Java compiler installed on your system. Here, the Java SDK 1.3.1 from Sun Microsystems has been used, but all JDK from 1.1 to 1.3.1 should work. For 1.4, you must add the option *-target 1.1* for the *lejosc* command.

Add the bin directory of your Java installation to your path. You should also set the *LEJOS_HOME* environment variable to point to where you installed leJOS, and add the bin directory under that to your path. Finally, the environment variable RCXTTY must be set to the port where your LEGO IR tower is connected.

NOTE

The setup examples, of course, have to be modified to reflect the specific installation directories for both leJOS and JDK.

- **Setting the Environment for Windows** This .bat file was used in Windows for setting the leJOS environment:

```
set JAVA_HOME=c:\jdk1.3.0_01
set LEJOS_HOME=c:\lejos_1_0_4alpha\lejos
set PATH=%PATH%;%JAVA_HOME%\bin;%LEJOS_HOME%\bin
set RCXTTY=COM2
set CLASSPATH=.
```

- **Setting the Environment for Linux** Source this script file on Linux for setting your leJOS environment (bash shell):

```
#! /bin/bash
JAVA_HOME=/usr/local/java/jdk1.3.1
```

```
LEJOS_HOME=~/lejos_1_0_4alpha/lejos
PATH=$JAVA_HOME/bin:$LEJOS_HOME/bin:$PATH
RCXTTY=/dev/ttyS1
CLASSPATH=.
export JAVA_HOME LEJOS_HOME PATH RCXTTY CLASSPATH
```

The *CLASSPATH* is used to define where you place your own Java programs and classes. As you can see, we have just set it to point to the current directory. Change this as necessary to meet your needs.

The next thing to do is transmit the leJOS firmware to the RCX. If your RCX has some other firmware installed like the standard LEGO one, it does not matter—it will be erased and leJOS will be downloaded instead. You just execute the command **lejosfirmdl –f**, which will transmit the firmware to the RCX. The *-f* option means *fast* and transmits the firmware four times faster. I have had limited success with the fast option, so I usually omit it, but try your luck.

After firmware download termination (signaled by a double beep), you are ready to start programming.

Using the lejosc Compiler

After setting up the environment, you are ready to begin programming. Just use your favorite text editor to write your leJOS Java program, save it, and execute **lejosc <yourprogramname>.java**. This should produce a file named <yourprogramname>.class. You then execute **lejos <yourprogramname>** which will convert your program and any necessary leJOS base classes, as well as any utility classes of your own, into one binary package and transmit that to the RCX for execution.

NOTE

> The **lejosc** command is just a wrapper setting the *-bootclasspath* command line option of the **javac** command to point to the location of the leJOS base classes when you have a JAVA2 environment (JDK 1.2 through JDK 1.4). For a Java 1.1 environment it will include those leJOS base classes at the beginning of the classpath.

You can specify the option *-o <file>* to the **lejos** command. This will dump the binary program package to <file>. You can then subsequently transmit it to the RCX using *lejosrun <file>*, which can be very convenient if you often experience download problems to the RCX, since it saves time in creating the binary package between subsequent download attempts.

WARNING

On a particularly sunny day, you may need to put a cardboard box over the tower and RCX to shield them from the sunlight, otherwise every single download attempt may fail.

Developing & Deploying…

Transmitting More Programs to the RCX

You can transmit multiple programs to the RCX at one time, just comma separate the names of the programs when supplying them to the **lejos** command, like this: **lejos <yourprogram1>,<yourprogram2>**. After transmission, you can select which program to run with the RCX **Prgm** button.

The LEGO Java Operating System

One of the greatest benefits of LeJOS is that it allows you to expand the capabilities of your LEGO robots, without the steep learning curve that comes with other replacement operating systems. You could say leJOS fits in between systems, pushing the limits of the standard LEGO firmware, like NQC, as well as systems which push the limits of LEGO hardware (legOS, for instance). Where NQC and the like have to move within the boundaries of both the LEGO ROM code and the LEGO firmware code, leJOS only leverages the ROM code. And, of course, legOS throws all LEGO code away to gain maximum power.

So why not just use legOS? Well, because you would like to do all the programming in Java, right? There are a few other good reasons as well. As mentioned earlier, the learning curve can be a lot steeper with legOS. Also, as legOS does not leverage the ROM code, you, as a programmer, are not protected by that code—that is, in some cases the code in the ROM actually protects you from accidentally destroying your RCX (for instance, leaving the IR-diode on in the long range mode for extended amounts of time can result in the burnout of that diode).

The limitations of using leJOS thus comes in two categories: limitations inherent in the ROM code, and limitations put there by the developers of leJOS.

Because leJOS was originally forged from the TinyVM Project, a lot of the present limitations date back to design decisions made in TinyVM. We are not saying that those decisions were wrong; when implementing a Java virtual machine for running in such a memory constrained device as the RCX, some tradeoffs are inevitable.

So here is a summary of the current limitations in leJOS as imposed by leJOS, not by the ROM:

- **No garbage collection** This is the main inconvenience if you are familiar with standard Java.

- **No switch statement** These can, of course, be simulated using *if else* constructs.

- **No arithmetic on the long variable type** However, casting is allowed on the long type from the integer type.

- **Maximum array length** The maximum array length is 511.

- *instanceof* This operator always returns true for interfaces. This is not so nice if you are used to designing your programs using interfaces, and base some functionality on certain classes implementing specific interfaces.

    Performing an *instanceof* on arrays (for example, *b instanceof int[]*) is not allowed by the linker.

- *java.lang.Class* This has no instances created, meaning the *.class* construct does not work, and that you cannot synchronize on static methods.

- *Class.forname* This always throws a *ClassNotFoundException*, as dynamic class loading is not supported.

- **J2SE API** This isn't always implemented, but when it is, it often behaves a little differently. Luckily, this doesn't occur in very dramatic ways.

Current drawbacks of this system are few. leJOS leaves about 12k for your own programs, but as RCX programs tend to be fairly small, this is usually not a problem.

I am really missing the switch statement. It generates way more compact Java bytecode than those nested, if-then-else constructs you need to make in its absence.

I am not too fond of the 511 bytes range limit on arrays either. I would like to be able to create one array spanning all the available memory, though I must admit I have never needed to do this.

From a Java language view, the fact that no object of *java.lang.Class* exists, and the consequence of that is that synchronization on static methods is not possible, which can be a little frustrating and confusing at times. But having those class objects created would use memory for something which you can easily work around.

One major thing to get used to with leJOS is that since it comes from standard Java, there is no garbage collection. When I mention this, most Java programmers ask "then how do you deallocate your objects?" The answer is: you don't. You just have to get used to writing your programs in a way where the number of objects are bounded, period. It's really not as hard as it sounds. It isn't even a unique feature of the leJOS environment. The same holds true for the Sun JavaCard specifications.

Many programmers consider this a bad thing and a future release of leJOS will probably contain a small (1KB or so) garbage collector. Personally, I don't mind the lack of garbage collection. As long as you know this going in, it isn't difficult to achieve a programming style which does not trash objects unnecessarily (this style can also help you improve performance of your "normal" Java programs, as object allocation and subsequent garbage collection are often performance eaters in those programs). So, my hope is that if a garbage collector eventually emerges for leJOS, it will be optional at the time of firmware download, letting you decide whether to sacrifice the extra memory needed for it.

Given the mentioned limitations, is leJOS in conflict with Sun Microsystems's view of Java as a platform on which you can run programs unaltered? Yes and no. In the beginning Sun seemed to have the "one Java size fits all" vision but later realized this wasn't possible. Now they have moved to different Java sizes for devices with different capabilities. To fit leJOS into the Sun picture, here's a quick rundown on the current state of affairs when it comes to different sizes of Sun virtual machines (VMs). (Note that these sizes refer to the VM size only, not the API size; you can think about the API size as following the VM size closely—the larger the VM, the larger the standard API.) From the top—Java for big iron machines—we have the Java 2 Enterprise Edition (J2EE), and then the Java 2 Standard Edition (J2SE). When it comes to the VM, J2EE is not different from the J2SE—the difference is which APIs are standard to the edition. The J2SE's current VM is the HotSpot VM; if you look at the file size of this, it is roughly 650KB (the older classic VM, which is also distributed with the J2SE, is roughly 280KB). Note that these are just the file sizes, which is a static picture of the VM. The default memory amount allocated by these VMs (when launching a Java program) is 1MB.

Then we have the J2ME. The J2ME was designed with memory-constrained devices, like mobile phones, pagers, and video phones in mind. Sun has partitioned different device types into what they call configurations. They currently have two: the Connected Device Configuration (CDC) and the Connected Limited Device Configuration (CLDC). For each configuration, they additionally define what they call profiles, which identify extra APIs for a more specific device. The most well-known profile is the MIDP (Mobile Information Device Profile), used in mobile phones and PDAs. These two configurations are based on two different VMs: the first, the KVM, is 65 to 80KB. The other, the CVM, is larger. As the RCX only has 32KB free, all of these VMs are way too large. But Sun also has a specification for something even smaller, called JavaCard. IBM has a VM implementation for JavaCard which is only 4KB, but JavaCard is even more restricted than leJOS (no threads, no floating point, no int, no String, only one-dimensional arrays). The leJOS VM is around 16KB (if you need something smaller but less feature-rich, the original TinyVM for the RCX is still available and takes up only 10KB). To complete the picture, Sun has also defined what they call Personal Java. This is an older attempt to divide Java into different sizes for different devices. It is still in existence though, and uses the standard J2SE VM. Sun, however, is transitioning Personal Java to become a Personal profile on top of CDC.

The TinyVM

The TinyVM was the first Java implementation for the RCX, and was solely developed by Jose Solorzano. It is a very small VM (only around 10KB), but still contains advanced Java features like preemptive threads, synchronization, and exceptions.

As briefly mentioned earlier, leJOS was culled from the TinyVM Project (which is still available). The reason for this was that Solorzano wanted a more feature-rich VM, yet still provide a VM that makes the best use of available memory. Because of this, for memory-intensive programs, TinyVM is a good choice.

The following lists most additions to the TinyVM in leJOS:

- **A Windows version** You can use TinyVM on Windows if you have CygWin installed. The Windows version for leJOS doesn't require it.

- **Floating point types and operations on these** These are nice, but remember: operations on floats are considerably slower than on *int*s. Use them only if you need to.

- **String constants** The benefit of this is you can now construct nicer user dialogs.

- **Casting between long and int** This makes it possible to more closely match the standard Java API, as it sometimes returns longs, for example, for the current time.

- **Download of multiple programs** This is a really nice feature, which you're probably familiar with from the standard LEGO programming environment. You can simply download a set of programs and select which to run by using the Prgm button on the RCX.

- **Implementation of *java.lang.Math*** This is not a complete implementation of *java.lang.Math* but it does contain methods for calculating sine, cosine, square roots, and so on. It is a must when programming advanced navigational robots.

- **Implementation of *notify*, *notifyAll*, and *wait* on *java.lang.Object*** This is a very important addition. Without it, it is nearly impossible to make different threads cooperate (at least in a predictable manner).

- **Marks object references in the call stack** This is not really something that will benefit you here and now, but it will make it possible for the leJOS developers to add a garbage collector in the future.

Jose Solorzano is no longer actively developing TinyVM or leJOS. The latter is now lead by Jürgen Stuber and Paul Andrews. While the former unfortunately is no longer maintained, it does work as is.

Overview of the leJOS Architecture

As you can see from Figure 5.1, leJOS leverages the RCX ROM code. The leJOS firmware lies directly above the ROM as seen from an architectural viewpoint. It implements the Java virtual machine, and is transmitted to the RCX using the **lejosfirmdl** command. But interesting ROM functionality, like motor control and sensor reading, is actually accessed from the leJOS base classes, defined in the josx.platform.rcx package.

Figure 5.1 The leJOS Architecture

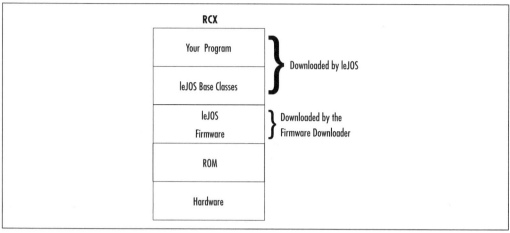

The neat thing is that those base classes are not part of the leJOS firmware, so only the actual classes needed by a particular program are transmitted to the RCX. As a result, unneeded classes do not take up precious memory. This functionality (implemented by the *lejos* command) also applies to your own programs as well. Only classes, which are directly and indirectly referenced from your main program class, will be packaged and transmitted to the RCX. Technically, the *lejos* command makes the transitive closure of all the classes used by your main program, and packs them into a leJOS-specific binary format, which is then transmitted to the RCX. The transitive closure is a graph theoretical term which means that, starting at a particular node in a directed graph, it will give you all nodes reachable from that node, once and only once. Applied to a Java programs class graph, this means that all classes used by the main class, as well as those used by those classes and so on, will be in the transitive closure exactly once. This is also what a linker normally does, but standard Java has a feature called dynamic class loading, which enables a programmer to dynamically load a class at runtime (perhaps the class name is even received as some user input). This feature makes it generally impossible to perform a transitive closure for a Java program. In leJOS, this particular feature (implemented by the *java.class.forName* method) is not implemented, and thus allows this transitive closure.

Exploring the josx.platform.rcx Package

In this section, we will go through the classes and interfaces in the package *josx.platform.rcx*. This package contains Java classes for interfacing to the main RCX features, including: motors, sensors, display, sound, buttons, and IR.

We will not go through every method of every class—only the most useful classes. The complete picture can be seen in the JavaDoc, or, if you are more of an adventurer, in the source code.

Using the Button and ButtonListener Classes

The *Button* class encapsulates the three RCX buttons **View**, **Prgm** and **Run** so you can utilize them in your own programs. The class contains three static instances of *Button*, one for each button; these are called (following the Java conventions) *VIEW*, *PRGM*, and *RUN* respectively. Also a static array called *BUTTONS* is declared which holds references to these methods in the order just listed:

- ***public void addButtonListener (ButtonListener listener)*** Adds a *ButtonListener* to this *Button*. (See the *ButtonListener* explanation later in this section.) You can add a maximum of four *ButtonListeners* per *Button*.

- ***public final boolean isPressed()*** Returns true if the button is pressed, false otherwise

- ***public final void waitForPressAndRelease () throws InterruptedException*** The calling thread execution is suspended until this button has been pressed and subsequently released.

The *ButtonListener* interface contains two methods, *buttonPressed* and *buttonReleased*; both get called with the actual *Button* as a parameter. You can implement this interface in your own class, which you then add to the button you wish to receive press/release events from. This way, the code you write in the method *buttonPressed* automatically gets executed when the button you add the listener to is pressed. This is actually basic event listener stuff, as you probably know from the standard Java Abstract Windowing Toolkit (AWT) event model. In this API, however, there are no event objects passed to the listener, the relevant parameters are passed directly to the method instead. Here is an example:

```
public class ButtonPressHandler implements ButtonListener {
    public void buttonReleased (Button b) {}
    public void buttonPressed (Button b) {
        //do something interesting
    }
    public static void main (Sting[] args) {
        Button.VIEW.addButtonListener (new ButtonPressHandler());
    }
}
```

Using the MinLCD, LCD, Segment, LCDConstants, and TextLCD Classes

The five classes/interfaces *MinLCD*, *LCD*, *Segment*, *LCDConstants*, and *TextLCD* are for controlling output to the LCD of the RCX.

MinLCD is minimal and low-level. It's handy if you have a larger program and need the extra memory LCD takes up. It only has two methods:

- ■ *public static void setNumber (int aCode, int aValue, int aPoint)* Outputs number *aValue* to the display with decimal point *aPoint*, and at the place given by *aCode*. Both *aCode* and *aPoint* take their value range from the *LCDConstants* interface. For *aCode*, the constants are *UNSIGNED*, *SIGNED*, and *PROGRAM*. The first two mean that the number to output is signed or unsigned. The last says to output the number in the one digit segment at the far right of the RCX display. The *aPoint* value range is *LCD_DECIMAL_0*, *LCD_DECIMAL_1*, *LCD_DECIMAL_2*, *LCD_DECIMAL_3* and indicates in which position to place the decimal point: *LCD_DECIMAL_0* meaning no decimal point, *LCD_DECIMAL_1* meaning one figure after the decimal point, and so forth.

- ■ *public static void refresh()* You need to call this to ensure the display is refreshed.

In addition to the methods defined by *MinLCD*, the *LCD* class describes the following:

- ■ *public static void showNumber (int value)* Shows a number on the display [0-9999]; *refresh()* does not need to be called.

- ■ *public static void showProgramNumber (int value)* Shows a number in the Program number part of the display [0-9]; *refresh()* does not need to be called.

- ■ *public static void setSegment (int code)* Sets an LCD segment to *on*—that is, it displays the segment; *refresh()* is needed for the effect to take place. The *code* parameter identifies the segment and can be one of the constants defined in the *Segment* section in the JavaDoc.

- ■ *public static void clearSegment (int code)* Clears an LCD segment so it does not show; *refresh()* needs to be called. The *code* parameter identifies the segment and is defined in *Segment* in the JavaDoc.

- ***public static void clear ()*** Clears the display; again, you must call *refresh()* before it takes effect.

Segment defines constants used by LCD to set or clear the various segments in the RCX display. See the *Segment* section in the JavaDoc documentation for the complete listing: *WALKING, STANDING, SENSOR_1_ACTIVE, BATTERY.*

NOTE

If you downloaded the JavaDoc documentation, and unpacked it in your LEJOS_HOME directory, it will be found in the apidocs directory there. Start viewing the index.html as usual.

The fourth class, *LCDConstants*, extends the *Segment* class to define constants for the number part of the display.

The fifth LCD control class, *TextLCD*, is the most complex and fascinating. It utilizes the display (originally designed to show numbers only) to show text messages. This occurs at the expense of greater memory—to be exact, *TextLCD* takes up 1560 bytes more than *MinLCD*! Also, remember that letters are approximated. The LCD on the RCX was not designed with letter output in mind, so the developer of this class had to make some compromises. There is only so much you can do with a display, of course, but the result seems a success:

- ***public static final void print (String text)*** Prints the string *text* on the LCD. Only the first five characters are displayed.

- ***public static final void print (char[] text)*** Prints the first five characters of the *text* array on the RCX display.

- ***public static final void print (char c, int pos)*** Prints the character *c* at position *pos* [1-4] counting from the right of the RCX display. You must call *LCD.Refresh()* for this to take effect in the display.

Using the Sound and MinSound Classes

The *Sound* and *MinSound* classes can be used for creating audible indications that a certain point has been reached in your program. If you are musically gifted, you may be able to make finer use of these classes.

The *MinSound* class, like the other classes with a "Min" prefix, is a small and low-level interface with RCX sound capabilities. It only contains one method, which is actually deprecated, so the use of this class is entirely discouraged.

The *Sound* class, on the other hand, is very useful. It contains six static methods:

- *public static void playTone (int aFrequency, int aDuration)* This is the most versatile method. It will play a tone in the range 1-20000Hz given by *aFrequency*. The tone is played for *aDuration*: the unit is1/100 of a second, so to play for 1 second, use the value 100. Also, it is truncated at 256, meaning that 2.56 seconds is the maximum duration possible with one call to the method.

- *public static void systemSound (boolean aQueued, int aCode)* This plays one of the predefined RCX system sounds. The *aQueued* parameter determines whether the sound is queued, meaning your program will continue running whether the sound is produced or not, or that your program will wait for the termination of the sound before continuing; true means queued. The sound is identified by the *aCode* parameter. The possibilities can be seen in Table 5.1.

Table 5.1 Available System Sounds

aCode	Resulting Sound
0	Short beep
1	Double beep
2	Descending arpeggio
3	Ascending arpeggio
4	Long low beep; error sound
5	Quick ascending arpeggio

- *public static void beep ()* Plays one beep; same as system sound 0, queued.

- *public static void twoBeeps ()* Plays two beeps; same as system sound 1, queued.

- *public static void beepSequence ()* Plays a sequence of beeps; same as system sound 2, queued.

- *public static void buzz ()* Plays a buzzing tone; same as system sound 4, queued.

Using the Sensor, SensorListener, and SensorConstants Interfaces

Sensors are configured using type and mode constants. Not all modes apply to all types of sensors. It does not, for instance, make sense to configure a rotation sensor in any other way than using the *SENSOR_TYPE_ROT*. In some situations, it is possible (and sometimes desirable) to configure a real sensor with a value normally used for another. Using, for instance, *SENSOR_TYPE_TOUCH* for a light sensor can make sense. Try it out!

The configuration constants are defined in the *SensorConstants* interface and are shown in Table 5.2. The possible sensor types can be seen in Table 5.3.

Table 5.2 Sensor Types

SensorConstants Constant	Applies to LEGO Sensor
SENSOR_TYPE_LIGHT	The light sensor
SENSOR_TYPE_TOUCH	The touch sensor
SENSOR_TYPE_TEMP	The temperature sensor
SENSOR_TYPE_ROT	The rotation sensor
SENSOR_TYPE_RAW	All

Table 5.3 Sensor Modes

SensorConstants Constant	Function
SENSOR_MODE_ANGLE	Angle measurement only applies to rotation sensors
SENSOR_MODE_BOOL	Boolean reading true/false
SENSOR_MODE_DEGC	Temperature in Celsius; (785-raw)/8, within the range [-20...70]
SENSOR_MODE_DEGF	Temperature in Fahrenheit; value of DEGC * 9/5 + 32
SENSOR_MODE_EDGE	Edge counting. 1 is added for each Boolean transition, from true to false, and from false to true.
SENSOR_MODE_PCT	Percentage. Calculated using 146-raw/7.
SENSOR_MODE_PULSE	Pulse counting. 1 is added for each Boolean transition from false to true.
SENSOR_TYPE_RAW	Raw value 0-1023

The different modes actually convert the raw values (0–1023) read into the appropriate format. For some modes, the conversion is simple: a cutoff, with a hysteresis value to prevent bouncing transitions from true to false around the cutoff for the Boolean mode, or the calculation of 146-raw/7 for the percentage mode. For other modes, the conversion made is much more complex—the Angle mode being the most complex of all, and beyond explanation here. Modes like edge, pulse, and angle also maintain an internal counter for representing the converted value.

To complete the mode configuration complexity, a mode value can be binary OR'ed with a slope value [0...31] but it only applies to *SENSOR_MODE_BOOL*. The value 0 corresponds to the normal Boolean mode (raw values less than 450 are true, and above 565 are false). A slope value between 1 and 31 changes that. Instead of having fixed values as a cutoff for true and false, the Boolean value change is instead based on how rapid the raw value changes. For instance, a slope value of 10 means that the raw value must decrease by 1023/10 = 102 between two subsequent sensor readings to make the Boolean value change from false to true, and in a similar way, increase by the same amount to switch the value back to false again. It no longer matters what the absolute value is; only the rate of change is a concern. Take a look at www.plazaearth.com/usr/gasperi/lego.htm for details on sensor modes and types, and information on how to build your own sensors. You can also find an explanation on how raw value conversions are made in the angle mode.

Even after configuring the sensor in your program according to the preceding values, you can still choose to read the sensor's raw-value, its Boolean value equivalent, as well as its converted value. The *SensorConstants* interface contains constants you can use for this in connection with the static method *readSensorValue(...)* in the *Sensor* class. These are rarely used, however, since the *Sensor* class has convenience methods defined for these purposes.

The final configuration you need to make if you are using a powered sensor is to call *activate()*. Some sensors (light and rotation) are powered, meaning that the RCX delivers power to them, and reads their measurements. For some applications, it might be desirable not to activate a light sensor. This will greatly reduce sensitivity of the sensor though, and there may, in truth, be no real use for this. Not activating a rotation sensor makes the sensor useless. Calling the opposite *passivate()* method for unpowered sensors is not necessary since it's the default sensor state.

NOTE

The reason one would keep the light sensor in the passive state is to avoid lighting the bright red LED, which shines light into the photo transistor, polluting its light measurements. A photo transistor needs power to work, however, so doing this defeats the purpose: Putting the sensor into passive state only supplies it a minimal power (power is designated to it even in the passive state, and is a consequence of the design of the electrical circuit of the RCX), thus greatly reducing the sensitivity. A far better approach to this is to block out the LED using undeveloped photographic film or other plastic material. See www.hempeldesigngroup .com/lego/lightsensor/index.html or http://philohome.free.fr/sensors/ ir_sensitivity.htm for more details on this.

The *Sensor* class contains three static variables (*S1, S2, S3*) of type *Sensor*, corresponding to the three sensor input ports on the RCX, and an array *SENSORS* containing the same objects at index 0 through 2.

The *Sensor* class has these methods defined:

- *public final void activate()* This method must be called to activate a sensor (powered sensors only).

- *public final void passivate()* Passivates a sensor; this is the default state.

- *public final void setTypeAndMode (int type, int mode)* Sets the sensor's type and mode to values defined in *SensorConstants* (if you wish to use the slope feature, OR it to the mode value).

- *public final void setPreviousValue (int value)* This is used to set the sensor's value to something predefined. This can be very useful for rotation sensors (or touch sensors in pulse or edge mode), as you will continue the counting from the value given to this method.

- *public final int readRawValue ()* Reads the raw value of the sensor [0…1023].

- *public final int readValue()* Reads the converted value of the sensor.

- *public final int readBooleanValue()* Reads the Boolean value of the sensor.

- *public final inf getId ()* Returns the ID of this sensor [0...2].

- *public static int readSensorValue (int sensorID, int valuetype)*
  This is a static low-level routine for reading the sensor value. You must
  supply the sensor identifier [0…2] and the type of value you wish to
  read (raw = *SensorConstants.RAW_VALUE*, boolean =
  SensorConstants.BOOLEAN_VALUE, converted =
  SensorConstants.CANONICAL_VALUE).

- *public void addSensorListener (SensorListener listener)* Adds a
  SensorListener to this sensor. A *SensorListener* is an interface you can
  implement, and by adding that implementation to a sensor your code
  can be executed whenever a sensor's reading changes. A maximum of
  eight *SensorListeners* can be added to one *Sensor*. You have to be careful,
  however, not to use synchronization inside your implementation of the
  SensorListener as this can lead to deadlocks.

The *SensorListener* interface is useful for getting notifications about changes in
sensor readings. You can implement this interface (one method only) and add it
to the *Sensor* you wish to monitor. This way your code is called on each sensor
value change.

The only method you must implement is:

- *public void stateChanged(Sensor source, int oldValue, int newValue)* Your
  implementation of this method gets called each time the sensor value
  changes. You get the following information: *source* is the *Sensor* value that
  changed, *oldValue* is the previous value, and *newValue* is the new value.
  For touch sensors in Boolean mode, the values supplied are 0 for false
  and 1 for true.

WARNING

You must be careful when implementing the *stateChanged()* method
for your *SensorListener* implementation. Not only can synchronization
within the implementation result in deadlocks, but also the method
will have to terminate fast, as it will otherwise tie up the sensor
reading thread, possibly resulting in lost sensor readings.

Using the ProximitySensor Class

This class utilizes a combination of sending short messages out of the RCX serial (IR) port and monitoring the value of a light sensor placed directly above or below the IR port. The LEGO light sensor happens to be very sensitive to infrared light, and thus will react to the reflection of the IR message when it bounces off some nearby object. You can then avoid the object even before hitting it, or grab the object with a robotic hand.

To use this class, just construct a *ProximitySensor* object using one of the two supplied constructors:

- **ProximitySensor (Sensor sensor, int threshold)**   Creates a new *ProximitySensor* instance; the supplied *Sensor* object is the one you must attach your light sensor to. This constructor will configure the *Sensor* and start sending messages out the IR port. The *threshold* determines how close to get to an obstacle before detecting it; larger values get you closer.

- **ProximitySensor (Sensor sensor)**   Same as the preceding, with a default threshold of 15.

The class only supplies two methods, of which only this one should be used by an application programmer:

- **public void waitTillNear (long timeout)**   Halts the calling thread until an object is near, or the supplied *timeout* is reached (0 means wait forever).

The other method you should not call directly is *ProximitySensor's* own implementation of the *SensorListener* interface method *stateChanged* (*ProximitySensor* implements *SensorListener*). This implementation checks whether the new value is greater than the old value by the threshold (supplied in the constructor of *ProximitySensor*), and then notifies any threads waiting in the *waitTillNear* method.

Here is a demo of this class. It will spin the RCX in place until it notices a near object (try waving something in front of the robot), then it will move towards the object for one second, stop, and sound the buzzer. Use a simple differential drive platform as shown in Figure 5.2, and connect the motors to port A and C. Then attach the light sensor to sensor port 1 and place the RCX above the sensor with the IR port facing the same way as the sensor. The demo is shown in Figure 5.3, which is provided on the CD accompanying this book.

Figure 5.2 A Simple Differential Drive with Light Sensor

Figure 5.3 Proximity Detection (proximity/Proximity.java)

```java
import josx.platform.rcx.Motor;

import josx.platform.rcx.Sensor;

import josx.platform.rcx.ProximitySensor;

import josx.platform.rcx.Sound;


public class Proximity {

    public static void main (String[] args) throws InterruptedException

    {

        ProximitySensor ps = new ProximitySensor (Sensor.S2, 30);

        Motor.A.setPower (4);

        Motor.C.setPower (4);

        Motor.A.forward ();

        Motor.C.forward ();

        ps.waitTillNear (0);

        Sound.twoBeeps ();

        Motor.C.backward ();

        Thread.currentThread ().sleep (1000);

        Motor.A.stop ();

        Motor.C.stop ();

        Sound.buzz ();
```

Continued

Figure 5.3 Continued

```
        Thread.currentThread ().sleep (1000);
    }
}
```

Using the Motor Class

The *Motor* class is used to control the RCX output ports, which you normally connect motors or LEGO lamps to.

The class contains three static *Motor* instances—*A*, *B*, and *C*—which represent the corresponding three output ports on the RCX. The class contains the following methods for controlling the motor:

- *public final void setPower(int power)* Sets the current power level of the motor [0...7]. This will not cause the connected motor to start moving unless it is already doing that.

- *public final int getPower()* Returns the current power level of the motor.

- *public final void backward()* Moves the motor backwards.

- *public final void forward()* Moves the motor forwards.

- *public final void flt()* Makes the motor float; similar to neutral in a car with automatic transmission.

- *public final void stop()* Brakes the motor.

- *public final void reverseDirection()* No matter which way the motor is turning, it makes it turn the other way.

- *public final boolean isMoving()* Returns true if the motor is moving.

- *public final boolean isStopped()* Returns true if the motor is stopped.

- *public final boolean isForward()* Returns true if the motor is going forward.

- *public final boolean isBackward()* Returns true if the motor is going backward.

- *public final boolean isFloating()* Returns true if the motor is floating.

- *public final char getId()* Returns the motor ID as A, B, or C.

NOTE

The direction a motor is turning is dependant on the wiring to the motor. So, if your program has set it to move forwards and your robot is actually moving backwards, you can turn the wire connection 90 degrees and make it go the other way. This can often save considerable program download time.

Using the Servo Class

The *Servo* class implements a servo (step-motor) by combining a rotation sensor with a motor. The amount of gearing in the mechanical connection between the motor and the rotation sensor (and between whatever the motor is driving) of course greatly influences the effect of this class when put to use.

You simply construct an object of the class using one of the constructors:

- ■ ***Servo (Sensor sensor, Motor motor, int slack)*** Creates a servo using a rotation sensor connected to the port represented by the supplied *Sensor* object, and a motor connected to the port represented by the supplied *Motor* object. The *slack* parameter is the precision tolerance you will accept when positioning the servo; 0 means no tolerance.

- ■ ***Servo (Sensor sensor, Motor motor)*** Just calls: *this (sensor, motor, 0)*.

The *Servo* is then very simple to use. Simply call this method to make it rotate to the desired position:

- ■ ***public boolean rotateTo (int pos)*** Rotates the motor to the supplied position. Returns true if the motor is already at that position; false if otherwise.

The class implements *SensorListener*, and its implementation of the *stateChanged* method will keep turning the motor until the position requested by the call to *rotateTo* is reached. At that point, it will stop the motor and notify any threads waiting on the *Servo* object instance. Figure 5.4, which is also provided on the CD, shows a small example that, when you connect a rotation sensor directly to a motor's shaft (without any gearing in between), will rotate the shaft by 360 degrees, and then sound the buzzer.

Figure 5.4 Demonstration of Servo (servo/ServoDemo.java)

```java
import josx.platform.rcx.Motor;

import josx.platform.rcx.Sensor;

import josx.platform.rcx.Servo;

import josx.platform.rcx.Sound;


public class ServoDemo {
    public static void main (String[] args) throws InterruptedException
    {
        Servo s = new Servo (Sensor.S3, Motor.B, 0);

        boolean isthere = s.rotateTo (14);
        if (! isthere) {
            synchronized (s) {
                s.wait();
            }
        }
        Sound.buzz ();
        Thread.currentThread ().sleep (1000);
    }
}
```

Be careful expanding this code since it actually contains a race condition between the sensor reading thread, and the main thread. It is possible that, if the *rotateTo* value is small enough, this value has been reached between the call to *rotateTo* and the call to *wait*, which may cause the program to deadlock. I have not been able to provoke this situation with the direct connection of the rotation sensor and the motor, but can easily do so by putting extra code between the two previously mentioned statements.

Using the Serial, Opcode, and SerialListener Classes

We will not cover these classes and this interface in depth here since they are covered elsewhere in the book. Instead, here's a quick rundown.

Opcode defines the original LEGO firmware opcode constants. This is very useful as these opcodes and their associated parameters are what is transmitted from the IR tower to the RCX, or from the LEGO remote control unit. You use these opcode constants when trying to parse packets received over the IR port.

Serial is a class used to communicate with the serial IR port of the RCX. It can transmit and receive data packets as defined by the original LEGO firmware. Have a look at Kekoa Proudfoot's opcode reference at http://graphics.stanford.edu/~kekoa/rcx/index.html if you are going to use this class.

SerialListener is an interface you can implement; it will be notified when a complete data package has been received over the IR port.

Using the Poll Class

This class is used to "poll" for state changes in RCX sensors, buttons, and the serial IR port. You set up a bit mask of events you wish to react to. Next, you call the poll method with this mask. Your calling thread will then be blocked until one of the resources specified in the bit mask has changed state. This class is used internally to notify listeners attached to *Button*, *Sensor*, and *Serial* objects. It only has a constructor, taking no arguments, and two methods:

- *public final int poll (int mask, int millis)* This polls for changes specified by the *mask*. It will block the calling thread for at most *millis* milliseconds (0 means forever). On termination, it returns a mask representing the changed resources. You must then check this returned mask to determine which of your monitored resources did, in fact, change.

- *public final void setThrottle (int throttle)* The throttle determines how many sensor reads must pass between each poll; 0 means poll as often as possible, while the default is 1. Remember that sensors are read in 3ms intervals.

The class also defines bit masks, which you can OR together to create your final mask. An excerpt is given here: *SENSOR1_MASK, ALL_BUTTONS, ALL_SENSORS, RUN_MASK, SERIAL_MASK*. See the JavaDoc section on *Poll* for the rest.

Figure 5.5 (also provided on the CD) shows a small example which will poll the **Run**, **View**, and **Prgm** buttons, and play a different system sound to match each. The **Run** button will additionally terminate the program.

Figure 5.5 Polling for Events Using Poll and Bit Masks (poll/PollDemo.java)

```
import josx.platform.rcx.Poll;
import josx.platform.rcx.Sound;

public class PollDemo {
```

Continued

Figure 5.5 Continued

```
public static void main (String[] args) throws InterruptedException
{
    Poll p = new Poll ();

    int org_mask = Poll.RUN_MASK | Poll.VIEW_MASK | Poll.PRGM_MASK;

    while (true) {
        int mask = p.poll (org_mask, 0);

        if ((mask & Poll.PRGM_MASK) != 0) {
            Sound.beep();
        }
        if ((mask & Poll.VIEW_MASK) != 0) {
            Sound.twoBeeps();
        }
        if ((mask & Poll.RUN_MASK) != 0) {
            Sound.buzz();
            Thread.currentThread ().sleep (1000);
            break;
        }
    }
}
}
```

Using the PersistentMemoryArea Class

The *PersistentMemoryArea* class provides you with a way to store data which will be preserved between subsequent runs of your program. Only removing the batteries from the RCX will erase the data you put here. At the moment, only individual bytes can be stored in this persistent area. The available methods are:

- ■ **static PersistentMemoryArea get (int magic, int size)** This method returns a new *PersistentMemoryArea* identified by the supplied *magic* value. This value makes it possible to have more than one *PersistentMemoryArea* identified by different magic values. At the moment, only one *PersistentMemoryArea* exists and it will be reinitialized if a different magic number is supplied. That may change in the future though. The *size* parameter specifies how many bytes you wish to allocate room for—the current maximum is 2037 bytes. Note that these bytes are allocated in a memory area within the RCX, which is not otherwise used by your leJOS programs, so the memory allocated here does not affect the available memory for your programs.

- ***public byte readByte (int i)*** This returns the value of the byte stored at index *i* in the *PersistentMemoryArea*. This method will throw an *ArrayOutOf BoundsException* if *i* exceeds the amount of bytes allocated for this *PersistentMemoryArea*.

- ***public void writeByte (int i, byte b)*** This writes the byte *b* at the index given by *i* in this *PersistentMemoryArea*. Again, an *ArrayOutOf BoundsException* can be thrown if *i* exceeds the amount of allocated memory.

Using the Memory, ROM, Battery, and MinuteTimer Classes

The *Memory* class is supposed to only be used internally. It provides an internal synchronization object for synchronizing access to memory from native code, and contains some methods for reading and writing absolute memory locations as well as getting the address occupied by an object. This class is useful only if you plan to do low-level things like modifying the leJOS base classes yourself. Its use can seriously jeopardize the stability of the leJOS and RCX runtime environment.

The ROM class contains methods for calling into the RCX ROM code directly, so use this class only if you are familiar with the RCX ROM. You can familiarize yourself with the ROM at Kekoa Proudfoot's RCX Internals page at: http://graphics.stanford.edu/~kekoa/rcx.

The *Battery* class provides three methods for returning the remaining voltage of the batteries. They are:

- ***public static int getVoltageInternal()*** This returns the RCX internal voltage representation. This representation is equal to the voltage in millivolts ★ 1560 / 43988.

- ***public static int getVoltageMilliVolt()*** This returns the battery voltage in millivolts.

- ***public static float getVoltage()*** This returns the voltage measure as a float; note that this is measured in volts, not in millivolts.

The *MinuteTimer* class can be used for one thing only: resetting the RCX's internal two-byte minute timer. It contains just one static method for this purpose: *reset()*.

Using leJOS: A Simple Example

Now, let's try to make a few simple RCX programs with leJOS. The first program will demonstrate a technique for finer motor control. The second example (actually two examples) will show you two different ways of reading sensor input. Knowing both ways will give you a choice when programming your own robots; sometimes it's useful to mix both reading methods in the same program.

The examples are very simple. Of the classes from the *josx.platform.rcx* package, you will only be using the *Motor* class in the first example. The last two examples will use the classes *Sensor*, *SensorListener*, and *SensorConstants* to read the sensor, and the *Sound* class to indicate a successful sensor read, before terminating the program.

Controlling Motors

A motor has only eight power levels, 0 thru 7, for you to exploit. This is actually a limitation in the ROM code, but for most applications it is fine. The thing to remember when you try to refine motor control is that the LEGO motor has an internal flywheel, which is good for preserving speed (at least with light loads). Now, the trick to slowing a motor down is to simply hit the brakes before lowering the power. The following simple program shown in Figure 5.6 (you can find this on the CD that accompanies this book) will demonstrate this technique by making the RCX perform a never-ending psychedelic dance. You can use the differential drive platform, as shown previously in Figure 5.2 located under the *ProximitySensor* heading, and again connect the motors to port A and C.

Figure 5.6 The Psychedelic Dance (dance/Dance.java)

```
import josx.platform.rcx.Motor;
import java.util.Random;
import java.lang.Math;

public class Dance {
    public static void doStep (Motor motor, int direction) {
        motor.stop();
```

Continued

Figure 5.6 Continued

```
        if (direction < 0) {
            direction = Math.abs (direction);
            motor.setPower (direction);
            motor.backward();
        } else {
            motor.setPower (direction);
            motor.forward();
        }
    }


    public static void main (String[] args) throws InterruptedException
    {
        Random rnd = new Random (42);
        while (true) {
            int a_power = rnd.nextInt () % 7;
            int c_power = rnd.nextInt () % 7;

            doStep (Motor.A, a_power);
            doStep (Motor.C, c_power);

            Thread.currentThread ().sleep ((rnd.nextInt() % 400) + 100);
        }
    }
}
```

Reading Sensors

You can design your program to use sensors in two ways. The first will periodically read the sensor value using the Sensor API directly; the other (and smarter)
way is to have the sensor reading thread call an object of yours (a listener) whenever the observed sensor's value changes. The reason this is better is because you
do not tie up an additional thread for the sole purpose of reading sensor values.
In fact, with this second method, you don't even have to think about threads.
Instead, you can concentrate on how you wish the RCX to act when a sensor is
triggered. Also, using listeners will make your programs more readable and maintainable, as they better separate the sensor reading code from the code handling

the read values. Again, what is designed here is basic event listener stuff, known from the J2SE AWT event model.

Here are two small programs demonstrating the two techniques. Both programs achieve the same end. They wait until a touch sensor attached to input port 1 is pressed, after which a buzz is heard for 1/10 of a second before the program terminates.

The first program, with sensor polling, is shown in Figure 5.7 (and can be found on the CD):

Figure 5.7 Reading Sensors Directly (sensorread/SensorPoll.java)

```
import josx.platform.rcx.Sensor;
import josx.platform.rcx.SensorConstants;
import josx.platform.rcx.Sound;

public class SensorPoll {

    public static void main (String[] args) throws InterruptedException
    {
        Sensor.S1.setTypeAndMode (SensorConstants.SENSOR_TYPE_TOUCH,
                            SensorConstants.SENSOR_MODE_BOOL);

        boolean auch = false;
        while (! auch) {
            auch = Sensor.S1.readBooleanValue ();
            //sensors are polled every 3 millisecs by the ROM,
            //so reading more often is a waste of time.
            Thread.currentThread ().sleep(3);
        }
        Sound.buzz ();
        Thread.currentThread ().sleep(100);
    }
}
```

And then using the listener technique, which we show in Figure 5.8 and on the CD that accompanies the book. Unfortunately, in this small example this technique seems rather awkward, as an infinite loop has to be made to prevent the main thread from falling out of the main method and thereby terminating

the program. If you're pulling your hair out because a program of yours terminates immediately, this is probably the cause. Many techniques exist, however, to
prevent this. A common one is to wait for the **Run** button to be pressed using
Button.RUN.waitForPressAndRelease(), but this does tie up your main thread,
which could be doing something useful instead. Therefore, it's common to do
this: create a lot of threads for doing the jobs your robot needs to get accomplished, and then stash each thread so it's out of the way, doing nothing but
waiting for the exit signal. Try to use that main thread for something useful,
which will at the same time prevent it from terminating the program, and also
use a *ButtonListener* for checking the **Run** button as a signal of program termination (you can, for instance, call *System.exit (0)* from within the *ButtonListener
.buttonPressed()* method). Okay, enough rambling. Here's the code:

NOTE

Occasionally, you may wish to actually do something when the sensor
reading does *not* change. In such cases, it is not possible to use the listener approach since your code is only executed when the sensor readings change.

Figure 5.8 Reading Sensors Using a *SensorListener* (sensorread/
SensorListen.java)

```
import josx.platform.rcx.Sensor;
import josx.platform.rcx.SensorConstants;
import josx.platform.rcx.SensorListener;
import josx.platform.rcx.Sound;


public class SensorListen
{
    static Thread mainThread = null;
    static boolean quit = false;

    public static class AuchHandler implements SensorListener {
        public void stateChanged(Sensor aSource,
                                 int aOldValue,
```

Continued

Figure 5.8 Continued

```
                                int aNewValue)
    {
    boolean auch = aSource.readBooleanValue();
        if (auch) {
            Sound.buzz();
            try {
                Thread.currentThread ().sleep(100);
            } catch (InterruptedException ie) {
                //do nothing
            }
            quit = true;
            mainThread.interrupt();
        }
    }
}


public static void main (String[] args) throws InterruptedException
{
    Sensor.S1.setTypeAndMode (SensorConstants.SENSOR_TYPE_TOUCH,
                              SensorConstants.SENSOR_MODE_BOOL);
    mainThread = Thread.currentThread();
    Sensor.S1.addSensorListener (new AuchHandler());

    while (!quit) {
        try {
            Thread.currentThread().sleep(10000);
        } catch (InterruptedException ie) {
            //do nothing
        }
    }
}
}
```

Summary

This chapter covered the leJOS system. The leJOS system is a very small Java runtime environment, much smaller than most of the known Java implementations from Sun. Only JavaCard for running Java on smartcards has a comparable size; for example, the smallest VM (KVM) for Sun's J2ME needs twice the memory the RCX has available.

The workstation environmental setups necessary for starting programming with leJOS were shown in this chapter for both the Linux and Windows platforms, and it was also demonstrated how the leJOS runtime system is downloaded to the RCX.

The leJOS system contains some limitations compared to standard Java, the lack of the garbage collector being the most prominent. A garbage collector might be added in the future, but until that happens, you need to design your programs in ways that bound the number of objects allocated.

To provide you with the information necessary to utilize RCX-specific features from leJOS, this chapter presented all the classes in the *josx.platform.rcx* package responsible for exposing those RCX features to Java programmers. It provided a few small demonstration programs to show you how to use some of these classes, like the ProximityDemo, which can detect objects using IR, and the ServoDemo, which demonstrates a 360-degree turn of an axle. It also provided programs demonstrating how to control the LEGO motors and reading sensors using leJOS, which are probably the most often used RCX features of all.

You should now be in a position where you can really start programming the RCX using leJOS, which is the topic of the next chapter.

Solutions Fast Track

Basic leJOS Usage Guidelines

- ☑ The leJOS environment (*PATH, RCXTTY, LEJOS_HOME, JAVA_HOME, CLASSPATH*) must be set up in order to start programming for leJOS.

- ☑ Compilation is done using *lejosc*, which is just a thin wrapper around *javac*.

- ☑ Conversion of Java class files to a leJOS binary format, and the transmission of that format to the RCX, is done using the *lejos* command line tool.

The LEGO Java Operating System

☑ LeJOS leverages the LEGO-provided ROM code, and thus inherits limitations imposed by the ROM—for instance, only eight power levels for the motors, and no sampling of sensors faster than 3 milliseconds.

☑ LeJOS gives you a common programming language (Java) and environment for the RCX. The learning curve is not as steep as other firmware replacements like legOS.

☑ A comparison to other Java environments shows the formidable achievement of cramming an entire Java VM into the RCX's 32KB of memory.

Overview of the leJOS Architecture

☑ Base classes are not part of the firmware. This is a great feature as it makes the firmware footprint smaller.

☑ Only classes needed by your program are actually downloaded to the RCX, since the *lejos* command line tool performs a transitive closure of class graphs of the main class.

☑ There is no garbage collector in leJOS—for now you have to live with that. The future might bring you one, and hopefully you will be able to choose whether or not to include it in your program.

☑ A switch statement is also missing, but may be available in the future.

Using leJOS: A Simple Example

☑ You can read sensor values in two different ways: by polling the sensor, and by listening for changes using an implementation of *SensorListener*.

☑ You should brake motors before changing power to ensure the power change can be noticed. This is necessary as the LEGO motor has an internal flywheel, which stores mechanical power.

Frequently Asked Questions

The following Frequently Asked Questions, answered by the authors of this book, are designed to both measure your understanding of the concepts presented in this chapter and to assist you with real-life implementation of these concepts. To have your questions about this chapter answered by the author, browse to **www.syngress.com/solutions** and click on the **"Ask the Author"** form.

Q: What happens if more than ten programs are downloaded to the RCX at once?

A: The 11th (and further) programs will appear in the program list, represented using blanks.

Q: What if a program does not bound the number of objects created?

A: The program will run out of memory, terminate with a buzz sound, and show a 6 at the far right of the LCD, assuming that the class *OutOfMemoryError* is number 6 (see Chapter 6 for details on this). Usually this happens to be the case.

Q: What if I have a LEGO tower connected to the USB port?

A: Set the RCXTTY environment variable to the value USB, instead of to a serial port value.

Q: What happens if I execute *lejosfirmdl* with leJOS already loaded?

A: The leJOS firmware will download once again. Any program of yours in the RCX memory at that time will have to be reloaded.

Q: I get a "Cannot unlock firmware failed" message when using *lejosfirmdl*. What should I do?

A: This usually happens when a previous attempt to download the firmware has failed. Turning the RCX off and then back on should remove the problem.

Q: I get an error message resembling:

```
Exception reading LCD
js.classfile.EClassFileFormat: Version not recognized: 46.0
```

from the *lejos* command. What is happening?

A: You are using JDK 1.4 and forgot to specify the option *-target 1.1* when you compiled your program with *lejosc*.

## Chapter 6

Programming for the leJOS Environment

Solutions in this chapter:

- Designing Java Programs to Run in leJOS

- An Advanced Programming Example Using leJOS

- Debugging leJOS Programs

- Testing leJOS Programs

☑ Summary

☑ Solutions Fast Track

☑ Frequently Asked Questions

Introduction

In the previous chapter, we laid the groundwork for programming the RCX using Java and the leJOS environment. This chapter will contain a more advanced programming example. We have chosen the classic line-following challenge because it is well known in the LEGO MINDSTORMS community, it is good for demonstrating program design, and it's very easy to understand. The challenge is to make a robot follow a black line drawn on white paper. The RIS comes with such a paper test course, suited exactly for this challenge.

Some of the pitfalls to watch for include creating objects which go out of scope, thereby trashing memory and tying up the event listener thread for too long, causing missed sensor readings. These pitfalls are related to leJOS in general. We'll also address specific problems concerning the line following example, like how to get the robot back to the line if it's diverted, or how to prevent the robot from leaving the line in the first place. We'll also explore a design paradigm for robotic control called *subsumption architecture* in an extension to the original line-following code. This architecture was originally developed by R.A. Brooks in 1986, and is built upon layering and prioritizing different lower behaviors to achieve a more complex higher order behavior. Further information can be found at http://ai.eecs.umich.edu/cogarch0/subsump.

For the design of your software, it's best to create a good object-oriented (OO) design, using your preferred notation (UML happens to be mine) to achieve the easiest maintainable and extendable code, once implemented. The subsumption architecture will allow you to focus on perfecting individual behaviors of the robot independently, thus allowing you to test a partly implemented system and then expand it by adding additional behavioral code all in a modular fashion.

Designing Java Programs to Run in leJOS

Since Java is an object-oriented programming platform, object-oriented design techniques apply to programs for Java on the RCX as well. But I encourage you to never forget while doing the program design that this is Java for a *memory-limited embedded device*. In my opinion, it is crucial, right from the design phase of the program, to understand and take into consideration the conditions under which a program will run. The old way of doing OO design taught people to "just do" OO design. It did not matter how the finished system would be run, nor which programming language should be used since these were implementation details.

Well, I can tell you that it does matter since it is excruciatingly difficult to follow an OO design using COBOL as your programming language. Also, some OO design patterns do not take into account that when implemented, many objects will need to be created. This, of course, is fine when your program is run on a mainframe, but you really need to bend the design in unfavorable ways to cram it into an RCX, for instance.

So, what is it we really need to take into account when designing a Java program for the RCX? Memory, memory, and more memory!

Using Memory Wisely

How can we best use the available RCX memory for our programs? Well, we have to remember two things. First, we do not have a lot of it to begin with, and second, if we allocate some of it, we cannot return it to the leJOS system to use it again. This basically boils down to a few guidelines (or warning signs) to look for in the code:

- Only allocate objects you really need.

- Design your objects to be mutable; this allows you to reuse them.

- Do not allocate objects inside loops (this is not always bad if they are really needed).

- Consider using *byte*s and *short*s instead of *int*s. They take up less memory and are usually quite adequate for holding sensor readings and so on.

- Use the main thread. Do not just park it.

With that said, try not to compromise on writing nicely OO separated code. It is possible to have a neat OO-designed Java program given the restrictions imposed on you, but remember, you do not get extra points for having lots of memory free, especially when your program terminates because of an unmaintainable and overly complex code. Of course, should you run into "memory trouble," you have to know what to look for, and how to improve the code. Having your program do what it is supposed to, with a clean design that happens to use up all the memory is far better than having sloppy code that has chunks of free memory it doesn't use.

If you are puzzled by the enormous amount of memory your program consumes, try looking at the implementation of some of the base classes you use. The code is not that hard to understand, as we'll demonstrate in the next section with *StringBuffer*.

Using the Right Java Classes (and Using Them Correctly)

A good way of demonstrating memory optimization for a number of allocated objects is the optimization of allocating instances of *java.lang.String*. The reason for this is that a *String* is immutable, which means that once a *String* is constructed, the characters it uses of can never be changed. Therefore, you have to create a new *String* object if you wish to represent another string. The standard Java solution for this is to use an instance of *StringBuffer* to build your dynamic string content and then turn that into a *String* (using *StringBuffers toString* method) for printing purposes and so on. This technique also applies to leJOS. Consider the program shown in Figure 6.1 (this can be found on the CD that accompanies this book, in the /string directory).

Figure 6.1 StringTest Shows the Usual Way of Manipulating String Objects (StringTest.java)

```
import josx.platform.rcx.TextLCD;
import josx.platform.rcx.Button;
import josx.platform.rcx.LCD;

public class StringTest {
    public static void main (String[] args) throws InterruptedException
    {
        String ha = "HA";
        TextLCD.print (ha);
        Button.VIEW.waitForPressAndRelease ();

        ha = ha + ' ' + ha;
        TextLCD.print (ha);
        Button.VIEW.waitForPressAndRelease ();

        LCD.showNumber ((int)Runtime.getRuntime().freeMemory());
        Button.VIEW.waitForPressAndRelease ();
    }
}
```

Well, it looks innocent enough, but actually there is no explicit use of the new statement, so at first glance it doesn't appear as if any objects are allocated. In truth, though, a lot of objects are created. First, the initial assignment of *ha* creates a *String* object, then in the line *ha = ha + ' ' + ha;* a *StringBuffer* is allocated using its default constructor, and 3 *append* methods on it are called. That does not sound frightening, but the leJOS version of the *StringBuffer*s default constructor allocates an internal *char* array of size 0, and upon each *append* call, this buffer is replaced with a new one if it does not have room for the characters you are about to append. To make matters worse, *String* (to preserve its immutability) allocates another *char* array when told to return itself as one using the *toCharArray()* method (which *StringBuffer* will call to append the *String*). *StringBuffer* also converts an appended *char* to first a *char[]* of size one, then a *String*, and then calls *append* with that *String*, which we just saw will make *String* create another *char* array. Finally, a *String* is created using the *StringBuffer*s *toString* method (whew!).

In total, that innocent-looking line allocates one *StringBuffer*, two *String*'s, and 9 *char[]*, for a total of 12 new objects, of which only two can actually be (re)used—the resulting *String* and the *StringBuffer*. As you can see, we finished the program by outputting the amount of available memory. The number says 2348!

So, let's check out the version shown in Figure 6.2 (also found on the CD), which is the standard Java solution to this problem, using a *StringBuffer* directly.

Figure 6.2 StringBuffer Shows the Usual Java Optimization for StringTest (StringBufferTest)

```
import josx.platform.rcx.TextLCD;
import josx.platform.rcx.Button;
import josx.platform.rcx.LCD;


public class StringBufferTest {
    public static void main (String[] args) throws InterruptedException
    {
        String ha = "HA";
        TextLCD.print (ha);
        Button.VIEW.waitForPressAndRelease ();

        StringBuffer bf = new StringBuffer (5);
        bf.append (ha);
        bf.append (' ');
```

Continued

Figure 6.2 Continued

```
        bf.append (ha);

        TextLCD.print (bf.toString());

        Button.VIEW.waitForPressAndRelease ();


        LCD.showNumber ((int)Runtime.getRuntime().freeMemory());

        Button.VIEW.waitForPressAndRelease ();

    }

}
```

Not much has actually happened. we have specified a size for the *StringBuffer*, which will eliminate the *char[]* allocated inside *StringBuffer* when it determines it doesn't have enough space allocated for the append operation to succeed, and that's all. The amount of memory available here hasn't improved dramatically—it's only up to 2364. A fast fix is to notice that TextLCD will actually print a *char[]* as well as a *String*, so changing the line *TextLCD.print (bf.toString();* into *TextLCD.print (bf.getChars());* will eliminate one *String* creation (and that *String*'s internal creation of a *char[]*) which will give you 2400 free bytes.

We still do not have a lot of free memory, and we are not really doing anything spectacular. The next move is to realize that *StringBuffer* itself is a fairly large class, so let us get rid of it entirely—Figure 6.3 (also found on the CD) shows a version which does that using *char[]* directly.

Figure 6.3 CharTest Shows the Ultimate Optimization (CharTest.java)

```
import josx.platform.rcx.TextLCD;

import josx.platform.rcx.Button;

import josx.platform.rcx.LCD;


public class CharTest {

    public static void main (String[] args) throws InterruptedException
    {
        char[] ha = "HA".toCharArray();

        TextLCD.print (ha);

        Button.VIEW.waitForPressAndRelease ();


        char[] bf = new char[5];

        byte curpos = 0;
```

Continued

Figure 6.3 Continued

```
    for (byte i = 0; i < ha.length; i++) {
      bf[curpos++] = ha[i];
    }
    bf[curpos++] = ' ';
    for (byte i = 0; i < ha.length; i++) {
      bf[curpos++] = ha[i];
    }
    TextLCD.print (bf);
    Button.VIEW.waitForPressAndRelease ();


    LCD.showNumber ((int)Runtime.getRuntime().freeMemory());
    Button.VIEW.waitForPressAndRelease ();

  }

}
```

How much did this version improve matters? Well, by getting rid of *StringBuffer* we have boosted the amount of free memory to 5774 bytes—rather good, don't you think?

Could it be improved even further? Yes, but not much. You can get rid of the initial *"HA"* string and place the individual characters in a *char* array directly. Thus, the initialization of variable *ha* will look like:

```
char[] ha = new char[2];
ha[0] = 'H';
ha[1] = 'A';
```

This will save you an additional 14 bytes, so it is hardly worth the trouble, unless you are really making large programs or collecting large amounts of data.

The lesson hopefully learned is that things are not always as they seem. The first version is definitely the least complex to understand, but it burns memory like crazy. And to understand fully what is going on, you have to look at the implementation of the used base classes. In this case, knowing the internal behavior of *String* and *StringBuffer* allows you to come up with a solution to the problem. But keep in mind that using *TextLCD* itself, of course, has a cost (as mentioned in the previous chapter), which amounts to around 1500 bytes. So, unless you really need the text output (it can often improve the usability of programs) use *LCD* instead.

By the way, what we've looked at is not leJOS-specific since the previous examples behave exactly the same in standard Java. The only difference is that in leJOS the space allocated is never reclaimed. Therefore, you pay more dearly for the unneeded memory allocations (and also the default size of a *StringBuffer* is 16 characters in standard Java, instead of 0 in leJOS).

An Advanced Programming Example Using leJOS

As mentioned earlier, we will show you how to program the classic line-following robot in leJOS—see the robot shown in Figure 6.4. This robot has two rear wheels powered by a single motor, and is steered by its one front wheel, which is turned by another motor. The downward-looking light sensor is placed in front of the steering wheel and turns with it. Because of the sensor's position, even small adjustments in steering will move the sensor a great deal. This will make the sensor contact the line's edge more quickly, and thus greatly reduce the chance of the robot steering away from the line. The robot uses only this single sensor and it can readily be built using a standard LEGO Robotic Invention System kit.

Figure 6.4 The Line-following Robot

The prerequisite of the line-following challenge is to stick to the left side of the line. At the edge, the light sensor will return a value between what is considered black and what is considered white. Initially, the robot will be placed on white, to calibrate the white value, and then placed on black for the same purpose. Afterward, when you place it on the line's edge, it will start following it. Path correction will involve turning right if the sensor returns a value considered "white," meaning we have strayed off the line to the left, and similarly turning left if the sensor reports "black," meaning the robot has now turned into the line. The driving motors will be set to full power so the robot follows the line as quickly as possible.

Let's start by making a nice OO design for it. From reading the preceding description, you can see you need some code for calibration, some for reading the light sensor, some for driving forward, and some for steering based on the value read by the sensor.

We have chosen to use the *TextLCD* for giving directions to the user under the initial calibration phase. Figure 6.5 is a UML class diagram showing the classes needed.

As you can see, a heavily used class is the *LineValueHolder*, but actually only one instance of it will be created. Objects aggregated from it will share the same instance.

The *LineValueHolder* is an example of a mutable object. It is used to synchronize access to the values supplied from the light-sensor (it is actually an implementation of a solution to the classical readers-writers problem). Here one class (the *LightReader*) will act as the only writer; it will be called when the light-sensor has changed its value, then it will update the current sensor reading held by the *LineValueHolder* by calling *setValue*, which will wake up any waiting readers.

The reader (in this case an instance of *Turner*) will continuously call *LineValueHolder*'s *getValue()*. This call will block until later notified by the *LightReader*'s call to *setValue*, signaling that a new value has become available. Notice that this code does not hold any queue, so it is possible that readers might miss some values, but for this application that probably does not matter as the light sensor tends to change values often. The *LineValueHolder* also holds the program's interpretation of white and black; those values are placed into it once at the start of the program using the *Calibrator*.

What about the user interaction? For simplicity's sake, we have chosen the not-so-pretty approach—that is, to place the user interface directly in the main class *LineFollower*'s constructor; the prettiest OO design would probably be to place the user interface and user interaction code into a separate UI class.

Figure 6.5 The UML Class Diagram for the Line-follower

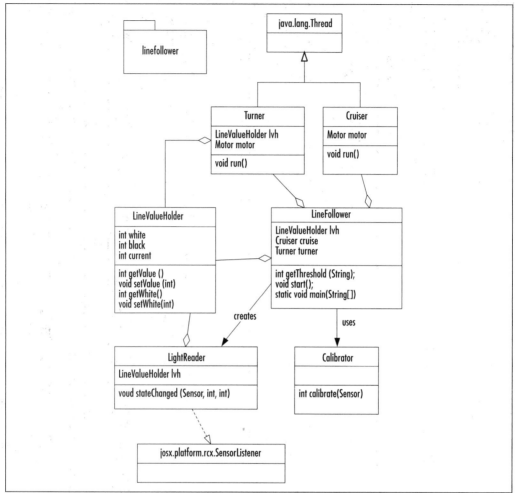

Finally, the two *Thread* subclasses, *Turner* and *Cruiser*, are responsible for movement of the robot, and as the name implies, *Turner* turns the robot left or right according to the current sensor reading, and *Cruiser* is responsible for driving forward as fast as possible.

Configuration of *Sensor.S1*, which the light-sensor is attached to, is done in the *LineFollower*'s constructor.

Now, let's take a look at the implementation of those classes one by one. First, the important *LineValueHolder*. (The code examples in Figures 6.6 through 6.11 are provided on the accompanying CD of this book in the /linefollower/original/linefollower directory for Chapter 6.)

Figure 6.6 LineValueHolder Contains Main Synchronization Between Sensor Reading Code and Steering Code (LineValueHolder.java)

```java
package linefollower;

public class LineValueHolder {
  public int white;
  public int black;
  public int current;
  public LineValueHolder() {
  }
  public synchronized void setValue (int value) {
    current = value;
    this.notifyAll(); //notify all waiting readers
  }
  public synchronized int getValue () throws InterruptedException {
    this.wait(); //wait until a new value is read
    return current;
  }
  public void setWhite (int value) {
    white = value;
  }
  public int getWhite () {
    return white;
  }
  public void setBlack (int value) {
    black = value;
  }
  public int getBlack () {
    return black;
  }
}
```

The most important and interesting methods are the two synchronized methods, *getValue* and *setValue*.

The *setValue* method's most important feature is that it is very short, and thus executes very fast. It will be called by the *LightReader* within its *stateChanged* method, which in turn is called by the leJOS sensor reading thread. So, the longer you tie up that sensor reading thread, the more sensor readings you will miss.

The two methods work in parallel, as calls to *getValue* will block until another call has been made to *setValue*. The reason this will work is that, as mentioned previously, sensor-readings will change! Let's now take a look at our *SensorListener*, which calls *setValue* (see Figure 6.7).

Figure 6.7 LightReader Is Responsible for Delivering Sensor Readings to the LineValueHolder (LightReader.java)

```java
package linefollower;
import josx.platform.rcx.SensorListener;
import josx.platform.rcx.Sensor;

public class LightReader implements SensorListener{
  LineValueHolder lvh;

  public LightReader(LineValueHolder lvh)
  {
    this.lvh = lvh;
  }
  public void stateChanged (Sensor sensor, int new_value, int old_value)
  {
    lvh.setValue (new_value);
  }
}
```

As you can see, the *stateChanged* method is very short, so it does not tie up the sensor reading thread as just mentioned. It simply calls the *LineValueHolder*'s *setValue* method (which, as you saw previously, was very short as well). This call transfers the new value as read by the *Sensor*.

Let's move on to the Cruiser, shown in Figure 6.8.

Figure 6.8 Cruiser Is Doing the Driving (Cruiser.java)

```java
package linefollower;
import josx.platform.rcx.Motor;

public class Cruiser extends Thread {
```

Continued

Figure 6.8 Continued

```
Motor motor;

public Cruiser(Motor motor) {
    this.motor = motor;
    motor.setPower (7);
}
public void run () {
    motor.forward();
}
}
```

As you can see, it simply sets the power level to maximum and then when it is started, sets the motor going forward.

The Turner thread (see Figure 6.9) is a bit more complicated, as it behaves differently based upon the light sensed.

Figure 6.9 Turner Is Responsible for Steering the Robot According to the Sensor Readings (Turner.java)

```
package linefollower;

import josx.platform.rcx.Motor;
import josx.platform.rcx.LCD;

public class Turner extends Thread {
    static final int HYSTERESIS = 4;
    Motor motor;
    LineValueHolder lvh;

    public Turner(Motor motor, LineValueHolder lvh) {
        this.lvh = lvh;
        this.motor = motor;
        motor.setPower (7);
    }
    public void run () {
        while (true) {
```

Continued

Figure 6.9 Continued

```
        try {
            int light = lvh.getValue();
//show the current reading, great for debugging
            LCD.showNumber (light);
            if (light < lvh.getBlack() + HYSTERESIS) {
              motor.forward();
            } else if (light > lvh.getWhite() - HYSTERESIS) {
              motor.backward();
            } else {
              motor.stop();
            }
        } catch (InterruptedException ie) {
            //ignore
        }
    }
  }
}
```

The logic in the *run()* method, which is implementing what is interesting, is pretty simple. It compares the light reading with what is considered black—if it is less, it spins the motor forward. With the right wiring, this will turn the wheel, and thereby the robot, left. Similarly, if it is greater than what is considered to be white, it spins the motor backward, which should turn the robot right. Otherwise, we do not need to turn so we stop the motor.

NOTE

Hysteresis actually means "lag of effect," a term that comes from physics, where it means a delay in the observed effect when forces on a body change. This term has crept into software lingo with the meaning that you need to take this lag of effect in the physical world into account when programming. This is often done (as in the example in Figure 6.9) by adding/deducting a value in a comparison. This will also allow a program to be more immune to noise in sensor readings.

Can that ever work? Of course not. Remember, white is probably the highest value we will see, and black the lowest. So we simply deduct/add a constant called *HYSTERESIS* before the comparison, which will make an interval of values considered too white or too black which we need to react to. Notice that it is rather small (only four), but for our lighting conditions this value seems to work. Plus, it's a place where you can tune your behavior.

The last of the helper classes is the *Calibrator*. Its *calibrate* method simply takes the average over 20 successive light-sensor readings, as shown in Figure 6.10.

Figure 6.10 Calibrator Is Used to Define the Interpretation of Black and White (Calibrator.java)

```java
package linefollower;
import josx.platform.rcx.Sensor;

public class Calibrator {
  private static final int  NUMBER_OF_SAMPLES = 20;
  Sensor sensor;

  public Calibrator(Sensor sensor) {
     this.sensor = sensor;
  }

  public int calibrate () {
      int sum = 0;
      for (int i = 0; i < NUMBER_OF_SAMPLES; i++) {
        sum += sensor.readValue ();
      }
      return sum / NUMBER_OF_SAMPLES;
  }
}
```

Now, look to Figure 6.11 for the main class, *LineFollower*, whose purpose is to set things up, drive the user interaction, and finally kickoff the controlling threads.

Figure 6.11 The Main Program Class Does Mainly Setup but also Drives the User Interface (LineFollower.java)

```java
package linefollower;

import josx.platform.rcx.LCD;
import josx.platform.rcx.TextLCD;
import josx.platform.rcx.Sound;
import josx.platform.rcx.Motor;
import josx.platform.rcx.Sensor;
import josx.platform.rcx.SensorConstants;
import josx.platform.rcx.Button;

public class LineFollower {

  LineValueHolder lvh = new LineValueHolder();
  Cruiser cruise;
  Turner turner;

  public LineFollower() throws InterruptedException {
    Sensor.S1.setTypeAndMode (SensorConstants.SENSOR_TYPE_LIGHT,
                              SensorConstants.SENSOR_MODE_PCT);
    Sensor.S1.activate();

    waitForUser ("white");
    lvh.setWhite (getThreshold());
    waitForUser (null);

    waitForUser ("black");
    lvh.setBlack (getThreshold());
    waitForUser (null);

    Sensor.S1.addSensorListener(new LightReader(lvh));

    cruise = new Cruiser (Motor.B);
    turner = new Turner (Motor.A, lvh);
  }
```

Continued

Figure 6.11 Continued

```
public void waitForUser (String message) throws InterruptedException
{
  if (message != null) {
    TextLCD.print (message);
  }
  Sound.twoBeeps ();
  Button.VIEW.waitForPressAndRelease();
}

public int getThreshold () {
  Calibrator calib = new Calibrator (Sensor.S1);
  int value = calib.calibrate ();
  //show calibration value, good for tuning the HYSTERESIS constant
  //in the Turner class
  LCD.showNumber(value);
  return value;
}

public void start ()
{
  //start threads
  cruise.start();
  turner.run();
}

public static void main(String[] args) throws InterruptedException {
  LineFollower lineFollower = new LineFollower();
  lineFollower.start ();
}
}
```

The code for *LineFollower* is fairly simple. A *LineFollower* object is created in the *main* method. Within the constructor, the *Sensor.S1* is then configured for light readings. Then the user is prompted with the text "white" which should serve as an instruction to place the robot's light-sensor over the white surface. When done, the user must press the **View** button for white calibration to begin, the calibration value is then displayed, and the user is again expected to press the **View** button to continue. This process resumes, but this time with the text "black" as prompt. When the user presses the **View** button at the end, the program continues its execution, so the user must place the robot near the left edge of the line, before doing the final **View** button press. Notice that we have also used a double beep to attract the user's attention, indicating something is needed from her. The rest of the program consists of only two things—first, attaching the *LightReader* as a listener to *Sensor.S1*, and the construction and start of the *Turner* and *Cruiser* threads. If all goes well, your robot will start following the black line.

Now, it was promised that some "mistakes" would be purposely included in the program to make it use more memory than actually needed. We will continue to refrain from correcting them (as long as we don't run out of memory), because they increase the readability and usability of the program. The memory optimized version can also be found on the accompanying CD in the /linefollower/optimized directory.

We will now go over the "mistakes" and at the same time explain how to remove them and thereby optimize the program.

- Notice in Figure 6.11 that the method, *getThreshold*, is called twice in the *LineFollower*'s constructor, and that within it a *Calibrator* is instantiated. That means two *Calibrator* instances and one *Calibrator* that does pure calculations. In fact, its sole method is actually thread-safe since it only works on method local variables, so a fast optimization is to simply make it into a static method and not allocate any *Calibrator* objects at all. If the *calibrate* method had not been thread-safe, we could still have done that because in our case, the calls to *calibrate* occur from only one thread, the main thread of the program.

- In the *LineValueHolder* (Figure 6.6) *int*s are the used type for the instance variables holding the sensor readings. But as light-sensor readings are percentages their values lies between 0 and 100, and a Java byte which has the range [-128:127] is quite adequate for holding those readings. So memory can be saved by using *byte*s instead of *int*s.

- It is really not so nice that three references to the *LineValueHolder* instance need to be kept at various places. The one in the *LineFollower* is easy to get rid of. Just move the construction inside the *constructor* and lose that *instance* variable. But to get rid of all three of them, we will instead apply the Singleton pattern, as identified in the book *Design*

Patterns by the Gang Of Four (Gamma, Helm, Johnson, and Vlissides). So, the changes to the *LineValueHolder* construction will look like:

```
...
private static LineValueHolder instance = null;
  public static LineValueHolder getInstance () {
    if (instance == null) {
      instance = new LineValueHolder ();
    }
    return instance;
  }


  private LineValueHolder() {
  }
...
```

- Now, take a look at the *Cruiser* thread (Figure 6.8). Actually the *run* method just starts the motor running and then terminates, thereby terminating the *Thread*. So it will be okay to just call the method directly from the *LineFollower's* *start* method (using the main thread). To improve things further, you can even remove the *Thread* extension, thereby making the constructed object smaller.

- Possible removal of a *Thread* extension also holds for the *Turner* thread because we used the already available main thread to call its *run* method directly, instead of indirectly through a *Thread.start()* call.

- *Cruiser* does not actually need to be instantiated at all, and can thus have its methods made static. We have not made that change, as it will make the use of *Cruiser* vastly different from that of the *Turner*.

- Finally, take another look at the *LineFollower* in Figure 6.11. All the methods are executed by the main thread, so no synchronization is needed. Thus, we do not really need to create any *LineFollower* objects. We can do that by turning *LineFollower's* instance methods into static equivalents. The constructor we will change into a static *init* method, which gets called by the *main* method.

We ran a slightly modified version of the original program with the one change that instead of continuously outputting the light reading, it outputted the amount of free memory. Then we did the same with the modifications just listed.

The result was that for the original, 3684 bytes were free, and for the modified version, 3814 bytes were free. Even though not much memory was saved, we haven't sacrificed any readability, usability, or maintainability of the program. Notice that in the optimized version on the CD we have chosen to keep the use of *TextLCD*, as opposed to using *LCD*, since it improves usability of the program.

Here is a list of other improvements you can try and implement yourself.

- As it is now, the program is stopped by pressing the **On-Off** button, which turns off the RCX completely. A nice feature would be a way to stop the program, perhaps by pressing the **Run** button; try adding a *ButtonListener* to do that. Its action could probably be to call *interrupt* on the main thread, to force it to break out of the endless loop in *Turner*'s run method. Notice that this demands a change in *Turner* as well, as it actually catches *InterruptedException*, ignores it, and continues with its business. And, of course, you need to keep a reference to the main thread somewhere (get that reference using the *Thread.currentThread()* method).

- The calibration routine could be improved to take the average of light readings made at different places along the course. This change would need some directions to the user to move the RCX between subsequent readings.

Designing & Planning...

Synchronization on Static Methods

Remember that no instances of *java.lang.Class* exist in leJOS, so you cannot synchronize on static methods. This is the reason you need to analyze your multithreaded programs. Make sure that when using static methods, no two threads will execute them simultaneously, or make sure the methods are thread-safe.

Controlling the Steering

If the robot, going too fast, passes entirely over the line to the right side of the black track, it will likely go into a never-ending spin around itself. This section will try to come up with two solutions for that.

The first solution will try to solve the problem by restricting the amount of turning allowed by the steering wheel, making it less likely that the robot will pass over the line.

The second solution is to try to find a way back to the left side of the line. This is achieved by determining that the line has been passed, and then over-ruling the robot's standard line-following behavior with a higher prioritized behavior which will hopefully bring the robot back on track; this solution introduces the subsumption architecture.

Before you attempt to control the steering, you will need to acquire some feedback of where the steering front wheel is positioned at any given time. To do this, we need to add a longer steering axle to the original design of the robot. This change allows us to put a rotation sensor on top of it, which is then connected to input 2 on the RCX. As a result, this rotation sensor gives us a way to measure the position of the wheel.

Restricted Steering

The first thing we'll do is make a programming change that controls how far to one side the wheel is allowed to turn. This, of course, will prevent the robot from making very sharp turns, but at least for the LEGO test pad we'll use here, no really sharp turns exist. The idea behind this is that, if the RCX doesn't do any sharp turns, it will not pass entirely over the line, and the spin-forever effect will go away.

In the program, we'll simply change *Turner* into a version utilizing not only a *Motor* but also a *Sensor,* or more specifically, a *Sensor* configured for rotational readings. To ease the programming, let's use the *Servo* class, which is precisely suited for this kind of control. The *Servo* combines a *Motor* and a *Sensor* so you can tell the *Motor* to turn to a certain axis point. It is important to notice that, as the servo keeps a number representing the absolute position of the *Motor,* you will need to start the robot with the steering wheel in a neutral position so it is going straight. The change is then to have a maximum turn of two to either side, a value determined from previous experiments. A lot of gearing exists between the rotation sensor and the motor, so that is the easiest way to find it. This solution actually solves the problem in a very simple manner. At least on this test course (in my experiences), the spinning behavior did not occur after the change was made. Prior to that, it was very frequent. In fact, usually two consecutive laps of the course could not be made before the spinning occurred.

Figure 6.12 shows the modified *Turner* code (for simplicity, we have chosen to refrain from my traditional approach where the *Motors* and *Sensors* used are determined in the main class and distributed to the objects using them, as parameters;

instead, this *Turner* version explicitly uses *Sensor.S2*). (You can locate a complete version of the line follower with this modification on the CD, in the /linefollower/ steering1/linefollower directory.)

Figure 6.12 A Limited Turn Turner (Turner.java)

```java
package linefollower;

import josx.platform.rcx.Motor;
import josx.platform.rcx.LCD;
import josx.platform.rcx.Servo;
import josx.platform.rcx.Sensor;

public class Turner extends Thread {

   static final int HYSTERESIS = 4;
   Servo servo;

   public Turner(Motor motor) {
      this.servo = new Servo (Sensor.S2, motor);
   }

   public void run () {
      LineValueHolder lvh = LineValueHolder.getInstance();
      while (true) {
         try {
            int light = lvh.getValue();
            LCD.showNumber (light);
            if (light < lvh.getBlack() + HYSTERESIS) {
               servo.rotateTo (-2);
            } else if (light > lvh.getWhite() - HYSTERESIS) {
               servo.rotateTo (2);
            } else {
               servo.rotateTo(0);
            }
         } catch (InterruptedException ie) {
            //ignore
```

Continued

Figure 6.12 Continued

```
            }
        }
    }


}
```

Getting Back to the Line

The second solution to the same "never-ending turn" problem is a much more advanced approach, involving the control concept called *subsumption architecture*. Also, the solutions tactic is a different one. It does not try to get the robot to avoid passing the line. Instead, it tries to determine when it has done so, and then runs some code in hopes of returning the robot to the left side of the line.

The idea of *subsumption architecture* is to first divide our program into subtasks or behaviors. Each subtask is responsible for controlling one specific behavior of our robot. This behavior can be simple, like backing up when a touch sensor is hit, or it can be complex, like our entire follow-the-line behavior. The next thing we need to do is prioritize the behaviors. The implementation is then made in a way so that only the highest prioritized behavior is actually running, this makes it possible to have multiple behaviors competing for the same resources (motors, sensors, display, and so on) to coexist. It is, of course, crucial that the individual behaviors release their control when they do not need it, to allow lower prioritized behaviors a chance to run.

Designing & Planning...

Line-following Software Design for a Differential Drive-based Robot

Had the robot been built using a differential drive as used in the previous chapter, the steering and driving straight behaviors would have been competing for the control of the motors, since this drive platform uses the same set of wheels for driving and steering. So, in this case, it would make perfect sense to use a subsumption-based architecture for programming the line following in the first place.

If our line-following program had been made using this architecture, the turning behavior would be a higher priority behavior than the drive forward behavior. However, these two behaviors in our example are totally independent of each other, and can therefore coexist without competing for the control of motors.

This example illustrates just one possible situation where this architecture shows its strength. Every time we have multiple behaviors, triggered by different situations (like sensor reading) but in need of the same actuators to perform the needed action, this architecture is a good way to modularize our code and keep it maintainable. Subsumption architectures are usually designed using diagrams like the one shown in Figure 6.13, which indicates that the sensors (*Wheel position* in the diagram) triggers certain behaviors together. The diagram also shows the priority of the different behaviors in that higher priority behaviors are drawn above lower priority ones. The round shape with the S, for *subsume*, shows that the higher priority behavior can take the control of a resource (here *Motors*) away from a lower priority one. This kind of diagram does not say anything about how each individual behavior is to be designed. They can then be made using standard OO techniques. The subsumption architecture can be viewed as a way to make objects cooperate. If you are familiar with design patterns, think of this architectural concept as a pattern.

Figure 6.13 Subsumption Architecture for Our Solution to the Spin Effect Problem

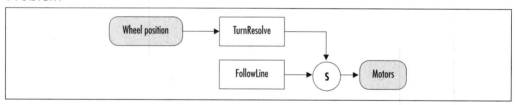

As explained earlier, the diagram is read from top to bottom and left to right, so the highest priority behavior is the new *TurnResolve*, and is somehow triggered by a wheel position. The lowest priority behavior is our existing line-following behavior, which is not triggered by anything but just runs continuously when not subsumed by any higher priority behavior.

To incorporate this into our program, let's use a class that resides in the *josx.robotics* package, named *Arbitrator*. What it does is perform arbitration of prioritized behaviors (just what we need). Let's take a look at the *Arbitrator* and its related *Behavior* interface.

NOTE

In addition to the *Arbitrator* class and *Behavior* interface used in our example of subsumption architecture in use, the *josx.robotics package* contains other classes useful for programming navigating robots. These classes come in two types. The first bases navigation on timing constraints (it takes *n* seconds to turn 90 degrees) and the other bases navigation on readings from rotation sensors. They are provided with a common interface, so you can easily switch between the two implementations.

Arbitrator

The *Arbitrator* class defines only one method, called *start*, which takes no arguments, so starting the arbitration is very easy. Before calling it, you need to construct an *Arbitrator* object, and its constructor takes an array of objects implementing the *Behavior* interface. These objects must be preordered in an array in such a way that the *Behavior* at index 0 corresponds to the desired behavior with the lowest priority, and so forth. Note that the *start* method does not start a separate thread, and thus never returns.

NOTE

In some designs, some behaviors actually have equal priority, which is not a problem as long as they are not competing for the same resources. This situation cannot be handled by the *Arbitrator* class, because its implementation enforces a strict hierarchy of priorities.

Behavior

The *Behavior* interface must be implemented by classes being arbitrated by the *Arbitrator* class. These implementations, in turn, are responsible for implementing the desired behavior for a given priority. The methods you must implement include:

- **public void action ()** This method must implement the task that is to be performed when this *Behavior* is in control. Notice that the method must not go into a never-ending loop, which will cause the arbitration process to no longer work.

- **public boolean takeControl ()** The implementation must return *true* if this Behavior wishes to take control. Whether it will actually take the control, of course, depends on its position in the priority hierarchy.

- **public void suppress ()** Your implementation of this method will stop the current running action (stopping motors and so on). The method should not return until the running action has terminated (but it must return eventually for the arbitration process to work).

Resolving the Never-ending Turn

We will use the same mechanical design as in the previous solution (see the "Restricted Steering" section), a rotation sensor attached to the top of a longer steering wheel axle.

The strategy will be as follows: whenever we, during the line-following process, end up having turned all the way to the right, that must mean we have crossed the line and engaged in that devious death spin. This situation is indicated by the rotation sensor having a value of 5 (experimentally determined). The behavior we will be implementing to escape from the spin is realized in the *TurnResolve* class. It will subsume the line-following behavior when the rotation sensor shows 5, and then do something clever to get it back on the line.

First, we need to turn our existing line-following code into something implementing the *Behavior* interface, so we can add it to an *Arbitrator* object. The change simply wraps the *Turner* and *Cruiser* instances in a class *LineFollowBehavior* (see Figure 6.14) implementing *Behavior*. This is an application of the standard wrapper pattern, known from the GOF book. Additionally, the *Cruiser* and *Turner* have themselves been turned into separate *Behavior* implementations. This way they can perhaps be reused as stand-alone behaviors in another setting. To complete the picture, they can be studied in Figure 6.15 and 6.16 respectively. (The code for Figures 6.14 through 6.16 can be found on the CD in the /linefollower/ steering2/linefollower directory.)

Figure 6.14 Making the Line-following Behavior Implementation (LineFollowBehavior.java)

```
package linefollower;


import josx.robotics.Behavior;


public class LineFollowBehavior implements Behavior
```

Continued

Figure 6.14 Continued

```
{

  Cruiser cruise;
  Turner turner;
  public LineFollowBehavior(Cruiser cruise, Turner turner) {
    this.cruise = cruise;
    this.turner = turner;
    turner.start();
  }

  public void action () {
     cruise.action ();
     turner.action ();
  }

  public boolean takeControl () {
    return true;
  }

  public void suppress () {
    cruise.suppress();
    turner.suppress();
  }
}
```

Figure 6.15 Cruiser as a Behavior Class (Cruiser.java)

```
package linefollower;
import josx.platform.rcx.Motor;
import josx.robotics.Behavior;

public class Cruiser implements Behavior{
  Motor motor;

  public Cruiser(Motor motor) {
```

Continued

Figure 6.15 Continued

```
      this.motor = motor;
  }

  public void action () {
     motor.setPower (7);
     motor.forward();
  }

  public boolean takeControl () {
    return true;
  }

  public void suppress () {
    motor.stop();
  }
}
```

As the main thread is now used to run the Arbitration process, the *LineFollowBehavior* will start the *Turner* instance as a separate thread (see Figure 6.16). This, in turn, will make the *takeControl* and *suppress* methods in *Turner* a little complicated. The idea is that a variable (*halted*) is used to signal if the steering is active. If it isn't, the thread is parked in a *wait* call. The Arbitrator's call to *action* will then wake up this thread again by calling *notifyAll*. Notice that both the *Turner* and *Cruiser* in their implementation of *takeControl* always return true, signaling they are always willing to run.

Figure 6.16 Turner as a Behavior Class (Turner.java)

```
package linefollower;
import josx.platform.rcx.Motor;
import josx.platform.rcx.LCD;
import josx.robotics.Behavior;

public class Turner extends Thread implements Behavior
{
  static final int HYSTERESIS = 4;
  Motor motor;
```

Continued

Figure 6.16 Continued

```
boolean halted = false;

public Turner(Motor motor) {
    this.motor = motor;
}

public synchronized void action () {
  motor.setPower (7);
  halted = false;
  notifyAll();
}

public boolean takeControl () {
    return true;
}

public synchronized void suppress () {
    motor.stop ();
    halted = true;
    notifyAll();
}

public void run () {
  LineValueHolder lvh = LineValueHolder.getInstance();
  while (true) {
    try {
      if (!halted) {
        int light = lvh.getValue();
        LCD.showNumber (light);
        if (!halted) {
          if (light < lvh.getBlack() + HYSTERESIS) {
            motor.forward();
          } else if (light > lvh.getWhite() - HYSTERESIS) {
            motor.backward();
          } else {
```

Continued

Figure 6.16 Continued

```
                motor.stop();
            }
        }
    } else {
        synchronized (this) {
            wait (); //block until notified
        }
    }
} catch (InterruptedException ie) {
        //ignore
    }
}
}
}
```

Second, we must implement our high priority *TurnResolve* behavior. Note that because the behavior is defined by a *Sensor* that does not change value as opposed to one that does change value, we cannot implement this using a *SensorListener* but must explicitly read the *Sensor* value at some interval.

The "clever" thing to do to get back on the line is really not that clever: We first slow down, and straighten up the drive wheel (it's best to actually keep it a little turned, so we curve back towards the line). Then because the line is relatively thin compared to our robot, we should assume that the robot will be spinning on the white surface, and also be on the white surface right after it has straightened out its steering wheel. So we keep driving until we hit a black surface. This should be the right edge of the line (as the robot follows the left edge, it must have passed the line and now be on the right-hand side of the line). We then keep going until we hit white again. At this point, the robot is probably at an angle somewhat perpendicular to the line, so we must turn the steering wheel, and try to curve back until we once again hit black. This should then hopefully be on the desired left side of the line. You can see the implementation of *TurnResolve* realizing this strategy in Figure 6.17 (also found on the CD in the /linefollower/steering2/linefollower directory).

Figure 6.17 Strategy for Finding the Way Back to the Line (TurnResolve.java)

```
package linefollower;

import josx.robotics.Behavior;
import josx.platform.rcx.Motor;
import josx.platform.rcx.Sensor;
import josx.platform.rcx.Sound;
import josx.platform.rcx.Servo;

public class TurnResolve implements Behavior
{
    static final int HYSTERESIS = 4;
    Motor drive;
    Motor turn;
    Sensor rot;

    Servo servo;

    boolean running = false;
    boolean first = true;

    public TurnResolve(Motor drive, Motor turn, Sensor rot)
    {
        this.drive = drive;
        this.turn = turn;
        this.rot = rot;
        servo = new Servo (rot, turn);
    }

    public synchronized void action ()
    {
        if (running) {
            return;
        }
        Sound.beepSequence(); //indicates we have now started finding back
```

Continued

Figure 6.17 Continued

```
running = true;

//curve back towards the line
try {
  turn.setPower (7);
  servo.rotateTo (1); //we will curve slightly towards the line
  synchronized (servo) {
    servo.wait();
  }
  drive.setPower(1);
  drive.forward();

  LineValueHolder lvh = LineValueHolder.getInstance();
  int light = -1;

  //assume we are spinning on white so go "straight" as
  //long as we are still on white
  do {
    light = lvh.getValue();
  } while (light > lvh.getWhite() - HYSTERESIS);

  //we should now be on black. Keep going until we reach white
  //again, and assume we crossed the line from the left side.
  do {
    light = lvh.getValue();
  } while (light < lvh.getBlack() + HYSTERESIS);

  //we should now be back on the left side of the line, so turn to
  //get onto the edge of the line again
  servo.rotateTo (2);
  drive.setPower(3);
  do {
    light = lvh.getValue();
  } while (light > lvh.getWhite() - HYSTERESIS);

  //we now hit the line from the left, so stop driving and
```

Continued

Figure 6.17 Continued

```
     //go straight

  } catch (InterruptedException ie) {
  } finally {
    servo.rotateTo (0);
    try {
      synchronized (servo) {
        servo.wait ();
      }
    } catch (InterruptedException ie) {}
    drive.stop ();
    running = false;
    notifyAll ();
  }
}


/**
 * Control will be taken when the rotation sensor is showing 5.
 **/
public boolean takeControl () {
   if (first) {
     first = false;
     return false;
   }
   if (running) {
     return true;
   } else {
     int current = rot.readValue ();
     if (current >= 5) {
        return true;
     }
     return false;
   }
}
```

Continued

Figure 6.17 Continued

```
/**
 * Called if higher priority behavior wishes to take control.
 **/
public synchronized void suppress () {
  while (running) {
    try {
      wait (200);
    } catch (InterruptedException ie) {
      //ignore
    }
  }
  Sound.systemSound(true, 3);
}


}
```

As mentioned earlier, this is not particularly clever, and to be honest, it only works to some degree (the first solution, with limited turning, works much better). But maybe you can come up with something far superior. The main point of this example has been to introduce you to the subsumption architecture, which is a good way to separate your behavioral logic.

Debugging leJOS Programs

Debugging your RCX programs is not an easy task compared to debugging programs on a workstation. Basically, you have to rely on the visual feedback provided by the LCD, as well as audio feedback from the sound capabilities.

Using Sounds and the LCD

One of my favorite ways to debug leJOS programs is to use the RCX sound capabilities. You can play different sounds when turning right and left, or when some sensor reading is above a particular value. This is really useful, especially in combination with the LCD. By using different sounds before displaying a value on the LCD, you can easily know what the displayed value represents—a low tone might signify a light-sensor reading, or a high tone might alert you to a temperature reading. Just remember that you often need to halt the program momentarily, using, for instance, *Button. VIEW.waitForPressAndRelease()*; otherwise, it will just be a mess of beeping and numbers flashing by in the display.

Exception Handling with leJOS

As you know from normal Java, exception handling is a great way to deal with errors in your programs. The throwing of exceptions in Java for signaling abnormal situations makes it possible to separate the functional logic of the code from the exception handling logic. This is the real benefit: separation of code into code for normal operation and code for error situations.

Normal Java exception handling applies to leJOS. For example, you can do constructs like the following:

```
try {
...
} catch (SomeException e) {
...
} finally {
}
```

And *throws* declarations can be put on method signatures, signaling to the method caller that it needs to handle the exceptions listed. Also, as in standard Java, only checked exceptions need to be handled with *try-catch* blocks, or declared in the *throws* clauses.

Of course, you can throw exceptions yourself, too, with constructs like:

```
throw new InterruptedException();
```

That allocated an object you cannot reclaim. If this code is executed often, you will eventually run out of memory. In these situations, you should allocate the *Exception* in a constructor and throw the same *Exception* instance when needed, like this:

```
public class SomeClass {
    InterruptedException ie = new InterruptedException();

    public void someMethod () throws InterruptedException
    {
        throw ie;
    }
}
```

On my wish-list is a construct like the one in JavaCard, where some exceptions have a static *throwIt(int code)* method declared. This method, when called, will throw a system-owned instance of that exception, which will eliminate pitfalls like the preceding one.

I must add though that in leJOS code, I usually do not throw many exceptions myself.

What about exceptions that are not caught inside your program, and travel all the way up to the leJOS runtime system? They will, of course, terminate your program—and while doing so, they will cause the buzzer to sound and show an exception number in the rightmost figure of the LCD, together with a method signature number in the main part of the display. See the "Using the leJOS Simulator" section for an explanation of how these numbers are to be interpreted.

Testing leJOS Programs

I find that testing leJOS programs can be quite entertaining. You think you have really come up with the perfect design and a really clever implementation and yet the outcome when run in the RCX is that your robot just circles in place, or a grabber opens the wrong way. The techniques using the RCX sound capabilities, mentioned previously are really helpful to determine what is going on. Remember, also, that turning a LEGO motor wire connection 90 degrees will reverse its operation. This often saves you from additional time-consuming downloads.

Before getting angry because the stupid thing misbehaves, remember that it only does as you instruct it! The RCX is a toy. It is supposed to be funny, creative, and, well, great to play with, and I really find that to be the case 100 percent of the time. So, relax and work those bugs out of your program.

Using the leJOS Simulator

Sometimes it is desirable to emulate the leJOS environment on your workstation. This often allows you to trace bugs more easily. The leJOS environment comes with two emulators, emu-lejos and emu-lejosrun, so do this:

```
emu-lejos -o <program-name>.bin <program-name>
emu-lejosrun -v <program-name>.bin
```

The *-v* option makes the emu-lejosrun output a bit more readable. For example, instead of outputting something like: *ROM call 1: 0x1946 (4096)*, it may instead resemble this: *set_sensor_active 0*. If exceptions are thrown, you will receive an output something akin to the following:

```
*** UNCAUGHT EXCEPTION/ERROR:
--   Exception class    : 14
--   Thread             : 1
--   Method signature   : 0
--   Root method sig.   : 0
--   Bytecode offset    : 8
```

Now, to really understand what is going on here you actually need to know which exception is represented as number 14, but this can easily be found if you put a *-verbose* option on the **emu-lejos** command (not the **emu-lejosrun** command); this will produce an output where (among other things) you can read:

```
...
Class 14: java/lang/InterruptedException
...
```

So, what was thrown upon you was an *InterruptedException* error. Now, if this was run on the RCX, the rightmost figure on the LCD would show 4, which is not the correct number (only one figure is used to display the number), illustrating the superior usability of the emulator.

More information is available, like which method threw the exception. Here the root method signature listing indicates the number 0, so you would again consult the verbose output, where you would see the signature numbers after the class numbers:

```
...
Signature 0: main([Ljava/lang/String;)V
...
```

So it was thrown from *main*, and the root method is also *main*. The root method refers to the method calling the guilty one. Finally, if you look at the bytecode, perhaps using the standard **javap** command, the bytecode offset will be 8, and you can thus exactly pinpoint the guilty statement.

If you use constructs like *Button.VIEW.waitForPressAndRelease()* in your program, you of course need to press the **View** button on your workstation. Unfortunately, such a button does not exist. Even worse, the present emulator does not define another button for the job. So, you need to eliminate such statements when running the emulator.

Note that the emulator uses a text-based interface, and it takes time to get the hang of it.

NOTE

On big endian machines like Sparc, you must use lejos instead of emu-lejos for creation of the binary package:

```
lejos -o <program-name>.bin <program-name>
emu-lejosrun -v <program-name>.bin
```

I actually prefer running my code in the RCX using the low-end debugging features described in Chapter 5, but that process might be bettered in the future. Andy Gombos' simulator, Simlink, for instance, contains (among other features) a graphical user interface (it's discussed in Chapter 7).

Summary

We covered a lot of ground in this chapter. The most important message to impose on you is to do good design first and then optimize as needed, although some design decisions have such a huge impact on the final implementation that you should keep in mind the constraints of the destination target while doing the design.

*String*s take up a lot of space, and manipulating them takes even more. This was explained in detail, and hopefully the benefits of creating your own classes in a mutable manner has since activated that little light bulb in your head, considering that most of the problems with *Strings* revolve about them being immutable.

We programmed a robot to follow the left edge of a black line, and tried different ways of making the robot either stay on that left side or find its way back to it should it happen to cross the line. This program was deliberately made in a way that could be optimized and the different optimizations explained.

You have also witnessed the useful robotic design technique named subsumption architecture. It was used to get the line-following robot back to the left side of the line in situations where the robot had crossed it. This architecture is not an alternative but rather a supplement to standard OO design. Its strength is that it allows you to separate your code into different robotic behaviors which can be individually programmed. The OO design on the other hand is more influenced with the internal design of those behaviors.

You have seen that debugging with leJOS on the RCX is tough work. The tools for debugging and testing are limited. Using sound and the LCD are probably the best ways at the moment, but better tools are on the horizon. How to use the leJOS emulator has also been explained, and even though its use is limited, it can sometimes save the day.

So, happy programming with leJOS, and play well.

Solutions Fast Track

Designing Java Programs to Run in leJOS

☑ When designing Java programs for leJOS, use the best OO design principles you know. It will make the final program much more maintainable.

☑ Pay attention to memory constraints even during the design phase. It is quite easy to do a beautiful OO design, which, when implemented, will use unnecessarily large amounts of memory.

An Advanced Programming Example Using leJOS

☑ The line-following type of robot can often become mired in a never-ending spin. Two techniques for avoiding that were presented.

☑ The subsumption architecture can be thought of as a design pattern for robotics programs.

Debugging leJOS Programs

☑ The best way to debug a leJOS program is to use the *Sound* and *LCD* classes in unison to provide you with feedback of the robot's state.

☑ Normal Java exception handling applies to leJOS, allowing you to separate code for normal operation and code for error situations.

Testing leJOS Programs

☑ When working out bugs, use emu-lejos and emu-lejosrun to emulate the leJOS environment on your PC. They use a text-based interface.

☑ When exceptions are output by the emulator, the output can be interpreted much more accurately than when displayed on the real RCX display.

Frequently Asked Questions

The following Frequently Asked Questions, answered by the authors of this book, are designed to both measure your understanding of the concepts presented   in this chapter and to assist you with real-life implementation of these concepts. To have your questions about this chapter answered by the author, browse to **www.syngress.com/solutions** and click on the **"Ask the Author"** form.

Q: I get an *OutOfMemoryException* (indicated by a number 6 displayed on the RCX), but I do not believe I have allocated any memory. What might have caused this?

A: Remember, only the last exception class digit is displayed on the RCX, so it might be exception 16 or 26 that bit you. Another possibility is that even though you do not allocate memory explicitly, you might be doing it implicitly by using *String* arithmetic for instance.

Q: I keep getting *IllegalMonitorStateException*. What is the reason for this?

A: This is standard Java behavior. When you call *wait*, *notify*, or *notifyAll* on an object, you must own that object's monitor (for example, have synchronized access to it).

Q: The *Arbitrator* doesn't seem to function properly. Why is this happening?

A: This is probably a case of either your *suppress* or your *action* method not terminating. They must terminate. If you need continuous running behavior, create your own thread in the *action* method. Remember that you must be able to suspend that thread when the *suppress* method is called by the *Arbitrator*. See Figure 6.16 for an example of this.

Q: I have synchronized a method but it does not seem to work—I get some strange values for the static variables it updates. How can this be?

A: Your method is probably static. leJOS does not allow you to synchronize on static methods, as no instances of *java.lang.Class* are created.

Q: I have a thread instance which has terminated, and am trying to restart it. Why do I get an exception?

A: The exception you get is an *IllegalStateException*. It is defined in Java that threads cannot be restarted. It is thus not a leJOS-specific feature you are observing.

leJOS Tools

Solutions in this chapter:

- **Programming Environments for leJOS**

- **Using the leJOS Visual Interface**

- **Using a leJOS Simulator: Simlink**

- **Additional Tips and Tools for leJOS**

☑ **Summary**

☑ **Solutions Fast Track**

☑ **Frequently Asked Questions**

Introduction

In this chapter we'll explain how to correctly configure and use various leJOS development environments, such as command-line (text) and GUI-based tools. We'll also take a look at the use and configuration of tools for effective leJOS development, such as RCXTools and Simlink.

While your choice of operating system may be different, many examples in this chapter were created with Windows in mind. All tools are either written in Java or provide ports to different platforms, allowing them to run anywhere you would like.

We'll show you some special development tips and tricks to ease you into leJOS development. This chapter serves as a guide for leJOS tools; other chapters cover the actual programs. Custom open-source software makes development easier; and you can create your own projects to help perform a specific task, such as a creating a script to compile and download a supplied robot program.

Programming Environments for leJOS

There are two different types of programming environments for leJOS—command-line-based and GUI-based. Each type has its own advantages and disadvantages in terms of ease-of-use and configurability. A command-line environment enjoys the greatest degree of configurability, as you can access any options that are available in the program, which is not always true of GUI-based environments. With this control, however, comes an ease-of-use penalty. Scripts can simplify the use of tools in a command-line environment, and are discussed at the end of the chapter.

GUI-based tools have the main advantage of being easy to use. However, depending on the interface used, control options can be sacrificed. For example, when integrating leJOS and *lejosc* (the command-line compiler) into an integrated development environment (IDE), you can lose some control over options such as output file type.

An IDE is typically designed to speed productivity and be easier to use than a command-line interface. Therefore, some time must be spent correctly configuring the IDE. Most command-line switches can be used, but the window disappears before you can gain any useful information. Again, to use options that are only easily available from the command line, it is better to *use* the command line. Dumping the verbose *lejos* output into a file for deciphering the displayed exceptions is easier than forcing an IDE to pipe in all of the program's output. This limitation can seem like a penalty for using a GUI-based tool over the command line.

In the following sections we'll take a close look at both types of environments. After reading about the characteristics of each, and the options they provide, you will be better able to make a decision on which style is more suited to you.

The next section will describe how to effectively use the command line in a leJOS environment. The sections "Existing IDEs" and "Using a Visual IDE for leJOS" describe how to set up and use a GUI-based tool with leJOS. In those sections, you will be able to more clearly see how a IDE limits advanced usage.

The Command-Line Tools that Interact with the RCX

The command-line tools that come with leJOS are the core of all GUI-based tools used to download and control LEGO MINDSTORMS robots. These command-line tools, along with Kekoa Proudfoot's *send.c* tool, can be used to download firmware, programs, and data to the RCX. Integrated into a development environment, programs can be compiled, tested, and downloaded with just a few mouse clicks.

Several tools are included in the leJOS package. These utilities, ranging from a compiler (*lejosc*), to a text debugger (*emu-lejos*), provide all the functionality you should need. These tools are:

- *lejosc*
- *lejos*
- *lejosrun*
- *lejosfirmdl*
- *emu-lejos*
- *emu-lejosrun*

We'll go over how to use each tool's options, and how to handle any possible problems you may encounter.

Using the *lejosc* Compiler

Lejosc is the command-line compiler for leJOS. It automates setting the correct classpath to compile the specified program. You should always use *lejosc* instead of *javac* to compile leJOS programs, letting *lejosc* configure the environment. This way, you are assured of compiling your leJOS programs so they run on the RCX. The *lejosc* command-line listing shown in Figure 7.1 shows the correct usage.

Figure 7.1 *lejosc* Usage

```
lejosc [Java file to be compiled]
```

Using *javac*, shown in Figure 7.2, bypassing *lejosc*, can also make compiling statements much longer.

Some of the necessary environment variables (such as *LEJOSHOME*) are determined automatically by *lejosc* for you. Others, like *CLASSPATH*, must be set by hand in order for *javac* to find the correct leJOS classes. There is no current way for *lejosc* to detect where the utility classes such as *Sensor* and *Motor* are located.

Figure 7.2 Compiling a leJOS Program Using *javac* on Windows

```
cd C:\lejos\examples\hworld
javac -classpath C:\lejos\classes\;. HelloWorld.java
```

As you can see, using *javac* is longer and more error-prone than using the supplied *lejosc* executable. A slight typo in the command can cause the compilation to fail. Also, the class file would be compiled in the incorrect endian byte order: the RCX's microprocessor uses big-endian order, while x86 architectures use little-endian order. These classes would not work on the RCX, assuming you even got them to download correctly.

Using the *lejos* Linker

lejos is the linker for leJOS that takes a compiled leJOS program using *lejosc* and translates it into a format that the underlying leJOS firmware can interpret. *lejos* can also download a program automatically into the RCX after it has been properly linked. The command-line listing for *lejos* is shown in Figure 7.3.

Figure 7.3 *lejos* Usage

```
lejos [options] class1, [class2 ...] [arg1, arg2 ...]
```

There are two options that can be specified with *lejos*. One is the *-o <path>* option, the other is the *-verbose* option. The *-o <path>* option is used to output a linked file into the specified path. This linked class file can then be downloaded with *lejosrun* (described in the next section). Using the *-o* option will not download the class to the RCX.

The *-verbose* option can be used to print out the method signatures used. It is a record of all native methods and JVM calls that are made in the produced linked file.

All *lejosrun* options are available under *lejos*, but are not listed in the usage listing. This listing is shown by typing **lejos** at the command line.

Using the lejosrun *Linker*

lejosrun can also be used to download the linked files generated by *lejos*. *lejosrun* provides the same downloading functions as *lejos* does, but it does not complete the linking step. The *lejosrun* usage listing is shown in Figure 7.4.

Figure 7.4 *lejosrun* Usage

```
lejosrun [options] filename
where options are:
--debug          Print out the raw bytes sent to the tower
-f,              fast  Use faster 4x downloading speed
-s,              slow Use slower 1x downloading speed (default setting)
--tty=TTY        TTY Tower connected to port TTY, e.g. COM1 or
                     /dev/ttyS1
--tty=usb        Tower is connected to a USB port - used with
                     the new 2.0 towers
-h,              help Display command line usage and options, then exit
```

The *--debug* option is not extremely useful unless you are trying to debug a connection error, such as a bad echo from the tower. Even then, these messages are usually printed out in text by *lejosrun* itself.

The *-fast* and *--fast* options can download programs at four times the normal rate. However, these modes are much more sensitive to light and other disturbances in the environment, which can make them problematic to use.

The *-s* and *--slow* options are the default settings, and download programs at the normal speed. This setting is much easier to setup correctly, and is much more flexible and insensitive to environmental conditions like light and the distance between the tower and the RCX.

To use a serial port with *lejosrun*, you must specify it either as an environment variable (RCXTTY), or on the command line using *--tty=TTY*, where TTY is the communications port to which you have connected the tower. These can be Windows-style ports such as COM1 or COM2, or UNIX-style designations such as /dev/ttyS0 or /dev/ttyS1.

The latest leJOS release has added Windows USB support, making it possible to use the new Robotics Invention System (RIS) version 2.0 USB tower. To enable USB support, use the *--tty=usb* option. RCXTTY can also be set to "USB," which will enable USB support. If you enable USB support, you will not have to set the serial port. This option is not yet available on Linux, though a Linux Lego USB driver is currently under development (see http://legousb.sourceforge.net).

The *-h* and *--help* options display the command-line arguments that *lejosrun* accepts. These arguments are the same as the ones we have listed here, but the explanations are less detailed in the command-line output.

Using the *lejosfirmdl* Downloader

lejosfirmdl is the customized firmware downloader for leJOS. It is based on Kekoa Proudfoot's *firmdl.c* tool, but modified to accept the longer line lengths contained by the leJOS firmware file. *Lejosfirmdl* has the same options as *lejosrun*, with one exception: the *-n* and *—nodl* options allow you to not download the firmware image, but rather check to see if the firmware file is found and the serial or USB port is configured correctly.

Figure 7.5 shows a complete development cycle from the command line. First, the PATH is set to point to the leJOS bin directory where the command line programs are stored, then RCXTTY is set to the correct communications port, which in this case is COM1. The directory is changed to an example directory supplied with the leJOS distribution. Before a program is downloaded, the firmware must be downloaded with *lejosfirmdl*, here using no special options. The example file (*HelloWorld.java*) is compiled with *lejosc*, then downloaded to the RCX, again using the default options.

Figure 7.5 An Example Session of leJOS Command Line Downloads on Windows

```
set PATH=C:\lejos\bin\;%PATH%
set RCXTTY=COM1
cd C:\lejos\examples\hworld
lejosfirmdl
lejosc HelloWorld.java
lejos HelloWorld
```

The Command-line leJOS Emulator

The provided *lejos* emulator, *emu-lejos*, is non-graphical and limited in its usefulness. One of its main advantages, however, is the ability to receive more detailed exception and trace information than that which is available on the RCX itself. Instead of deciphering a numeric exception code on the RCX's LCD screen, you get a text message that describes the exception that was thrown.

In addition to providing exception information, using the *--verbose* option tells you what commands were called, translating the ROM's hex calls into text.

Using the *emu-lejos* Emulator

Emu-lejos is the emulation equivalent of *lejos*. It accepts the same command-line options, but must be used with the *-o* option to emulate. Using *lejos -o* will result in a linked file that *emu-lejosrun* will not accept. Using *emu-lejos* changes the magic number of the linked file, identifying it as an emulation link, and allows hex ROM codes to be translated into text. It also links the file into little endian byte order instead of the big endian order used by the RCX.

If you are running leJOS on a SparcStation or another big endian byte order architecture, you will need to use *lejos* instead of *emu-lejos* to link, since *emu-lejos* orders for a little endian byte order.

Using the *emu-lejosrun* Linker

Emu-lejosrun is the emulation version of *lejosrun*. However, it does not accept all of *lejosrun*'s options, supporting only the *--v* option to translate the hex commands. *Emu-lejosrun* only accepts *emu-lejos*-linked files.

Using Exisiting IDEs

To use an existing IDE with leJOS, you need to know how to set it up. Although commercial IDEs are available, we'll explain how to set up the free Forte IDE for Java.

Other free Java IDEs, such as Borland's JBuilder Personal Edition and IBM's Eclipse do not provide the ability to change every aspect of the Java Development Kit (JDK) configuration. Therefore, they cannot easily be used with a non-standard JDK such as leJOS, and especially one with an incomplete set of classes. Due to these apparent limitations of the other free IDEs, this section will only discuss the Forte IDE.

Forte for Java (available at www.sun.com/forte/ffj), is an IDE written completely in Java. While this may cause the interface to be slightly less responsive than a native interface, only a slight lag should be noticeable. Like JBuilder, Forte provides a visual GUI creator, a debugger, and compilation functions—all the expected parts of an IDE. Forte also has the seemingly unique ability to configure the compiler and Java runtime you use. Neither JBuilder nor Eclipse provide this ability.

This section assumes that you have a basic knowledge of your IDE and can already perform tasks such as creating a new project or editing a new file. It only covers how to change the paths so *lejosc* is started for *javac*, and *lejos* is started for *java*.

Configuring Forte

This section is written using the interface from Forte for Java Community Edition, version 3.0. However, the basic process should be the same on any version since 1.0, although the menu item names may have changed.

Unfortunately, compiler settings cannot be set across the entire IDE. They must be set for each individual project. Create a new project, then go into the project settings through **Project | Settings**. This dialog (shown in Figure 7.6) has a tree node named **Compiler Types**. Click on it, and you will see a tree leaf called **External Compilation**. In Figure 7.6, this leaf is highlighted.

Figure 7.6 Forte Options Dialog

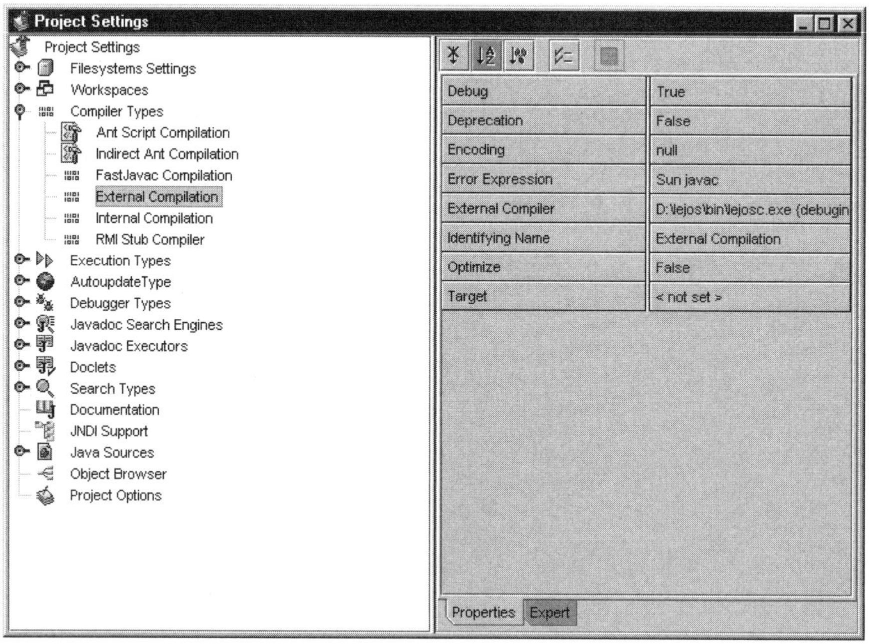

The field *External Compiler* is where the compiler setting is changed. Change this field to *leJOS_Home\bin\lejosc*, where *leJOS_Home* is your home directory for leJOS. Change the arguments setting simply to *{files}*, so the current project's files will be compiled with *lejosc*.

Now that the compiler type is set up, we can work on setting *lejos* as *java*. To do this, click on the *Execution Types* node in the tree. As before, edit the *External Execution* field, setting the path containing *lejos*. Because any automatically-generated path would include the incorrect base classes, you must specify the exact leJOS classpath. In the **Arguments** text field, you must add **–cp leJOS_Home/classes {classname}**. This will ensure that only leJOS classes are found when linking occurs.

Compile and run (download) a program to the RCX and see if it works. If not, verify all that all of your paths are correct.

Using the leJOS Visual Interface

There are many Java IDEs that can be set up for use with leJOS. Some, such as the free professional IDEs described above, can be setup to automatically compile and run leJOS programs. Others, which are classified as powerful text editors like Jtext and jEdit, can be configured to work with leJOS without the large overhead and startup times of most IDEs. This section is not a thorough description of the available IDEs, but more of a brief overview.

Custom IDEs and IDE components, such as the leJOS Visual Interface and RCXDownload, can be used in place of a more complicated and powerful IDE. These programs provide functions that are specifically tailored to leJOS and are a great substitute for any other tool.

The leJOS Visual Interface

The leJOS Visual Interface (lVI) is a custom IDE that is specially authored and configured by Andy Gombos for use with leJOS. The options in the **Tools** menu allow you to automatically compile, link, and download programs; as well as download firmware. After setting the necessary environment variables and settings, you can create, edit, compile, and link a file in a few simple steps. In the words of Jonathan Knudsen, "Essentially, it's a pint-sized editor for leJOS."

The main window (See Figure 7.7) contains the menu bar and an internal window that holds the current code. The instances of this coding window support automatic indention and syntax colorization, but the current implementation has some problems, which are discussed on the CD.

The menu bar provides access to standard functions such as saving and loading, as well as the leJOS-specific commands and configuration commands.

Figure 7.7 The Main leJOS Visual Interface Window

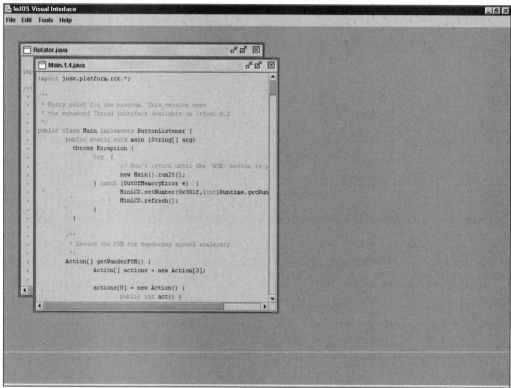

Installing lVI

Installation of lVI can be slightly tricky. To create the preferences directory that lVI uses for storage, and to copy over the default options for their first use, run *java install* from the command line. As of release 1.2.0, the *install* class outputs the directory that was created and used for the options directory. You can then just copy the outputted directory to transfer your settings to another computer with lVI installed.

Due to the installation procedure, some problems can arise when installing lVI. It seems that if lVI is installed once, attempting to install it again overwrites the old directory and preferences and gives the error message "Error creating .lvi directory". As of release 1.2.0, use the *java install -d* option. This deletes the current preferences, then copies over the new files. As long as there are no changes listed in the preferences format, simply starting a new lVI version should work fine.

Setting Up lVI

Setting up lVI is as simple as setting the preferences. The *Interface Preferences* dialog (See Figure 7.8) has multiple tabs that divide the preferences into categories, each of which deals with a particular setting.

Figure 7.8 The First Tab of the Interface Preferences Dialog

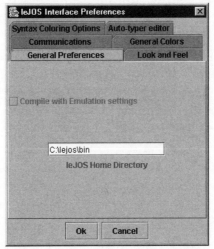

The dialog allows you to set all the required paths and settings to enable all of lVI's built-in functions. The dialog also allows you to set syntax colorization preferences, automatic completion sequences, and global editor settings.

On the first tab, **General Preferences** (shown in Figure 7.8), you must set the directory into which leJOS is installed. If this path is incorrect, lVI will be unable to locate the command-line programs used by leJOS to compile, link and download (such as *lejosc*). The emulation settings box is left disabled for now, but it may be enabled at a later date.

In the **Look and Feel** tab, you can select the Java *Look and Feel* (L&F) you want to use. The Java L&F is the default, cross-platform look and feel. The Motif L&F is a UNIX-style Look and Feel, and is the default for the native window manager under that platform. Due to licensing issues, the Windows L&F is only available on Windows platforms.

The **Communications** tab allows you to set the serial port used by the tower or enable USB support. USB support is only as good as the current leJOS release, since lVI uses the leJOS tools.

By accessing the **General Colors** tab, you can change the background color of the lVI window, the text area background color, the default non-colorized text color, and several other colors. The only color change that works reliably is the background text area change, due to the fact that Sun Microsystems's JavaKit colorization package changes the text area and default text colors.

The **Syntax Coloring Options** tab will allow you to change the colors that the JavaKit package uses to colorize the code. Currently, most colors do not affect anything when changed. The Readme file on the CD describes this in more detail.

From the **Auto-typer editor** tab (See Figure 7.9), you can set what words or phrases will signify a longer section of code, such as *main* signifying *public static void main (String args []) { }*.

Figure 7.9 The Auto-typer Managing Window

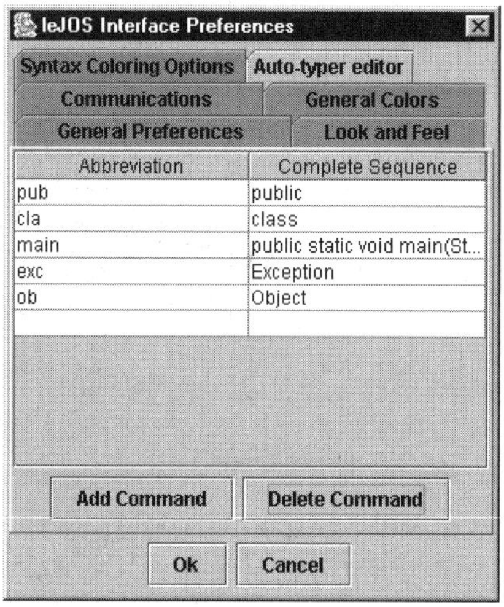

To add a new command, click the **Add Command** button. This button opens up the **Add an Abbreviation** editor window, where you can define the new abbreviation. (See Figure 7.10)

The **Command Abbreviation** text field is where the shortened version of the new command goes. The current window is set up for the *main* example above. As soon as *main* is typed in, then the full replacement is inserted in the **Full Command** area.

To delete a command that has been entered incorrectly or entered twice, you can use the **Delete Command** button. Unfortunately, there is currently no **Edit** button. If you enter an abbreviation a second time without deleting the old sequence, then the oldest (first) abbreviation to appear in the manager window's list will be the one executed, not the last one as you might expect.

Figure 7.10 Adding a New Abbreviation

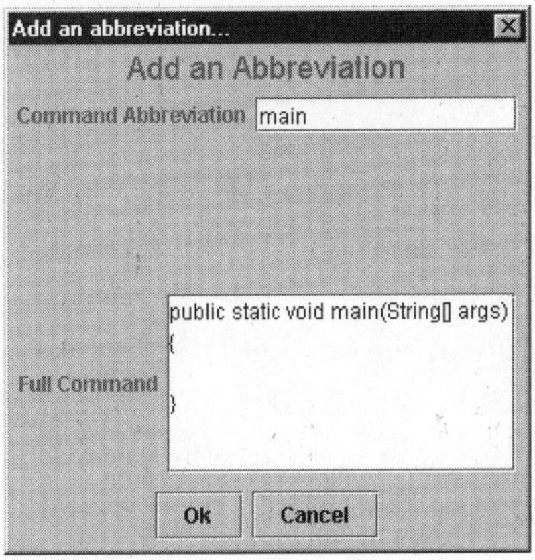

![Add an Abbreviation dialog]

Basic Usage

To test out lVI's functions, it is best to start with a good example. Go to your leJOS directory and load the HelloWorld example (leJOS_Home/examples/hworld/HelloWorld.java). To compile this example, make sure the text area containing the HelloWorld example is selected, and click **Tools | Compile**. If you get a dialog box that looks like Figure 7.11, check the red highlighted area. If this area is incorrect, then that means you have wrongly entered your leJOS home path in the preferences. For example, in this example, I put my home directory as C:\lejos\bin. This causes lVI to look for *lejosc* in C:\lejos\bin\bin, which obviously is not the correct path.

Figure 7.11 A Path Generated Error

If there are errors when you compile your program, then you can look in the *javac* dialog box to see what errors occurred. In a future release (possibly 1.3), the output will be piped into a dialog so you can scroll through the errors.

The next step is to download the firmware, if you haven't already done this. This can be done via **Tools | Download Firmware**. Again, if there are any errors, they will show up in the dialog box in which the process is running.

The last step is to download the compiled class to the RCX. The lVI interface combines the linking and downloading steps together, so there is no need to do an extra step. If there are errors related to the download itself, then you will need to troubleshoot your connection, discussed later.

If you have successfully done these steps, then you are ready to see if it correctly runs on the RCX. Hit the **Run** button. If "Hello World" scrolls across the LCD, it is working correctly. If not, try compiling and linking again, making sure the firmware is correctly installed.

From the last page, you can see that all lVI does is create the correct paths and environment settings, then call the default leJOS tools; *lejosc, lejos,* and *lejos-firmdl.* This just shows that for each new tool created for use with leJOS, the command-line portions are the base of the functionality for that tool.

Using a leJOS Simulator: Simlink

The Simlink leJOS simulator, also authored by Andy Gombos, is a linking set of classes and interfaces for the Rossum Project and leJOS. *Rossum's Playhouse* (the release name of The Rossum Project's efforts) is a two-dimensional robotic simulator generalized for use to all roboticists, whether they construct with LEGO bricks or carbon fiber beams. LeJOS is specifically targeted to the LEGO MINDSTORMS RCX using the H8/3297 chip from Hitachi. There obviously needs to be an interface of some sort between Rossum's Playhouse and the low-level APIs leJOS provides, and that is exactly what Simlink is designed to do.

At the most basic level, Simlink is just an abstraction layer between the two APIs, facilitating communications between them. To create the layer, some leJOS classes were completely changed to provide the correct interface while still offering the same public methods. This means very little modification will be required for your robot code, while major modification will have to be done to the leJOS classes when a new class release comes out.

Getting Started with Simlink

The main Simlink window (see Figure 7.12) consists of a managing pane on the left side and a visual RCX model on the right. The managing pane displays which robot is currently being simulated, all exceptions that have been caught, and whether or not the simulation is being saved for later playback. The exception list shows all non-fatal exceptions that have been thrown. The exceptions will be listed, but the simulation will end.

Figure 7.12 The Main Simlink Window

www.syngress.com

Debugging...

Using Simlink to Debug Programs

Using Simlink to debug programs can be tricky, since there is no indication to tell which line of code is currently executing. In future versions, a Java Platform Debugger Architecture (JPDA) interface will be implemented, allowing a trace of lines to be output. In its current form, however, Simlink is mainly useful for altering robot motions, checking line following or other algorithms, and navigation techniques.

Programs can also be debugged in the normal manner by displaying a value on the LCD that coincides with a snippet of code. This method is useful, since a message that is sent to the LCD also triggers a log message. Evaluation of the log can reveal many details about the program's execution, including motor activation, sensor readings, and IR communications requests.

You can also log events on the real robot, then compare that log to the Simlink log, to gauge simulation accuracy for example. Simlink's logging and, later, debugging features make it a valuable tool for debugging the embedded RCX system.

The right side of the window is a rendered diagram of the RCX. The sensor and motor ports change from gray and black to red when they are read or activated, respectively. This shows if sensors are being read when they are supposed to be, or when a motor is being turned on; to aid in debugging. The model also contains Tim Rinken's *TextLCD* class, which acts as a virtual LCD to print messages and numbers when specified. The four buttons on the rendered image correspond to the actual buttons on the RCX. These buttons are attached to any listeners that a robot program may create, and send an event when pressed. This allows the simulation to be controlled just as in real life. When serial IR communications are implemented, the IR window above the sensor pads will also change to red when active to show communications between the RCX and the IR tower.

In this section, we will work through installation, configuration, and running your first simulation. Each step will be described in detail, aiding in the simulation process.

Installing and Configuring Simlink

Installing Simlink is much less complex than installing lVI. A graphical installer will guide you through installation, and set up the simulation environment. The *Rossum Playhouse* (which is available at http://rossum.sourceforge.net), must be downloaded and uncompressed to a temporary directory. The installer will ask you for this directory later, so as to copy over the needed files. LeJOS must also be uncompressed to a temporary directory, but the standard installation will work fine.

To set up the simulator for the first time, start the setup with *java install*. The installer will request your current leJOS and Rossum directories, and where you would like the new, modified directories to be placed. The default leJOS package will be copied into the correct directory, then the modified classes will be copied over the old versions. This ensures that no class is left out by the current release of Simlink, nor will any extra helper classes be incorrectly copied. Now you are ready to configure Simlink.

1. Start Simlink with *java simInterface.Main* in the directory to which you told the installer to install Simlink. The installer program will automatically set the correct leJOS, Rossum, and Simlink paths for you.

2. However, you will still get a dialog box saying you have not yet configured Simlink due to the fact that default preferences have not been set yet. Click **OK**.

3. Enter the **Configure Global Options** dialog in the **Tools** menu (See Figure 7.13). In this dialog, the paths for your Rossum and leJOS classes can be changed, as well as aspects such as simulation speed and logging preferences.

Figure 7.13 Simlink Options Dialog

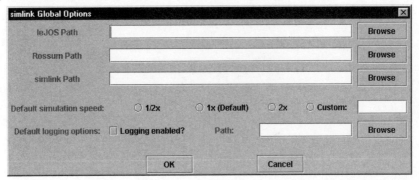

4. By default, the simulation speed is 1x (real time), and logging is turned off. The custom simulation speed takes a floating point number, such as 3.0, 4.6, or 0.25, and uses that as the speed at which to run. Think of it as a scaling factor—2.0 would cause the simulation to run twice as fast as normal, while 0.5 would cause it to run half as fast. Logging will start out with a few things logged such as sensor state changes and motor activation, but should get more complete over time.

Running Your First Simulation

Now you are set to run your first simulation. Complete the following steps.

1. To set up a robot simulation run, go to the **File | Configure New Run** menu item (see Figure 7.14). In this dialog, you can set the path where your robot's classes are saved, as well as a specific run's logging options and simulation speed. You must also set the body layout class for the robot and the floor plan to be used. These will both be discussed in detail later on. If the logging and speed arguments are not supplied, then the defaults from the Global Options dialog will be used. The robot class path must be specified, since it will be changed for each new simulation. Along with the path for the classes, the main class itself must be input so that Simlink knows the class with which to begin the simulation control.

Figure 7.14 Dialog to Create a New Simulator Run

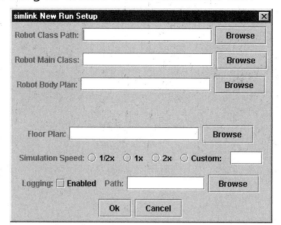

2. As an example, suppose the HelloWorld.java example from the leJOS distribution has been compiled with *lejosc* and placed in the directory C:\simlink\robots\. In this directory, the ClientZero.java file from the Rossum distribution has also been compiled and placed in the directory. The floor plan, WhiteRoom.txt, also from the Rossum distribution, can be copied.

3. To run this simulation, set the classpath to C:\simlink\robots, the robot class to *HelloWorld.class*, and leave the simulation speed and logging at the defaults you set earlier. If this is an early release, they may not be enabled yet anyway. Then set the body plan to the class copied earlier (*ClientZero.class*), and the floor plan to WhiteRoom.txt.

4. Now you are ready to begin the simulation. Go to the **Tools** menu and select **Run simulation**. All this example will do is print "Hello World" to the model RCX's LCD screen.

5. If this works, then you have correctly set up and configured the simulator. If not, run through the steps again, making sure you are inputting the correct values for each step.

Designing a Floor Plan for Simlink

Rossum floor plans have a special syntax and format all their own, essentially making them a "floor plan scripting language." This language is automatically parsed by the Rossum simulator, and has a few simple keywords, or declarations.

Note that a specification is defined in the Rossum User's Guide to be a one-line statement, while a declaration is more than one line, enclosed in braces. We are going to follow this style here, to better interface with the User's Guide.

NOTE

The version of Rossum available for download at the time of this writing is version .49. This section describes the features found in Rossum version .50, which at the time of this writing was still a pre-release version. Obstacles, for example, are an addition found in version .50.

Declarations and specifications in the floor plan format:

- units
- caption
- wall
- obstacle
- target
- placement
- paint
- node
- link

When we describe the format of the different declarations, we will use several common terms that can be used to specify different options. These terms are:

- *fillColor* If a filled polygon is used as the shape, this specifies the inside color.
- *lineColor* This is the color of the line surrounding the declaration's geometry.
- *color* This is a combination of the fillColor and lineColor specifications; it sets the same color for both.
- *label* This labels the current declaration that will be shown on the simulator GUI, as an identifying mark.

These terms can be used simply by adding them into the declaration before the closing brace. This will all make sense for each of the keywords.

Non-visual Declarations

The *units* specification indicates the unit you want Rossum to use when interpreting your floor plan (see Figure 7.15). Obviously, if you wanted a wall 13 feet long, but the unit was in centimeters, you would end up with an unexpected result..

Figure 7.15 Specification of Units

```
units: meters, centimeters, feet, or inches;
```

Depending on what unit you want to use to specify measurements, you can select meters, centimeters, feet, or inches. You can have as many *units* specifications as you want, so it's possible to declare the walls in meters, then the target radius in centimeters.

The declaration caption sets the title of the window Rossum opens as the GUI for the floor plan (See Figure 7.16). This caption can describe the loaded floor plan or any other data you wish to be placed in the title area.

Figure 7.16 Specification of Caption

```
caption: "Title bar text";
```

Visual Declarations

The first visual declaration is *wall*, or a solid barrier that causes sensor events to be fired and prevents target "light" from passing through (see Figure 7.17). It is just like a wall of your house: solid and immovable.

Figure 7.17 Declaration of Wall

```
wall a {
    geometry: x1, y1, x2, y2, thickness;
    [fillColor: color];
    [lineColor: color];
    [color: color];
    [label: text];

}
```

Let's go through this one a section at a time.

```
wall a {
```

This statement says that a new wall, called "a", will be specified here.

```
geometry: x1, y1, x2, y2, thickness;
```

Here we say that the wall will start at the coordinates (x1, y1) and end at the coordinates (x2, y2). It will also be a filled box with a width of a certain number of units. The default Rossum unit is the meter, but can be changed with the *units* specification as discussed earlier. Using the default meter, a statement of:

```
geometry: 0, 0, 0, 2, .01;
```

will create a wall two meters long with a thickness of one hundredth of a meter, or a centimeter. Because walls are specified with four coordinates and a thickness, they must form straight lines.

```
[fillColor: color];
[lineColor: color];
[color: color];
[label: text];
```

The parts of the declaration that are enclosed in square brackets are optional. As discussed above, these options set the color of the specific parts, blue or green, for example. The *label* argument is simply the text you want displayed, enclosed in double quotation marks (" ").

Each visual declaration must have a set of opening and closing braces before and after the arguments, just as in a Java method or class.

The next declaration, *obstacle*, is new to Rossum version .50 (See Figure 7.18). It defines a wall that can accept more geometry arguments (to create a octagonal object for example). It is essentially a wall with more geometry coordinates allowed, as it blocks target influence and causes sensor events. There is one restriction with the geometry arguments: *Every shape created must be a polygon that does not intersect itself.*

Figure 7.18 Declaration of Obstacle

```
obstacle box {
    geometry: x1, y1, x2, y2, xn, yn;
    [offset: x1, y1;]
    [orientation: degrees;]

}
```

Instead of using the geometry statement, Rossum provides a polygon statement that creates a round; *n*-sided shape for you, with the specified number of sides and radius.

```
polygon: numberOfSides, radius;
```

Besides walls, any shape created with a geometry or polygon statement can be supplied an offset and a rotation. If a polygon was created with 4 sides and a radius of 1.0, then an offset of (1.0, 1.0) would put the polygon at (1.0, 1.0), and it would be drawn from that point. An orientation statement allows you to rotate the shape a specified number of degrees, to make a flat square into a rhombus, or a turn a chair model so it faces the room instead of the wall. The offset and orientation statements handle rotation and translation for you, so you can create an object at (0,0), then move it to the correct spot more easily.

Targets are 2 dimensional point sources of "light," modeling objects like candle flames and flashlights (See Figure 7.19). A flashlight can be modeled by placing two walls at angles to the target, creating an area that, while it cannot be passed through, can block the target's influence, creating a virtual cone of light.

Figure 7.19 Declaration of Target

```
target Goal {
    geometry: x1, y1, radius;
    [fillColor: color;]
    [lineColor: color;]
    [color: color;]
    [label: text;]
}
```

The (x1, y1) *geometry* argument is the center of the target, and the radius creates a circle around the target for human reference only. The actual detection range is controlled by *RsBodyTargetSensor*, which is discussed later.

Placements are declarations where Rossum places the robot at the beginning of the simulation (See Figure 7.20). In the current Simlink version, this cannot be specified, and is called "home" by default. Later versions will take advantage of a new .50 feature, random placements. This method, when enabled, will cause the Rossum simulator to place the robot at a random defined location. Every random spot must still have a placement, but any placement available can be chosen.

Figure 7.20 Declaration of Placement

```
placement Home {
     geometry: x1, x2, r botOrientation, radius;
     [fillColor: color;]
     [lineColor: color;]
     [color: color;]
     [label: text;]
}
```

The geometry coordinate (x1, y1) is the position of the robot's center (pivot point) when placed at that placement. The *robotOrientation* is the number of degrees the robot is to be turned from 0°, which is a straight line to the right. The radius is the approximate radius used when Rossum draws the "home plate" icon, signifying a placement position.

To use a line-following robot, you must use the floor paint feature or line elements (See Figure 7.21). These lines have selectable colors and regions, which allow them to be differentiated between by humans and the robot, respectively. These lines must be detected by a *RsBodyPaintSensor*, as it is the only sensor that looks down.

Figure 7.21 Declaration of Floor Paint

```
paint blackLine {
     geometry: x1, y1, x2, y2, xn, yn;
     color: color;
     region: region;
}
```

Floor paint geometry is described with a set of coordinates much like the ones used in specifying obstacles. A given geometry statement can span multiple lines, by putting each coordinate pair on a separate line, ending with a comma. The last line will instead have a semicolon, like this.

```
paint longLine {
     geometry: 0, 0,
               1, 1,
               2, 2;
}
```

See how the geometry line has been extended over multiple lines, each with their own comma, and ending with a final semicolon? You can do this for any geometry statement, whether to make it more readable, organized, or any other reason you see fit.

Navigational Declarations

The two navigational declarations, *node* and *link*, provide a way to create a virtual system of roadways that a robot can use to navigate—useful for maze robots, path finding robots, or any other problem that requires a preset path to work. You might want to spend some time optimizing the path-finding algorithm rather than facing errors from the path detection section. This will also help improve the theoretical performance, while further acting as permanent "floor paint."

The *node* declaration specifies a point in the floor plan that will form an endpoint of a segment or segments that define the navigational network (See Figure 7.22). These nodes can form endpoints, corners, loops, and other paths possible with floor paint.

Figure 7.22 Declaration of a Node

```
node start {
    geometry: x1, y1;
    [label: text;]
}
```

For nodes and links, the *lineColor* and *fillColor* statements have no effect, although they are allowed in the code. Every node or link is drawn in a light cyan color. The label is for human reference only, and can be used for node identification.

Links are the actual roads between node markers (see Figure 7.23). These links form the lines a robot can follow as it makes its way across a floor plan, just as highways and intersections form real roadways.

Figure 7.23 Declaration of Link

```
link startLink {
    nodes: node1, node2;
}
```

Links can only connect to one node, but one node can connect to multiple links. Links do not support *lineColor* or *fillColor* labels , but as with *node*, they do not reject their inclusion.

While the system of nodes and links is not currently implemented in Simlink, you could implement it in your custom robot code. There is no comparable functionality for leJOS as the floor paint feature is designed for the purpose. Since using this network could be classified as "cheating," it will most likely remain unimplemented. Use floor paint for a navigational gridwork or guide.

NOTE

Andy Gombos hopes to develop a floor plan generator to make this design process easier. You will have selectable components, which you can then use to draw a floor plan out graphically, with no measurement required. Look for this and other tools in a future Simlink release.

Creating a New Simlink Robot Body

Robot bodies in Simlink are represented as Java classes, with Rossum classes allowing you to create simple designs. Currently, only a differential system (where a motor drives each wheel independently) is available. This system is also limited to two wheels, so your mobility options are limited. Therefore, the main reason to currently create a new robot body is for correct sensor positioning and correct wheel modeling. There are several important classes used to create a new robot model.

Physical RsBody derived classes include:

- *RsBodyArt*
- *RsBodyShape*
- *RsWheelSystem*

Physical sensor representations include:

- *RsBodyContactSensor*
- *RsBodyTargetSensor*
- *RsBodyRangeSensor*
- *RsBodyPaintSensor*

These classes allow you to create a working, interactive, visual model to use in simulations. The base class is *RsBody*. *RsBody* is a container class for all the other body elements and serves as an easy way to represent a given design in the Simlink and Rossum worlds. The only method in *RsBody* that is important in creating a robot design is *addPart(RsBodyPart part)*, which registers a new design piece to be drawn.

Creating a body is much like creating the same body with LEGO bricks. Each section, whether it be the chassis, a moveable arm, or a sensor, is created from the same beams and plates as a truck or a city. The Rossum classes all derive from *RsBody*, and those base classes—*RsBodyArt*, *RsBodyShape*, and *RsWheelSystem*—form the beams and plates of the Rossum world.

Creating a Body: Passive Components

The first classes we will cover are the base classes, or the classes related to the main body of the robot, listed previously as derived from *RsBody* in the table.

The *RsBodyArt* class provides a way to represent lines, numbers, letters, and shapes as drawings on the robot body. These representations do not interact with the environment, however; they are strictly for accurate identification or representation, much like a sign or label. The constructor for *RsBodyArt*, shown in Figure 7.24, requires a list of points, and the number of points in the list. In this aspect, it is similar to a geometry statement for a floor plan.

Figure 7.24 RsBodyArt Constructor

```
RsBodyArt (double[] pointList, int nPointList)
```

The point list is specified as a series of (x,y) coordinates, listed in *x1, y1, x2, y2,...* format, with one coordinate occupying one array element. The *nPointList* argument is half the total length of the array, or the number of complete (x,y) coordinates that can be created from the array data. You can easily reuse parts of drawings, and then extend them by putting in, say, twenty coordinate pairs, then specifying *nPointsList* as fifteen. Then, the last five coordinate pairs can be used by passing the full twenty point value, and you will get whatever the last five coordinates represented, such as another letter. Keep in mind that while you can limit reading the end of the array, you cannot change the beginning.

RsBodyShape is the base class for all physical parts that interact with the Rossum environment. The classes derived from *RsBodyShape* describe the chassis, or body, of the robot, as well as active components such as sensors. To create a body that is a shape other than a circle, you must supply a set of coordinate pairs, just as with floor plan declarations and *RsBodyArt*. As with *RsBodyArt*, the coordinates are inserted into the array as *x1, y1, x2, y2, ...*. See Figure 7.25 for *RsBodyShape*'s constructor, which also shows that you must specify the number of coordinates contained in the array.

Figure 7.25 RsBodyShape Constructor

```
RsBodyShape (double point[], int nPoint)
```

The coordinate system for *RsBodyShape* and *RsBodyArt* is different than that of the floor plans. The robot design is centered around (0,0), with (1,0) being one meter to the right of the robot. This can lead to some errors in the design, so remember that you start in the center of the robot. Also, as with floor plan obstacles, you cannot have an intersecting polygon. If your robot is in the shape of two triangles with their points together, then each triangle is a separate body piece, since to make it one would violate this rule. This will not be an issue with most robots, especially since an intersecting LEGO MINDSTORMS design would be fairly hard to do.

If you are creating a circular body shape, such as the demonstration ClientZero body provided in the Rossum distribution, there is the *RsBodyCircle* class to make it easier. This class functions much like a floor plan's polygon statement, where you specify the center point and the radius (See Figure 7.26).

Figure 7.26 RsBodyCircle Constructor

```
RsBodyCircle (double xCenter, double yCenter, double radius)
```

The (*xCenter, yCenter*) coordinate pair is the center of the circle. A center of (0,0) is the center of the robot body, while centers of (1,0) and (-1,0) would produce an "OO" shape, assuming radii of one meter. The radius of the circle is measured in meters, so a radius of one meter would equal a circle two meters across. Since the default unit is the meter, any units for robot body design must be in meters, as presently there is no way to define a unit for use.

The *RsBodySensor* derivative classes, *RsBodyContactSensor*, *RsBodyTargetSensor*, *RsBodyRangeSensor*, and *RsBodyPaintSensor*, are the active parts of the robot design (the chassis parts, or the passive parts, were discussed previously). For our purposes, *RsWheelSystem* is considered active here due to its motion control properties, although it is discussed as a passive part in the Rossum User's Guide.

Active Body Classes: Sensors and Wheels

RsWheelSystem defines how a simulated robot moves—its speed, turning radius and wheel base are all definable. To have the *Motor* class function correctly, some explanation needs to be given about how it is written.

The Rossum simulator has no way to control individual motors, or even motors themselves. The robot is simply propelled by calling an *RsTransform* on it, telling the drawing methods to move the robot, with all of its parts in the *RsBody* container class, to a new location. Therefore, there was a need for a way to hack the simulator into allowing control of different motors. This is done by calculating how many wheel "clicks" it will take to get out of the floor plan from the given location and speed, then using that as a base value. It modifies the values, such as movement speed and the number of clicks to move each wheel, to provide the correct motor actions. Because of this, speed is set in several ways. In later releases, there should be options to control how speed is regulated, but for now, it is simply done by the wheel system setup. The speed is calculated by the maximum wheel system speed, the number of clicks in a full rotation, and the current power level.

The number of clicks in a rotation and the maximum wheel speed are both set by the *RsWheelSystem* constructor, shown in Figure 7.27. These values are used as the basis of motor movement, and determine the main physics at work.

Figure 7.27 *RsWheelSystem* Constructor

```
RsWheelSystem (double wheelBase, double radius, double thickness,
    double nStepPerRevolution, double maxStepsPerSecond)
```

The *wheelBase* parameter is the distance between the wheels, measured in meters. The radius is how tightly a robot can turn in a circle, just like a car or other wheeled vehicle's turning radius. The thickness parameter is how thick the wheels are, measured in meters. The parameters *nStepPerRevolution* and *maxStepsPerSecond* are the main basis for movement calculations. For purposes of compatibility with a rotation sensor implementation in a later release, this should be equal to the number of counts you get on a rotation sensor for every complete turn of your robot's wheel. It also affects the resolution of the movement, but for LEGO MINDSTORMS-sized projects, the inaccuracies should be slim to none. The *maxStepsPerSecond* parameter specifies the maximum speed of the motor. This value should be used in conjunction with *nStepPerRevolution* to set the speed of the motor and gear assembly—If a wheel has sixteen counts for every rotation, but can only rotate two times a second, then the maximum distance that can be traveled is thirty-two steps. Different gear trains can affect this value, but it should be set at power level eight—changing the power level could result in incorrect behavior.

The various sensor classes can be used to detect every kind of object in the floor plan. Target sensors, contact sensors, ranging sensors and paint sensors comprise the Rossum sensor toolkit. In future releases, it is expected that a Simlink-compatible light sensor and source will be developed. This sensor, along with a rotation sensor, will provide a more accurate and useful environment in which LEGO MINDSTORMS robots will be simulated. Although their expected implementations are described later, they may change as they are implemented.

The first sensor that is actually implemented is the contact sensor. Due to automatic sensor type detection algorithms, there are specific names that sensors must have in order to be registered. For example, if a sensor is on port one, then it is required to be named "Sensor1," and a sensor on port three is required to be named "Sensor3." All of the necessary conversions and manipulations are performed based on the detected sensor types, allowing existing leJOS code to go unbroken. The sensor name must be set with the *setName(String name)* method— the given name in the designing class will not matter.

The contact sensor is rather easy to set up. As with most sensors and other body parts, you must supply an array of coordinate pairs and the number of supplied coordinates, as shown in Figure 7.28.

Figure 7.28 *RsBodyContactSensor* Constructor

```
RsBodyContactSensor (double[] points, int nPoints)
```

The point array will generally be a square, to describe the square gray touch sensor block. However, if your sensor is attached to a semi circular bumper on the left side, this must be drawn and modeled as well in order to provide accurate detection. As always, the units are meters. *nPoints* is the number of supplied coordinates, but changing this value doesn't really help, as it will be attached to the same sensor space. Raw mode for contact sensors always returns 800 + a random number in the range of zero to fifty, in order to simulate average contact sensor values. Unfortunately, multiple sensors on a single port are not currently supported, although a special flag may make it possible to differentiate between them.

Target sensors require some more explanation about how they are hacked to be used as light sensors. The target, while a point source, is used as a temporary light source. Therefore, the light sensor detects the targets, and some simple algorithms are used to convert the values into the raw and percentage values. Therefore, the bins (or divisions) of area and ranges should be set to reflect the average light sensor, but modified for your conditions. For example, the "perfect" light sensor would be configured with 1023 bins for distance to match up with the 1023 values that a raw value can provide. This is necessary for correct raw mode readings, and conversion to percentages. Since Simlink is not completed, Andy cannot yet say if firing 1023 events in a short time will bog down the software, but he suspects it will. In this case, a value lower than 1023 can be used, with each bin scaled to meet the needed resolution.

A bin is a section of a sensor's view, like a virtual grid laid over the area. The values specified by the sensor detection area width and height are used to determine the size of each bin; 200 bins over a large detection area may be smaller than 20 bins over a smaller area. Customize this value for your application to get the most accurate readings.

You can also define the *int getRangeBins(int nRangeBins)* method to return the number of bins used by the light sensor. If this method is not defined, then the default 1023 value will be assumed; if it is smaller than 1023, then it will be appropriately scaled.

The basic constructor of a target sensor, shown in Figure 7.29, is much more complicated than any other constructor used thus far. The myriad of variables you can use define the exact characteristics of the target sensor, many of which must be guessed at for the real sensor model.

Figure 7.29 *RsBodyTargetSensor* Constructor

```
RsBodyTargetSensor(double[] point, int nPoint,double xDetector,
    double yDetector,
double sightAngle, double width, double maxRange, int nWidthBin, int
    nRangeBin)
```

The point array is comprised of the coordinate pairs describing the sensor. Since the light sensor is a rectangle, your sensor should be as well; for accurate depiction and detection of targets. The *xDetector* and *yDetector* values specify the (x,y) coordinate for the detection point of the sensor. For the target sensor, this area should be on the front and slightly left of center. Since Rossum is a two-dimensional environment, there is no height setting, nor does the sensor detect different height values.

The *sightAngle* parameter specifies the angle from 0° to which the sensor is oriented. 0° is specified as the front of the robot, facing to the right at construction time. For example, the sensor is looking down from the top, with the sensing phototransistor facing "up". The 0° mark is a perpendicular line from the y axis, or the positive x axis.

The *width* and *maxRange* describe the detection area for which the sensor can be used. Since a light sensor can detect different amounts of light, these values must be chosen for the specific application. If you add a one-hole beam to the front of the sensor, the effective width value will be lower. This value is the angular measurement in radians, which can be converted from degrees by the formula:

radians = degrees * PI / 180

The *maxRange* argument is the number of meters at which the sensor can detect a target on the floor plan. This value can be very large, as you will get a value proportional to distance. However, if you want to simulate a room in semi darkness, this value should be set appropriately to model a less powerful light source.

The *nWidthBin* and *nRangeBin* arguments are used to set the sensitivity of the sensor. A sensor event will be fired for each change from one bin to another. As mentioned before, it might be a good idea to limit the fired events in order to keep the simulator from bogging down, so choose appropriate values. Higher values get more precision, accuracy, and realism, while lower values result in fewer listener events your robot program must handle. Also, in the future, a threshold value may be specified in the run configuration for the number of bin changes to report.

A note on the target sensor—a light sensor is expected to be developed, along with a light object, for the floor plan in later releases. This sensor will have more natural parameters, but to make it more useful to developers, the parameters will be similar to the target sensor values.

The range sensor can function as either an ultrasonic range sensor, such as those constructed by John Barnes, or as a proximity sensor, such as the IRPD sensors like those sold by Pete Sevcik. This sensor can also be used in place of the IR radar that is used as proximity detection with the light sensor. This sensor is set up much like the target sensor, as shown in Figure 7.30.

Figure 7.30 *RsBodyRangeSensor* Constructor

```
RsBodyRangeSensor(double[] point, int nPoint, double xDetector, double
    yDetector,
double sightAngle, double maxRange, int nRangeBin)
```

The *point* and *nPoint* parameters are the same as other sensors. The *xDetector* and *yDetector* values are the same as the target sensor—the virtual point where the transceiver is placed on the sensor. The *sightAngle* is the angle from 0° that the sensor is pointing at; a wall on this virtual axis will be registered as the distance. The *maxRange* and *nRangeBin* values must be set to the sensor's set specifications. For example, John Barnes' ultrasonic sensor must be set to a distance of ~1.82 meters and have 100 bins. This matches exactly with the values the sensor returns, so your distance readings will be accurate. Other sensors will have different characteristics, and must be set accordingly.

Paint sensors are simply downward looking light sensors that can only detect paint strips on the floor generated in the floor plan (See Figure 7.31). The paint sensor operates on the premise of regions, when you create the strip, you specify a region. The paint sensor is only sensitive to that region, and will change states when entering or exiting the area. All lines are assumed to be black or another dark color, so a state change to *hot* will cause the reported percentage value to drop. In a later release, these colors should be configurable.

Figure 7.31 *RsBodyPaintSensor* Constructor

```
RsBodyPaintSensor(double[] point, int nPoint, double xDetector,
    double yDetector)
```

All parameters are the same as a light sensor, with the *xDetector* and *yDetector* doubles specifying the point that paint will be sampled for under the sensor. The *setRegionSensitivity(int region)* method allows you to set the region, or color of floor paint, to which the sensor is sensitive.

For any sensor, the *setHotFillColor(java.awt.Color c)* and *setHotLineColor (java.awt.Color c)* methods can be used to specify the colors shown when a sensor has a hot detection. The default color is a translucent orange color. The default, or normal, colors can be set with the *setFillColor(java.awt.Color c)* and *setLineColor(java.awt.Color c)*. Setting this to *null* will cause the sensor to not be rendered, but still be active for detections. The contact sensors in ClientZero.java demonstrate this. Having a sensor not be rendered can be uesful in many cases —in a robot where the body is the actual touch sensor, for example. In this case, the area can be defined but you will not see an incorrect depiction of a sensor which is not visible in real life.

One final note—when adding parts to the *RsBody* class, the parts added last are rendered on top of the parts added earlier; that is, they overwrite the robot body underneath.

Creating a Simple Robot Design

Designing a robot from these base classes can be challenging. Let's build on an example from *Building Robots with LEGO MINDSTORMS* by Mario and Giulio Ferrari; see Figure 7.32 for the simple differential drive configuration. We will add a light sensor, so the robot very simply consists of a six-inch (15.24 cm) square body with some wheels and a light sensor on one end. However, it provides a good example of how to create a robot manually based on the Rossum classes. Figure 7.33 shows how the rendered robot will appear on the Rossum screen. The comments in the code explain why each value was passed due to a certain parameter. One note however—the light sensor values were picked as reasonable for a given environment, but other values are probably more suitable to your situation. They were merely picked out of thin air, so I wouldn't use them as a base.

Figure 7.32 Simple Robot Design

Figure 7.33 Robot Rendered on the Rossum Screen

To start, make a list of the sensor and body classes needed in this example. By adding a light sensor, we will need the following classes:

- *RsBodyShape*
- *RsWheelSystem*
- *RsBodyTargetSensor*

The finished class is shown in Figure 7.34, and can be found on the CD that accompanies this book. We'll discuss the structure of the class, and how the specific classes are initialized, later in this section.

Figure 7.34 Listing of SimpleRobot.java

```java
import rossum.*;
import java.awt.Color;

public class SimpleRobot{
    public static RsBody build() {
        RsBody body = new RsBody("SimpleRobot");
        double[] bodyShape = {
            -0.064, 0.064,
             0.128, 0.064,
             0.128, -0.064,
            -0.064, -0.064};

        RsBodyShape shape = new RsBodyShape(bodyShape, 4);
        shape.setFillColor(Color.lightGray);
        shape.setLineColor(Color.lightGray);
        body.addPart(shape);

        RsWheelSystem wheels = new RsWheelSystem(
            .160,           //Wheelbase of 16cm
            .0248,          //Radius of wheels - 49mm / 2
            .028,           //Wheel thickness - 28mm
            16,             //Steps per revolution, set for rotation
                                sensor
            32);            //Max steps per second, limits speed to 2
                                rotations per second
```

Figure 7.34 Continued

```
    wheels.setFillColor(Color.black);
    wheels.setLineColor(Color.black);
    body.addPart(wheels);

    double[] lightC = {
        0.112,  0.008,
        0.144,  0.008,
        0.144, -0.008,
        0.112, -0.008};

    RsBodyTargetSensor lightSensor = new RsBodyTargetSensor(
    lightC,                 //Coordinates for sensor
    4,                      //Number of coordinates
    144,                    //X focal point coordinate
    0,                      //Y focal point coordinate
    45 * Math.PI / 180,     //Angle sensor can see in radians
    3,                      //Distance sensor sight area is wide
    3,                      //Distance sensor can "see"
    15,                     //Number of bins wide
    1024);                  //Number of bins across 1023 for accurate
                               light sensor

    lightSensor.setName("Sensor0");
    lightSensor.setFillColor(Color.blue);
    lightSensor.setLineColor(Color.blue);
    body.addPart(lightSensor);

    return body;
    }

public int[] getDriveMotors() {
    int[] motors = new int {0, 1}
    return motors;
    }
}
```

Note how the *lightSensor* object's name is set with *setName(String name)*. This is very important: the sensors must be named Sensor0, Sensor1, and Sensor2 to be detected and correctly set up by the *Sensor* class. Also, a new method was used. This method *int[] getDriveMotors()* is required by Simlink. It defines which motor ports are used as the driving wheels. 0 corresponds to *Motor.A*, and 1 corresponds to *Motor.B*. Without this method, a *MethodNotFoundException* error will be thrown.

Bricks & Chips...

Converting Bricks and Feet to Rossum Meters

When creating a Rossum robot, you may wonder how you convert twenty-six studs to a meter value for use in the class initialization. The simple answer is that one stud equals eight millimeters, or .008 meters. Therefore, two studs equal sixteen millimeters, or .016 meters.

If you prefer to think of the dimensions in English units, one stud equals .32 inches, or eight millimeters multiplied by .04 (8 * .04).

One stud is also equal to .02625 feet, so a robot that is thirty-eight studs long is almost one foot.

The chart below lists the conversion factor to convert feet into meters. To use the chart, multiply the feet by the number listed to get the value.

English Unit	Metric Conversion Factor
One inch	25.4 millimeters
One inch	2.54 centimeters
One foot	0.3048 meters
Three feet	0.9144 meters

Future Tools for Designing Robots

In the future, Andy Gombos will be creating a body plan editor and floor plan editor, with which you can pick the class to be used, then draw out the component to be placed. Further, adding order will be adjustable, so that a sensor can be rendered on top of the body.

When these tools are finished, they will be accessible from a toolbar on the top of the Simlink screen, like a new simulator run. This improvement will be available in the first Simlink release, or one soon thereafter. More improvements will be made as bugs are found, or new features are thought of. Simlink is his main priority though, so don't expect it for some time.

Additional Tips and Tools for leJOS

Many tricks and tips can be used to ease development of leJOS programs. Some of these, such as creating a program to automatically compile, and (if no errors are found) download, can be relatively simple. Others, like adding a module to your IDE for compiling and downloading shortcuts can be harder, depending on your IDE. Configuring your IDE was discussed earlier in this chapter under the section "Using Existing IDEs," so refer to that section for more information.

There are also tools available that are useful for checking your code for the simple mistakes that are hard to debug on the RCX, including these two:

- Jlint (http://www.ispras.ru/~knizhnik/jlint/ReadMe.htm)
- Jad (http://kpdus.tripod.com/jad.html)

Jlint is a Java version of the popular *lint* for C programs. Jlint can be useful, since debugging programs on the RCX, especially ones that deal with a logic errors (such as an incorrect loop structures), can be difficult. It can also detect other "assumptions" you may have made, and tells you if they are incorrect. Jlint, along with Simlink, can be used to debug programs more easily than on the RCX.

Jad allows you to retrieve a compiled class file for editing, even if you have lost the source. This can be especially useful when an unwanted modification is saved, causing the program not to function. If you have compiled the class before, then a tool like Jad can help you use the class as a backup copy, though no comments are preserved.

Jad can also be used to decompile other Java robot files that may have only been distributed in class form. Decompiling a program you did not create can help you learn programming styles, ways to implement complex functions, or just how to better code for the RCX. As you gain further experience in the leJOS API, the uses of these tools and scripts will become more apparent.

Another useful development tool is the RCXTools package by Tim Rinkens, which includes RCXDownload and RCXDirectMode. These two programs, which we'll cover in the next two sections, allow you to interface with the RCX from a PC. Also, the package allows you to download programs, read sensor values, and play tones, all from your PC. However, the current release does not support USB connectivity, which means it is incompatible with the RIS 2.0 system. This functionality is planned for an upcoming release.

RCXDownLoad

RCXDownload (part of the RCXTools package, as we just mentioned) is much like lVI, but without the editing aspect. The main window, shown in Figure 7.35, contains several buttons and a text area where errors and informative messages are displayed.

Figure 7.35 RCXDownload Main Window

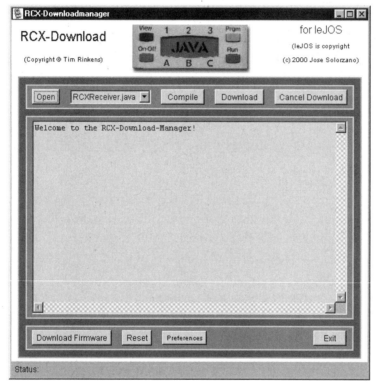

The Buttons at the top (**Open**, **Compile**, **Download**, and **Cancel Download**) are all related to the file shown in the drop down box, currently shown as RCXReciever.java, which was chosen via the **Open** button. The other buttons compile, then download the program to the RCX. If the download needs to be canceled for some reason, the **Cancel Download** button can stop the download.

The mail text area shows any informative messages from RCXDownload, as well as any compilation errors, or communications errors when downloading.

The buttons on the bottom (**Download Firmware**, **Reset**, **Preferences**, and **Exit**) deal with the configuration of the RCX and RCXDownload.

Download Firmware allows you to download the leJOS firmware easily. **Reset** clears the text area and drop down file list box. The area to be cleared is selectable, so a new compilation can start in an empty text area, and a new project can have the file area cleared. **Exit** quits RCXDownload.

The **Preferences** dialog, shown in Figure 7.36, allows you to set the leJOS and Java home directories, as well as which communications port to use. The colors can also be set to Normal (green and yellow), Mauve (light purple and dark purple, the default Swing colors), or System, which on Windows is gray and blue.

Figure 7.36 RCXDownload Preferences Dialog

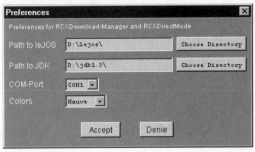

RCXDownload allows you to access the static functions of the RCX, or those that do not require a program to be running on the RCX. It also serves as a graphical build utility, which, in conjunction with your favorite IDE, can form a full leJOS editing environment without a special IDE configuration .

RCXDirectMode

RCXDirectMode's main window provides direct, instant control over a robot's motor functions, as well as return sensor readings. RCXDirectMode can also create noises through the RCX's internal speaker. It does all of this by downloading a control program to the RCX, which then allows RCXDirectMode to poll sensors and control the motors. This main window, shown in Figure 7.37, has buttons and sliders to control your robot.

The sliders and buttons under the labels for **A**, **B**, and **C** control the motors. The sliders control motor power, while the buttons control direction and state (on or off). The button **Stop all** stops all the motors currently running, as it's name implies.

The Sensors panel contains the controls for sensors 1, 2, and 3. Sensor types can be set here, then the value polled by using the **Value** button. The received sensor value is put into the white text field where −1, -2, or -3 is currently displayed.

Figure 7.37 RCXDirectMode Main Window

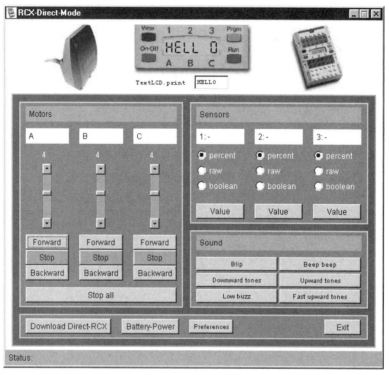

The **Sound** panel allows you to create tones and sequences of tones that are played on the RCX's internal speaker. While this functionality does not require the downloaded program stub, it does require firmware to be loaded.

The bottom panel contains the **Download Direct-RCX**, **Battery-Power**, **Preferences,** and **Exit** buttons. The **Download Direct-RCX** button allows you to download a small leJOS program to the RCX to allow you to control the motors and sensors. The **Battery-Power** button returns the battery voltage of the batteries in the RCX, both in a raw value and in millivolts.

The **Preferences** button displays the dialog shown in Figure 7.36. Each dialog not only modifies its own settings, but also those of the other programs, so a change in RCXDirectMode affects RCXDownload.

The RCXTools package provides a simple, intuitive interface to RCX interaction. Its ability to download programs, directly control the RCX, and download the firmware make RCXTools one of the most downloaded leJOS extensions available. Combined with an IDE and leJOS distribution, the RCXTools package can create a complete leJOS editing and development environment.

Summary

If you have successfully configured the various different editors and software packages described in these preceding pages, then congratulations! Correctly setting the environment variables and paths for each new program, especially when one may cancel the other's changes, can be very frustrating.

Using the command-line programs allows you, the developer, more control than using an IDE. However, there's tradeoff between convenience and control, and the ease-of-use factor can make an IDE useful in many instances. Configuring a standard IDE (like Forte) may be possible—you need to check and see what options are provided. Tools like lVI and RCXTools come pre-configured for use with leJOS, which makes setup and use a snap.

Debugging on the RCX can be difficult at times, and in some cases, downright impossible. Simlink provides a way to gather more exception information than previously possible, leading to easier development cycles. Interpreting an exception on the RCX's LCD could result in the wrong error being tracked down, as the least significant digit only of the exception is displayed.

Controlling a robot from afar can be very difficult when trying to use the buttons on the RCX. A program like RCXDirectMode can help you turn off motors without the use of the LEGO remote. IDEs like lVI or RCXDownload can enable you to compile and download your new leJOS creations with just a few mouse clicks. Configuring your favorite IDE for use with the leJOS command-line programs can allow you to use all of its features when creating a robot.

All of these tools and techniques can increase your enjoyment while using leJOS, LEGO bricks, and LEGO MINDSTORMS. Each new third-party tool is a new building block upon another, just like the bricks and beams of your robots.

Solutions Fast Track

Programming Environments for leJOS

☑ The command line tools provide ultimate control in terms of the options you can use, but sacrifice ease-of-use.

☑ GUI-based tools can simplify the use of the command-line tools, but sacrifice some elements of control.

☑ Command-line tools included in the leJOS package include *lejosc, lejos, lejosrun, lejosfirmdl, emu-lejos,* and *emu-lejosrun.*

☑ The free IDE called Forte provides a visual GUI creator, a debugger, and compilation functions. Unlike JBuilder and Eclipse, it provides the seemingly unique ability to configure the compiler and Java runtime you use.

Using the leJOS Visual Interface

☑ The leJOS Visual Interface (lVI) is a custom IDE especially configured for use with leJOS.

☑ The options in the Tools menu allow you to automatically compile, link, and download programs, as well as download firmware.

☑ After graphically setting the necessary environment variables and settings, you can create, edit, compile, and link a file.

Using a leJOS Simulator

☑ Simlink is designed to be an interface between Rossum's Playhouse and the low level APIs provided by leJOS.

☑ The Rossum simulator has a syntax and format of its own; using its navigational and other declarations and specifications, you can create visual and non-visual elements of floor plans.

☑ Robot bodies in Simlink are represented as Java classes, with Rossum classes allowing you to create simple designs.

☑ Note that sensors and motors under simulation do not work exactly as in real life.

Additional Tips and Tools for leJOS

☑ Java tools like Jlint and Jad can be used on leJOS programs.

☑ The RCXTools package provides a clean interface to many RCX functions, while also allowing you direct control.

☑ The LCDText class included with RCXDirectMode can be used to test LCD words before they are downloaded to the RCX.

Frequently Asked Questions

The following Frequently Asked Questions, answered by the authors of this book, are designed to both measure your understanding of the concepts presented   in this chapter and to assist you with real-life implementation of these concepts. To have your questions about this chapter answered by the author, browse to **www.syngress.com/solutions** and click on the **"Ask the Author"** form.

Q: lVI seems to forget my preferences and other settings. What's wrong?

A: This is a known problem with no known solution. The author of lVI says a later release will fix this issue.

Q: Why will Simlink not render my robots correctly?

A: You may have an issue with out-of-order coordinates. Make sure they are in the right order, and add a final ending coordinate to form a complete shape.

Q: Why is there no option for USB on lVI or RCXTools?

A: USB support will be added to RCXTools in a future release, the latest lVI release includes USB support.

Q: I keep receiving the error "No response from RCX." What's going wrong?

A: Try downloading the firmware again. To remove the current firmware, take out the RCX's batteries, then reinsert them.

leJOS Internals

Solutions in this chapter:

- **Advanced Usage of leJOS**

- **Examining leJOS Internals**

- **Extending leJOS with Native Methods**

- **Additional Tips and Tricks with leJOS**

☑ **Summary**

☑ **Solutions Fast Track**

☑ **Frequently Asked Questions**

Introduction

In this chapter we will look at the internals of leJOS and the RCX, and delve into some topics that are a little more advanced than those we've covered in the previous chapters. We'll start with a section about some advanced features (such as multiprogram downloading) that will let you load several unrelated programs at the same time, which is useful for demos or competitions.

After that, we will take an in-depth look at the internal workings of leJOS, in particular the linker and the virtual machine. Knowing about the internals will give you a better understanding of what leJOS can do and why there are certain limitations inherent to the program. By exposing the system we also hope to give you a framework to help you find your way around the leJOS internals, should you one day need to explore them yourself—For example, you may want to know for sure how a certain function is implemented, or you may need to implement a feature that is not present but is still very important to you. Since leJOS is open source software, there is nothing to stop you from changing it, once you know how.

In the next section we take a more hands-on approach and look at native methods. Native methods are the standard tool for extending the system via proper C routines, if you need to do some special things with the hardware or have especially demanding timing constraints, for example. We explain in detail the steps you have to take in order to successfully implement a native method.

We'll also show you a few useful tricks, like changing the stack size or accessing the memory with the already existing native methods.

Be aware that leJOS is still evolving (in fact, while writing this book, we discovered that quantum-mechanical systems and computer systems have something in common: both change before your very eyes!). While the system will stay pretty much the same, by the time you are holding this book in hand some of the details may have changed slightly.

Advanced Usage of leJOS

There are some features of leJOS that are rarely needed in everyday use, but are still quite handy in special situations. In this section we explore two of them. *Multiprogram downloading* can be useful for demos or competitions, where you want to load several unrelated programs onto the RCX at the same time and be able to easily change between them. Unrestricted access to the memory of the RCX can be useful for exploring the internals of the RCX, and for accessing objects in ways that are forbidden by the Java type system. It can also be used to implement a *persistent storage* area in a previously unused space of memory.

Multiprogram Downloading

Like the original LEGO MINDSTORMS firmware, leJOS supports the simultaneous loading of several programs into the RCX. This is particularly useful if you want to run several unrelated programs in your RCX. For example, in a competition you might want to load the programs of several competitors on one standard robot in order to avoid unnecessary delays. Or you might want to demo several of your programs on the same robot. Perhaps you want to quickly exchange the RCX between different robots without reloading the program. Another application where multiprogram downloading is not strictly needed is to give parameters to your program; for example the different programs may just set their network address and then use a common class for the main part of their work.

In short, being able to load several programs into the RCX at once gives you more flexibility and avoids the delays associated with loading different programs, and since common classes are shared, the memory overhead is minimal. However, unlike with the LEGO MINDSTORMS firmware, it is not possible to load several programs into the RCX incrementally; changing one program means that you must reload all of them.

We will illustrate the creation of a multiprogram binary by a simple example that contains two programs, Main1 and Main2. Each of these entry classes needs to contain a program entry point method:

```
public static void main (String[] arg)
```

First, compile the classes as usual. The easiest way is to put them all into the same directory and to execute the following command:

```
$ lejosc *.java
```

If you are running a competition you may also want to just accept the .class files from your competitors directly, without doing the compilation yourself.

Now use the leJOS linker to link the entry classes. The linker will link them into a single binary, together with any other classes that are used:

```
$ lejos  Main1,Main2 -o Main.bin
```

Download this binary to the RCX:

```
$ lejosrun Main.bin
```

On the RCX you can now select the program you want to run by using the **Program** button, and running the desired program.

NOTE

LeJOS does not support starting a program by using the LEGO remote control.

You can easily extend this method to more than two entry points, to give a number of RCX unique addresses in a small network, for example. The maximum number of program entry points is limited to 255, which in practice is more than enough. Note that for program entry points with a number greater than nine, the program number display will be blank, but you can still select and start them.

Storing Persistent Data

As an example of direct memory access we will implement a simple store for persistent data that survives stopping and restarting the leJOS program, and even reloading a corrected program, as long as the persistent data's format remains the same. This is very useful if you want to preserve valuable data from one run to the next:

- You might have set some parameters by pressing a lot of buttons, and you don't want to repeat that for every run.

- You have calibrated your robot (for example, the light sensor, or the distance the robot travels in a certain amount of time).

- Your robot may need to remember the last positions of its joints because it has no sensors for finding out their absolute position.

- You want your robot to create and remember a map of the surroundings.

Normal leJOS objects do not survive stopping and restarting a program, because leJOS reinitializes its object memory when it starts a program. To pass values from one program run to the next we will use a memory area between the two ROM data areas near the top of the address space. This area is unused by the ROM and the leJOS firmware up to version 1.0.4. Later versions of leJOS use this space for the leJOS heap, but the beginning of this memory area is used last, so you can expect it to be free at the start of your program. The data will in fact survive as long as the memory has power. Since it is so useful we have already added the class *josx.platform.rcx.PersistentMemoryArea* to the leJOS library (see Figure 8.1).

NOTE

The version of *PersistentMemoryArea* in Figure 8.1 is only useful as an example. Newer versions of leJOS contain a suitable version in their library. Versions 1.0.4 or earlier need to access memory via the *Native* class instead of *Memory*. A version for leJOS 1.0.4 or earlier is available on the CD that accompanies this book.

Figure 8.1 PersistentMemoryArea.java

```java
package josx.platform.rcx;

/**
 * A memory area for persistent storage.
 * Only removing batteries will delete it.
 *
 * The magic number should be different for each application
 * (use a random integer).
 * At the moment there can be only one PersistentMemoryArea,
 * that will be reinitialized if you change the magic number.
 * This may change in the future, with more than one area and
 * magic number used to distinguish them.
 */

public class PersistentMemoryArea
{
  private static final int MAGIC_ADDRESS = 0xf001;
  private static final int SIZE_ADDRESS  = MAGIC_ADDRESS+2;
  private static final int START_ADDRESS = MAGIC_ADDRESS+4;
  private static final int END_ADDRESS   = 0xfb80;
```

Continued

Figure 8.1 Continued

```java
private static PersistentMemoryArea singleton = null;

private int size;

private PersistentMemoryArea ()
{
}

public static PersistentMemoryArea get (int magic, int size)
  throws OutOfMemoryError
{
  if (singleton == null) {
    if (START_ADDRESS + size > END_ADDRESS) {
      throw new OutOfMemoryError ();
    } else {
      synchronized (Memory.MONITOR) {
        if (Memory.readShort (MAGIC_ADDRESS) != magic
            && Memory.readShort (SIZE_ADDRESS) != size) {
          // not what we are looking for, need to reinitialize
          for (short i = 0; i < size; i++) {
            Memory.writeByte (START_ADDRESS+i, (byte)0);
          }
          Memory.writeShort (MAGIC_ADDRESS, (short)magic);
          Memory.writeShort (SIZE_ADDRESS, (short)size);
        }
      }
    }
    singleton = new PersistentMemoryArea ();
    singleton.size = size;
  }
  return singleton;
}

public byte readByte (int i)
  throws ArrayIndexOutOfBoundsException
```

Continued

Figure 8.1 Continued

```
{
    if (i >= 0 && i < size) {
        return Memory.readByte (START_ADDRESS+i);
    } else {
        throw new ArrayIndexOutOfBoundsException();
    }
}

public void writeByte (int i, byte b)
    throws ArrayIndexOutOfBoundsException
{
    if (i >= 0 && i < size) {
        Memory.writeByte (START_ADDRESS+i, (byte)b);
    } else {
        throw new ArrayIndexOutOfBoundsException();
    }
}
}
```

In Figure 8.1 you can see the use of all the methods in *josx.platform.rcx .Memory*: that is, *readByte, readShort, writeByte* and *writeShort* (read and write bytes and shorts, respectively). You also see the use of *Memory.MONITOR*, which locks the memory so that two concurrent threads will not interfere with each other. You should also use *Memory.MONITOR* if you call native methods that modify memory. As an example, you can look at *Button.readButtons*, which also uses the auxiliary memory area defined in the *Memory* class.

Accessing memory directly is dangerous; you can easily crash your RCX by writing into the wrong places. In our example we check that the access stays within the allocated memory area and raise an exception if this is not the case.

To test it you can use the test program *PersistentMemoryAreaTest* in Figure 8.2, which is also available on the CD that accompanies this book.

Figure 8.2 PersistentMemoryAreaTest.java

```
import josx.platform.rcx.*;

/**
```

Continued

Figure 8.2 Continued

```
 * This program tests PersistentMemoryArea
 * */

public class PersistentMemoryAreaTest implements LCDConstants
{
  private static PersistentMemoryArea pmem;
  private static int index;

  public static void main (String[] arg)
  {
    pmem = PersistentMemoryArea.get (6125417, 10);
    index = 0;

    while (Button.RUN.isPressed());
    display();
    while (!Button.RUN.isPressed()) {
      if (Button.VIEW.isPressed()) {
        index++;
        display();
        while (Button.VIEW.isPressed());
      }
      if (Button.PRGM.isPressed()) {
        pmem.writeByte (index, (byte)(pmem.readByte(index)+1));
        display();
        while (Button.PRGM.isPressed());
      }
    }
    while (Button.RUN.isPressed());
  }

  private static void display ()
  {
    LCD.setNumber (LCD_SIGNED, pmem.readByte(index), LCD_DECIMAL_0);
    LCD.showProgramNumber (index);
  }
}
```

This program allocates 10 bytes of persistent memory and lets you view and change it with the buttons. The **View** button increments the bytes for viewing, which is indicated by the variable index, and the **Prgm** button increments the currently viewed byte. When you go past the 10 bytes, *readByte* throws the *ArrayIndexOutOfBoundsException*. This is intentional; we're testing the bounds-checking. The magic number should be different for each application so that the data doesn't get mixed up.

Examining leJOS Internals

In this section we will examine the internal structure of leJOS from several different points of view. The high-level view we'll take on the data flow will show you how the leJOS tools work together to transform Java source code into an executable program on the RCX. After this global view, we'll take a closer look at the linker, which is the most important tool in this chain. Next, we'll look at the RCX, starting with the running Java code and its communication with the external world. We will also take a closer look at both the logical structure and the memory layout of the software in the RCX, from the Java executable down to the ROM. Finally, we will show you how the source code of the various leJOS components is organized.

From Source Code to Execution

Figure 8.3 shows the data flow from the Java source code through compiler, linker and loader to the executable program in the RCX.

1. The compiler *lejosc* takes several Java source files and produces several class files containing Java byte code. This is essentially a standard Java compiler inside a thin wrapper that sets the class path and some other parameters appropriately.

2. The linker *lejos* takes the class files from the first step plus any class files that are needed from the library, and builds a single executable binary in an internal leJOS format.

3. The loader *lejosrun* takes this binary, either directly from *lejos* or via an intermediate .bin file, and downloads it into the RCX via infrared (IR) communications.

4. A loader routine inside the RCX receives the binary and copies it into memory verbatim. The loader uses the underlying ROM routines for the actual IR transfer.

5. When you run the program, the virtual machine reads the program and constant data in the code section, works on the data in the section, and communicates with the outside via the ROM routines.

Figure 8.3 Data Flow in leJOS

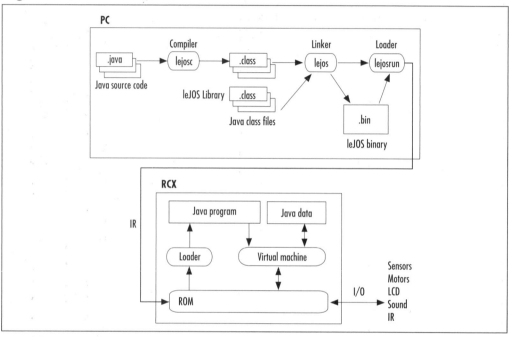

Continued

and all work equally well with leJOS. Other bricks in the LEGO MIND-STORMS range (the Scout, the CyberMaster and the MicroScout) cannot be programmed in leJOS, as they lack a sufficient amount of RAM and have a fixed firmware inside their ROM.

The most important chip in the RCX is the 8-bit H8/3292micro controller from Hitachi. It runs at 16MHz, has 16KB internal ROM and 512B internal RAM, which is extended by 32K external RAM. It also supports the RCX's I/O devices, with analogue inputs to read the sensors, a serial interface that is used for IR communication, and digital I/O lines for buttons, the LCD display and the motors. Hitachi provides a data sheet for the H8/3297 (Hitachi Single-Chip Microcomputer H8/3297 Series Hardware Manual at http://semiconductor.hitachi.com/products/pdf/h33th014d2.pdf). The motors are not controlled directly by the RCX, but rather via three motor controller chips, which can put the motor output into four states: forward full voltage, backward full voltage, outputs disconnected (float) and outputs short circuited (brake or stop). Motor power is controlled in software by rapidly switching between float and one of the three other states. The motor controllers use the full battery voltage, while the power supply for the micro controller part is regulated to 5V.

The most important leJOS–specific components in this chain are the linker and the virtual machine, which we will discuss in detail in the following sections.

Inside the leJOS Linker

The leJOS linker is a program written in Java inside a small wrapper written in C that calls the Java Virtual Machine and supplies it with the necessary command line arguments.

The C Wrapper

The source code for the C wrapper is called "javaexec.c," and can be found in the tools subdirectory. It is used both for *lejos* (the linker for the RCX) and *emu-lejos* (the linker for the emulator). To be specific, it executes a command line consisting of the following parts:

- **The JVM executable** Either the contents of the environment variable *JAVA*, or *java* by default if *JAVA* is not set. Thus you can select a different Java virtual machine by setting *JAVA*.

- **–Dtinyvm.write.order=WRITE_ORDER**   Sets the *tinyvm.write.order* Java system property to determine the byte order used by the Java main program of the linker for the leJOS binary. *WRITE_ORDER* is set in the Makefile when javaexec.c is compiled to either *BE* for big-endian in *lejos* or *LE* for little-endian in *emu-lejos*.

- **–Dtinyvm.loader=LOADER_TOOL**   Sets the loader tool for the Java main program. *LOADER_TOOL* is set in the Makefile at compile time to either *lejosrun* or *emu-lejosrun*.

- **–Dtinyvm.home=tinyvm_home**   Sets the leJOS home directory for the Java main program. Tinyvm_home is determined at runtime as the parent directory of the directory where the linker executable resides.

- **js.tinyvm.TinyVM**   The Java class that contains the program entry point for the linker.

- **–classpath $LIBPATH:$CLASSPATH**   Defines the Java class path to search for the Java classes that are to be linked. *LIBPATH* is currently tinyvm_home/lib/classes.jar and *$CLASSPATH* may be set in the environment, if you want to add your own libraries, for example. Note that for Windows the path separator is a semicolon instead of a colon.

Any other arguments given on the command line follow.

The wrapper also sets the *CLASSPATH* environment variable to tinyvm_home/lib/jtools.jar, so that the Java virtual machine can find the Java main program for the linker.

NOTE

The use of the name "tinyvm" in some of the names has historical reasons, as tinyvm was leJOS' predecessor.

The Java Main Program

The program entry point of the leJOS linker is the *js.tinyvm.TinyVM* class in the file jtools/js/tinyvm/TinyVM.java. It accepts the following command-line options and arguments:

- **-classpath pathname** Sets the class path for linking. This is set by the C wrapper.

- **-verbose[=level]** Sets the verbosity level to 1 by default. On level 1 the linker prints the class and signature indices.

- **-o filename** Specifies the output filename.

- **-gb** Sets the output format to the format needed by the Nintendo Game Boy (we'll explain this shortly).

- **entry_classes** A single non-option argument that contains the entry classes, separated by commas.

The main program reads the following Java system properties:

- **tinyvm.home** Contains the leJOS home directory.

- **tinyvm.loader** Contains the name of the loader (*lejosrun* or *emu-lejosrun*). The loader executable must be in the bin subdirectory of the leJOS home directory.

- **tinyvm.temp.dir** Contains a directory for temporary files. However, this is only used for the Game Boy. The linker uses the file __tinyvm_temp.tvm__ in the current directory to pass the leJOS binary to the loader.

- **tinyvm.class.path** An alternative way to pass the class path, but it is not used by the wrapper.

- **tinyvm.write.order** Contains the desired write order as either *BE* (big-endian) or *LE* (little-endian).

After parsing the command line, the linker builds a binary, starting with the entry classes and recursively including all of the classes that are used. This binary is dumped in little-endian or big-endian order according to the Java property *tinyvm.write.order*, with some extra processing for the Game Boy.

Using it directly, you have access to the Nintendo Game Boy option, which is not available through the standard C wrapper. However, as the current developers don't have a Game Boy, it will be necessary to adapt the Game Boy-specific code to recent developments before it will work. We will not go into further details about how the support for the Game Boy works in this chapter.

Building the Binary

Building the binary proceeds in several stages, called successively from the *js.tinyvm.Binary.createFromClosureOf* method:

- **Load classes** First the special classes, then the entry classes and finally all other classes that are referenced are loaded. For each class, the class file is read by the *js.classfile* reader, resulting in a *JClassFile* object that represents the class and contains all the information from the class file.

- **Extract information** Retrieves the data needed by the leJOS binary about constants, methods, fields, code, exceptions etc. from the *JClassFile* objects and builds records for them. This is done by the various *processX()* methods.

- **Store** Organizes the various records for the binary into a sequence. This is done in *Binary.storeComponents()*.

- **Compute offsets** Computes the offsets by which the records will refer to each other in the binary, where the offsets are relative to the beginning of the binary.

- **Post-process code** Computes indices into tables, weakens some opcodes with respect to type checking, and refuses opcodes that are not implemented (namely the operations on values of type long, the operations *lookupswitch* and *tableswitch* that implement the switch statement, and operations with wide operands that are not needed due to size limitations in leJOS). The modifications are simple per-opcode changes, so the structure of the code and the addresses of opcodes are not modified. For details see *CodeUtilities.processCode(byte[] aCode)*.

- **Report** Generates the report of class and method indices for the *-verbose* option.

- **Dump** Writes the sequence of records to the binary file.

In the Java class file format classes, methods, fields, etc. are referred to by indices into the constant pool. In the leJOS binary format these are removed from the constant pool and the references are replaced by the offset for the referenced record. As a consequence, choosing long identifiers does not increase the size of the binary.

The leJOS Binary Format

The output format is suitable as a memory image of the Java program. It is loaded verbatim into the Java data area on the RCX, and the virtual machine operates directly with this format. You can peruse the various dump methods to find out about the exact format, or you can look into the definition for the VM in vmsrc/language.h, which contains most of the definitions. Here we will just summarize the sizes of the various records, giving an indication how much it costs to add a class or a method to a given program:

- **Master record**   one per binary, 16 bytes

- **Class record**   one per class, 10 bytes

- **Static state**   one per static field, uses the length needed for representing the value. Strings are encoded as references. In the VM this is the storage area for static fields; on startup it is initialized to all zeros, followed by the static fields assignments.

- **Static field record**   one per static field, 2 bytes. This is the table that points to static field values.

- **Constant record**   one per int, long, float, double or String constant in the program, 4 bytes. Table that points to constant values.

- **Method record**   one per method, 11 bytes + 1 padding

- **Exception record**   one per exception handler, 7 bytes + 1 padding

- **Instance field record**   one per instance field, 1 byte. Encodes the type of the field.

- **Code sequence**   one per method or initializer, of variable length.

- **Constant value**   one per int, long, float, double or String constant in the program, uses the length needed for representing the value. Strings are written out as UTF-8-encoded Unicode like in the Java class file.

- **Entry class index**   one per entry class, 1 byte

The format follows the Java class format relatively closely, but leaves out any features that are not implemented by leJOS, such as flags for access control and checking for correct use of interfaces. Also note that the data for all the classes are pooled together.

The command *emu-dump* prints information about a class or constant contained in a leJOS binary. The binary must be linked with *emu-lejos* for *emu-dump* to work. For example, the following command dumps information about the class with index 0 (*java.lang.Object*) in the leJOS binary View.emubin:

```
emu-dump View.emubin class 0
```

Another command that is useful for looking at internals is *lejosp*. It is a wrapper around *javap*, the class file disassembler. It sets the classpath in the same way as *lejosc* does for *javac*.

Developing & Deploying...

The ROM in the RCX

The RCX contains 16KB of read-only memory (ROM), which is used for low-level interaction with the hardware. It contains routines for booting and downloading the firmware, other infrared communications, reading sensors and buttons, and controlling the motors and the LCD. To handle these tasks in parallel, it contains several interrupt routines. The most important for leJOS is the so-called OCIA interrupt routine, which is called every millisecond. It counts time, switches motors on and off to implement the power levels, plays sounds, and every 3ms it starts the A/D conversion for the sensors.

Kekoa Proudfoot has extensive documentation on the ROM (RCX Internals at http://graphics.stanford.edu/~kekoa). He also has a page that describes how to download the contents of the ROM from the RCX in srec format, which you can then disassemble using the objdump utility. Looking at the disassembled ROM is sometimes useful to find out exactly what the various ROM routines do.

Inside the leJOS Firmware

We now come to the second big part of leJOS, the firmware. In Figure 8.3 you can see how the data flow continues inside the RCX for loading and running a leJOS program. The loader receives the binary via IR and allows you to select a program entry point with the **Prgm** button and to start execution with the **Run** button. This will cause the loader to create the boot thread and start the Java virtual machine, which begins executing the loaded byte codes. Note that all communication with the external world is handled by routines in the ROM. Most of them are called via the generic ROM calls, but some (sensors, for example) have their own native code interface.

The Structure of the leJOS Virtual Machine

Once the initialization is done, the main loop of the byte code interpreter in vmsrc/interpreter.c is started, and executed once for every instruction. The instructions themselves are very close to the instructions defined in the Java virtual machine specification, with some modifications made to the operands that replace references to the constant pool by offsets, as explained in the section on the linker. The instructions are called from a large switch call. These instructions are included from files with the .hc extension.

Everything that is done in the main loop directly influences performance, because it is done for every executed byte code instruction. The main loop must check whether it is necessary to interrupt the normal execution and call the scheduler (if, for example, a hardware event happened or the time slice for the current thread was used up). To minimize the overhead, the single flag *gMakeRequest* is checked on every iteration. It is set either if some piece of code requests a call to the scheduler, or at least every millisecond in the OCIA interrupt. If the flag is set, the action to be taken is determined by looking at *gRequestCode*. If it is just a timer tick, then the ticks are counted and the scheduler is called only when the time slice is used up; if thread switching is requested it is called directly; and if there is an exit request, the interpreter terminates. Note that the correct way to create a scheduler request is to use this:

```
schedule_request (REQUEST_SWITCH_THREAD);
```

instead of manipulating *gMakeRequest* and *gRequestCode* directly.

On a higher level, the execution is organized in threads. Each thread has its own program counter and stack, and executes independently of the other threads. The scheduler's job is to switch between threads; this occurs in the *switch_thread* function. Its source code resides in vmsrc/threads.c. It also handles most of the life cycle of a thread. A thread is always in one of the following states:

- **NEW** A newly created thread that has no thread id, no stack allocated and is not queued.

- **STARTED** A new thread with ID, the stack is allocated and queued, but is not yet executing.

- **RUNNING** A thread that is in the process of execution.

- *SLEEPING* A thread that is sleeping. It will awake at a certain time.

- *CONDVAR_WAITING* A thread that is waiting for notification or timeout.

- *MON_WAITING* A thread that is waiting on a lock.

- *DEAD* A thread that is dead. The scheduler will deallocate its stack and remove it from the queue.

A thread is alive if it is neither NEW nor DEAD. Figure 8.4 shows the state transitions that a thread can take. Note that an uncaught exception causes a return from the *main* or *run* method and thus causes the death of the thread.

Figure 8.4 Execution States of a Thread

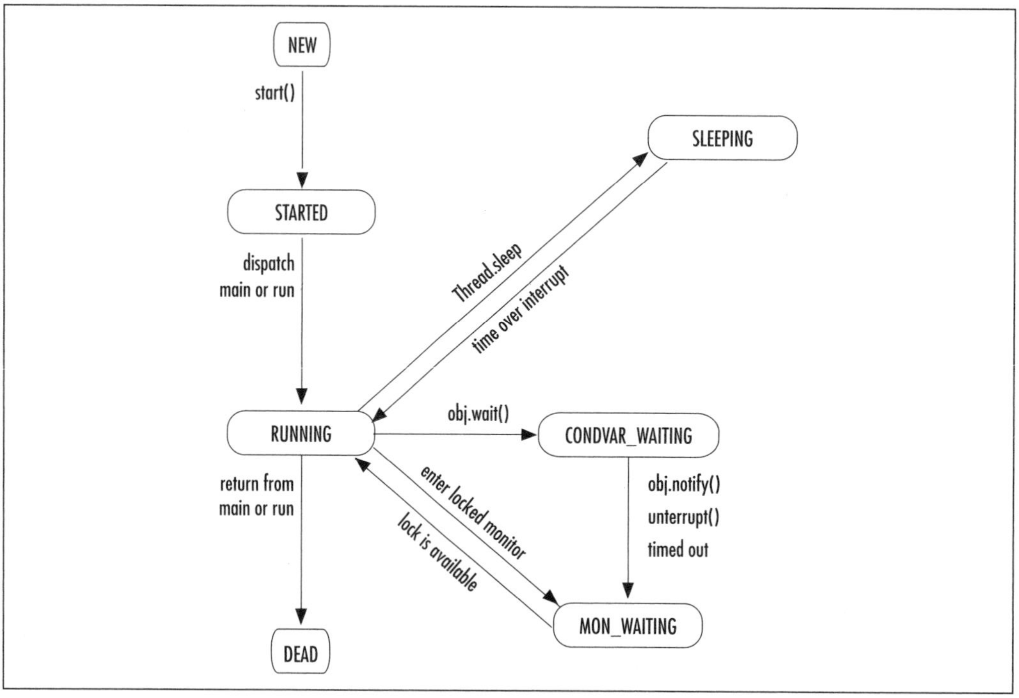

Real-Time Behavior

leJOS is intended for building systems that react in real time. It is therefore important to know on which time scales leJOS' different levels operate, and how you can achieve faster reaction times if you really need to.

The highest level is that of a Java program. Here you can expect reaction times on the order of ten milliseconds at best, even if you have a single thread that runs in a rather short loop. For larger programs with several threads, reaction time is more likely to be on the order of 100ms. A thread that does not yield the processor itself currently gets a time slice of 20ms, but this can be changed in platform_config.h via the *TICKS_PER_TIME_SLICE* constant, where a tick equals one millisecond. The ticks are generated by the OCIA interrupt that is activated every millisecond, and which also controls motors, A/D conversion for sensors, sounds, and the global millisecond timer that is read by *System .currentTimeMillis()*. As specified by the Java Language Specification, threads are scheduled strictly according to their priority. As long as high-priority threads want to run, all lower priority threads must wait. Threads of the same priority are scheduled in a round-robin fashion.

To achieve faster reaction times than those possible in Java code, you can add code to the virtual machine itself. This is facilitated by using one of the hooks into the byte code interpreter provided by the virtual machine :

- *instruction_hook()* Called before every instruction executed by the VM. Beware that using it will slow down leJOS considerably.

- *tick_hook()* Called at least every millisecond before the next instruction is executed, but possibly more often if there is scheduling activity. This has a relatively low impact on speed.

- *idle_hook()* Called when no thread wants to run.

- *switch_thread_hook()* Called after every call of the scheduler.

These hook into the main interpreter loop in vmsrc/interpreter.c, and their platform-specific values are defined in rcx_impl/platform_hooks.h and unix_impl/platform_hooks.h. The leJOS firmware currently uses only *tick_hook()* for sensor reading. The sensor values need to be processed on each A/D-conversion (which happens every 3ms), otherwise rotation sensors and pulse- and edge-counting on touch sensors will not work properly. To avoid this, a single transitional value leads to a miscount for the rotation sensor; as is the case for the RCX firmware, we require a value to be preset during two consecutive measurements before it can be counted. This reduces the maximal speed for the rotation sensor to 625 rotations per minute, which is still well above the raw speed of the gear motor in the Robotics Invention Set. It reliably eliminates the miscounts except for very low rotation speeds, where miscounts can still occur when there are two intermediate values in a row. The figure of 625 rpm is determined by the following equation:

$60s/(2*0.003*16) = 625$

RCX Memory Layout

At the lowest level, the memory layout of the RCX is the layout of the H8/3292 micro controller:

- **0x0000–0x3fff** ROM
- **0x4000–0x7fff** Reserved
- **0x8000–0xfb7f** External RAM
- **0xfb80–0xfd7f** Reserved
- **0xfd80–0xff7f** Internal RAM
- **0xff80–0xff87** External RAM
- **0xff88–0xff8f** Reserved
- **0xff90–0xffff** Hardware control registers

According to the H8 Hardware Manual, the reserved areas should not be accessed. The first two arise because they are in the address spaces for the ROM and the internal RAM, but the 3292, which is at the low end of the H8 controller range of, doesn't fill them completely with its internal ROM and RAM. In principle it would be possible to enable the external RAM in the area 0xfb80–0xff80 also, but this is not done in the ROM boot code, and at later stages it becomes difficult because the ROM data, interrupt vectors and stack are in this area.

The next higher level is that of the ROM. Since we want to reuse leJOS' ROM routines, we have to respect the data areas used by the ROM. The layout of the data areas in the RAM (from the point of view of the ROM) is as follows:

- **0x8000–0xef31** leJOS firmware and data. The uppermost part is used by the ROM main loop before the firmware is loaded. Since the only way back to the ROM loop is a full reset, this data is no longer needed when leJOS is running.
- **0xef32–0xf000** ROM data area.
- **0xef01–0xfb7f** Free RAM, unused
- **0xfb80–0xfd7f** Reserved by hardware
- **0xfd80–0xfd8f** ROM data, used by *init_timer*
- **0xfd90–0xfdbf** RAM interrupt vectors
- **0xfdc0–0xff7f** Stack, starts with the stack pointer (SP) pointing at 0xff7e and grows downwards

The file rcx_impl/rcx.lds describes the memory layout inside the RCX for the GNU linker *ld*, which uses it to place code and data in the appropriate regions of memory when linking the leJOS firmware. It is also used to define the particular addresses needed to access ROM data and hardware control registers.

Now let's look closer at how leJOS organizes the area **0x8000–0xef31** (the first part is taken up by the firmware, after that comes the loaded Java, and at the end comes the program data):

- **0x8000–MEM_START** Firmware code and data
- **MEM_START–mmStart** Java binary
- **mmStart–MEM_END** Java data
- **0xef02–0xfb7f** Java data (in leJOS versions later than 1.0.4).

The symbols *MEM_START*, *MEM_END* and *mmStart* are used in rcx_impl/main.c. *MEM_START* and *MEM_END* are defined as *_end* and *romdata1*, respectively, which in turn are defined in rcx_impl/rcx.lds. *mmStart* is the word-aligned beginning of the free space after the firmware is loaded. In leJOS versions up to 1.0.4 only the word-aligned *mmStart* is passed to the virtual machine's memory manager by a call to *init_memory*. Later versions use a different scheme where more than one memory region can be used for the heap. The initialization code first calls *memory_init* and then *memory_add_region,* with the lower and upper bound of each region without alignment. The memory manager does the necessary aligning and adds the regions to a linked list, with pointers to the next region and the end of the current region in the first four bytes of each region (see vmsrc/memory.c). The region that is added last is allocated first, beginning at its upper end. The layout of the firmware is done by the C linker according to rcx_impl/rcx.lds. The layout of the leJOS binary is created by the leJOS linker (explained above). Note that there is no relocation of offsets for obtaining the final address in the VM; each time a VM operation needs to access something in the leJOS binary, it computes the absolute address anew from the load address and the offset.

Now let's take a look at how the Java data are managed and how Java objects are represented. The memory is organized in blocks that begin with a header containing information about the type and size of the block. The format is defined in vmsrc/classes.h.

The first two bytes specify whether the block is allocated or not. If it is allocated, its length is specified; if the block is not allocated, it is specified whether it is an object or array. For objects, the first two bytes also contain the class index, which allows the memory manager to look up the size of the memory area for the object in the class record. For arrays, the first two bytes specify element type and size, which allows us to compute the size of the memory area used by the array. For objects and arrays, the subsequent two bytes contain the monitor count and possibly the thread that has obtained the lock associated with the object. They are followed by the instance variables or array elements. Besides defining objects, vmsrc/classes.h also defines the layout of the other special classes: *Thread*, *Runtime* and *String*.

All these definitions must agree with the definition in the Java library or leJOS will crash. Types are encoded in 4 bits as defined in vmsrc/constants.h, which allows the memory manager to determine the memory required to store one element of that type. There is a table with the sizes at the beginning of vmsrc/memory.c. Objects inside arrays or other objects are always stored as references, which makes them uniform in size. In addition to the Java-defined types, there is a leJOS-specific type for stack frames (*T_STACKFRAME*), which allows us to build an array of stack frames without using an indirection through *T_REFERENCE*.

Each thread has its own stack, which consists of an array of integers providing storage for the stack, and an array of stack frames storing the information to be preserved on method invocation. Stack frames store the program counter, the stack pointer and the base pointer for local variables, as well as information related to locking. The definition of the type *StackFrame* is in vmsrc/threads.h. Currently each thread is allocated a stack of 70 four-byte slots and an array of ten stack frames, which together with the thread data take up approximately 400 bytes of memory.

The Emulator

The emulator uses the same virtual machine as the RCX firmware, but differs in the loader in terms of the native code interface and its use of the VM hooks; also, it emulates the OCIA interrupt in software. Contrary to the virtual machine on the RCX, the emulator uses little-endian byte order. Loading the executable into the emulator is trivial, it just loads the file into memory. Currently the emulator always executes program number 0. For native code routines that call ROM routines there is no RCX equivalent, instead the memory address of the routine and its parameters are printed to standard output. The emulator is still very useful for regression testing and debugging.

In particular, there is a regression test suite in the main leJOS directory's regression subdirectory that you should run after making modifications to the virtual machine. To do this, change into the regression subdirectory and run the *run.sh* shell script. This will compile a large number of examples, run them using the emulator, and log the output in regression.log. At the end it will display the differences between the output produced by your run and a reference output in regression.gold. Often there will be minor differences, either due to your changes or due to the nondeterminism inherent in the execution of threads. It is up to you to judge whether the differences represent bugs or not. If you are satisfied that everything is working correctly you can copy regression.log to regression.gold to make it the new reference.

The leJOS Source Code

The leJOS source code is organized into several subdirectories within the main leJOS directory. It is quite diverse, since there are parts written in both C and Java, and there are two target architectures; the host computer and the RCX.

- **Main directory** Contains some global files, like README and RELEASENOTES. It also contains the file LICENSE, which contains the legalese giving you the right to use, modify and redistribute leJOS, as well as the obligation to make available the source code to any changed version of leJOS that you redistribute. From a technical point of view, the global Makefile is very interesting, it contains commands for the various steps needed in the compilation of leJOS. To compile the firmware you need a Makefile.config with the options set according to your environment, Makefile.config.renameme serves as a template for that.

- **bin** Contains the executable files for the host computer and the firmware in the file lejos.srec.

- **classes** Contains the Java classes for the RCX, organized according to the package hierarchy. classes/java/lang contains a subset of the standard Java classes, whose functionality is restricted to that which is most important for leJOS. classes/josx/platform/rcx contains all the RCX-specific classes for interfacing to the hardware.

- **common** Contains the files that are used to generate code for both the linker and the virtual machine. Currently, it creates constant definitions for special classes and signatures (mostly those of native methods), but also some with a special meaning for the VM, like *main*, *run* or *<init>*.

- **docs** Contains some documentation, mostly related to programming the virtual machine.

- **examples** Contains some examples that show the use of leJOS, and can be used for testing to verify whether everything is working correctly.

- **gameboy_impl** Contains the platform-specific files for the Nintendo Game Boy. Note that they are not up-to-date, they need to be adapted to recent developments.

- **jtools** Contains Java code for the host computer. jtools/js/tinyvm contains the leJOS linker, which relies heavily upon the Java class file reader in jtools/js/classfile. The directory jtools/js/tools contains the Java program for generating the files with constant definitions for the linker and the VM from common/*.db.

- **lib** Contains the Java class libraries (.jar files) for both the RCX and the host computer.

- **rcx_impl** Contains the RCX-specific C code for the firmware; for loading the binary and initializing it, plus some low-level code that deals with sensors and timers.

- **regression** Contains a regression test suite for leJOS.

- **tools** Contains C code for the leJOS tools.

- **unix_impl** Contains the C code that is specific for the emulator.

- **vmsrc** Contains the C code for the virtual machine. It is mostly independent of the architecture on which it runs, (with the architecture-dependent parts in unix_impl and rcx_impl).

You can obtain the leJOS source code in several ways. The easiest is to download a release from the leJOS website (currently at http://sourceforge.net/project/showfiles.php?group_id=9339). There are two kinds of releases, lejos and lejos-win32, which both contain the complete source code. Lejos-win32 additionally contains the executable programs for Windows, while lejos contains only the source code and is intended for Linux and UNIX systems.

File releases are usually a few weeks or months old. You can get the most recent version of the source code from the CVS server at sourceforge.net by issuing the following command:

```
cvs -z3 -d:pserver:anonymous@cvs.lejos.sourceforge.net:/cvsroot/lejos co
lejos
```

This will create the lejos directory containing the source code. Both kinds of releases and the CVS version contain the compiled firmware. You only need to install the h8300 cross-compiler if you want to make your own modifications to the firmware.

Developing & Deploying…

Compiling the leJOS Firmware

The leJOS firmware is developed using the GNU tools. These are the standard tools under Linux, but they also exist as part of the Cygwin system for Windows. To compile the leJOS firmware you need a special version of the GNU tools that targets the h8300 architecture of the micro controller in the RCX. Some Linux distributions (Debian, for example), already contain a package with a h8300 cross-compiler, which only needs to be installed. However, this is currently GCC version 2.95, which does not produce the most compact code. For the official releases of leJOS we use version 3.0, which reduces code size by something on the order of one KB. To obtain your own gcc-3.0 cross compiler, take a look at http://h8300-hms.sourceforge.net. The compiler is available as an RPM package, though you can also obtain the sources and compile it (and the associated binary tools) yourself. This is less complicated than it sounds, and there is a detailed description at the site that works very well.

The other thing that you need in order to compile the firmware is Kekoa Proudfoot's *librcx* library, available at http://graphics.stanford .edu/~kekoa/rcx/librcx.tar.gz. It contains some basic definitions and code for initialization, ROM calls and some arithmetic.

Now that you have everything together, you just need to tell the Makefile where to find the cross compiler and the library. You do this by adding suitable definitions in Makefile.config. For example, this is what I have in mine:

```
BINDIR = /usr/local/src/hms-gcc/bin

BINPREFIX = h8300-hms-

LIBRCX_HOME = /home/juergen/Sonst/Lego/librcx-2000-12-16

export BINDIR

export BINPREFIX

export LIBRCX_HOME
```

Now **make lejos_bin** or **make all** can be used to compile the firmware.

Extending leJOS with Native Methods

Normal methods in a Java program are written in Java, compiled to byte codes and executed by the virtual machine's byte code interpreter. They can only manipulate data inside the virtual machine; they don't have any access to the outside world. Native methods, on the other hand, are executed as native machine code; they can access data both inside and outside the JVM. So native methods are necessary for communicating with the outside world, and for doing anything useful at all.

Execution of native methods is also faster than the execution of methods in byte code. Further, native methods cannot be preempted by the scheduler. This makes them useful for real-time programming, when especially rapid responses are needed, for example; or when several operations must be tied together into one that is atomically executed.

In this section we will explain step-by-step how to add a native method to leJOS. But before we start writing our own native methods we will first look a little at what native methods can do in leJOS, and which native methods are already present in the package.

Native Methods in leJOS

Compared to the Java Native Interface (JNI), leJOS' native methods are more directly part of the virtual machine. They also are more limited. For example, it is not possible to call Java from C, as Java byte code can not be executed while a native method is running. You can however dispatch a method that will be called after your native method has finished. With respect to the manipulation of data, however, native code is not restricted in any way, it has full access to the virtual machine's internals. There is less support for accessing Java data than in JNI, but you can work directly on the data structures using the C functions of the leJOS virtual machine. A leJOS native method in one class can coexist with non-native methods of the same name and signature in another class. However, since native methods are identified only by their signature and not their class, there can be only one native method for each signature.

The existing native methods in leJOS are used by the leJOS Java library to interface with the RCX hardware and with certain internal aspects of the virtual machine.

- Hardware access is done via classes in *josx.platform.rcx*, in particular *josx.platform.rcx.ROM*, which contains methods for calling *ROM* routines, and *josx.platform.rcx.Memory*, which contains methods for directly accessing memory. Some other native methods occur in *Serial*, *Sensor* and *Poller*, but most of the classes in *josx.platform.rcx* use ROM calls to access the hardware. Note that in previous versions the methods now in *ROM* and *Memory* were in *Native*, and were not publicly accessible. *Memory* also contains a native method to get the memory address for any object, which allows it to access the internal data structures of the virtual machine

- Communication with the virtual machine is done via native methods in special classes within the java.lang package. These classes, in particular *Object* and *Thread*, interact with the virtual machine in special ways. For example, *Thread* contains native methods to start a thread, sleep, set the priority, etc. (in other words, actions that interact with the scheduler). The *Object* class contains the native methods used for waiting and waking up a waiting process, which can be used to make locking more efficient. The internal structure of instances for these classes are defined both in Java and in the C code of the virtual machine. Their respective definitions must match or leJOS will crash.

Adding a Native Method

To add a native method to leJOS, we first need to write a declaration in some Java class. The declaration is like that of an ordinary method, except that the modifier *native* is added and there is no *method* body.

All other modifiers except *abstract* and *strictfp* are allowed, and by convention the native modifier should come last. As an example we will implement native methods for determining the stack usage in a thread.

We first add a class *VMStatistics* to *josx.platform.rcx* (shown in Figure 8.5 and available on the CD).

Figure 8.5 VMStatistics.java

```
package josx.platform.rcx;

/**
 * Provides statistics about execution in the virtual machine
 */
public class VMStatistics
{
```

Continued

Figure 8.5 Continued

```
public static native int getStackSize (Thread t);
public static native int getStackMaxUsed (Thread t);

public static int getStackMinFree (Thread t)
{
    return getStackSize (t) - getStackMaxUsed (t);
}
}
```

Next we have to declare the signatures of the new native methods. We append the lines in Figure 8.6 to common/signatures.db.

Figure 8.6 Lines Appended to File common/signatures.db

```
# josx.platform.rcx.VMStatistics
getStackSize(Ljava/lang/Thread;)I
getStackMaxUsed(Ljava/lang/Thread;)I
```

The line format in common/signatures.db is as follows:

```
methodName(argumentTypes)resultType
```

This is the name of the method followed by a method descriptor as specified in Section 4.3.3 of the Java Virtual Machine Specification. Types are encoded by field descriptors, which are summarized in Table 8.1.

Table 8.1 Encoding of Java Types in Signatures

Java Type	Encoding
void	V
boolean	Z
char	C
byte	B
short	S
int	I
long	J
float	F

Continued

Table 8.1 Continued

Java Type	Encoding
double	D
package.....package.Class	Lpackage/.../package/Class;
array	[(type of elements follows)

The important thing about this encoding is that it completely specifies signature and return type, so that no two distinct methods can be confused. But note that this format does not distinguish class and instance methods, and that it is in general not necessary to add a class that contains a native method to the special classes in common/classes.db.

From the signatures we generate include files for the linker and the virtual machine by executing the following command in the main lejos directory (normally this is done automatically by **make all**):

```
% make generated_files
```

This creates the two files vmsrc/specialsignatures.h and jtools/js/tinyvm/SpecialSignatureConstants.java. These associate a number to each native method in a consistent way. The linker will map names of native methods in the class files to numbers in the leJOS binary using a table constructed from this file, and the virtual machine will then use the numbers to select the native code it executes. For this to work, the numbers must be the same for the linker and the virtual machine, or leJOS will call the wrong code and crash. Essentially this is a change to the leJOS binary format. To ensure that the binary created by the linker and the firmware are compatible, the linker puts a magic number inside the binary, which is checked when the binary is loaded on the RCX. If they mismatch you will get this error message:

```
Magic number is not right. Linker used was for emulation only?
```

You should change this magic number whenever you add a native method. The magic number for the virtual machine is defined in vmsrc/magic.h; we increase it by one:

```
#define MAGIC 0xCAF3
```

For the linker it is defined in jtools/js/tinyvm/Constants.java; we change it to the same value:

```
    public static final int MAGIC_MASK = 0xCAF3;
```

Next we take a look into vmsrc/specialsignatures.h and find definitions for our new native methods:

```
#define getStackSize_4Ljava_3lang_3Thread_2_5I 43
#define getStackMaxUsed_4Ljava_3lang_3Thread_2_5I 44
```

As you see, there has been some name mangling done to make the signatures acceptable as identifiers. Now it remains to do the implementation of the native methods in the VM. We add the code in Figure 8.7 to the end of the switch statements in rcx_impl/native.c and unix_impl/nativeemul.c.

Figure 8.7 Code Added to Files rcx_impl/native.c and unix_impl/nativeemul.c

```
case getStackSize_4Ljava_3lang_3Thread_2_5I:
  push_word (get_stack_size ((Thread *) word2ptr(paramBase[0])));
  return;
case getStackMaxUsed_4Ljava_3lang_3Thread_2_5I:
  push_word (get_stack_max_used ((Thread *) word2ptr(paramBase[0])));
  return;
```

Note that leJOS may be ported to more platforms in the future, and that you may need to extend the corresponding files there as well. It is however not strictly necessary to provide an implementation for the functioning of the system; not providing one will not cause leJOS to crash. If a native method is not implemented, an exception is raised whenever it is called, but otherwise the system functions normally.

Arguments to a native method are accessed via the pointer *paramBase*. The layout follows the standard Java VM convention:

- When an instance method is called, *paramBase[0]* contains a reference to the instance and *paramBase[1]* to *paramBase[n]* contain the arguments that are passed to the method.

- When a class method is called, *paramBase[0]* to *paramBase[n]* contain the arguments that are passed to the method.

Note that each long or double parameter takes up two slots. Since they are used so often, the function *dispatch_native* in rcx_impl/native.c contains abbreviations *paramBase1* for paramBase+1 and *paramBase2* for paramBase+2, which avoids doing the index computation over and over again (it exists only for those two, as no index computation is needed for *paramBase[0]*; and *paramBase[3]* and higher are not used often). By defining *paramBase2* and using it instead of *paramBase[2]*, which occurs 9 times, a total of 18 bytes were saved. This may not seem like much, but on such a small machine every byte counts, and here we can get them almost for free.

In our example we are implementing a class method so the thread argument is passed in *paramBase[0]*. It is represented by a four-byte integer, which the function *word2ptr* converts to a C pointer. Our two C functions return a 16-bit value, which is pushed on the stack as a 32-bit Java int.

Our native methods call the C functions *get_stack_size* and *get_stack_max_used*. To implement their functionality we will put a mark just beyond every newly created stack frame, like a high water mark. Then we just have to search for the highest mark to get the maximal stack usage. The stack is initialized with zeros when it is allocated, so we will only need to search for the highest non-zero slot to find our mark.

In vmsrc/threads.c we allocate one more integer, so that *STACK_SIZE* has enough space for the mark:

```
// Allocate actual stack storage (STACK_SIZE * 4 bytes)
thread->stackArray = ptr2word (new_primitive_array
                                (T_INT, STACK_SIZE+1));
```

In vmsrc/stack.h we let the function *is_stack_overflow* (which checks for stack overflow) put in the mark and add the functions for stack size and maximal usage (see Figure 8.8).

Figure 8.8 Modification of vmsrc/stack.h

```
static inline boolean is_stack_overflow (MethodRecord *methodRecord)
{
  STACKWORD *newStackTop = stackTop + methodRecord->maxOperands;
  STACKWORD *stackEnd = stack_array() + STACK_SIZE;
  boolean is_overflow = newStackTop >= stackEnd;

  if (!is_overflow) {
    *newStackTop = 1;
  }
  return is_overflow;
}
```

Continued

Figure 8.8 Continued

```
static inline int get_stack_size (Thread *t)
{
  return STACK_SIZE;
}


static inline int get_stack_max_used (Thread *t)
{
  STACKWORD *t_stack_array
    = (STACKWORD *) ((byte *) word2ptr(t->stackArray) + HEADER_SIZE);
  STACKWORD *p = t_stack_array + STACK_SIZE;

  while (*p == 0)  p--;
  return p - t_stack_array;
}
```

Note that we used *inline* for these functions as they are used only once. By making the C compiler inline them in the switch, we avoid the overhead for calling the function and passing arguments.

Now that everything is in place you can recompile leJOS by executing the following command:

```
make all
```

This will recompile the library and compile the leJOS firmware and the emulator. You can load your new firmware onto the RCX with lejosfirmdl, as usual. At this point, however, we still need to test the native method. The following class will do an increasingly deep recursion and display the stack usage at each iteration. The computations inside *recurse* serve only to consume some space on the stack (see Figure 8.9—this is also available on the CD).

Figure 8.9 StackTest.java

```
import java.lang.System;
import josx.platform.rcx.*;


public class StackTest
{
```

Continued

Figure 8.9 Continued

```
private static int sum = 0;

private static void recurse (int depth)
{
  int a = sum + depth;
  int b = sum + a;

  if (depth <= 0) {
    return;
  } else {
    recurse (depth-1);
  }
  sum = a + b;
}

public static void main (String[] arg)
  throws InterruptedException
{
  Thread t = Thread.currentThread();

  LCD.showProgramNumber (0);
  LCD.showNumber (VMStatistics.getStackSize (t));
  Thread.sleep (500);
  for (int i = 1; i < 10; i++) {
    recurse (i);
    LCD.showProgramNumber (i);
    LCD.showNumber (VMStatistics.getStackMaxUsed (t));
    Thread.sleep (500);
  }
  LCD.showProgramNumber (10); // invisible
  LCD.showNumber (sum);
}
}
```

After working on the virtual machine, it is a good idea to not only test whether it is still working (the View example in examples/view is suitable for that), but whether the performance has suffered, using the PerformanceTest example in examples/performance_test. Doing this shows that, with the new methods, we have about 150 bytes less free memory in the VM. Since memory is tight and these methods are only rarely useful, it is probably not a good idea to add them to a release version of leJOS.

If you try to optimize for memory, check that the optimized version is indeed smaller. Often it is not, as storing and retrieving the value causes some overhead, especially if this exhausts the available registers. From two versions with the same footprint, choose the clearer one. For example, if you are iterating over an array *item[LENGTH]* and want to access the elements by a pointer *item_ptr*, there are two possibilities for writing the *for* loop, this one:

```
for (i=0; i < LENGTH; i++) {
  item_ptr = &item[i];
```

or the common C idiom:

```
for (i=0, item_ptr = item; i < len; i++, item_ptr++) {
```

C programmers usually prefer the second variant, which has the advantage of replacing the multiplication in the index computation by an iterated addition, which is likely to run somewhat faster. However, in leJOS, space is more important than speed, and the second version often (though not always) uses more space. Also, the first version is clearer, as it makes the meaning of *item_ptr* more

Debugging...

Debugging the leJOS Firmware

Debugging programs for an embedded system like the RCX pose some problems, as you cannot easily look inside the RCX as you can on a PC. Here are some techniques you can use:

> **Debugging in the emulator** The emulator is a standard C program on your PC, so you can use your favorite C debugging techniques with it. For example, you can insert *print* statements that produce debug output, and you can run the emulator inside the GNU debugger gdb. This is especially useful for work on the VM.

Continued

Debugging on the RCX If your modifications to leJOS involve the RCX hardware, you are less fortunate. However, all is not lost. As with Java programs, you can use the I/O facilities of the RCX to produce debug output. Most useful is the LCD display, where you can display values that interest you. A good technique is to use the four-digit part to display the value and the program number to indicate the point in the program at which you are. This is especially useful if leJOS crashes, as the last value will stay visible on the LCD. Another useful form of output is sound, especially for output that is too fast to read on the LCD. A useful routine to produce both forms of output is the trace routine in rcx_impl/main.c.

Using assertions Assertions are checks within a program that state that a certain property must hold. They not only serve to find bugs, but are also useful for documenting the conditions inside the code. They are implemented by a macro that only activates them when in debugging mode, otherwise they act as comments. By default, assertions are active in the emulator version of leJOS but not in the RCX version. The assertion check may be any Boolean expression, which is evaluated and, in the event that it is false, causes the program to abort with an error message. See the main interpreter loop in vmsrc/language.c for examples.

explicit, and if there are only a few occurrences of *item[i]* you may even use that directly. So before you use the second version, check whether it is worthwhile.

Additional Tips and Tricks with leJOS

We'll end the chapter with a few useful tricks to help you get to know and extend the capabilities of leJOS. First we'll briefly mention how to increase the size of the stack in case your program needs more stack space or deeper recursion than is available by default. Another important issue is to know the amount of free memory, as memory is usually the scarcest resource in leJOS; we'll show you how to determine the amount of free memory. The third issue is timing, which is often critical for real-time systems. We'll use an example with two communicating threads to demonstrate how to measure latency, and how good programming style can avoid having a thread wait for and unnecessarily long time.

Changing Stack Sizes

Now that you know how much of the stack your threads use (thanks to the native method example), you might see that they actually use only a small fraction of their generously allocated stack. If you have many threads and you are having problems trying to fit your program into memory, you might be tempted to decrease the stack size. In theory you may also run into problems with a stack that is too small for your needs, though as far as I know this has not yet happened. Changing leJOS' stack size is not difficult. There are two parameters: the *stack size*, which limits the amount of memory used, and the *number of stack frames*, which limits the recursion depth. Both values can be changed globally by editing vmsrc/configure.h and recompiling the leJOS firmware.

Determining the Amount of Free Memory

Since memory is rather scarce in leJOS, it is often useful to find out how much memory remains for you to use. For this you can use the method *freeMemory()* in the class *java.lang.Runtime*. To use it, type:

```
(int)(Runtime.getRuntime().freeMemory())
```

The method returns a long, as required by the Java API Standard. Since most of the operations on long are not implemented in leJOS, in order to save space, you need to cast the long to an int (or if you like, to a short). There is also a similar method, called *totalMemory*, that gives you the total amount of memory in the system.

Measuring Latency

In programs where the reaction time is crucial, it is sometimes useful to measure latencies. This is simple with the global millisecond timer, which can be used as a stopwatch. The code in Figure 8.10, which is also provided on the CD, is a simple example of how this works.

Figure 8.10 LatencyTest.java

```
import josx.platform.rcx.*;

public class LatencyTest
{
    static int startTime;
    static int maxLatency = 0;
```

Continued

Figure 8.10 Continued

```
static boolean flag = false;

public static void main( String[] arg)
    throws InterruptedException
{
  Thread t1 = new Thread () {
      public void run()
      {
        while (true) {
          while (flag)
            Thread.yield();
          startTime = (int)System.currentTimeMillis();
          flag = true;
        }
      }
    };


  Thread t2 = new Thread () {
      public void run()
      {
        while (true) {
          while (!flag)
            Thread.yield();
          flag = false;
          int stopTime = (int)System.currentTimeMillis();
          if (stopTime - startTime > maxLatency)
            maxLatency = stopTime - startTime;
        }
      }
    };


  while (Button.RUN.isPressed());

  t1.start();
```

Continued

Figure 8.10 Continued

```
    t2.start();


    while (!Button.RUN.isPressed()) {
      LCD.showNumber (maxLatency);
      Thread.sleep (100);
    }
    while (Button.RUN.isPressed());
    System.exit (0);

  }

}
```

Here we create two threads (*t1* and *t2*), that communicate in a very simple way via a Boolean flag. The first thread envoys the message by setting *flag* to *true*, and the second thread waits for *flag* to become *true*, which means that the message has arrived. To measure latency, the first thread records the time before it sends the message, and the second thread computes the time duration that the passing message took after receiving it. Since we are interested in the maximum latency, the second thread keeps a running maximum of the duration in *maxLatency*, which is displayed by the main program every 100 milliseconds. Since the measurement starts before sending and stops after receiving, the latency that is displayed is an upper bound of the actual latency.

The threads in this example are well behaved, as they yield when they are waiting in a loop. This allows other threads to run; so here the second thread reacts relatively quickly, as the maximum latency displayed is only two milliseconds. If you remove the *Thread.yield()* in the *while* loop of the sending thread, it keeps running until it is preempted at the end of its full time slice. The second thread can only then react, with a latency of as much as 20 milliseconds. It is generally a good idea to put a *Thread.yield()* wherever a thread is waiting. However, if the sending thread has a higher priority than the receiver, this is not enough; you will have to either sleep or wait on a locked object to give up the processor for the other thread.

Summary

Advanced techniques such as multiprogram downloading and persistent storage of data can help you to make your robots more useful and flexible. To load several Java programs simultaneously onto the RCX you can link them together into a single multi-program binary and load them onto the RCX together. This allows you to easily switch among the different programs, for running a competition or a demo, for example. To store data persistently on the RCX you can use the class *josx.platform.rcx.PersistentMemoryArea* in the leJOS library. Persistent data is not deleted on every run of a leJOS program as is the case with normal data, but rather it survives as long as the RCX has battery power. *PersistentMemoryArea* also serves as an example for the use of direct memory access using the class *josx.platform.rcx.Memory*.

leJOS uses the standard Java compiler inside a wrapper that sets the classpath appropriately. The leJOS linker transforms a Java program in the form of several Java class files into a leJOS binary that can be loaded onto the RCX. The linker starts with the entry point classes and recursively loads all classes that are referenced, until the program is complete. It dumps the program into a special binary format that can be loaded into the leJOS virtual machine and executed without modification.

The leJOS firmware consists of the loader and the virtual machine. The loader loads the binary via IR communications and allows the user to select the entry point and start the program. It also initializes memory and creates the boot thread. The virtual machine executes byte codes in its main loop. Periodically or upon request, the scheduler preempts a thread and selects a new one to run. If they are not running, threads may be sleeping or waiting on a lock. The scheduler is also responsible for initializing new threads and removing dead threads. The RCX's RAM is used for the leJOS firmware, the program binary and for the heap containing Java objects, in that order. Memory can be allocated as needed, but there is currently no garbage collection. Java stacks are allocated on the heap, they are freed after the thread dies.

Native methods are special methods that are implemented by native machine code instead of Java byte code. Native code has no restrictions with respect to the objects in memory it can access. It is also faster than Java code and can be used to program atomic operations that cannot be interrupted by the scheduler. LeJOS uses native methods for accessing the hardware, either by native methods for ROM calls, or by special native methods, for accessing sensors, for example. It also uses native methods to communicate with the virtual machine, for example to implement the special methods in *java.lang.Object* and *java.lang.Thread*. Native methods become part of the firmware. They are identified by their signature index, which is known both to the linker and the firmware, in the form of special constants. For each native method there are implementations for various platforms, currently these are the RCX and the emulator.

Finally there are a few useful tricks, like changing the stack size in vmsrc/configure.h or determining free memory by using *java.lang.Runtime.freeMemory()*. When you have several threads you should be careful when selecting priorities. To reduce latency, threads should yield or sleep whenever they are waiting in a loop, or they should wait on a lock instead.

Solutions Fast Track

Advanced Usage of leJOS

☑ You can link several programs into a single binary by calling the linker with a comma-separated list of the entry classes containing the *main* method.

☑ You can store data persistently by using thelibrary's *josx.platform.rcx.PersistentMemoryArea* class.

☑ You can inspect and modify the contents of the RCX's memory by using the methods in the library class *josx.platform.rcx.Memory*.

Examining leJOS Internals

☑ leJOS uses the standard Java compiler, but employs a leJOS-specific linker on the host computer and a leJOS-specific virtual machine in the firmware on the RCX.

☑ The linker reads the Java class files and produces a leJOS binary that can be loaded into the firmware without any modification. Class, method and field names are replaced by offsets into the binary.

☑ The firmware contains a loader that loads the binary and a virtual machine that executes it. The virtual machine executes slightly modified Java byte code instructions.

☑ Threads are scheduled strictly according to priority, and round-robin within the same priority. They are preempted after a time-slice of 20 milliseconds.

☑ Each thread uses approximately 400 bytes of memory for its stack and other data structures.

Extending leJOS with Native Methods

☑ Native methods are used to interface with the hardware and with the virtual machine.

☑ To add a native method to the VM you need to add its signature to common/signatures.db, and you need to provide an implementation for the RCX in rcx_impl/native.c and for the emulator in unix_impl/ nativeemul.c.

☑ To optimize for memory you can use variables for common expressions. Always test whether your optimization is better than the original.

Additional Tips and Tricks with leJOS

☑ You can determine the amount of free memory with the method *freeMemory* in the class *java.lang.Runtime*.

☑ You can change the stack size by modifying the values in vmsrc/configure.h and recompiling the leJOS firmware.

Frequently Asked Questions

The following Frequently Asked Questions, answered by the authors of this book, are designed to both measure your understanding of the concepts presented in this chapter and to assist you with real-life implementation of these concepts. To have your questions about this chapter answered by the author, browse to **www.syngress.com/solutions** and click on the **"Ask the Author"** form.

Q: I'm using JDK version 1.4. Why do I get the following error message?

```
js.classfile.EClassFileFormat: Version not recognized: 46.0
```

A: Sun has changed the default class file format from 1.1 to 1.2 in the Java SDK 1.4. Give *lejosc* the additional option *-target 1.1* to make the compiler create the old format.

Q: Can we add a method to class *java.lang.Object* to free an object?

A: The classes in *java.lang* have a standard interface that is defined in the Java API Specification. It is not a good idea to change that. This also applies to other standard classes in *java.lang* and to other methods you might want to add.

Q: Why is the *switch* statement not implemented? Shouldn't we add that to leJOS?

A: The Java compiler translates a *switch* statement into a *lookupswitch* or *tableswitch* virtual machine operation. Compared to other VM instructions they are rather complicated, and implementing them would probably cost several hundreds of bytes in the leJOS virtual machine. The same functionality can be achieved by using conditional statements, so the cost of having *switch* would probably outweigh the benefit. However, if you want to try it and come up with some hard numbers that prove us wrong, you're welcome to do it.

Q: Why isn't garbage collection implemented?

A: Real time garbage collection is not easy, so nobody has done it yet. Also, the code for garbage collection would eat up memory, and some people fear that there would not be enough memory left, no matter how useful garbage collection would be.

Q: What virtual machine does leJOS use? Is it related to the Java 2 Micro Edition (J2ME) or to JavaCard?

A: leJOS contains its own virtual machine, which is neither an implementation of J2ME nor of JavaCard. J2ME is intended for bigger machines with a memory of at least 128KB. JavaCard has the right size but is aimed at a totally different application area (smart cards).

Q: Does leJOS implement the Real-Time Specification for Java?

A: No. The Real-Time Specification for Java is too large for such a small machine.

## Chapter 9

Programming LEGO MINDSTORMS with Jini

Solutions in this chapter:

- Overview of Jini

- A Simple Jini Service Example

- Proxies and Service Architectures

- A RCX Jini Proxy Service

- Using the RCX Jini Service: Example Server and Client

☑ Summary

☑ Solutions Fast Track

☑ Frequently Asked Questions

Introduction

Jini, which is pronounced like "genie," is the name of Sun's Java technology that is a framework for distributed computing. As such, its purpose is to allow computers and electronic devices to not only communicate with each other but also to be "plug and play" enabled, allowing devices to find one another on a network. There is a large amount of information available to support the developer who wants to work with Jini, ranging from the documentation distributed with Sun's Jini Technology Starter Kit (TSK) to a number of books and Web sites, including an online Jini community at http://jini.org.

Since Jini allows devices to communicate with each other, and since robots are devices, they are suitable for utilizing the Jini framework. However, there is a limitation of running a Jini service inside of the robot itself. But by using a proxy on a host PC, a Jini service can still be implemented for the RCX. In this chapter, we will provide an overview of Jini, and cover all the requirements for installing and running Jini services before exploring a simple example of an actual Jini service and client. After this, we will focus on Jini's potential applications with the RCX, and show a number of MINDSTORMS robots interacting with one another using Jini technology.

Overview of the Jini Architecture

Jini is a form of middleware that aims to make networks much more dynamic in that devices can be readily added or removed from the network with very little administrative overhead. The devices form a "federation," which is essentially a collection of available services, and the clients that make use of those services.

Jini is not a client/server architecture. It is very much a device-to-device architecture, where any device may make services available to the network, and any device may be a client of those services. The only requirement is that there be at least one *lookup service* on the network. The lookup service forms a kind of central repository that providers of services can register their available services with, and that clients can request the availability of services from.

Figure 9.1 demonstrates how this may appear in practice. In this example, the telephone and fax machine devices may register services with the lookup services. The workstation and the Personal Digital Assistant (PDA) (which may be operating via a wireless link such as 802.11b) could then discover these services through requests to the lookup service and then make use of the services.

Figure 9.1 A Federation of Devices Using a Jini Lookup Service

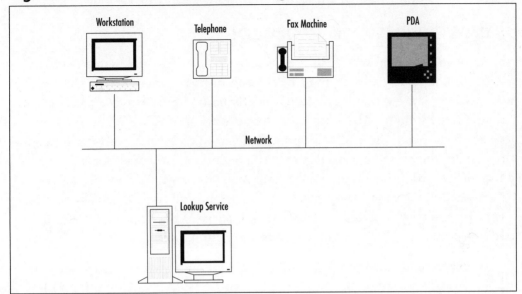

So, what kind of scenarios would be good candidates for using Jini? Really, any network where a disparate set of devices may be added or removed at various times and where maximum interoperability and minimum administrative overhead is required. This probably describes just about any computing network anywhere, but a good illustration is the concept of a home appliance control system.

Imagine that you have a wall-mounted control unit in your living room, connected via an IP-based network to a number of devices in your house (for example, refrigerator, coffee machine, and microwave oven), and an early summer arrives. You purchase a new Jini-enabled air conditioning unit, bring it home and plug it into your home network. Immediately your control unit detects the presence of the air conditioner; in fact it not only detects its presence but is also able to display the air conditioner's user interface. You haven't installed any drivers; it just works!

What then does Jini have to do with LEGO? Well, as you will see as we progress through this chapter, Jini is remarkably useful in networking embedded devices that may require obscure communications protocols and allowing them to appear as simple Java objects. And since the RCX is an embedded system that does indeed require a fairly obscure protocol, Jini is the ideal technology for network-enabling the RCX for all kinds of distributed LEGO scenarios; imagine robots that can find each other in a network and communicate with their brothers to work together as a team. They could take over the world...

Jini as a Network Protocol

Jini is not in itself a protocol, but it does serve to hide any underlying network protocols. The remote objects must be written in Java (or at least in a language that produces Java byte code), and the underlying transport must be Java Remote Method Invocation (RMI)—or a very close imitation of RMI. What Jini does is leverage technologies like RMI to provide a very high level of network abstraction. Taking the example from Figure 9.1, the workstation could obtain a telephone object from the lookup service and make standard method calls against it as if it was a regular local Java object. These method calls would actually be executing on the telephone, and so a call such as *phone.Dial("Home")* replaces the traditional process which would have gone something like this:

- Determine a custom protocol for sending messages to a telephone device, including defining such messages as DIAL, HANGUP, XFER, and so on, as well as response messages.

- Implement a socket server at the telephone end that will accept connections, and a socket client at the workstation end.

- Establish a socket connection between the two devices, and manage the formation and parsing of the various messages that must be sent between the two devices.

Clearly, some kind of network protocol is being implemented, but it is hidden from the developer by RMI and Jini. The developer does not need to know anything at all about how the messages are being handled at a network protocol level, which is quite handy if you don't know too much about the inner workings of your new refrigerator!

It's also quite handy if you want to talk to some LEGO MINDSTORMS devices that are scattered around your network. Instead of having to concoct a complex protocol for talking to the machines that are connected to the RCXs and manage all of the complexities of establishing connections, transmitting and receiving messages, and handling network errors, it would be magnificent to be able to talk to the MINDSTORMS devices as if they were local Java objects. In the examples that follow, we will show how it's possible to do just that, and by the end of the chapter you will understand how these robots can communicate with each other and influence one another's actions.

A Simple Jini Service Example

To illustrate just how a simple Jini service is built, we will discuss a simple service that can calculate a checksum on a character string. In order to test such a service we will first investigate the various supporting services that must be installed and configured. After covering this rather simplistic example, we will move on to a more complex case that will demonstrate how multiple RCXs can interact with one another in a network.

What's Required for Installing and Running Services

In order to install and run your own Jini services, you will need the Jini .jar files installed on any machine that will be acting as a client or that will be providing a service. Furthermore, you will require access to a Jini lookup service. Fortunately, Sun's Jini Technology Starter Kit includes the required .jar files, as well as a set of sample service implementations that can be used for development and testing. The included services are shown in Table 9.1.

Table 9.1 Jini Services Available in the TSK v1.2

Service Name	Description
Reggie	Reggie is a Jini Lookup Service, which will be used extensively in the examples in this chapter.
Fiddler	Fiddler is a Jini Lookup Discovery Service.
Mahalo	Mahalo is a Jini Transaction Manager Service. Jini includes rich transaction management functionality.
Norm	Norm is a Jini Lease Renewal Service.
Outrigger	Outrigger is a pair of JavaSpaces Services.
Mercury	Mercury is a Jini Event Mailbox Service that can be used in conjunction with Jini Lookup Services to store events on another entity's behalf.

The first step is to download and install the Jini TSK. At the time of writing, this was at version 1.2, available from http://java.sun.com/jini. For the purposes of the following examples, we will assume that Jini has been installed on a Windows 2000 platform in c:\jini1_2. Obviously, you will have to adjust the examples if you have installed the Jini TSK to a different location, or if you are running on a different platform.

The lookup service implementation that comes with the TSK is called *reggie*, and it has a few dependencies. You will need to run the RMI Activation Daemon (*rmid*), and you will also need an HTTP server. A simple HTTP server has also been provided in Sun's Jini starter kit, although you may choose to use another, such as Microsoft IIS or Apache. Figure 9.2 shows the relationship between these services. The shaded boxes in the figure represent the three programs we will set up in this section, and which will be depended on by all of the examples in this chapter. The boxes without shading represent client programs and services that will be developed in the examples. Note that any of the five components in Figure 9.2 can theoretically be run anywhere on the network (or at least on the one subnet), but for initial development purposes it is possible to run them all on one machine.

Figure 9.2 Basic Components of a Jini Federation

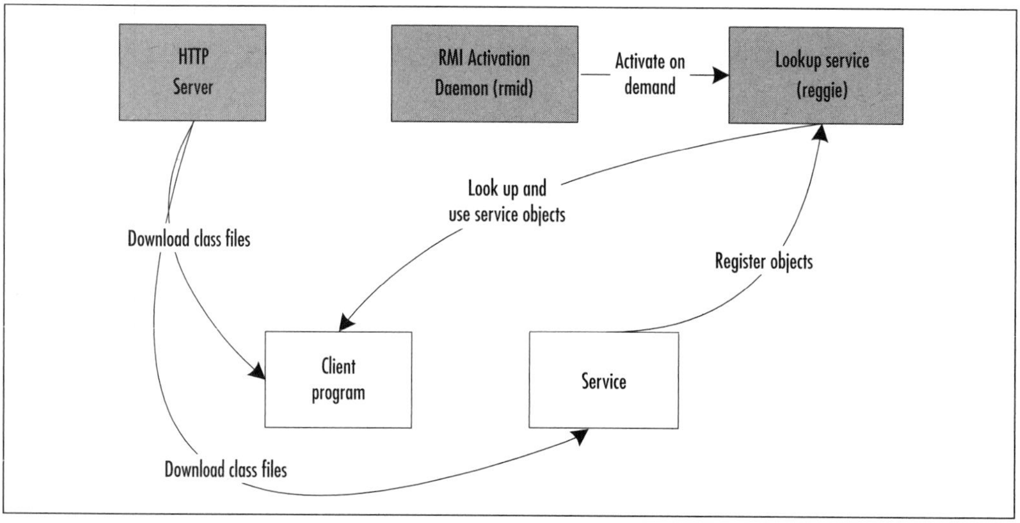

The first step is to run the HTTP server. The following batch file will start the Jini TSK implementation on port 8081; you could use another port, including the default HTTP port of 80. The important thing is that the server can provide HTTP access to various archives of class files that will be downloaded by clients and services. The *–verbose* option helps in debugging; you can see a trace of HTTP requests. The *–trees* option should also be specified; this causes the HTTP server to examine each of the jar files in its root directory and serve up any class files found within them.

In the example batch file that follows, the HTTP server will serve files from the folder c:\httproot. Initially this folder will contain the file *reggie-dl.jar*, which contains the client-side code for programs that will access the lookup service. Make sure you copy this jar file from the lib directory of your Jini installation to the directory from which your HTTP server will serve files, then start the HTTP server:

```
rem
rem starthttp.bat
rem
rem Start up the Jini TSK HTTP server
rem
java -jar c:\jini1_2\lib\tools.jar -port 8081 -dir c:\httproot -trees
-verbose
```

If successfully started, the HTTP server should display a list of the archive files that it will serve from its root directory; in our case, this should be *reggie-dl.jar*.

The second step is to start up the RMI Activation Daemon. It is not necessary to specify a port, as the default one will be adequate. For a test scenario such as this, we can essentially bypass security checking by using *-J-Dsun.rmi.activation .execPolicy=none*; in a production environment, you would be sensible to specify an appropriately-configured policy file.

```
rem
rem startrmid.bat
rem
rem start up the RMI Activation Daemon without enforcing any
rem security policy.
rem
rmid -J-Dsun.rmi.activation.execPolicy=none -log c:\temp\rmidlog
```

Finally, the lookup service itself can be started. One thing to note about this is that it is not really run as a daemon. Instead, *reggie* registers itself with RMI, and then exits. RMI will then activate *reggie* on demand. It is important to note at this stage that the log directory for *reggie* must *not* exist when *reggie* is started; otherwise, *reggie* will abort with an exception.

The *reggie* lookup service also requires some additional parameters for startup. The URL of the *reggie-dl.jar* file is required as the first parameter; this file will be served by the HTTP server that we previously started, in this case on port 8081; just make sure you use a true hostname or IP address for this – do not use *localhost* as this will not be accessible to remote machines. Additionally, a security policy file is required; for our purposes, it will be adequate to use the sample provided in the Jini TSK. The final mandatory parameter is the log directory.

```
rem
rem startreggie.bat
rem
java -jar c:\jini1_2\lib\reggie.jar http://myreggieserver:8081/reggie-dl
  .jar c:\jini1_2\policy\policy.all c:\reggielog
```

You should observe that after a short delay this script will terminate due to the fact that *reggie* registers itself with RMI and exits. From this point on, RMI will invoke *reggie* as required.

Developing & Deploying...

Potential reggie Pitfalls

There are several things you should take note of when attempting to start *reggie*, the lookup service implementation provided by Sun:

- The first of these is that *reggie* relies on being *activated* by *rmid*, the RMI activation daemon. This means that the first time *reggie* is manually run, it registers itself with *rmid* and exits. It should not be manually run again, as *rmid* will activate it as required. It "remembers" that it has been run previously through its log files: if the directory where its log files are stored is not empty, it cannot be run. Likewise, *rmid* remembers its previous state, including the fact that *reggie* is registered with it through its log files – and these log files will even span the machine being restarted. So, if you ever have to re-register *reggie* (for example, the IP address of the HTTP server has changed), or if you need to reset *rmid* for any reason, you will have to stop the *rmid* process (using *rmid -stop*), delete the log directories for both *rmid* and *reggie*, restart *rmid* and then manually restart *reggie* so it will be re-registered with *rmid*.

- The second thing to remember is that any programs that access *reggie* (*rmid* itself, as well as Jini clients and services) will need to dynamically obtain *reggie*'s client-side code via a URL, probably using HTTP. This is a similar process to the one used by browsers when they download the code for applets. This is why an HTTP server is required. Depending on the

Continued

operating system you are using, you may also find that the machine will have to be connected to a network when this is set up, even if you are running all the components on a single machine.

- The third thing to be aware of is that *reggie* requires a security policy file. If you look at the sample policy files provided with the Jini download, you can see that their implementation can be non-trivial. For this reason, the examples in this chapter make use of the sample "policy.all" file. This file is really not recommended for use in any kind of production environment, but is certainly the easiest way to get an example implementation running. RMI is a powerful mechanism, but it can also open up a wide array of security holes. Please remember that if you are going to implement a Jini federation in a network that requires security, you really need to become familiar with security policy files.

A Simple Service and Client

For our simple example, we will register a service that can examine a message in the form of a byte array, and generate a calculated checksum. We will also construct a client program that will be able to access this service and make use of it. In order to build this example, we will need to create four Java source files and compile them:

- **ChecksumCalc.java** One requirement if Jini services and clients are to operate together is to have one or more interfaces known to both client and service. The ChecksumCalc.java file will define a public interface that will be implemented by the service object and will allow the client to know how to look up the service object and invoke the *calcChecksum()* method. This file is located on the accompanying CD in the /shared directory.

- **ChecksumCalcClass.java** This is the class that will be instantiated as the service object itself. The server obviously needs intimate knowledge of this class (via having the compiled class file in its classpath) in order to instantiate it prior to registering it. The client will also need this knowledge but not at compile time (the interface is sufficient for that); the client will actually access the class file via HTTP at runtime as described in more detail momentarily. This file is located on the accompanying CD in the /checksum directory.

- **ChecksumService.java** This top-level class will be run as the server itself; it will be responsible for instantiating the service object (as an instance of *ChecksumCalcClass*) and registering it with the lookup service. This file is located on the accompanying CD in the /checksum directory.

The first requirement is a well-known contract interface (this has to be known to both service and client). We will define it in a package called *shared* (see Figure 9.3).

Figure 9.3 ChecksumCalc.java

```
/**
 * ChecksumCalc.java
 *
 */


package shared;

import java.rmi.Remote;

public interface ChecksumCalc {

    public byte calcChecksum(byte[] message);
}
```

The next two classes will reside in the *checksum* package. The first is called *ChecksumCalcClass*, shown in Figure 9.4, which is the service's actual implementation of the interface we defined in Figure 9.3.

Figure 9.4 ChecksumCalcClass.java

```
/**
 * ChecksumCalcClass.java
 *
 */
```

Continued

Figure 9.4 Continued

```
package checksum;

import shared.ChecksumCalc;
import java.io.Serializable;

public class ChecksumCalcClass
        implements ChecksumCalc, Serializable {

    public byte calcChecksum(byte[] message) {

        //
        // Calculate checksum as XOR of all bytes
        //

        byte retVal = 0;

        for (int ix=0; ix<message.length; ix++) {
            retVal ^= message[ix];
        }

        return retVal;
    }
}
```

The second class in this package is the one that will be responsible for service registration and lease renewal (see Figure 9.5).

Figure 9.5 ChecksumService.java

```
/**
 * ChecksumService.java
 *
 */

package checksum;
```

Continued

Figure 9.5 Continued

```
import net.jini.core.discovery.LookupLocator;

import net.jini.core.lookup.ServiceRegistrar;

import net.jini.core.lookup.ServiceItem;

import net.jini.core.lookup.ServiceRegistration;

import net.jini.core.lease.Lease;

import net.jini.lease.LeaseRenewalManager;

import net.jini.lease.LeaseRenewalEvent;

import net.jini.lease.LeaseListener;

import java.io.Serializable;

import java.io.IOException;

import java.rmi.RMISecurityManager;

import java.rmi.RemoteException;

import java.net.MalformedURLException;


public class ChecksumService
        implements Serializable, LeaseListener {

    // The LeaseRenewalManager will ensure that the
    // lease with the locator serivce is regulalry
    // renewed.
    protected LeaseRenewalManager leaseManager
        = new LeaseRenewalManager();

    static public void main(String args[]) {

        new ChecksumService();

        // Ensure service runs indefinitely so
        // we can keep renewing the lease. If
        // we don't keep running, the lease will
        // expire and the service registration
        // will lapse.
        Object keepAlive = new Object();
        synchronized(keepAlive) {
            try {
                keepAlive.wait();
```

Continued

Figure 9.5 Continued

```
        } catch(java.lang.InterruptedException e) {
            // do nothing
        }
    }
}

public ChecksumService() {

    // Lookup using Unicast (i.e., specify the address of
    // a single lookup service), using the default port.
    LookupLocator lookupLocator = null;

    // Make sure to specify the correct
    // address of the running lookup service.
    try {
    lookupLocator =
        new LookupLocator("jini://192.168.100.3");
    } catch (MalformedURLException e) {
        System.err.println(e.toString());
        System.exit(1);
    }

    // The Service Registrar is the proxy
    // through which we communicate with
    // the lookup service.
    ServiceRegistrar serviceRegistrar = null;

    try {
        serviceRegistrar =
            lookupLocator.getRegistrar();
    } catch (IOException e) {
        System.err.println(e.toString());
        System.exit(1);
    } catch (ClassNotFoundException e) {
        System.err.println(e.toString());
```

Continued

Figure 9.5 Continued

```
            System.exit(1);
    }


    // Register our implementation class
    // as a service.
    ChecksumCalcClass cCImplementation =
        new ChecksumCalcClass();
    ServiceItem serviceItem =
        new ServiceItem(
            null,
            cCImplementation,
            null);


    // Request a 10 second lease duration. This
    // means that the lease will require renewing
    // at least once every 10 seconds.
    ServiceRegistration serviceRegistration = null;

    try {
        serviceRegistration =
            serviceRegistrar.register(
                serviceItem,
                10000L);
    } catch (RemoteException e) {
        System.err.println(e.toString());
        System.exit(1);
    }


    // Configure the lease manager
    // to keep on renewing our lease
    // indefinitely.
    leaseManager.renewUntil(
            serviceRegistration.getLease(),
            Lease.FOREVER,
            Lease.ANY,
            this);
```

Continued

Figure 9.5 Continued

```
    // If all has gone well, we have a service ID and
    // clients can now invoke the service.
    System.out.println(
        "Successful Registration - Service ID: " +
        serviceRegistrar.getServiceID());

    }


    public void notify(LeaseRenewalEvent evt) {
        // Will receive events concerning abnormal
        // lease behaviour. Ignored in this
        // example.

    }
}
```

We have already covered the concept of registration with a lookup service, but what is *lease renewal* and why do we need it? The answer is probably best explained by stating why we need it: in a distributed environment like this, it may not always be beneficial to register a remote service as being available indefinitely; if the implementation of the service is no longer available (for reasons ranging from physical malfunction to intentional decommissioning), we may not want the registration of that service to remain in force indefinitely. The answer is the lease concept: a service provider asks to register its service and is in return granted a lease which will expire after a certain time. It is then the responsibility of the service provider to periodically request that the lease be renewed. Obviously, if the service provider fails or is shut down, the lease will expire and the service will no longer be registered.

Jini service providers can handle lease renewals in a number of ways, but in the examples in this chapter we will use the simplest of all—the *net.jini.lease .LeaseRenewalManager*, which will handle the job of lease renewal automatically.

Finally, we need some client code to make use of the service. This code will contact the lookup service and request an object matching the interface we defined previously. It can then make use of that object remotely without any knowledge of the implementation or of the communication methods; the object appears as if it was local to the client. We will define this class in a package called *checksumClient* (see Figure 9.6).

Figure 9.6 ChecksumClient/Client.java

```
/**
 * Client.java
 *
 */

package checksumClient;

import shared.ChecksumCalc;
import net.jini.core.discovery.LookupLocator;
import net.jini.core.lookup.ServiceRegistrar;
import net.jini.core.lookup.ServiceTemplate;
import java.rmi.RMISecurityManager;
import java.rmi.RemoteException;
import java.net.MalformedURLException;
import java.io.IOException;

public class Client {

    static public void main(String args[]) {

        new Client();
    }

    public Client() {

        // Lookup using Unicast (i.e., specify the
        // address of a single lookup service),
        // using default port.
        LookupLocator lookupLocator = null;

        // Make sure to specify the correct
        // address of the running lookup service.
        try {
```

Continued

Figure 9.6 Continued

```
        lookupLocator =
                new LookupLocator(
                    "jini://192.168.100.3");
    } catch (MalformedURLException e) {
        System.err.println(e.toString());
        System.exit(1);
    }


    // The Service Registrar is the proxy
    // through which we communicate with
    // the lookup service.
    ServiceRegistrar serviceRegistrar = null;

    try {
        serviceRegistrar =
            lookupLocator.getRegistrar();
    } catch(IOException e) {
        System.err.println(e.toString());
        System.exit(1);
    } catch(ClassNotFoundException e) {
        System.err.println(e.toString());
        System.exit(1);
    }


    // Construct a template for looking up
    // a service that matches the
    // commonly-known ChecksumCalc interface.
    Class [] classArr =
        new Class[] {ChecksumCalc.class};
    ServiceTemplate svcTemplate =
        new ServiceTemplate(
            null,
            classArr,
            null);
```

Continued

Figure 9.6 Continued

```
// Request a remote copy of the matching
// object from the lookup server.
ChecksumCalc checksumRemoteObj = null;

try {
checksumRemoteObj =
    (ChecksumCalc)serviceRegistrar.lookup(
        svcTemplate);
} catch(RemoteException e) {
    System.err.println(e.toString());
    System.exit(1);
}
if (null == checksumRemoteObj) {
    System.err.println(
        "No valid service object found");
    System.exit(1);
} else {
    // We now have a valid object
    // which can be called locally.

    // Get the checksum for a binary message.

    // Define a message as an array of
    // arbitrary values:
    byte[] msg = new byte[] {
        (byte)0x34, (byte)0xa1, (byte)0x22
    };

    int csum = 0;

    csum = (int)
        checksumRemoteObj.calcChecksum(
            msg);

    // Print out the checksum in hex,
```

Continued

Figure 9.6 Continued

```
            // remembering that the Java byte
            // is a signed type.
            System.out.println("Checksum is: " +
                    Integer.toHexString(
                        csum >= 0 ?
                        csum : csum+256));
        }
    }
}
```

To test this simple service, make sure you have the HTTP server, the RMI Activation Daemon, and *reggie* all running as described previously (remembering that you should only have to start up *reggie* once; subsequently, it should be invoked automatically by *rmid*). Then register the service. In order to do this, you may have to specify a security policy as shown. Also make sure your CLASSPATH correctly includes jini-core.jar and jini-ext.jar:

```
java -Djava.security.policy=c:\jini1_2\policy\policy.all
  -Djava.security.manager checksum.ChecksumService
```

If this registers successfully, it should receive a unique service identifier and you should see something like the following output:

```
Successful Registration - Service ID: 546e76ab-2c47-4b29-bb29-
  9638e920ee58
```

Because the client will need to execute *ChecksumCalcClass* code without actually having *ChecksumCalcClass.class* in its CLASSPATH, it will need to obtain this code via HTTP. To enable this, you will have to do two things:

1. Create an archive (jar) containing *ChecksumCalcClass.class* and place it in the directory that the HTTP server is configured to serve files from (the same directory you previously copied *reggie-dl.jar* into), and restart the HTTP server. This time the HTTP server should output the names of both *reggie-dl.jar* and the newly-created archive—for example, *checksum.jar*. To create a jar file containing class files, you can run the jar tool specifying −*c* (to create a new archive), -*v* (for verbose output), and −*f* (to specify the archive filename). Also, the −*C* option can be used to

change the directory, so that the following command line will produce an archive named *checksum.jar* containing *ChecksumCalcClass.class*:

```
jar cvf checksum.jar -C checksum/ ChecksumCalcClass.class
```

2. Specify a CODEBASE property when you start the client so that it knows to download the *checksum.jar* archive from the HTTP server when required.

Starting the client will also require specifying a security policy, and the following command line demonstrates all of the required parameters (remembering to replace *myhttp* with the actual machine name or IP address of your HTTP server):

```
java -Djava.rmi.server.codebase=http://myhttp:8081/checksum.jar -Djava.
  security.policy=c:\jini1_2\policy\policy.all -Djava.security.manager
  checksumClient.Client
```

If all goes well, it should obtain the desired object and calculate the checksum. The following shows the expected output after running the client:

```
Checksum is: b7
```

In order to really understand what has just taken place here, we need to consider which Java Virtual Machines (JVMs) each component is running in. Each JVM is an executable program, and whether or not our client and service run on the same machine or different machines (in practice they would be on different machines), they certainly run in different JVMs. So what happens to the object of type *ChecksumCalcClass* as it progresses through its lifecycle?

1. Our service program instantiates an object of type *ChecksumCalcClass* within its own JVM, just as one would create any normal object in Java.

2. The object is *serialized* (which is why it implements *serializable*), and registered with *reggie*. This means that the object's *state* (in other words, a snapshot of its data at the time it was serialized) is stored away until required.

3. Our client program receives the serialized object from *reggie* and reconstructs it as an object within its own JVM.

4. The client then starts making local method calls against the object, as if it was a regular Java object that had been instantiated locally by the client.

These four steps are shown in Figure 9.7.

Figure 9.7 Flow of Execution in the Simple Example

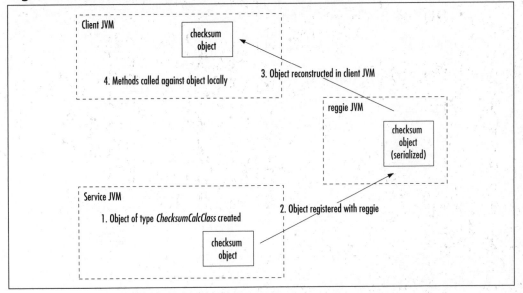

So, what's so simplistic about this scenario? Well, in the case where the checksum object doesn't interact with any other objects or systems, this works just fine. However, what if that object created by the service had referenced another object in the JVM of the service? This reference would be meaningless when the client came to access it in its JVM, regardless of whether it was on the same machine or not. And what if the object created by the service expected to access a LEGO MINDSTORMS RCX via a serial port on that machine? It certainly won't work if a client on a completely different computer uses it!

What we have achieved so far is to transport an object between two Java Virtual Machines fairly painlessly, but obviously something more is required. We clearly need a mechanism whereby we don't transmit the object itself but rather we implement a process like this:

1. The service creates an object within its JVM just as before.

2. Instead of the service object being registered with *reggie*, an identical-looking *stub* object is registered with *reggie*.

3. The object that is reconstructed in the client's JVM is actually the service *stub* object.

4. The client makes method calls against the object just as before.

5. However, the *stub* object does not implement the code within those method calls; it knows how to communicate back to the original service object, which may well be running on another machine, and that original object does all of the processing.

This flow is shown in Figure 9.8.

Figure 9.8 The Use of RMI Stubs in a Jini Architecture

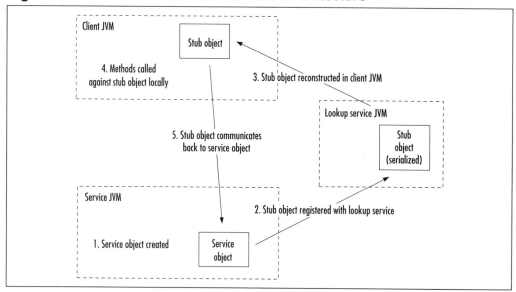

Now that would make sense; if the service object was expecting to communicate with an RCX via a serial port, then it still could because the object would be invoked in the original JVM that created it. And if that object held references to other objects, these references would still be valid for the same reasons.

The only problem is that we have to write an absolutely enormous amount of code to achieve this complex interaction between objects across the network, right? Wrong! Fortunately, Jini's use of RMI means that this can be achieved with essentially no coding whatsoever! There are several ways to implement this, but the one we will use in the examples is by extending a class known as *java.rmi.server.UnicastRemoteObject*. Basically, the steps required are as follows:

1. Make sure that the class of the object that is to be registered as a service extends *UnicastRemoteObject* (and also ensure that it still implements *Serializable*).

2. When you compile your service's class (for example, *MyCoolService.class*), run the RMI compiler against it to produce a stub class.

3. Make sure that the stub class file is accessible to the client via the HTTP server.

That's it! That's all you have to do; the RMI compiler will generate all of the code required for the stub so that the stub and the original object know how to communicate across JVMs and even across a network. You still specify the original class name in your code; Jini knows to instantiate the stub and register that with *reggie* instead of your local object.

Generating the stub class using the RMI compiler is no trouble at all. The compiler executable is *rmic*, and the argument is the class file that the stub is being produced for. The output is the class name followed by an underscore, followed by *Stub*, followed by the .class extension. So, if the original class was called *MyCoolServiceClass.class*, the generated stub would automatically be called *MyCoolServiceClass_Stub.class*.

The most commonly used options for *rmic* in this context are:

■ **-keep** Suppresses the deletion of intermediate files. The RMI compiler actually generates a .java source file on its way to generating the .class file, and this option stops the source file from being deleted; handy if you want to understand a little more about what's going on behind the scenes.

■ **-v1.2** Under Java 1.1, the standard was to produce stub and skeleton files, with "_stub" and "_skel" suffixes. The skeleton files are no longer required, so this option suppresses their creation.

So, running the command:

```
rmic -v1.2 mindstorm.MindstormProxy
```

would create a single stub file called *MindstormProxy_Stub.class* in the *mindstorm* directory.

Proxies and Service Architectures

Having now covered some of the basics of registering and using a Jini service, we also need to consider how to decide on the correct architecture for a specific situation, and most appropriately in this context, how to select the right architecture for a situation involving LEGO MINDSTORMS and Jini.

Selecting the Right Architecture

As with most things, there are good and bad ways to approach the architecture of a Jini federation, but often no "right" or "wrong" way. The following sections will serve as a guide to how your particular solutions may be designed.

Using Proxies

As we have already covered, Jini is often considered appropriate as a technology for allowing the services of a wide range of devices to be readily discovered and utilized in a distributed environment. If you think about it, it makes perfect sense that a large device such as a household air conditioning unit may contain enough computing power to run Java, (including RMI), a TCP/IP stack, and Jini, so that it can register its own services. What then if the device contained a much less powerful embedded system (perhaps an 8- or 16-bit microcontroller), with only a primitive communications facility (perhaps RS-232) and limited RAM (measured in Kbytes rather than Mbytes or Gbytes)? That's when you would need a proxy.

A proxy in the Jini context is a service that runs on a more powerful computing platform (such as a PC or perhaps a home control system) and which stands between the client and something like an embedded device. The thing about the proxy is that to the client, the proxy appears to actually be the service itself. However, the reality is that the proxy is a layer of abstraction; it handles all of the communication with the device that is physically performing the service (over RS-232 in our previous example), and it handles such tasks as service registration and lease renewal. Figure 9.9 shows the basic architecture of a system where a single object acts as a proxy, and the physical service is carried out by a LEGO MINDSTORMS device.

A RCX Jini Proxy Service

In this section, we will delve into building an example Jini service and client that will allow multiple LEGO MINDSTORMS to interact with each other. This will follow a design similar to that shown in Figure 9.9, where a proxy architecture is used.

Why a Proxy?

If you were thinking that our discussions about embedded devices with limited computing powers and primitive communications abilities could apply to the

RCX, you're absolutely right. Despite the fact that people have been able to implement a form of Java Virtual Machine within the RCX, it really doesn't come close to having the computing power required to run Jini.

Figure 9.9 The Use of Proxies for Embedded Devices

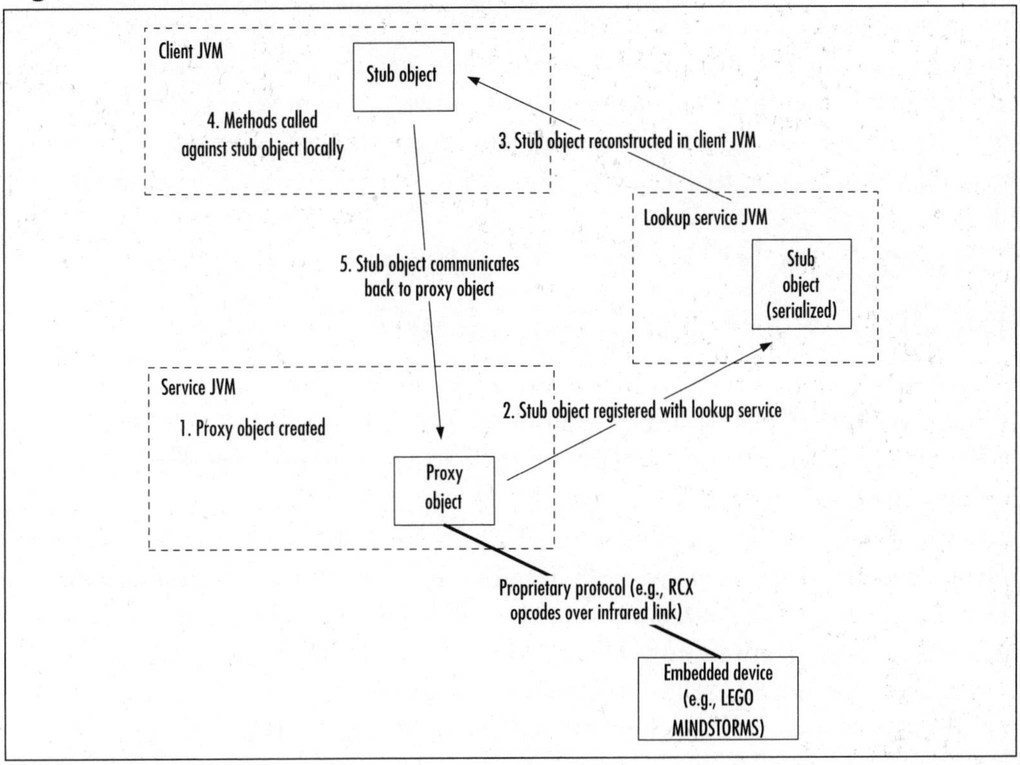

That said, the Jini proxy architecture makes perfect sense in the case of the RCX. Since the only way it has of connecting to a network is via an infrared link connected to some form of more powerful computer, that computer is the ideal candidate to act as proxy. So, a Jini federation of MINDSTORMS is a very real possibility; one or many machines connected to infrared towers register proxy services. To the client or clients, these proxy services appear as the services them-selves—the client calls a method *DoWhateverRobotsDo()*, and the robot responds by doing it. What has really taken place though is that the proxy has interpreted the method call and executed it by sending and receiving a set of RCX opcodes over the infrared connection.

Interfacing with the RCX Java API

There are multiple mechanisms by which the Jini proxy could interface with the RCX—in our example, we shall use the RCX Java API. We will create a service program that will instantiate a proxy object (and its corresponding stub), and register this with the lookup service, and we will run more than one instance of this program (using more than one RCX, each connected to its own machine). When a client invokes methods against these proxy objects, the proxies will actually make use of the RCX Java API to send and receive the RCX opcodes to command the RCX to behave a certain way and to receive feedback from the RCX.

Using the RCX Jini Service: Example Server and Client

Now we will cover a more complex example scenario that involves one or more LEGO MINDSTORMS. In this example, the MINDSTORMS will effectively communicate with each other (via a central client program) to perform a kind of synchronized dance.

The desired outcome is this: for a pair of MINDSTORMS, the first will perform a certain "dance step" (actually one of eight predefined movements); the second will imitate the exact movement, wait several seconds, and then perform its own randomly chosen movement. This will then be imitated by the first, and so on until the program is terminated or the batteries run out!

If there is only one MINDSTORMS robot in the Jini Federation, it will just have to be content with imitating its own movements. Likewise, if there are more than two robots, they will form a "daisy chain," with each one copying the moves of the previous one in the chain before deciding on its own original step.

Figure 9.10 shows the basic scenario for this example, assuming two robots. As you can see in this diagram, the PCs which are connected to the infrared towers will act as proxies for RCX units themselves. Also, because some of the components of this system are likely to reside on different machines (or at least in different JVMs in the case where one machine may control multiple RCXs via multiple serial ports), the proxy objects must be executed in the JVM of the service that registers them. Therefore, it will actually be stub objects that will be registered with *reggie* and these stub objects will communicate via RMI with the proxies.

Figure 9.10 Example Scenario for Jini and the RCX

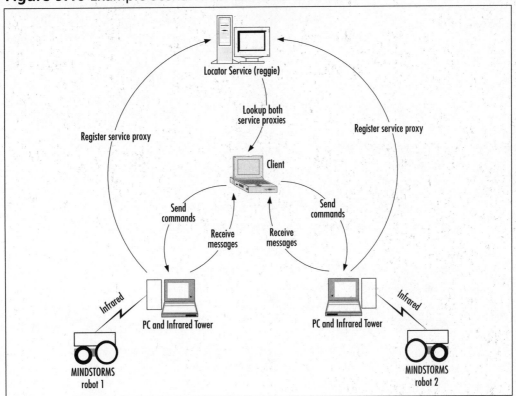

A RCX Jini Server

The first step is to create an interface that can be known to both client and service. Again, as in the simple Jini example shown previously, we will create this interface in a package called *shared* (see Figure 9.11). The interface defines some methods to allow certain attributes to be retrieved, as well as the method *imitateThis()*, which is a command to a MINDSTORMS robot to imitate a certain dance step.

Figure 9.11 Mindstorm.java

```
/**
 * Mindstorm.java
 *
 */
```

Continued

Figure 9.11 Continued

```
package shared;

import java.rmi.Remote;
import java.rmi.RemoteException;
import net.jini.core.event.RemoteEventListener;

public interface Mindstorm
    extends Remote {

    // Define the two possible message types:
    // EVENT_RCX_MSG is a message from a remote RCX.
    // EVENT_DANCE_STEP is a notification that a Mindstorm
    // has completed a dance step.
    public final int EVENT_RCX_MSG = 1;
    public final int EVENT_DANCE_STEP = 2;

    // Method to retrieve the ID of a Mindstorm.
    public String getRcxId() throws RemoteException;

    // Tell a Mindstorm to imitate a dance step.
    public void imitateThis(int danceStep) throws RemoteException;

    // Retrieve the most recent RCX Message received. Should
    // be called in response to receiving an EVENT_RCX_MSG.
    public byte[] GetLastRCXMessage() throws RemoteException;

    // Retrieve the most recent dance step performed
    // by an RCX. Should be called in response to
    // receiving an EVENT_DANCE_STEP.
    public int GetLastStepPerformed() throws RemoteException;

    // Allow the client to register a listener
    // to receive events from the service.
    public void RegisterRemoteListener(RemoteEventListener listener)
```

Continued

Figure 9.11 Continued

```
        throws RemoteException;


}
```

The proxy class will be called *mindstorm.MindstormProxy*. It will make extensive use of the RCX Java classes, so make sure you are familiar with the RCX Java mechanisms before you embark on this one. This proxy will also make use of multithreading; it will spawn a new thread of execution and return, before proceeding through the cycle of imitating a dance step, pausing for 10 seconds, and then deciding on another dance step to perform. This is so that the client program is not held up for the entire 10-plus seconds, and it is a very common technique to use for this kind of scenario in Java. In this case, the class that will process the additional thread (*Imitation Thread*) has been implemented as an *inner class*. It is a class declared within another class, which has implicit access to the members of the enclosing class and is not visible outside of that class. Just remember that when *MindstormProxy.java* is compiled, two .class files will be produced—*MindstormProxy.class* and *MindstormProxy$ImitationThread.class*—and that both these files must be in the Java runtime's CLASSPATH for the example to work.

The other thing to note about this class is that instances of it will be required to execute on the machine that they were created on (because they will be communicating out a physical serial port to an RCX device), so we will be required to register an instance of a proxy that will be capable of communicating back with the equivalent object of this class from a remote client. As already discussed, we are very fortunate that RMI can provide this functionality with very little effort on our part. As can be seen from the following code, the proxy class will extend *UnicastRemoteObject*. The only other thing you must remember to do is run the RMI compiler against the compiled class file to produce a stub class. You can invoke the compiler with a command such as:

```
rmic -v1.2 mindstorm.MindstormProxy
```

After running *rmic*, you should now have produced a file called *MindstormProxy_Stub.class* in the /mindstorm subdirectory; this file is the proxy code (see Figure 9.12). That certainly beats coding it by hand!

Figure 9.12 MindstormProxy.java

```java
/**
 * MindstormProxy.java
 *
 */

package mindstorm;

import java.rmi.server.UnicastRemoteObject;
import net.jini.core.event.UnknownEventException;
import net.jini.core.event.RemoteEvent;
import net.jini.core.event.RemoteEventListener;
import shared.Mindstorm;
import java.io.Serializable;
import java.rmi.RemoteException;
import rcx.RCXListener;
import rcx.RCXPort;

public class MindstormProxy
    extends UnicastRemoteObject
    implements Mindstorm, Serializable, RCXListener {

    // Make sure to generate a stub class using the
    // RMI compiler since this class extends
    // UnicastRemoteObject.

    protected static final byte FORWARDS = (byte)0x80;
    protected static final byte BACKWARDS = (byte)0x00;
    protected static final byte ON = (byte)0x80;
    protected static final byte OFF = (byte)0x40;
    protected static final byte MOTOR_A = (byte)0x01;
    protected static final byte MOTOR_C = (byte)0x04;
    protected static final byte MOTOR_DIR = (byte)0xe1;
    protected static final byte MOTOR_ON_OFF = (byte)0x21;

    // Store our unique ID so that the client
```

Continued

Figure 9.12 Continued

```
    // can differentiate between robots.
    protected String rcxId = null;

    protected RCXPort rcxPort = null;

    protected RemoteEventListener remoteListener = null;

    // Store any message received from the RCX
    // as a raw byte array for retrieval by the client.
    // Note that any subsequent message will overwrite
    // the existing one and if messages are retireved
    // in quick succession, data may be lost. A more
    // robust implementation could be employed for a
    // production system...
    protected byte[] lastRCXEvent = null;

    // Similarly for the most recent dance step performed...
    protected int lastDanceStep = 0;

    protected long seqNo = 0;

    public MindstormProxy() throws RemoteException {
    }

    public String getRcxId() {
        return rcxId;
    }

    protected void setRcxId(String id) {
        rcxId = id;
    }

    protected void openRcxPort(String port) {
        // Open a specific serial port
        rcxPort = new RCXPort(port);
```

Continued

Figure 9.12 Continued

```
    // Register as a listener with the RCX
    rcxPort.addRCXListener(this);
}

protected void executeMovement(int movementId) {
    // Execute one of our robot's 8
    // spectacular dance steps.
    System.out.println("Executing step: " + movementId);
    switch(movementId) {
        case 0:
            // Directly forward
            setMotorDir(FORWARDS,
                (byte)(MOTOR_A | MOTOR_C));
            motorOn((byte)(MOTOR_A | MOTOR_C));
            break;
        case 1:
            // Directly back
            setMotorDir(BACKWARDS,
                (byte)(MOTOR_A | MOTOR_C));
            motorOn((byte)(MOTOR_A | MOTOR_C));
            break;
        case 2:
            // Rotate right
            setMotorDir(FORWARDS, MOTOR_A);
            setMotorDir(BACKWARDS, MOTOR_C);
            motorOn((byte)(MOTOR_A | MOTOR_C));
            break;
        case 3:
            // Rotate left
            setMotorDir(BACKWARDS, MOTOR_A);
            setMotorDir(FORWARDS, MOTOR_C);
            motorOn((byte)(MOTOR_A | MOTOR_C));
            break;
        case 4:
            // Forward right
```

Continued

Figure 9.12 Continued

```
                setMotorDir(FORWARDS, MOTOR_A);
                motorOn(MOTOR_A);
                break;
            case 5:
                // Forward left
                setMotorDir(FORWARDS, MOTOR_C);
                motorOn(MOTOR_C);
                break;
            case 6:
                // Reverse right
                setMotorDir(BACKWARDS, MOTOR_A);
                motorOn(MOTOR_A);
                break;
            case 7:
                // Reverse left
                setMotorDir(BACKWARDS, MOTOR_C);
                motorOn(MOTOR_C);
                break;
        }
        // Each dance step is of a 0.3 second duration
        try {
            Thread.sleep(300);
        } catch(InterruptedException e) {
            //
        }
        motorsOff();
    }

protected void motorOn(byte motors) {
    // Turn one or both motors on
    byte[] msg = new byte[] {};
    sendToRcx(
        new byte[] {
            MOTOR_ON_OFF,
            (byte)(ON | motors)});
```

Continued

Figure 9.12 Continued

```
    }

    protected void motorsOff() {
        // Turn both motors off
        sendToRcx(
            new byte[] {
                MOTOR_ON_OFF,
                (byte)(OFF | MOTOR_A | MOTOR_C)});
    }

    protected void setMotorDir(byte dir, byte motors) {
        // Set direction for one or both motors
        sendToRcx(
            new byte[] {
                MOTOR_DIR,
                (byte)(dir | motors)});
    }

    protected void sendToRcx(byte[] msg) {

        System.out.println(
            "Sending to port: " +
            byteArrayToString(msg));

        if (!rcxPort.write(msg)) {
            System.err.println("Error writing to port");
        }
    }

    public void imitateThis(int danceStep)
        throws RemoteException {
        // This should be the dance step that the other
        // robot has just performed. We will attempt to
        // imitate it. Handle this from a new thread.
        new ImitationThread(danceStep, this).start();
```

Continued

Figure 9.12 Continued

```
    }

public void receivedMessage(byte[] msg) {
    // Receive messages from the RCX
    if (null != msg) {
        System.out.println(
            "RCX message: " +
            byteArrayToString(msg));

        if (null != remoteListener) {
            // Store the event contents
            // for retrieval by the listener
            lastRCXEvent = msg;

            // Notify the listener of the event.
            // Listener will have to call back to
            // obtain the details.
            RemoteEvent evt =
                new RemoteEvent(
                    this,
                    EVENT_RCX_MSG,
                    seqNo++,
                    null);
            try {
                remoteListener.notify(evt);
            } catch(UnknownEventException e) {
                System.err.println("Event exception");
            } catch(java.rmi.RemoteException e) {
                System.err.println("Remote exception");
            }

        }
    }
}
```

Continued

Figure 9.12 Continued

```
protected String byteArrayToString(byte[] msg) {

    // Convert an array of bytes to a human-readable
    // string

    StringBuffer sBuf = new StringBuffer();

    for(int ix = 0; ix < msg.length; ix++) {
        int dm =
            msg[ix] >= 0 ?
            (int)msg[ix] :
            ((int)msg[ix]) + 256;
        sBuf.append(
            Integer.toHexString(dm) + " ");
    }

    return sBuf.toString();
}

public void receivedError(String err) {
    // Receive errors from the RCX
    System.err.println("RCX error: " + err);
}

public byte[] GetLastRCXMessage() {
    // This will be called by the client
    // to retrieve details of the last message
    // after we have sent a notification.
    return lastRCXEvent;
}

public int GetLastStepPerformed() {
    // This will be called by the client
    // to retrieve details of the last step
    // after we have sent a notification.
    return lastDanceStep;
```

Continued

Figure 9.12 Continued

```
    }

    public void RegisterRemoteListener(
        RemoteEventListener listener) {
        // Called by the client to register its
        // listener object (which should also extend
        // UnicastRemoteObject so that we can notify it
        // remotely).
        remoteListener = listener;
    }


// Declare this thread class as an inner class
class ImitationThread extends Thread {

    protected int step;
    protected MindstormProxy proxy = null;

    public ImitationThread(
            int danceStep,
            MindstormProxy proxy) {

        // Store the reference to the
        // object that created us as well
        // as the dance step to execute.
        this.proxy = proxy;
        step = danceStep;
    }

    public void run() {

        // Firstly execute the move in
        // imitation of the other robot.
        executeMovement(step);

        // Then wait 10 seconds
        try {
```

Continued

Figure 9.12 Continued

```
                Thread.sleep(10000);
        } catch(InterruptedException e) {
            // Do nothing
        }

        // Now randomly pick a new movement
        // (between 0 and 7 inclusive).
        int newMovement;
        newMovement = (int)(8 * (Math.random()));

        // Perform our randomly-selected movement.
        executeMovement(newMovement);

        // Now let the remote client
        // know that we just performed it.
        //
        // The client will have to call back
        // to get the details.
        lastDanceStep = newMovement;
        if (null != remoteListener) {
            RemoteEvent evt =
                new RemoteEvent(proxy,
                    EVENT_DANCE_STEP,
                    seqNo++, null);
            try {
                remoteListener.notify(evt);
            } catch(UnknownEventException e) {
                System.err.println("Event exception");
            } catch(java.rmi.RemoteException e) {
                System.err.println(e.toString());
            }
        }
    }
  }
}
```

Having now defined a proxy class, we will move on to examine a sample server that will instantiate a proxy object, register its stub with any lookup services on the network, and keep it alive and keep the lease renewed.

There are a number of differences between this service and the one we looked at in the preceding simple example. One of these differences is that we will be using multicast instead of unicast lookups to find instances of *reggie* (the lookup service). Whereas, in the checksum example, we specified the IP address of a specific lookup service instance, here we will use multicast to find any number of lookup services that may exist on our network. Once we find them, we will register the proxy object (actually its stub) with each of them.

Another difference between this and our simple example is that in this scenario we are expecting multiple services on the network to register objects implementing the same common interface. This is because this scenario involves multiple MINDSTORMS robots, and we need some way to differentiate between them. Because there is no distinguishing identifier inherent in the basic RCX firmware, we will assign an identifying name to each proxy object instead. This will be passed in as a command line parameter to the service as a string; it can be any name at all as long as you use a different name for any other robots you register.

Along with the robot's identifier, we will expect another command line parameter: the port identifier. This is the actual port name to be used by RCX Java, such as "COM1" for a Windows machine.

It is important that this service keep itself alive after it has done the job of registering the proxy with the lookup service. This is not just for the purpose of lease renewal, but also because we are really only registering a stub for remote use, and the proxy object itself will run in the JVM of this service and will receive calls remotely from the client via RMI. If this JVM goes away, so does the proxy, and the client will start to see all kinds of remote exceptions and no responses from the robot.

The code for the service is as shown in Figure 9.13.

Figure 9.13 MindstormService.java

```
/**
 * MindstormService.java
 *
 */


package mindstorm;
```

Continued

Figure 9.13 Continued

```java
import net.jini.discovery.LookupDiscovery;

import net.jini.discovery.DiscoveryListener;

import net.jini.discovery.DiscoveryEvent;

import net.jini.core.lookup.ServiceRegistrar;

import net.jini.core.lookup.ServiceItem;

import net.jini.core.lookup.ServiceRegistration;

import net.jini.core.lease.Lease;

import net.jini.lease.LeaseRenewalManager;

import net.jini.lease.LeaseRenewalEvent;

import net.jini.lease.LeaseListener;

import java.io.Serializable;

import java.io.IOException;

import java.rmi.RMISecurityManager;

import java.rmi.RemoteException;


public class MindstormService
    implements
        Serializable, LeaseListener, DiscoveryListener
{
    // This service will be responsible for creating
    // an instance of the proxy and registering it
    // with the Jini locator service.
    protected MindstormProxy proxy = null;


    // The LeaseRenewalManager will ensure that the
    // lease with the locator service is regularly
    // renewed.
    protected LeaseRenewalManager leaseManager
        = new LeaseRenewalManager();


    // Store our own ID so we can be differentiated from
    // any other MINDSTORMS in the federation.
    static protected String rcxId = null;
```

Continued

Figure 9.13 Continued

```
// The name of the serial port.
static protected String portId = null;

static public void main(String args[]) {

    // Since reggie is running with a security policy,
    // we will have to as well. This assumes that
    // the policy file is located at
    // c:\jini1_2\policy\policy.all
    // Adjust this for specific installations.
    System.setProperty(
        "java.security.policy",
        "c:\\jini1_2\\policy\\policy.all");
    System.setSecurityManager(new SecurityManager());

    // Check that the correct arguments were passed in
    if (args.length < 2) {
        System.err.println
            ("Usage: java MindstormService RcxId Port");
        System.exit(1);
    }

    rcxId = args[0];
    portId = args[1];

    new MindstormService();

    // Ensure service runs indefinitely so
    // we can keep renewing the lease.
    Object keepAlive = new Object();
    synchronized(keepAlive) {
        try {
            keepAlive.wait();
        } catch(java.lang.InterruptedException e) {
            // do nothing
```

Continued

Figure 9.13 Continued

```
            }
        }
    }

    public MindstormService() {

        try {
            // Lookup using Multicast (i.e., look for any lookup
            // services on the network). We will receive a
            // callback to the discovered() method with a
            // list of all lookup services found.
            LookupDiscovery lookupDiscovery =
                new LookupDiscovery(
                    LookupDiscovery.ALL_GROUPS);
            lookupDiscovery.addDiscoveryListener(this);

        } catch(IOException e) {
            System.err.println(e.toString());
            System.exit(1);
        }
    }



    public void discarded(DiscoveryEvent event) {
        // Must be implemented from the
        // DiscoveryListener interface.
    }

    public void discovered(DiscoveryEvent event) {

        //try {
        // Must be implemented from the
        // DiscoveryListener interface.

        // This method will be called with a list
```

Continued

Figure 9.13 Continued

```
// of all lookup services found
// (actually their registrar proxies).
ServiceRegistrar[] regArray = event.getRegistrars();

try {
    proxy = new MindstormProxy();
} catch (RemoteException e) {
    System.err.println(e.toString());
    System.exit(1);
}

proxy.setRcxId(rcxId);

// Turn off security management while
// opening the comm port. This requires
// holding a reference to the existing
// security manager so it can be
// restored again.
SecurityManager sm =
    System.getSecurityManager();
System.setSecurityManager(null);

// Request that the serial port
// be opened.
proxy.openRcxPort(portId);

// Turn security management back on again
System.setSecurityManager(sm);

// Iterate through the array of
// lookup services that were found
// on the network.
for (int ix = 0; ix < regArray.length; ix++) {
    ServiceRegistrar svcRegistrar = regArray[ix];
```

Continued

Figure 9.13 Continued

```
                    // register ourselves as a service

                    ServiceItem serviceItem = new ServiceItem(
                        null, proxy, null);

                    // Request a 60 second lease duration. This
                    // means that the lease will require renewing
                    // at least once every 10 seconds.
                    ServiceRegistration serviceRegistration = null;

                    try {
                        serviceRegistration =
                            svcRegistrar.register(
                                serviceItem,
                                Lease.FOREVER);
                    } catch (RemoteException e) {
                        // If the service registration
                        // fails, we can still try with
                        // any other lookup services
                        // on the network.
                        System.err.println(e.toString());
                        continue;
                    }

                    // Request the Lease Renewal Manager
                    // to perform regular renewals of the
                    // lease indefinitely.
                    leaseManager.renewUntil(
                        serviceRegistration.getLease(),
                        Lease.FOREVER,
                        Lease.ANY,
                        this);
                    System.out.println(
                        "Successful - Service ID: "
                        + svcRegistrar.getServiceID());
```

Continued

Figure 9.13 Continued

```
    }
  }

public void notify(LeaseRenewalEvent evt) {
    // Will receive events concerning abnormal
    // lease behavior. Ignored in this
    // example.
}
}
```

Debugging…

Troubleshooting the Jini Federation

Debugging Jini services and clients should be relatively straightforward, provided you are well aware of which JVMs the various components are running in. For example, in our simplistic initial example, where the service object was actually run locally by the client, the debugger could be run against the client program provided it had access to the Java source code of the service. In the case of debugging our more advanced example involving the RCXs, things are a little different but really no more difficult. In this case, the proxy object would be debugged within the server JVM itself; just be aware that a number of threads will be running and the methods in the object will actually be invoked as a result of receiving network messages from the stub object in the remote JVM.

There are several additional tricks that may help in debugging your Jini solutions:

- To debug the calls into a stub object on the client, it may be beneficial to have the source code for the stub class available. To achieve this, just remember to specify the –keep option when you run the RMI compiler to generate the stub class or classes.

Continued

- Use plenty of *System.out.println()* calls in your client and service code to provide ample information of what is taking place at runtime.
- When starting either the client or the server, there are two additional options that can be set in the command line to enable additional debugging information: *-Dnet.jini.discovery.debug=1* and *-Djava.rmi.server.logCalls=true.*

A RCX Jini Client

Now that we have generated all of the files required to provide the service, we can turn our attention to a client program that will make use of a number of instances of these services (see Figure 9.14). As outlined previously, this client will be capable of interacting with any number of such services, as long as they have a unique identifier attached to them.

Just as with the preceding service code, the client will use the multicast mechanism to find any available lookup services on the network. Then, for each of these, it will examine any registered objects that implement the *Mindstorm* interface defined previously. It will compare the string identifier that was given to each of these and determine whether it has already come across an instance with this identifier. If it is the first time it has seen such an object, it will add it to its list. This list is being stored in a Java object called a *Vector*, which is a very handy mechanism for storing a variable number of objects of different types.

Figure 9.14 MindstormClient/Client.java

```
/**
 * Client.java
 *
 */


package mindstormClient;

import shared.Mindstorm;
import net.jini.discovery.LookupDiscovery;
import net.jini.discovery.DiscoveryListener;
import net.jini.discovery.DiscoveryEvent;
import net.jini.core.lookup.ServiceRegistrar;
```

Continued

Figure 9.14 Continued

```
import net.jini.core.lookup.ServiceTemplate;

import net.jini.core.lookup.ServiceMatches;

import net.jini.core.event.RemoteEventListener;

import net.jini.core.event.RemoteEvent;

import net.jini.core.event.UnknownEventException;

import java.rmi.RemoteException;

import java.rmi.server.UnicastRemoteObject;

import java.rmi.RMISecurityManager;

import java.util.*;

import java.io.Serializable;

import java.io.IOException;


public class Client

    implements DiscoveryListener {


    // This client will control multiple Mindstorms. Use

    // the Vector object as a flexible container for

    // holding a variable number of objects.

    protected Vector mindstorms = new Vector();


    static public void main(String args[]) {


        // Since reggie is running with a security policy,

        // we will have to as well. This assumes that

        // the policy file is located at

        // c:\jini1_2\policy\policy.all

        // Adjust this for specific installations.

        System.setProperty(

            "java.security.policy",

            "c:\\jini1_2\\policy\\policy.all");

        System.setSecurityManager(new SecurityManager());


        new Client();


        // Ensure client runs indefinitely.
```

Continued

Figure 9.14 Continued

```
        Object keepAlive = new Object();
        synchronized(keepAlive) {
            try {
                keepAlive.wait();
            } catch(java.lang.InterruptedException e) {
                // Do nothing
            }
        }
    }

    public Client() {

        // Lookup using Multicast (i.e., look for any lookup
        // services on the network).
        LookupDiscovery lookupDiscovery = null;

        try {
            lookupDiscovery =
                new LookupDiscovery(
                    LookupDiscovery.ALL_GROUPS);
        } catch (IOException e) {
            System.err.println(e.toString());
            System.exit(1);
        }
        lookupDiscovery.addDiscoveryListener(this);

    }

    public void discarded(DiscoveryEvent event) {
        // Must be implemented from the
        // DiscoveryListener interface.
    }

    public void discovered(DiscoveryEvent event) {
```

Continued

Figure 9.14 Continued

```
// Must be implemented from the
// DiscoveryListener interface.

// This method will be called with a list
// of all lookup services found
// (actually their registrar proxies).
ServiceRegistrar[] regArray = event.getRegistrars();
Class [] classes = new Class[] {Mindstorm.class};
ServiceTemplate svcTemplate =
    new ServiceTemplate(null, classes, null);

for (int ix = 0; ix < regArray.length; ix++) {
    ServiceRegistrar svcRegistrar = regArray[ix];

    // For each lookup service, there could be
    // 0 or many registered matching objects.
    // Request a maximum of 10.
    ServiceMatches matches;
    try {
        matches =
            svcRegistrar.lookup(svcTemplate, 10);
    } catch (RemoteException e) {
        System.err.println(
            "Remote exception in lookup");
        continue;
    }
    for (int iy = 0;
        iy < matches.totalMatches;
        iy++) {
        Mindstorm matched = (Mindstorm)
            (matches.items[iy].service);

        if (null != matched) {
            // Call ProcessMatch() to either
            // add it to the collection
```

Continued

Figure 9.14 Continued

```
                        // or ignore it.
                        try {
                            ProcessMatched(matched);
                        } catch (RemoteException e) {
                            // This will likely be old
                            // services that are no longer
                            // available.
                            continue;
                        }
                    }
                }
            }


    System.out.println("Finished list");
    if (mindstorms.isEmpty()) {
        // Client cannot operate if no Mindstorm
        // services have been found.
        System.err.println(
            "Could not find any Mindstorms");
        System.exit(1);
    } else {
        // All OK; we have at least one Mindstorm
        // service.
        // Start it off by getting the first
        // Mindstorm to perform the first dance step.
        try {
            ((Mindstorm)mindstorms.
                firstElement()).
                imitateThis(0);
        } catch (RemoteException e){
            // If we can't invoke the first
            // Mindstorm, then there's no point
            // continuing.
            System.err.println(e.toString());
            System.exit(1);
```

Continued

Figure 9.14 Continued

```
            }
        }
    }


    protected void ProcessMatched(Mindstorm matched)
            throws RemoteException {


        // matched represents a Mindstorm object
        // that may or may not be a duplicate instance
        // of one we already have.


        String foundId =
            matched.getRcxId();


        // Only add the Mindstorm to the
        // collection if we don't
        // already have it.
        if (IsUnique(foundId)) {


            mindstorms.add(matched);
            System.out.println("Found ID: " + foundId);


            // Create a new listener
            // object to receive events
            // from this Mindstorm.
            matched.RegisterRemoteListener(
                new EventListener(matched, foundId));
        } else {
            System.out.println("Ignoring ID: " + foundId);
        }


    }


    protected boolean IsUnique(String id) {
```

Continued

Figure 9.14 Continued

```
        // Iterate through the list of Mindstorms and
        // determine whether we already have this one.

        for (Iterator iter = mindstorms.iterator();
                iter.hasNext();) {
            String existingId = null;
            try {
                existingId = ((Mindstorm)iter.next()).
                    getRcxId();
                if (id.equals(existingId)) {
                    return false;
                }
            } catch(RemoteException e) {
                System.err.println(
                    "Caught: " + e.toString());
            }
        }
        return true;
    }


protected void NotifyNextMindstorm(String id, int step) {

        // One of the Mindstorms has notified us of a
        // step performed; notify the next one.

        // Firstly loop through the Vector of
        // Mindstorms until we find the match
        for (Iterator iter = mindstorms.iterator();
                iter.hasNext();) {
            String currId = null;
            try {
                currId = ((Mindstorm)iter.next()).getRcxId();
                if (id.equals(currId)) {
                    // We have the match. Either get the
                    // next from the list or the first
```

Continued

Figure 9.14 Continued

```
                          // in the list.
                          // If there's only one, it will just
                          // notify itself...
                          if (iter.hasNext()) {
                              ((Mindstorm)iter.next()).
                                  imitateThis(step);
                          } else {
                              ((Mindstorm)mindstorms.
                                  firstElement()).
                                  imitateThis(step);
                          }
                      }
                  } catch(RemoteException e) {
                      System.err.println("Caught: " +
                          e.toString());
                  }
              }
          }


class EventListener extends UnicastRemoteObject
        implements RemoteEventListener, Serializable {

          // This class must extend UnicastRemoteObject
          // because it needs to receive calls back
          // from a remote JVM. Remember to generate a
          // stub class for it using the RMI compiler!

          protected String rcxId = null;
          protected Mindstorm remoteMindstorm = null;

          public EventListener(
                  Mindstorm mindstorm, String rcxId)
              throws RemoteException {

              // Call the default constructor for
```

Continued

Figure 9.14 Continued

```
            // the parent class.
            super();

            // Keep a reference to the remote object that
            // we're listening to.
            this.remoteMindstorm = mindstorm;

            // Keep a copy of the remote ID so we don't have
            // to make round trips to look it up.
            this.rcxId = rcxId;
        }

    public void notify(RemoteEvent evt)
            throws UnknownEventException, RemoteException {

            // Will receive notification messages from
            // the service that it is associated with.
            switch ((int)evt.getID()) {

                case Mindstorm.EVENT_RCX_MSG:
                    // We have received some form
                    // of message from the remote RCX.
                    byte[] msg;
                    msg = remoteMindstorm.
                        GetLastRCXMessage();

                    // We could process the message here
                    // in some way.
                    break;

                case Mindstorm.EVENT_DANCE_STEP:
                    // This is a notification from a remote
                    // Mindstorm that it has just completed
                    // a dance step. We must query the
                    // service to find out what the
```

Continued

Figure 9.14 Continued

```
                            // step was.
                            int step;
                            step = remoteMindstorm.
                                GetLastStepPerformed();
                            System.out.println(
                                "Received step: "
                                + step
                                + " from: "
                                + rcxId);

                            // Pass the dance step along
                            // the list of robots.
                            NotifyNextMindstorm(rcxId, step);
                            break;
                    }
                }
            }
        }
```

Note that the *mindstormClient.Client* class also contains an inner class, named *EventListener*, which extends *UnicastRemoteObject*. The *EventListener* class will be instantiated locally, and a corresponding stub object passed across the network (or at least across JVMs) to the service proxy. This then allows the service proxy to communicate notifications back to the client by calling the stub locally, which will in turn communicate back to the remote client. This complex combination of local and remote objects is diagrammed in Figure 9.15.

Now we're ready to start one or more instances of the service (depending on how many RCXs and computers we have on hand), and then start the client.

So long as the HTTP server and the RMI activation daemon are still running as described previously, and as long as our computer has a working installation of RCX Java, we can now start up the service. You can see one other difference from the preceding example; in the main() function, we are now setting the security policy and security manager programmatically so these will not need to be passed in as parameters in the command line. Notice also that the security manager is momentarily removed (in the *discovered()* method) while the serial port is initialized; otherwise, an exception would result. Once the port has been opened, we can write to it and read from it with the security manager in place.

Figure 9.15 The Complex Interactions Between Components in the Jini/RCX Example

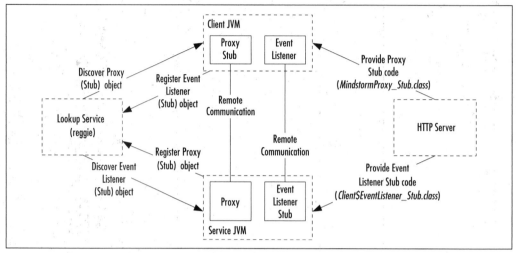

We have described previously how to use the RMI compiler to generate the stub class file for the proxy class. Before running this example, you will also need to generate the stub class file for the *EventListener* inner class. Since *EventListener* is an inner class of *Client* (within the *mindstormClient* package), the Java compiler will have generated a file named Client$EventListener.class, so you can generate the stub file by running:

```
rmic -v1.2 mindstormClient.Client$EventListener
```

After running this command, you should have a new class file named *Client$EventListener_stub.class* in the mindstormClient directory.

The next step is to package each stub class file into an appropriate jar file so that they can be served by the HTTP server. For the purposes of this example, we will assume that they are in mindstorm.jar and mindstormClient.jar; we have previously described the use of the jar tool, and the following command lines can be used to generate the two jar archive files:

```
jar cvf mindstormClient.jar -C mindstormClient/ Client$EventListener
_stub.class
jar cvf mindstorm.jar -C mindstorm/ MindstormProxy_stub.class
```

When all of the class files, including stubs, have been compiled and the jar files produced, you will need to make the stub files accessible via HTTP. If you are running the HTTP server that came with the Jini TSK, the jar archives will need to be copied to the directory from where the HTTP server will serve files, and the HTTP Server will have to be restarted.

At around this time, you may be thinking there has to be an easier way to execute the steps of compiling the Java source files, generating RMI stubs, and producing the jar archives. In fact, there is a tool available to assist in this, although at the time of writing it is only an alpha release. The tool, appropriately named BuildTool, is downloadable from http://developer.jini.org/exchange/projects/outofbox/buildtool/index.html (after creating a login account), and can perform the following three tasks:

- Compile the Java source files.
- Generate the RMI stub files.
- Generate jar archive files.

The tool comes with enough documentation to get it up and running, and includes a GUI interface that makes it very easy to use. A screenshot of the GUI interface for *BuildTool* can be seen in Figure 9.16.

Figure 9.16 The BuildTool User Interface

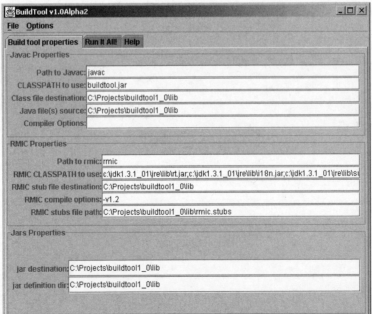

Starting up an instance of the server on a Windows machine with a serial port named COM1 can then be done as follows, remembering that the server will have to download the class file for the *EventListener* stub via HTTP:

```
rem
rem startmindstorm.bat
rem
rem replace 'myhttp' with your HTTP server's machine name
rem or IP address.
java -Djava.rmi.server.codebase=http://myhttp:8081/mindstormClient.jar
 mindstorm.MindstormService Barney COM1
pause
```

This will assign the arbitrary name "Barney" to the proxy (in this case, to distinguish it from "Fred" and possibly "Wilma"). The output should initially look something like that shown in Figure 9.17.

Figure 9.17 Successful Registration of an RCX Service Proxy

Once you have successfully started one or more server instances, starting the client is similarly straightforward. The following script shows how to do this:

```
rem
rem startmindstormclient.bat
rem
rem replace 'myhttp' with your HTTP server's machine name
rem or IP address.
java -Djava.rmi.server.codebase=http://myhttp:8081/mindstorm.jar
```

```
mindstormClient.Client
```
```
pause
```

When the client executes, you should see output similar to that in Figure 9.18. In this instance, the client program has detected three valid service registrations on the network. At the point in time that this screenshot was taken, the following had just taken place:

- The client program had discovered three service proxy objects with unique IDs: Wilma, Barney, and Fred.

- The client program had instructed Wilma to perform step 1 (it starts the process by sending step 1 to the first RCX proxy in its list).

- Wilma had completed step 1, and 10 seconds later randomly chose to perform step 6, which was sent back to the client as a notification.

- The client had instructed Barney to imitate step 6, and after the 10-second pause, Barney chose to perform step 1 and notify the client.

- The client then told Fred to imitate step 1. From Figure 9.18, you can see that Fred executed step 1 and then chose to perform step 6 and notify the client.

Figure 9.18 A Snapshot of the Client Program Output

```
C:\WINNT\System32\cmd.exe                                        _ □ ×

C:\Projects>java mindstormClient.Client
Found ID: Wilma
Found ID: Barney
Found ID: Fred
Finished list
Received step: 6 from: Wilma
Received step: 1 from: Barney
Received step: 6 from: Fred
_
```

Figure 9.19 shows the output from one of the services. This screenshot was captured as part of the same trial run as that in Figure 9.18. As you can see, this service was run with an RCX ID of "Fred". The snapshot shows that Fred has executed step 1 in imitation of Barney, and has then chosen to perform step 6.

You can also clearly see from this screenshot that the proxy object is in fact executing in the same JVM that the service was run in; all of the trace output has been generated by the proxy object which is both transmitting opcodes to the RCX and receiving messages back from the RCX.

Figure 9.19 A Snapshot of the Output of One of the Services

Bricks & Chips...

Two Robots Are Better than One

This chapter demonstrates how Jini can be used to allow interaction with and between multiple LEGO MINDSTORMS on a network. There are a few practicalities that you should bear in mind if you are going to try this:

- There is no simple way for the infrared tower to differentiate between RCX units, and vice versa. This means that if two or more RCXs are in range of the one tower, they will all respond to the signals they receive, and they will all transmit signals back to the tower. This may make the tower (or your software) quite confused.

- While this chapter has shown a way to differentiate between RCXs by giving their proxy objects unique identifying names, this identifier only applies to the proxy; if one RCX was to move out of range of the proxy's tower and another move into its range, the newly-accessible RCX would continue to respond as if it were the original one.

Continued

■ In order to give RCXs their own identifier within the firmware, you would have to reprogram the firmware and download a unique identifier into the MINDSTORMS device. Then one infrared tower could control multiple RCXs independently; they would have to be programmed to respond only to commands addressed to their unique ID. You may like to attempt this by combining what you have learned in this chapter with the knowledge on leJOS gained from other chapters in this book.

As you can see from Figure 9.20, we found office desk partitioning to be a very effective infrared screen, allowing us to test the interaction of a pair of "Roverbot" robots at reasonably close range. The Jini solution works very effectively; the client discovers the registered services, and away they go—a synchronized LEGO dance! Because the services determine their own dance steps randomly, the average number of forward and right movements should be roughly equivalent to the average number of backward and left movements respectively so the robots shouldn't wander too far away, but it might be a good idea not to let them dance too long unattended.

Figure 9.20 Two LEGO MINDSTORMS Interacting via Jini

Summary

Jini is a Java technology that is built upon Java Remote Method Invocation (RMI), and which enables devices to communicate in a network. At the heart of a Jini network or "federation" is one or more lookup services. Jini services can register themselves with these lookup services, and Jini clients can "discover" the services through them. In this way there is very little administrative overhead.

Jini can not only be useful in networking very powerful devices such as computers, but also embedded devices that could include the RCX. In the case of a device like the RCX that is not powerful enough to run Jini, another device such as a personal computer can function as a *proxy* Jini service and will then talk to the embedded device over whatever mechanism is available.

In this chapter we looked at an example of a fairly simplistic Jini service and client, and then moved on to cover a more substantial example involving multiple RCXs; this illustrated how a proxy architecture can be used with the RCX so that multiple RCXs can interact with one another.

Solutions Fast Track

Overview of Jini

- ☑ Jini is a Java technology built on top of RMI, enabling clients and services to interact in a network with very little administrative overhead.

- ☑ One feature of Jini is that it is vary applicable to embedded devices, including devices like the RCX.

- ☑ The Jini Technology Starter Kit (TSK) includes all of the required jar files as well as some service implementations such as *reggie*, an implementation of a lookup service.

A Simple Jini Service Example

- ☑ We covered an example of a simple Jini service to calculate checksums and a client that made use of the service.

- ☑ The example showed how to register a service with a single known lookup service, as well as how a client could discover the registered service by querying the known lookup service.

☑ The service example was quite simplistic, especially in that the client actually executed the service object within its own JVM.

Proxies and Service Architectures

☑ Solutions that make use of Jini can be implemented according to various architectures.

☑ One such service architecture involves the use of a *proxy* object that is registered as a service, but actually abstracts the real service and communicates with it behind the scenes.

☑ The proxy architecture is especially suitable when providing services for devices that are not capable of running Jini themselves.

A RCX Jini Proxy Service

☑ Since the RCX is not capable of running Jini itself, it is a very good candidate for the proxy architecture, where a proxy object would run on a machine, which would then communicate with the RCX via the infrared tower.

☑ A single machine with a single infrared link could potentially control multiple RCXs if the firmware were modified. This would require a unique identifier to be stored in each of the RCXs' firmware.

☑ Another architecture (as used in the example in this chapter) involves one infrared tower per RCX, and the proxy objects themselves storing the unique identifiers of the respective RCXs.

Using the RCX Jini Service: Example Server and Client

☑ We covered a much less simplistic example that involved the networking of a number of RCX units.

☑ This example showed how servers and clients could dynamically discover lookup services on a network by using multicast, and also showed the use of RMI stub objects to make method calls across a network.

☑ The outcome was that RCXs could interact with one another, performing a synchronized dance.

Frequently Asked Questions

The following Frequently Asked Questions, answered by the authors of this book, are designed to both measure your understanding of the concepts presented   in this chapter and to assist you with real-life implementation of these concepts. To have your questions about this chapter answered by the author, browse to **www.syngress.com/solutions** and click on the **"Ask the Author"** form.

Q: Is the word "Jini" an acronym?

A: No, "Jini" doesn't actually stand for anything. However, it has been said that it could stand for "Jini Is Not Initials"—a variation on the "GNU's Not Unix" self-defining acronym.

Q: If a Java Virtual Machine can be run on the RCX, why can't Jini run directly on the RCX instead of having to deploy a proxy?

A: The basic guideline for a machine to run Jini is a 32-bit CPU with around 8MB of RAM and full networking capabilities. Since the RCX only has 32KB of RAM and simple point-to-point infrared communication ability, it falls well short of these requirements.

Q: How is Jini different from RMI?

A: Jini makes extensive use of RMI, especially in RMI's facilities for calling methods on objects in remote JVMs and for enabling the downloading (for example, via HTTP) of class files to remote users of objects as required. Jini is somewhat different to RMI in a few areas, however: Jini objects can use other protocols for remote communication and are not bound to using RMI stubs (making Jini quite flexible for communicating with a wide variety of devices), and Jini allows multicast discovery of the lookup service which makes it a lot more flexible both for Jini clients to discover available services on a network, and for Jini services to register themselves on a network that they have very little specific knowledge of.

Q: Can a Jini service provide a user interface to be displayed by a client?

A: Yes, it is absolutely possible for a Jini service to export a graphical user interface (GUI). There are a number of possible architectural approaches to doing this; you can find out more about it at Web sites such as http://jini.org.

Q: Where can I dig up more information on Jini?

A: There are numerous sources of information. The following list is a starting point:

- There is extensive documentation included in the Jini TSK download, covering both the service implementations and the API.

- Sun's Web site—http://java.sun.com/jini

- The online Jini community—http://jini.org

- The "Jiniology" articles at artima.com—www.artima.com/jini/jiniology

Appendix A

Resources

There's quite a large amount of reference material to be found regarding MIND-STORMS inventions, including some very good books, and hundreds of Internet sites that cover specific topics and show interesting models. We apologize in advance for the significant number of interesting sites that we surely (and unintentionally) omitted from the list.

Every link of this appendix has been checked, but as you know, the Internet is a dynamic animal and we cannot guarantee they will be still valid at the time you read the book. If you find any broken links, use the descriptive information we provided beside each site address to hunt for it using your favorite search engine.

A few of the links point to commercial sites, or to sites that, besides providing information about the making of some custom part, also sell a kit or the finished product. We have no direct or indirect interest, nor any connection with them; we included the links simply as a help to the reader.

General Interest Sites

LEGO MINDSTORMS (http://mindstorms.lego.com)
The first site to mention is, of course, the LEGO MINDSTORMS official site. It contains tons of stuff: technical tips, a gallery of inventions, events, contests, answers to frequently asked questions (FAQ), and more. The official LEGO MINDSTORMS FAQ site is: http://mindstorms .lego.com/products/whatis/faq.asp.

LUGNET (www.lugnet.com)
The LEGO Users Group Network (LUGNET) is the most comprehensive Internet resource for LEGO, and it's difficult to describe in a few words. It features a database containing all the LEGO sets ever released, as well as a reference list citing all the single LEGO parts. But, more important, its newsgroups are the meeting point of LEGO fans of any age and from any part of the world, and it's one of the friendliest places on the Internet. Don't miss the LUGNET newsgroups, where you can ask any number of questions and be answered with completeness, competence, and patience.

- www.lugnet.com/robotics The general robotics LUGNET newsgroup

- www.lugnet.com/robotics/rcx/java The LUGNET newsgroup specifically devoted to Java programming for the RCX

Fred Martin's Unofficial Questions and Answers about MIT Programmable Bricks and LEGO MINDSTORMS (http://fredm.www.media.mit.edu/people/fredm/ mindstorms/index.html)

Fred Martin tells the story of the Programmable Brick and provides some other useful information about the RCX.

LEGO MINDSTORMS Internals (www.crynwr.com/ lego-robotics)

Russell Nelson maintains a page that contains many technical details about the MINDSTORMS system as well as many useful links. This site also includes a directory of individuals who contributed to the reverse engineering of the RCX.

Artificial Intelligence and Machine Learning (www.home.zonnet.nl/bvandam)

Bert van Dam's site is a mine of information about artificial intelligence in general. If you find the subtle link to Miscellaneous | General Information, you will discover a whole world of LEGO projects!

MINDSTORMS RCX

RCX Internals (http://graphics.stanford.edu/~kekoa/rcx)
Kekoa Proudfoot documents all the internals of the LEGO firmware and ROM routines. He made the development of firmware like legOS and pbForth possible.

Ole Caprani's RCX Manual (www.daimi.au.dk/dArkOS/ Vaerktoejer.dir/RCX.vejledning.dir/Vejledning.html)
Ole Caprani from the University of Aarhus, Department of Computer Science, has created a very informative manual about the internals of the RCX. It includes information on how the I/O ports of the microcontroller are connected to the hardware.

MINDSTORMS RCX Sensor Input Page (www.plazaearth.com/usr/gasperi/lego.htm)
Michael Gasperi's site describes the various sensors that can be constructed; used in a leJOS environment, this is the starting point for any investigation into using sensors. The site also contains Brian Stormont's suggestion to combine a touch sensor and a light sensor on the same

port, and Tom Schumm's trick to connect touch sensors in the AND configuration.

Gordon's Brick Programmer (www.umbra.demon.co.uk/gbp.html)

With its graphic-textual interface, Gordon's Brick Programmer (GBP) acts as a bridge between RCX Code and the pure textual programming environments.

Languages, APIs, and Tools

legOS (http://legos.sourceforge.net)

The legOS homepage. The latest releases, downloads, and developer notes for legOS can be found here.

LegoSim (www.informatik.hu-berlin.de/~mueller/legosim)

LegoSim is a UNIX-based simulator for legOS with an Applet-GUI, written by Frank Mueller, Thomas Röblitz, and Oliver Bühn.

emulegOS (http://sourceforge.net/projects/emulegos)

This is the homepage for the legOS emulator, which lets you run and debug your legOS programs on your Win/Linux PC. Started by Mario Ferrari and Marco Berti, emulegOS is currently an open source project managed by Mark Falco.

Java Communications API (http://java.sun.com/products/javacomm/index.html)

The Java Communications API can be used to write platform-independent communications applications for MINDSTORMS robots.

RCXPort—Java Interface to the LEGO MINDSTORMS RCX (www.slewis.com/rcxport)

Scott Lewis' RCXPort site for the Java interface he created for the purpose of interacting with a LEGO MINDSTORM RCX from a Java Virtual Machine.

RCXJava (www.escape.com/~dario/java/rcx)

A platform-independent Java library used to develop RCX applications, developed by Dario Laverde.

Forte Tools—Forte for Java (www.sun.com/forte/ffj)

Forte is an IDE written completely in Java. Forte provides a visual GUI creator, a debugger, and compilation functions—all the expected parts of an IDE. Forte also has the seemingly unique ability to configure the compiler and Java runtime you use.

Jini (www.javacommerce.com/tutorial/jini)

Jan Newmarch's Jini Tutorial featuring a chapter on LEGO MIND-STORMS

Jad (http://kpdus.tripod.com/jad.html)

Jad allows you to retrieve a compiled class file for editing, even if you have lost the source. This can be especially useful when an unwanted modification is saved, causing the program not to function. Decompiling a program you did not create can help you learn programming styles, ways to implement complex functions, or just how to better code for the RCX.

Jlint (www.ispras.ru/~knizhnik/jlint/ReadMe.htm)

Jlint is a Java version of the popular *lint* for C programs. Jlint can be useful, since debugging programs on the RCX, especially ones that deal with logic errors (such as an incorrect loop structures), can be difficult. It can also detect other "assumptions" you may have made, and tells you if they are incorrect.

An Operating System in Java for the LEGO MINDSTORMS RCX Microcontroller (www.usenix.org/publications/library/proceedings/usenix2000/freenix/nikander/nikander.pdf)

A scientific paper by Pekka Nikander presented at the 2000 USENIX Annual Technical Conference

NQC—Not Quite C (www.enteract.com/~dbaum/nqc/index.html)

Dave Baum's NQC site contains the compiler and the documentation.

Bricx Command Center (http://hometown.aol.com/johnbinder/bricxcc.htm)

Formerly known as the RCX Command Center, and based on Mark Overmars' original source code (see LEGO Robot Pages), John Hansen's Bricx Command Center (BricxCC) supports all the LEGO Programmable Bricks and introduces many new and interesting features. If you use NQC on a PC platform, this is a "must have."

LEGO Robot Pages (www.cs.uu.nl/people/markov/lego)
The site of the original RCX Command Center, a very good IDE for NQC originally developed by Mark Overmars but not updated to the current version (see Bricx Command Center).

Visual NQC (http://home.hetnet.nl/~myweb1/VisualNQC.htm)
Ronald Strijbosch's Visual NQC has its roots in the RCX Command Center, but is completely rewritten in Visual Basic. A very functional and complete IDE to NQC.

NQCEdit (http://hem.passagen.se/mickee/nqcedit)
Another front-end IDE for NQC, written by Mikael Eriksson. Currently less sophisticated than the RCX Command Center and Visual NQC, it's an effective and solid alternative.

NQC API Programmer's Guide (www.cybercomm.net/ ~rajcok/nqc)
Mark Rajcok's guide to NQC API lists all NQC functions, their syntax, their supported programmable bricks and a few examples.

General Paranoyaxc RCX Tools (www.rainer-keuchel.de/rcx/ rcx.html)
A package that contains a port of the NQC compiler, a simple editor, and a remote control program to access your RCX from WinCE platforms.

Hempel Design Group (www.hempeldesigngroup.com/lego/ index.html)
Ralph Hempel's site contains a copious amount of tools and information. Some of the highlights include

- Information about Ralph's maze solver, an application demonstrated during the 1999 MindFest at MIT.

- Extremely helpful information on how to improve the reading range of the LEGO light sensor.

- Information about Ralph Hempel's programmable brick FORTH (pbForth) for MINDSTORMS (www.hempeldesigngroup.com/ lego/pbFORTH/index.html).

- Schematics and detailed instructions on how to interface R/C Servos to the RCX.

■ Home page of Ralph Hempel's famous double-acting compressor. The same site also contains his Pressure Switch (www.hempeldesigngroup.com/lego/pressureswitch/index.html).

Reactive Languages and LEGO MINDSTORMS (www.emn.fr/richard/lego)

Martin Richard's Web site about using synchronous languages (Esterel, Lustre, Grafcet) to play with the LEGO MINDSTORMS kit.

ADA for MINDSTORMS (www.usafa.af.mil/dfcs/adamindstorms.htm)

An ADA pre-processor to NQC. Also consult some of the documentation at www.faginfamily.net/barry/Papers/AdaLetters.htm.

Bot-Kit (www.object-arts.com/Bower/Bot-Kit/Bot-Kit.htm)

An interface to programming the RCX in Smalltalk (based upon Dolphin Smalltalk).

Brick Command (www.geocities.com/Area51/Nebula/8488/lego.html)

A simple textual programming language that incorporates a complete IDE.

The PowerBook Source (www.pbsource.com/features/LEGO_and_Macs.shtml)

Information on how to control LEGO MINDSTORMS from a PowerBook with Common LISt Processing (LISP).

QC (http://digilander.iol.it/ferrarafrancesco/lego/qc/index.html)

Francesco Ferrara's QC, a mini OS (no multitasking) meant as an interface between C code and the ROM routines of the RCX.

TCL—RCX (www.linux.org/docs/ldp/howto/mini/Lego/tcl.html)

Laurent Demailly and Peter Pletcher's TCL RCX can either compile a TCL script into RCX bytecode, or it can remotely control the robot via either a script or an interactive TCL shell.

WinVLL (www.research.co.jp/MindStorms/winvll/index-e.html)

A simple tool by Shigeru Makino to control and program the Micro Scout from a PC.

For Inspiration

Ben's LEGO Creations (http://unite.com.au/~u11235a/lego)
Ben Williamson has created some very cool robots!

BrickBots (www.brickbots.com)
BrickBots is Richard Sutherland's repository of building contests and best solutions. This is a nice site where you can attend "remote" challenges. Although the contests are no longer running on a regular basis, the current repository of contest entries provides builders with great ideas.

MindScope (http://baserv.uci.kun.nl/~smientki/Lego_Knex/ Lego_electronica/Mindscope.htm)
Stef Mientki's graphing utility is able to continuously monitor the sensors and produce a chart from the sampled values.

Programming the LEGO Micro Scout (http://eaton.dhs.org/ lego)
Doug Eaton explains how to program the Micro Scout through bar codes.

Programming LEGO MINDSTORMS with Java Fast Track

This Appendix will provide you with a quick, yet comprehensive, review of the most important concepts covered in this book.

❖ Chapter 1: Introducing LEGO MINDSTORMS

The LEGO MINDSTORMS RIS Kit

☑ The MINDSTORMS series comes from a collaboration between the LEGO Company and the Massachusetts Institute of Technology (MIT) Media Lab that led to the creation of a "programmable brick."

☑ The Robotic Invention System (RIS) is the basic kit, and the starting point for every MINDSTORMS robot of more than basic complexity.

☑ The RIS includes everything you need to build and program robots: the RCX unit, three sensors, two motors, an infrared (IR) tower, manuals, more than 700 TECHNIC pieces and a software CD-ROM.

RCX: The Robot's Brain

☑ The RCX is a microcomputer than interfaces with input and output devices. Programs can be written on a PC and then downloaded to the unit through the IR tower.

☑ The RCX uses two types of memory: read-only memory (ROM) and modifiable random access memory (RAM). The latter stores both user-written programs and the system firmware, which is the RCX's operating system.

☑ The RCX can be expanded in two ways: using a different programming software like NQC or the Java APIs, or replacing the default firmware with a new one (legOS, pbForth, and leJOS solutions).

The RIS Software Environment

☑ The RIS kit contains RCX Code, which is the standard programming language from LEGO. It contains tools for downloading firmware and a visual programming interface that makes writing code a very easy task.

☑ RCX Code is targeted at kids and beginners; its capabilities are too limited for the development of more complex robots.

RCX Bytecodes

☑ The RCX architecture uses an interpreter-based virtual machine to execute commands statement by statement.

Chapter 1 Continued

☑ Opcodes, the assembly commands, are used both by the RCX's stored programs and the IR emitting devices, like a PC with an IR tower or a remote control.

LEGO Expansion Kits

☑ There are other robotics kits besides the RCX-based system: CyberMaster, Scout, Micro Scout, and Code Pilot. Each of these kits features only a subset of the full RIS' capabilities.

☑ Standard LEGO TECHNIC pieces can be used to expand building possibilities, as can sensors and other spare pieces that are available separately.

☑ MINDSTORMS can be expanded with kits that contain sensors, motors, and special pieces. Further, Vision Command (VC) is a LEGO video camera with an advanced visual recognition system that can be used to add more functionalities to your LEGO MINDSTORMS robots.

❖ Chapter 2: The Java Communications API

Overview of the Java Communications Extension API

☑ The Java Comm API provides the mechanism for port enumeration and ownership as well as event driven notification of change of ownership.

☑ Asynchronous and synchronous I/O is possible due to the standard Java-style event-driven architecture.

☑ The *SerialPort* and *ParallelPort* classes provide a clean encapsulation for supporting the many platforms for which the JCE API is available.

Installing and Configuring the Java Communications API

☑ There are three deliverables: a jar file, a properties file, and a native shared runtime library.

☑ Several options are available depending on ease-of-use versus ease-of-configuration. The simplest is to keep the three deliverable files together in the same folder so long as it is the application's working folder.

Chapter 2 Continued

☑   There are possible version control caveats, but fortunately the API has stabilized enough such that it's not a big issue.

Reading and Writing to Serial Ports

☑   The Java Communications API comes with several simple examples that illustrate the usage of both parallel and serial ports.

☑   Adding event-driven notifications is straightforward using *EventListeners.*

☑   Working with the parallel ports is similar to working with any port that extends the *CommPort* abstract class.

Debugging with Serial Ports: The Black Box Example

☑   A close look at a specific advanced Java sample program that comes with the JCE illustrates all functionality of the serial port by serving as a serial port analyzer and line monitor.

☑   The BlackBox sample program can be used as is as a serial proxy or sniffer tool without modifications.

☑   The way that the output and input streams were used in the BlackBox example can be used as the basis of custom applications that provide similar functionality.

Extending the Java Communications API

☑   The mechanism for adding new functionality exists via the *CommDriver, CommPort* and *CommPortIdentifier* classes.

☑   A step-by-step process of how a customized USB driver was implemented for use with the RCX 2.0 USB tower.

☑   The limitations shown include the inability to add external packages as the source for new port drivers. This would break the package naming convention of not adding to or changing the classes in the *javax.comm* hierarchy.

❖ Chapter 3: Communicating with the RCXPort API

Overview of the RCXPort Java API

☑ The code in the RCXPort Java API establishes a connection with your infrared (IR) tower through the appropriate serial port. It relies on the Java Communications package to control the port. USB support is not included.

☑ The *RCXPacket* class wraps commands into a format that the RCX can understand before they are sent to the tower.

☑ *RCXCmd* includes all of the standard opcodes that are used to control the RCX. These bytes are declared as static in the *RCXCmd* class so that they may be called from other classes without instantiating an *RCXCmd* object.

☑ Existing RCXPort functionality does not allow for the running of Java code directly on the RCX or for high-level Java code to be compiled into byte code for downloading to the RCX. This functionality is forthcoming.

Programming the RCX Using RCXPort

☑ By inserting RCX commands into a Java program that runs on your PC, you can control the RCX in direct mode, provided your RCX remains within range of the IR tower for the duration of the program's execution.

☑ When running programs in direct mode, there is a slight delay between commands as the data is sent from the computer's serial port to the IR tower, then on to the RCX.

☑ Programming in direct mode allows for the increased power and flexibility of the Java programming language, yet limits you to keeping the RCX within range of the tower.

Downloading Programs with RCXPort

☑ RCXPort also provides functionality to download byte code files to the RCX, where they are stored in random access memory (RAM) and can be run by pressing the **Run** button.

☑ Storing programs on the RCX frees you from having to stay near the tower when running a program.

Chapter 3 Continued

☑ Programs can be written manually in byte code, or written in a high-level language, such as 'Not Quite C' (NQC), then compiled into byte code.

Interfacing External Software with RCXPort

☑ NQC, a high-level language based on C syntax, can be compiled into byte code that is understood by RCX's firmware. This allows you to take advantage of more advanced control structures such as loops, events and functions.

☑ RCXPort is capable of downloading compiled NQC byte code to the RCX.

☑ These programs, once stored on the RCX, can be run by themselves or called from an RCXPort-based program that is running on your personal computer.

An Advanced Example Using RCXPort

☑ Our example uses a hard-coded value to represent the light threshold between two colors. This value could vary widely due to different amounts of light and different colored candies used in your experiment. This simple branch in the code could also be used to sort the "darks" and "lights" from a bag of multicolored candies. Alternatively, you could assign ranges to your different colors and check for read values that are within these ranges.

☑ Programs stored on the RCX can be called from Java code when controlling the RCX in direct mode. This allows you to better control the timing of RCX operations that would otherwise be thrown off by variance in the infrared communications.

❖ Chapter 4: Communicating with the RCXJava API

Designing an RCXJava Communications Architecture

☑ The use of the Java Communications API facilitates the automatic search for an available serial port, and use of the rcx.comm package gives us USB capability in a platform-neutral manner. Allowing the configuration of the port to be based on the port name improves ease-of-use.

Chapter 4 Continued

☑ Management and encapsulation of RCX protocol details is hidden from the application user.

☑ The use of standard Java design patterns and Java interfaces enables us to use new and different types of ports without changing a line of code.

Overview or the RCXJava API

☑ The RCXJava API is an open source and extensible API.

☑ It supports serial, USB and new ports such as sockets.

☑ It lays the groundwork for a full-fledged programming environment for the RCX by using high level methods that follow the same method signature naming convention of other Java efforts like leJOS.

Using the RCXLoader Application

☑ The RCXLoader is an out-of-the-box utility and test tool for interfacing with the RCX.

☑ It provides a convenient lookup table of all the opcodes and their arguments.

☑ It provides the starting point or template for creating more advanced examples.

Beyond Serial Port Communications: The RCXApplet Example

☑ Control of an RCX can not only be enabled from a stand-alone application but also over the Internet using a Java-enabled Web browser, providing the same GUI as one would get with the stand-alone application.

☑ Using *RCXSocketPort*, one could control a number of RCXs over a network and the network via a proxy server.

☑ Use of the direct control API methods gives you the capability of creating complex frameworks similar to the visual-programming interface that comes with the LEGO MINDSTORMS kit.

Chapter 4 Continued

Direct Control Programming for the RCX Using Java

☑ With direct control programming, we are using the RCX's "brain" to pass commands from a proxy "brain" residing on a PC. There are significant advantages to programming tasks to run on the PC's resources rather than running tasks inside the RCX.

☑ Tasks can run on the PC in near real time (there is a noticeable time lag).

☑ We can add Artificial Intelligence (AI) capabilities when programming our RCX robots. Neural network programming allows an RCX to "learn" the right response to stimuli all on its own.

❖ Chapter 5: The leJOS System

Basic leJOS Usage Guidelines

☑ The leJOS environment (*PATH, RCXTTY, LEJOS_HOME, JAVA_HOME, CLASSPATH*) must be set up in order to start programming for leJOS.

☑ Compilation is done using *lejosc*, which is just a thin wrapper around *javac*.

☑ Conversion of Java class files to a leJOS binary format, and the transmission of that format to the RCX, is done using the *lejos* command line tool.

The LEGO Java Operating System

☑ LeJOS leverages the LEGO-provided ROM code, and thus inherits limitations imposed by the ROM—for instance, only eight power levels for the motors, and no sampling of sensors faster than 3 milliseconds.

☑ LeJOS gives you a common programming language (Java) and environment for the RCX. The learning curve is not as steep as other firmware replacements like legOS.

☑ A comparison to other Java environments shows the formidable achievement of cramming an entire Java VM into the RCX's 32KB of memory.

Chapter 5 Continued

Overview of the leJOS Architecture

☑ Base classes are not part of the firmware. This is a great feature as it makes the firmware footprint smaller.

☑ Only classes needed by your program are actually downloaded to the RCX, since the *lejos* command line tool performs a transitive closure of class graphs of the main class.

☑ There is no garbage collector in leJOS—for now you have to live with that. The future might bring you one, and hopefully you will be able to choose whether or not to include it in your program.

☑ A switch statement is also missing, but may be available in the future.

Using leJOS: A Simple Example

☑ You can read sensor values in two different ways: by polling the sensor, and by listening for changes using an implementation of *SensorListener*.

☑ You should brake motors before changing power to ensure the power change can be noticed. This is necessary as the LEGO motor has an internal flywheel, which stores mechanical power.

❖ Chapter 6: Programming for the leJOS Environment

Designing Java Programs to Run in leJOS

☑ When designing Java programs for leJOS, use the best OO design principles you know. It will make the final program much more maintainable.

☑ Pay attention to memory constraints even during the design phase. It is quite easy to do a beautiful OO design, which, when implemented, will use unnecessarily large amounts of memory.

An Advanced Programming Example Using leJOS

☑ The line-following type of robot can often become mired in a never-ending spin. Two techniques for avoiding that were presented.

Chapter 6 Continued

☑ The subsumption architecture can be thought of as a design pattern for robotics programs.

Debugging leJOS Programs

☑ The best way to debug a leJOS program is to use the *Sound* and *LCD* classes in unison to provide you with feedback of the robot's state.

☑ Normal Java exception handling applies to leJOS, allowing you to separate code for normal operation and code for error situations.

Testing leJOS Programs

☑ When working out bugs, use emu-lejos and emu-lejosrun to emulate the leJOS environment on your PC. They use a text-based interface.

☑ When exceptions are output by the emulator, the output can be interpreted much more accurately than when displayed on the real RCX display.

❖ Chapter 7: leJOS Tools

Programming Environments for leJOS

☑ The command line tools provide ultimate control in terms of the options you can use, but sacrifice ease-of-use.

☑ GUI-based tools can simplify the use of the command-line tools, but sacrifice some elements of control.

☑ Command-line tools included in the leJOS package include *lejosc, lejos, lejosrun, lejosfirmdl, emu-lejos,* and *emu-lejosrun*.

☑ The free IDE called Forte provides a visual GUI creator, a debugger, and compilation functions. Unlike JBuilder and Eclipse, it provides the seemingly unique ability to configure the compiler and Java runtime you use.

Using the leJOS Visual Interface

☑ The leJOS Visual Interface (lVI) is a custom IDE especially configured for use with leJOS.

Chapter 7 Continued

☑ The options in the Tools menu allow you to automatically compile, link, and download programs, as well as download firmware.

☑ After graphically setting the necessary environment variables and settings, you can create, edit, compile, and link a file.

Using a leJOS Simulator

☑ Simlink is designed to be an interface between Rossum's Playhouse and the low level APIs provided by leJOS.

☑ The Rossum simulator has a syntax and format of its own; using its navigational and other declarations and specifications, you can create visual and non-visual elements of floor plans.

☑ Robot bodies in Simlink are represented as Java classes, with Rossum classes allowing you to create simple designs.

☑ Note that sensors and motors under simulation do not work exactly as in real life.

Additional Tips and Tools for leJOS

☑ Java tools like Jlint and Jad can be used on leJOS programs.

☑ The RCXTools package provides a clean interface to many RCX functions, while also allowing you direct control.

☑ The LCDText class included with RCXDirectMode can be used to test LCD words before they are downloaded to the RCX.

❖ Chapter 8: leJOS Internals

Advanced Usage of leJOS

☑ You can link several programs into a single binary by calling the linker with a comma-separated list of the entry classes containing the *main* method.

☑ You can store data persistently by using the library's *josx.platform.rcx.PersistentMemoryArea* class.

Chapter 8 Continued

☑ You can inspect and modify the contents of the RCX's memory by using the methods in the library class *josx.platform.rcx.Memory*.

Examining leJOS Internals

☑ leJOS uses the standard Java compiler, but employs a leJOS-specific linker on the host computer and a leJOS-specific virtual machine in the firmware on the RCX.

☑ The linker reads the Java class files and produces a leJOS binary that can be loaded into the firmware without any modification. Class, method and field names are replaced by offsets into the binary.

☑ The firmware contains a loader that loads the binary and a virtual machine that executes it. The virtual machine executes slightly modified Java byte code instructions.

☑ Threads are scheduled strictly according to priority, and round-robin within the same priority. They are preempted after a time-slice of 20 milliseconds.

☑ Each thread uses approximately 400 bytes of memory for its stack and other data structures.

Extending leJOS with Native Methods

☑ Native methods are used to interface with the hardware and with the virtual machine.

☑ To add a native method to the VM you need to add its signature to common/signatures.db, and you need to provide an implementation for the RCX in rcx_impl/native.c and for the emulator in unix_impl/nativeemul.c.

☑ To optimize for memory you can use variables for common expressions. Always test whether your optimization is better than the original.

Additional Tips and Tricks with leJOS

☑ You can determine the amount of free memory with the method *freeMemory* in the class *java.lang.Runtime*.

☑ You can change the stack size by modifying the values in vmsrc/configure.h and recompiling the leJOS firmware.

Chapter 9 Continued

❖ Chapter 9: Programming LEGO MINDSTORMS with Jini

Overview of Jini

☑ Jini is a Java technology built on top of RMI, enabling clients and services to interact in a network with very little administrative overhead.

☑ One feature of Jini is that it is vary applicable to embedded devices, including devices like the RCX.

☑ The Jini Technology Starter Kit (TSK) includes all of the required jar files as well as some service implementations such as *reggie*, an implementation of a lookup service.

A Simple Jini Service Example

☑ We covered an example of a simple Jini service to calculate checksums and a client that made use of the service.

☑ The example showed how to register a service with a single known lookup service, as well as how a client could discover the registered service by querying the known lookup service.

☑ The service example was quite simplistic, especially in that the client actually executed the service object within its own JVM.

Proxies and Service Architectures

☑ Solutions that make use of Jini can be implemented according to various architectures.

☑ One such service architecture involves the use of a *proxy* object that is registered as a service, but actually abstracts the real service and communicates with it behind the scenes.

☑ The proxy architecture is especially suitable when providing services for devices that are not capable of running Jini themselves.

Chapter 9 Continued

A RCX Jini Proxy Service

☑ Since the RCX is not capable of running Jini itself, it is a very good candidate for the proxy architecture, where a proxy object would run on a machine, which would then communicate with the RCX via the infrared tower.

☑ A single machine with a single infrared link could potentially control multiple RCXs if the firmware were modified. This would require a unique identifier to be stored in each of the RCXs' firmware.

☑ Another architecture (as used in the example in this chapter) involves one infrared tower per RCX, and the proxy objects themselves storing the unique identifiers of the respective RCXs.

Using the RCX Jini Service: Example Server and Client

☑ We covered a much less simplistic example that involved the networking of a number of RCX units.

☑ This example showed how servers and clients could dynamically discover lookup services on a network by using multicast, and also showed the use of RMI stub objects to make method calls across a network.

☑ The outcome was that RCXs could interact with one another, performing a synchronized dance.

Index

A

AC/DC jack adapter, 6

ACodes for system sounds, 182

Add-on building elements, 24–25

addPortOwnershipListener() method, 38

AI. *See* Artificial intelligence (AI)

Air conditioning units, 335, 356

AllMessagesListener interface in RCXJava API, 127

Analyzing data and protocols, 57

Andrews, Paul, 15, 170, 177

Apache HTTP servers, 338

API. *See* Bluetooth Java API; Java Communications Extension API (JCE API); RCXJava API; RCXPort API

Apple Macintosh. *See* Macintosh (Mac OS)

Applets

building and extending, 139–147

signing, 131

Application programming interfaces (APIs). *See* Bluetooth Java API; Java Communications Extension API (JCE API); RCXJava API; RCXPort API

Arbitrator class, 226–227

Architecture

event-based, 43–45

Java communications, 112–124

Jini federation, 356

LEGO Java Operating System (leJOS), 177–195

subsumption, 204, 225–226

Array length, maximum, 174–175

ArrayToString(byte[] array) method, 122

Artificial intelligence (AI), 150–163

Assembly code for RCX, 20–21

Asynchronous event-based I/O, 42–43

Automatic Binding Brick, 3

AWT. *See* Java Advanced Window Toolkit (AWT)

B

Barcodes, 23

Batteries, 16, 150

Battery class, 194

Baud rate, 45

Baum, Dave, 12–13

Behavior, real-time, 306–307

Behavior interface, 227–232

Big blocks, 18

Binary code

building, 302

format, 303–304

Bit masks, 192–193

BlackBox sample program, 57–64

Blocking light sensors, 185

Blocking the input stream, 42

Bluetooth Java API, 67

Books

Building Robots with LEGO MINDSTORMS, 5, 18, 151, 162, 277

Constructopedia manual, 4–5, 93

Design Patterns: Abstraction and Reuse of Object-Oriented Design, 220–221

Rossum User's Guide (Simlink manual), 263

See also CD-ROMs; Companion CD-ROM; Documentation

Braking, 131

Brick, smart or programmable. *See* Robotics Command Explorer (RCX)

BricxCC integrated development environment (IDE), 13

Broad Blue Chess Robot, 163

Building applets, 139–147

Building Robots with LEGO MINDSTORMS book, 5, 18, 151, 162, 277

BuildTool, 389

Button class, 179

ButtonListener class, 179

Bytecodes. *See* Opcodes

C

Calibrator.java, 217

Callback listener, 38

Candy sorter, 97–105

CandySorter.java class, 99

CD-ROMs

LEGO MINDSTORMS, 16

RIS software, 4–5

Ultimate Builders Set projects, 24

See also Books; Companion CD-ROM; Documentation

CDC. *See* Connected Device Configuration (CDC)

CharTest.java, 208–209

ChecksumCalcClass.java, 341–343, 352–353

ChecksumCalc.java, 341–342

ChecksumClient/Client.java, 348–351

ChecksumService.java, 342–347

Chess robot, 150–163

Circuit board, 8

Class loading, dynamic, 178

Class record, 303

Classes

event listener classes, 33

listener classes, 33

rcx.★ package, 125–126

RCXJava API, 125–126

See also leJOS classes

CLASSPATH environment variable, 46–47, 120, 172, 300

CLDC. *See* Connected Limited Device Configuration (CLDC)

Clock, four-digit, 16

Code base, shared, 135

Code blocks, 18

Code Pilot expansion kit, 23

Code sequence, 303

Command-line leJOS emulator, 251

Command-line options, 57, 92

Command-line programming environment, 246

Command-line switches, 246

Command-line tools

javac compiler, 247–248

lejosc compiler, 172–173, 247–248, 330

lejosc linker, 248–249

lejosfirmdl downloader, 250

lejosrun linker, 249–250

Command types, 21

Commands, formatting for RCX, 82–84

CommDriver interface, 33, 48, 65–66, 68–69, 71

comm.jar library, 46–47, 48, 97

CommPort abstract class, 33, 35, 37, 72

CommPortIdentifier class

central point for port control, 37

controlling system ports, 35, 38

native driver, hiding selection of, 43

no documentation, 68

non-public helper classes, 43

port factory, 33

shared libraries, finding and loading, 46

source code, 68

CommPortOwnershipListener interface, 38

Communication

architecture, 112–124

basic, 113–120

network, 132–139

Communication towers. *See* Towers

Companion CD-ROM

Calibrator.java, 217

CandySorter.java class, 99

CharTest.java, 208–209

ChecksumCalcClass.java, 341–343, 352–353

ChecksumCalc.java, 341–342

ChecksumService.java, 342–347

Cruiser.java, 214–215, 229–230

dance/Dance.java, 195–196

Dispense.nqc, 98–99

LatencyTest.java, 324–326

LightReader.java, 214

LightRover.nqc, 94–96

LineFollowBehavior.java, 228–229

LineFollower.java, 217–222

LineValueHolder.java, 213–214

linuxusb.so shared library, 113

macusb.shlib shared library, 113

MyRCX.java, 87

PersistentMemoryArea.java, 293–295

PersistentMemoryAreaTest.java, 295–297

poll/PollDemo.java, 192–193

proximity/Proximity.java, 187–189

RCXControlApp.java, 139

RCXNeuralBrain.java, 160–162

RCXNeuralTest.java, 151–162

RCXPort code re-architecture, 86

RCXSimpleTest.java, 127–128

sensorread/SensorPoll.java, 197

servo/ServoDemo.java, 190–191

SimpleRobot.java class, 278–279

SimpleWriteRead.java, 112, 119

StackTest.java, 320–321

StringBufferTest, 207–208

StringTest.java, 206

TestEnumeration.java code, 35

TestOwnership.java code, 38

Turner.java, 215–216, 224–225

TurnResolve.java, 232–236

USB support *rcx.comm* package, 75

VMStatistics.java class, 315–316

See also Books; CD-ROMs; Documentation

Comparison table of kits, 23

Compatibility

  Macintosh, 14, 28, 65

  RCX versions, 17

  RIS versions, 5

  video camera, 14

Compiling

  Java, 85

  LEGO Java Operating System (leJOS), 171–173, 313

  Not Quite C, 93, 96

Components of RCX, 9–11

com.sun.comm. ★ package, 65

Configuration

  infrared (IR) towers, 16

  Java Communications Extension API (JCE API), 48–50

Connected Device Configuration (CDC), 176

Connected Limited Device Configuration (CLDC), 176

Constant pool, 302

Constant record, 303

Constant value, 303

Constants for opcodes, 84–85, 90

Constructopedia manual, 4–5, 93

Converting opcodes from RCX Code, 10

Corso, Tom, 57

Cruiser.java, 214–215, 229–230

CyberMaster expansion kit, 3, 22–23, 123

CygWin, 177

Cygwin system for Windows, 313

D

-d compiler option, 49, 50

Dacta, 6

Dance/Dance.java, 195–196

Dancing example

  client, 378–388

  debugging, 377–378

  description, 358–359

  interface, 361

  MindstormClient/Client.java, 378–387

  Mindstorm.java, 359–361

  MindstormProxy.java, 361–370

  MindstormService.java, 371–377

  proxy class, 361–370

  running, 388–393

  server, 371–377

Dark Side Developer Kit (DSDK), 23

Data

  monitoring and analyzing, 57

  persistent, 292

Data bits, 45

Data control, 45

Data flow, 297–298

DC/AC jack adapter, 6

Dead threads, 306

Debugging
dancing example, 377–378
Jad debugger, 281
Jlint debugger, 281
LEGO Java Operating System (leJOS), 236–238, 322–323
lint debugger, 281
RCXJava API, 145–147

Decompiling Java, 281

Design
future tools, 280–281
line-following robot, 210–212
simple robot, 277–280

Design Patterns: Abstraction and Reuse of Object-Oriented Design, 220–221

Development environment, 48–50

Devices, embedded, 204, 335, 356–357

Devices, federation of, 334–335

Differential drive, 188

Differential drive-based robot, 225

Direct-control programming, 21, 147–163

Direct memory access, 292, 295

Direct mode technique, 83, 85–86, 92, 98–99

Dispense.nqc.java, 99

Documentation
Java Communications Extension API (JCE API) installation, 46, 53
LEGO Java Operating System (leJOS), 170–171
LEGO MINDSTORMS 2.0 SDK, 64, 72, 112
none for *CommPortIdentifier,* 68
Robotics Command Explorer (RCX) internals, 62
See also Books; CD-ROMs; Companion CD-ROM

Downloading
*downloadProgram()*method, 91
lejosfirmdl downloader, 177, 202, 250
MINDSTORMS SDK 2.0 download, 17
multiprogram downloading, 290–292
Not Quite C (NQC) compiler, 96
RCXDownLoad program, 282–283
RCXDownload/RCXDirectMode, 16
RCXPort API, 91–93
SDK 2.0, 17
See also Web sites

*downloadProgram()*method, 91

Droid Development Kit, 3, 23

Dynamic class loading, 178

E

Eclipse IDE (IBM), 251

Embedded devices, 204, 335, 356–357

emu-lejos emulator, 251

emu-lejosrun linker, 251

Emulation mode, 145–147

Emulator, LEGO Java Operating System (leJOS), 251, 310–311

Encapsulation of native ports, 43

Encoding of Java types in signatures, 316–317

Entry class index, 303

Entry points, 292

Environment variable RCXTTY, 171, 202, 250

Environments, alternative, 11

Error messages, 131

ErrorListener interface in RCXJava API, 127

Event-based architecture, 43–45

Event-based I/O, asynchronous, 42–43

Event listener classes, 33

Exception handling, 127–129, 131, 237–238, 243

Exception record, 303

Expanding RCX brain, 11–16

Expansion kits. *See* LEGO expansion kits

Exploration Mars kit, 25

Extending
applets, 139–147
Java Communications Extension API (JCE API), 64–75

LEGO Java Operating System (leJOS), 314–323
Extension folder, 47, 48
Extreme Creatures kit, 25

F

Federation of devices, 334–335
Ferrari, Mario and Giulio, 5, 88, 151, 277
Fiber-optic cable, 4
Fiddler service in Jini, 337
Firewire, 68
firm0328.lgo release of RCX, 17
Firmware, replacement. *See* LEGO Java
 Operating System (leJOS); legOS
 replacement firmware; pbForth language
Firmware for Infrared (IR) towers, 10–11
Firmware for LEGO Java Operating System
 (leJOS)
 debugging, 322–323
 description, 304–305
 leJOS Virtual Machine, 305–306
 scheduler, 305
 thread states, 305–306
Firmware for Robotics Command Explorer
 (RCX)
 description, 10, 17
 installing, 16
 new features, using, 28
 reloading, 10–11
 replacing, 14–16
 See also LEGO Java Operating System
 (leJOS); legOS replacement firmware;
 pbForth language
Floating, 131
Floor plans, Simlink, 262–269
Flow control, 45
Flow of data, 297–298
Format of binary code, 303–304
Format of opcode messages, 83–84
Forte IDE (Sun)
 configuration, 252
 Web site, 251

FORTH language, 15
Frameworks
 direct-control, 150–163
 distributed computing (Jini), 334
 Java Media Frameworks, 144
 port access, 34–43
Freeware, 12
Frequency, polling, 144
Future design tools, 280–281

G

Game Boy, 301
Gamma, Erich, 221
Garbage collection, 174–175, 330
Gasperi, Michael, 24
GCC-3.0 cross-compiler for leJOS, 313
getAvailableSerialPorts() method, 37, 120
getBatteryPower() method, 150
getCurrentOwner() method, 38
getName() method, 35
getPortIdentifier(), 120
getPortIdentifiers() static method, 35
getPortType() method, 35
GNU tools, 313
Gombos, Andy, 240, 253, 258, 280
GUI-based programming environment, 246

H

Hacking, 60
Handling exceptions, 127–129, 131, 237–238, 243
Hardware
 TECHNIC series, 3, 24
 See also Kits; Robotics Command Explorer
 (RCX); Sensors; Towers
Heap, LEGO Java Operating System (leJOS), 292
Heat problems, 173
HelloWorld.java, 250
Helm, Richard, 221
History of Robotics Invention System
 (RIS), 3

Hitachi H8 microprocessor, 7, 299, 308
Home appliance control systems, 335, 356
Hooks, 307
HTTP servers, 338–340, 351–352, 388–389
Hysteresis, 216

I

I/O, event-based, 42–43
Identifiers, long, 302
IDEs. *See* Integrated development
        environments (IDEs)
idle_hook(), 307
IEEE 1284 parallel ports, 63–64
Infinite loop required, 197–198
Infrared (IR) proximity detector, 24
Infrared (IR) towers
    commands, echoing, 84
    configuring, 16
    description, 4
    firmware, reloading, 10–11
    port, naming, 91
    port variations, 64
    RCXPort connections, 84
    reliability of infrared signal, 86
Infrared (IR) transmitter, 4
Input Buffersize property, 42
Input devices, 4
Input stream, blocking, 42
Installation of JCE API, 46–48
Installing RCX firmware, 16
Instance field record, 303
instanceof operator, 174
instruction_hook(), 307
Integrated development environments (IDEs),
        12, 13, 251–253
Interchanging streams between serial ports,
        62–64
Interfaces
    AllMessagesListener in RCXJava API, 127
    Behavior, 227–232
    CommDriver, 33, 48, 65–66, 68–69, 71
    CommPortOwnershipListener, 38

dancing example interface, 361
ErrorListener in RCXJava API, 127
Java Native Interface (JNI), 66, 314
Jini user interface, 397
RCX Code language improved interface, 6
RCXCommPort in RCXJava API, 126, 132
RCXListener in RCXJava API, 127
SensorConstants, 183–186
SensorListener, 186–187
See also leJOS Visual Interface (lVI)
Interfacing external software with RCXPort
        API, 93–96
Interpreting, 20
IR. *See* Infrared (IR) transmitter
isCurrentlyOwned() method, 38

J

J2EE. *See* Java 2 Enterprise Edition (J2EE)
J2ME. *See* Java 2 Micro Edition (J2ME)
J2SE. *See* Java 2 Standard Edition (J2SE)
Jad debugger, 281
Java
    communications architecture, 112–124
    compiling, 85
    decompiling, 281
    runtime *(jview),* 49
    sizes, 175–176
    types, encoding in signatures, 316–317
Java 2 Enterprise Edition (J2EE), 175
Java 2 Micro Edition (J2ME), 170, 176, 331
Java 2 Standard Edition (J2SE), 174–176
Java Advanced Window Toolkit (AWT), 179
Java application programming interfaces
        (APIs). *See* Java Communications
        Extension API (JCE API); RCXPort
        API
Java Communications Extension API (JCE
        API)
    asynchronous event-based I/O, 42–43
    BlackBox sample program, 57–64
    comm.jar library, 47
    configuration, 48–50

-*d* compiler option, 49, 50

development environment, 48–50

encapsulation of native ports, 43

event-based architecture, 43–45

features, 34

framework for port access, 34–43

installation, 46–48

javax.comm package, 33

javax.comm.properties configuration file, 37, 47–49

limitations, 34

native library, 33, 46–47

overview, 32–34

port discovery and enumeration, 34–37

port ownership management, 37–42

pure-Java interface, 32, 34, 112, 124

reading from serial ports, 50–53

Universal Serial Bus (USB), 66–75

update plans, 78–79

Web sites, 32

writing to serial ports, 54–56

See also rcx.* package; *rcx.comm.** subpackage

Java Media Frameworks, 144

Java Native Interface (JNI), 66, 314

Java Remote Method Invocation (RMI), 336, 338–341, 354–355, 361, 377

Java Runtime Environment (JRE), 83, 167

Java Swing, 167

Java Virtual Machine (JVM)

  LEGO Java Operating System (leJOS), 93

  needed for Java APIs, 13

  selecting, 299

  separate JVMs, 352–355, 377

  TinyVM, 15, 176, 300

javac compiler, 247–248

JavaCard, 176, 238

java.class.forName method, 178

javah command line tool, 66

java.lang.Class, 174–175, 222

java.lang.Math, 177

java.lang.Object, 177

javax.comm package, 33

javax.comm.properties configuration file, 37, 47–49, 68

javax.usb extension API for USB devices, 67

JBuilder Personal Edition IDE (Borland), 251–252

JCE API. *See* Java Communications Extension API (JCE API)

jEdit text editor, 253

Jini

  BuildTool, 389

  ChecksumCalcClass.java, 341–343, 352–353

  ChecksumCalc.java, 341–342

  ChecksumClient/Client.java, 348–351

  ChecksumService.java, 342–347

  community Web site, 334

  description, 334

  distributed computing framework, 334

  event mailbox service (Mercury), 337

  federation architecture, 356

  HTTP servers, 338–340, 351–352, 388–389

  information Web sites, 397

  Java Remote Method Invocation (RMI), 336, 338–341, 354–355, 361, 377

  JavaSpaces services (Outrigger), 337

  lease renewal, 347

  lease renewal service (Norm), 337

  lookup discovery service (Fiddler), 337

  lookup services (reggie), 334, 337–341, 351–353

  multiple RCX units, 356, 392

  network protocol, 336

  overview, 334–336

  proxies, 356–358

  registering services, 334, 340–342, 347, 351

  Robotics Command Explorer (RCX) API, 358

  security manager, 387–388

  security policy file, 341, 352

  service example, 337–355

  services available, 337

  stub objects, 353–355

Technology Starter Kit (TSK), 337

transaction manager service (Mahalo), 337

user interface, 397

See also Dancing example

Jlint debugger, 281

JNI. *See* Java Native Interface (JNI)

Johnson, Ralph, 221

josx.platform.rcx package, 170, 177–195, 314–315

josx.platform.rcx.PersistentMemoryArea class, 193–194, 293

josx.robotics package, 226

jre folder, 46, 48

js.tinyvm.TinyVM class, 176, 300

Jtext text editor, 253

jview (Java runtime), 49

JVM. *See* Java Virtual Machine (JVM)

K

Kits

comparison table, 23

CyberMaster, 3, 22–23, 123

Dark Side Developer Kit (DSDK), 23

Droid Development Kit, 3, 23

Exploration Mars, 25

Extreme Creatures, 25

Java Advanced Window Toolkit (AWT), 179

Jini Technology Starter Kit (TSK), 337

Micro Scout, 4, 22–23

RCX Code standard kit, 4

RoboSport, 25

Robotics Invention System (RIS), 2

Scout, 22–23, 123

See also LEGO expansion kits

Knudsen, Jonathan, 253

L

Languages

FORTH, 15

Logo, 18

new, 12

Not Quite C (NQC), 12–13, 93, 96

pbForth, 15

RCX Code, 4, 6, 10, 18–19

Latency, measuring, 324–326

LatencyTest.java, 324–326

Laverde, Dario, 13, 86

LCD class, 180

LCDConstants class, 180–181

Lease renewal, 347, 352

LEGO Dacta, 6

LEGO educational branch Web site, 6

LEGO expansion kits

add-on building elements, 24–25

alternative processing units, 22–23

comparison table, 23

overview, 21–22

LEGO Java Operating System (leJOS)

advanced programming example, 210–236

advanced usage, 290–297

allowing Java code, 85, 90, 93

architecture, 177–195

Behavior interface, 227–232

benefits, 173

Bit masks, 192–193

compiling, 171–173, 313

debuggers, 281

debugging, 236–238, 322–323

description, 15–16, 170

documentation, 170–171

emulator, 251, 310–311

exception handling, 237–238

extending, 314–323

firmware, 304–311, 322–323

free memory, 324

GCC-3.0 cross-compiler, 313

heap, 292

hooks, 307

infinite loop required, 197–198

Jad debugger, 281

javac compiler, 247–248

Jlint debugger, 281

josx.platform.rcx package, 170, 177–195, 314–315

josx.robotics package, 226

leJOS linker, 299–304

leJOS Visual Interface (lVI), 16, 253–258

lejosc compiler, 172–173, 247–248, 330

lejosc linker, 248–249

lejosfirmdl downloader, 250

lejosrun linker, 249–250

librcx library, 313

limitations, 174, 204–205

Linux environment, 171–172

memory layout, 308–310

motors, controlling, 195–196

multiprogram downloading, 290–292

native methods, 314–323

OCIA interrupt routine, 303

poll masks, 192–193

programming environments, 246–253

RCXDirectMode program, 283–284

RCXDownLoad program, 282–283

RCXDownload/RCXDirectMode, 16

real-time behavior, 306–307

sample programs, 195–199

SensorConstants interface, 183–186

SensorListener interface, 186–187

sensors, reading, 196–199

simulator (Simlink), 258–281

source code, 311–312

stateChanged() method, 186

string objects, manipulating, 206–210

testing, 238–240

timing, 306–307

tricks and tips, 281, 323–326

Universal Serial Bus (USB), 202

Web site for downloading, 170

Windows environment, 171

Windows Universal Serial Bus (USB) support, 250

See also leJOS classes; leJOS Visual Interface (lVI); Line-following robot; Stacks; Steering

legOS replacement firmware, 14–15

leJOS. *See* LEGO Java Operating System (leJOS)

leJOS classes

  Arbitrator, 226–227

  Battery, 194

  Button, 179

  ButtonListener, 179

  class selection, 206

  js.tinyvm.TinyVM, 176, 300

  LCD, 180

  LCDConstants, 180–181

  Memory, 194

  MinLCD, 180

  MinSound, 181–182

  MinuteTimer, 194–195

  Motor, 189

  no *java.lang.Class*, 222

  Opcode, 191

  PersistentMemoryArea, 193–194, 293

  Poll, 192

  ProximitySensor, 187–189

  ROM, 194

  Segment, 180–181

  Sensor, 185

  Serial, 191–192

  SerialListener, 191–192

  Servo, 190–191

  Sound, 181–182

  TextLCD, 180–181

  VMStatistics.java class, 315–316

leJOS linker

  binary code, building, 302

  binary code, format of, 303–304

  C wrapper, 299–300

  Java main program, 300–301

  js.tinyvm.TinyVM class, 300

  JVM executable, 299–300

  lejosp command, 304

leJOS Visual Interface (lVI)

  configuration, 255–257

description, 16, 253–254
installation, 254
preferences bug, 287
Universal Serial Bus (USB), 287
usage, 257–258
lejosc compiler, 172–173, 247–248, 330
lejosc linker, 248–249
lejosp command, 304
lejosrun linker, 249–250
Lewis, Scott, 13, 82, 85, 90
Libraries
  comm.jar, 46–47, 48, 97
  Java Communications Extension API (JCE
    API), 46–47
  LEGO Java Operating System (leJOS), 313
  librcx, 313
  libSolarisSerialParallel.so, 46
  linuxusb.so, 113
  macusb.shlib, 113
  native, 33, 46–47
  rcxport.jar, 97
  shared libraries, finding and loading, 46
  Solaris, 46–47
  win32com.dll, 46, 49, 112–113
  win32usb.dll, 112–113
librcx library, 313
libSolarisSerialParallel.so native library, 46
Light sensors, 4, 185, 187–189
LightReader.java, 214
LightRover.nqc, 94–96
LightRover.nqc.java, 94–96
Limitations of RCXPort, 85–86
Line-following robot
  Calibrator.java, 217
  Cruiser.java, 214–215
  design, 210–212
  LightReader.java, 214
  LineFollowBehavior.java, 228–229
  LineFollower.java, 217–222
  LineValueHolder.java, 213–214
  Turner.java, 215–216

LineFollowBehavior.java, 228–229
LineFollower.java, 217–222
LineValueHolder.java, 213–214
Linkers
  emu-lejosrun linker, 251
  leJOS linker, 299–304
  lejosc, 248–249
  lejosrun, 249–250
lint debugger, 281
Linux
  Java Communications Extension API (JCE
    API), 32
  Java USB reference implementation, 67
  javax.usb extension API for USB devices, 67
  LEGO Java Operating System (leJOS)
    environment, 171–172
  LEGO USB driver Web site, 250
  RCXPort and USB, 86
  Universal Serial Bus (USB) tower drivers, 65
linuxusb.so shared library, 113
Listener classes, 33
Listeners
  callback, 38
  limit of one, 41
Logical structure of RCX, 9–11
Logo programming language, 18
Long identifiers, 302
Lookup services, 334
Low-level instructions. *See* Opcodes
LVI. *See* leJOS Visual Interface (lVI)

M

Macintosh (Mac OS)
  compatibility, 14, 28, 65
  Java Communications Extension API (JCE
    API) download, 32
  Mac OS X, 65
  no Universal Serial Bus (USB) tower driver,
    65
macusb.shlib shared library, 113
Magic number, 317
Mahalo service in Jini, 337

Mangling names, 318
Martin, Fred, 3
Master record, 303
Maximum array length, 174–175
Measuring latency, 324–326
Memory
  available, 28
  conservation, 204–210
  direct access, 292, 295
  free space, 324
  layout, 308–310
  persistent, 292–297
  types, 8–9
  See also Random-Access memory (RAM);
    Read-Only memory (ROM)
Memory class, 194
Mercury service in Jini, 337
Message format, 83–84
Messages, 83–84, 122, 127, 131
Method record, 303
Method signatures
  encoding of Java types, 316–317
  name mangling, 318
  native method identification, 314, 316
  source code, 311
  throws declarations, 237
  verbose output, 239, 249, 301
Methods, native, 314–323
Micro Scout expansion kit, 4, 22–23
Microcomputer, RCX, 2
Microprocessor, Hitachi H8, 7, 299, 308
Microsoft IIS HTTP servers, 338
Microsoft Windows. *See* Windows
MIDP. *See* Mobile Information Device Profile
  (MIDP)
MindstormClient/Client.java, 378–387
Mindstorm.java, 359–361
MindstormProxy.java, 361–370
MINDSTORMS for school. *See* ROBOLAB
MINDSTORMS SDK 2.0 download, 17
MindstormService.java, 371–377
MinLCD class, 180

MinSound class, 181–182
MinuteTimer class, 194–195
Mobile Information Device Profile (MIDP),
  176
Monitoring data and protocols, 57
Motor class
  LEGO Java Operating System (leJOS), 189
  RCXJava API, 126, 139, 144
Motors
  choosing via opcodes, 105
  controlling, 195–196
  fundamental, 4
Multifunctional commands, 21
Multiple RCX units, 162, 356, 392
Multiprogram downloading, 290–292
MyRCX.java, 87

N

Name mangling, 318
Native libraries, 33, 46–47
Native methods in LEGO Java Operating
  System (leJOS), 314–323
Native ports, 34, 43
Network Communications, 132–139
Neural networks code, 151, 162
Never-ending turn, 228
New threads, 305
Nintendo Game Boy, 301
NoClassDefFoundError exception., 49
Noga, Markus, 14
Nonprogrammers, 16
Norm service in Jini, 337
Not Quite C (NQC) language
  compiler, downloading, 96
  compiling opcodes from, 93, 96
  description, 12–13
  Web site, 93

O

objdump utility, 304
OCIA interrupt routine, 303
100 percent Java. *See* Pure-Java interfaces to
  Robotics Command Explorer (RCX)

Opcode class in LEGO Java Operating System
      (leJOS), 191
Opcodes
   abstraction, 90
   assembly code for RCX, 20–21
   bit representation, 89
   command types, 21
   commands written in bytecodes, 83, 85
   compiling from Not Quite C code, 93, 96
   constants for, 84–85, 90
   conversion from RCX Code, 10
   definition, 2, 82
   echoed back to tower, 84
   examples, specific, 91, 121
   interpreting, 20
   layer, abstracting, 90
   message format, 83–84
   motors, choosing, 105
   packaged by *getBytes()*, 84
   processing bytecodes, 11, 20
   RCX internal commands, 12, 83, 121
   RCXCmd class, 84–85
   RCXPort, compiling from, 109
   receiving, program for, 127–129
   reverse engineering, 59–62, 83
   sending, program for, 127–129
   use of, 20
Operational codes. *See* Opcodes
Origin of Robotics Invention System (RIS), 3
OutOfMemoryException, 243
Output Buffersize property, 43
Output devices (motors), 4
Outrigger service in Jini, 337
Overheating, 173
Ownership management of ports, 37–42

P

Packages
   com.sun.comm.,* 65
   javax.comm, 33
   josx.platform.rcx, 170, 177–195, 314–315
   josx.robotics, 226
   rcx.,* 125–135
   rcx.comm.,* 66, 69–71, 75, 120, 124
   RCXTools, 281–284, 287
Packet sniffing, 83
Papert, Seymour, 3
Parallel ports. *See* Ports, parallel
paramBase pointer, 318–319
Parity, 45
pbForth language, 15
Persistent data, 292
PersistentMemoryArea class, 193–194, 293
PersistentMemoryArea.java, 293–295
PersistentMemoryAreaTest.java, 295–297
Personal Java, 176
Physical structure of RCX, 9–11
Poll class, 192
Poll masks, 192–193
poll/PollDemo.java, 192–193
Polling frequency, 144
Pool, constants, 302
Ports
   arbitrary, 132
   common properties, 42–43
   identifying, 71
   naming, 91
   ownership management, 37–42
   parallel, 63–64
   socket RCX port, 132–139
   TCP sockets, 124, 132
   Universal Serial Bus (USB), 68–75, 124
   variations, 64
Ports, serial
   access framework, 34–43
   data control, 45
   discovery and enumeration, 34–37
   encapsulation, 43
   flow control, 45
   interchanging streams, 62–64
   reading from, 50–53
   writing to, 54–56

Processing units, alternative, 22–23
Program commands, 21
Program entry points, 292
Programmable brick. *See* Robotics Command Explorer (RCX)
programmable brick Forth. *See* pbForth language
Programming
    advanced example, 210–236
    big blocks, 18
    class selection, 206
    code blocks, 18
    decompiling Java files, 281
    direct-control, 21, 147–163
    environments, alternative, 11
    hysteresis, 216
    LEGO Java Operating System (leJOS), 210–236
    memory conservation, 204–210
    string objects, manipulating, 206–210
    testing, 238–240
    text *versus* graphical (visual), 12
    See also Sample programs; Steering
Programs, sample. *See* Sample programs
Properties
    common properties of ports, 42–43
    Input Buffersize, 42
    javax.comm.properties configuration file, 37, 47–49, 68
    Output Buffersize, 43
    Receive Framing, 43
    Receive Threshold, 42, 78
    Receive Timeout, 42
Protocols, monitoring and analyzing, 57
Proudfoot, Kekoa
    firmdl.c tool, 250
    librcx library, 313
    RCX internals (opcodes), 12, 112, 121, 192, 194
    RCX virtual machine, 20
    reverse engineering, 59, 83
    ROM documentation, 304

send.c tool, 247
Proxies
    Jini, 356–358
    serial, 60
Proximity detector, infrared (IR), 24
proximity/Proximity.java, 187–189
ProximitySensor class, 187–189
Proxy server, 136–139
Psychedelic Dance program, 195–196
Pure-Java interfaces to Robotics Command Explorer (RCX)
    Java Communications Extension API (JCE API), 32, 34, 112, 124
    RCXJava API, 112, 124
    RCXPort API, 82

R
Random-Access memory (RAM), 8–10
RCX. *See* Robotics Command Explorer (RCX)
RCX Code language
    bytecode conversion, 10
    improved interface, 6
    standard kit, 4
    visual programming tool, 18–19
*rcx.** package
    classes, 125–126
    exceptions, 127–129
    interfaces, 126–127
    RCXLoader utility program, 129–131
    RCXSocketPort.java, 132–135
    Unified Modeling Language (UML) diagram, 125
RCXApplet.java, 131–132, 140
RCXCmd class, 84–85
*rcx.comm.** subpackage, 66, 69–71, 75, 120, 124
RCXCommPort interface in RCXJava API, 126, 132
RCXControlApp.java, 139
RCXControl.java, 140–144
RCXDirectMode program, 283–284
RCXDownLoad program, 282–283

RCXDownload/RCXDirectMode, 16
RCXJava API
  artificial intelligence (AI), 150–163
  classes, 125–126
  communication, basic, 113–120
  communications, 123
  components, 122–123
  CyberMaster expansion kit, 123
  debugging, 145–147
  direct-control programming, 147–163
  emulation mode, 145–147
  error handling, 122
  exceptions, 127–129
  interfaces, 126–127
  message parsing, 122
  origin, 13
  overview, 124–129
  ports, arbitrary, 132
  ports, configuring, 122
  protocol management, 122
  pure-Java interface, 112, 124
  remote-control application, 147–150
  Scout expansion kit, 123
  TCP sockets, 124, 132
  tower communications, 123
  Universal Serial Bus (USB), 124
  versus RCXPort API, 167–168
RCXListener interface in RCXJava API, 127
RCXLoader class, 126
RCXLoader utility program, 129–131
RCXNeuralBrain class, 152
RCXNeuralBrain.java, 160–162
RCXNeuralTest.java, 151–162
RCXOpcode class, 126
RCXPacket object, 84
RCXPort API
  basic example, 86–91
  code re-architecture, 86
  commands, formatting, 82–84
  compiling Java, 85
  compiling opcodes from, 109

  connections, 84
  direct mode technique, 83, 85–86
  downloading programs, 91–93
  interfacing external software, 93–96
  limitations, 85–86
  object model, 84–85
  overview, 82–86
  programming the RCX, 86–91
  pure-Java interface, 82
  RCXPacket object, 84
  reliance on Java Communications Extension
    API (JCE API), 86
  source code, Web site for, 82
  troubleshooting, 96–97
  versus RCXJava API, 167–168
RCXPort class, 126
RCXPort object, 84
rcxport.jar library, 97
RCXResult protected class, 108
RCXSensorEmulation.java, 145–146
RCXSerialPort class, 126
RCXServer class, 126
RCXServer.java, 136–139
RCXSimpleTest.java, 127–128
RCXSocketPort class, 126
RCXSocketPort.java, 132–135
RCXTest.java, 147–149
RCXTools package, 281–284, 287
RCXTTY environment variable, 171, 202,
  250
RCXUSBPort class, 126
Reaction times, 306–307
Read-Only memory (ROM), 8–10, 304
Reading from serial ports, 50–53
Real-time behavior, 306–307
Receive Framing property, 43
Receive Threshold property, 42, 78
Receive Timeout property, 42
reggie service in Jini, 334, 337–341, 351–353
Register file, 20
Registering services in Jini, 334, 340–342,
  347, 351

Release, firm0328.lgo, 17

Release compatibility, 5, 17

Reliability of infrared signal, 86

Reloading RCX firmware, 10–11

Remote-control application, 147–150

Replacement firmware. *See* LEGO Java
    Operating System (leJOS); legOS
    replacement firmware; pbForth language

Replacing RCX firmware, 14–16

Reserved areas of memory, 308

Resnick, Mitchel, 3

Response messages, 131

Restricted steering, 223–225

Reverse engineering RCX opcodes, 59–62,
    83

Reverse Polish notation (RPN), 15

Rinkens, Tim, 281

RIS. *See* Robotics Invention System (RIS)

RMI. *See* Java Remote Method Invocation
    (RMI)

ROAPI project, 82

ROBOLAB, 13–14

RoboSport kit, 25

Robot body, simulating, 269–277

Robotics Command Explorer (RCX)
  API components, 122–123
  artificial intelligence (AI), 150–163
  assembly code, 20–21
  brain, expanding, 11–16
  circuit board, 8
  command types, 21
  commands, formatting for RCX, 82–84
  commands in RCX opcodes, 12, 83
  communication, basic, 113–120
  communication test program, 129–131
  components, 9–11
  data flow, 297–298
  description, 7
  direct-control programming, 147–163
  firm0328.lgo release, 17
  interfacing external software with RCXPort
      API, 93–96

  internal commands, 12, 83, 121
  Java communications architecture, 112–124
  logical structure, 9–11
  memory, 8–10
  memory layout, 308–310
  microcomputer, 2
  microprocessor, Hitachi H8, 7, 299, 308
  multiple RCX units, 162, 356, 392
  opcodes, 21
  pbForth language, 15
  physical structure, 7–9
  programmable brick, 3, 15
  programming sequence, 10–11
  programming using RCXPort API, 86–91
  remote-control application, 147–150
  reverse engineering, 59–62, 83
  second RCX unit, 25
  TCP-to-RCX proxy server, 136–139
  troubleshooting with RCXPort API, 96–97
  version compatibility, 17
  virtual machine, 20–21, 90, 298
  See also Firmware for Robotics Command
      Explorer (RCX); Pure-Java interfaces to
      Robotics Command Explorer (RCX)

Robotics Command Explorer (RCX) API
    Jini, 358

Robotics Discovery Set, 3

Robotics Invention System (RIS)
  contents, 4–7
  history, 3
  Java Application Programming Interfaces
      (APIs), 13
  kit, 2
  Not Quite C (NQC), 12–13
  software, replacing, 11–14
  version compatibility, 5

Robots, specific
  Broad Blue Chess Robot, 163
  Chess robot, 150–163
  Differential drive-based robot, 225
  Room explorer robot, 151

Simple robot design, 277–280
Simple Steering Drive Robot (Roverbot), 88, 93
See also Line-following robot
ROM. *See* Read-Only memory (ROM)
ROM class, 194
Room explorer robot, 151
Rossum Playhouse. *See* Simlink
Rossum User's Guide (Simlink manual), 263
Rotation sensors, 24
Roverbot (Simple Steering Drive Robot), 88, 93
RPN. *See* Reverse Polish notation (RPN)
RS232/434. *See* Ports, serial
RTS/CTL, 45
Running threads, 305

S
Sample programs
BlackBox, 57–64
candy sorter, 97–105
CandySorter.java, 100–105
HelloWorld.java, 250
LEGO Java Operating System (leJOS), 195–199
Psychedelic Dance, 195–196
RCXApplet.java, 131–132, 140
RCXControl.java, 140–144
RCXSensorEmulation.java, 145–146
RCXServer.java, 136–139
RCXSocketPort.java, 133–135
RCXTest.java, 147–149
reading example, 50–53
steering line follower, 18–19
TestUSB.java, 73–74
writing example, 54–56
See also Companion CD-ROM
Sargent, Randy, 3
Scout expansion kit, 22–23, 123
SDK 2.0 download, 17
Security manager, 387–388
Security permissions, 131

Security policy file, 341, 352
Segment class, 180–181
SelectProgram command, 21
Sensor class in LEGO Java Operating System (leJOS), 185
Sensor class in RCXJava API, 126, 139, 144
SensorConstants interface, 183–186
SensorListener interface, 186–187
sensorread/SensorPoll.java, 197
Sensors
calibration, 14
fundamental, 4
Infrared (IR) proximity detector, 24
light, 4, 185, 187–189
modes, 183
reading, 144, 196–199
rotation, 24
sources, 24
types, 183
Web sites, 24, 184
Serial class, 191–192
Serial ports. *See* Ports, serial
Serial proxies, 60
Serial towers, 6–7, 28
SerialListener class, 191–192
SerialPort class, 35, 37, 44–45
Servers, HTTP, 338–340, 351–352, 388–389
Services, registering in Jini, 334, 340–342, 347, 351
Servo class, 190–191
servo/ServoDemo.java, 190–191
Shared code base, 135
Signatures. *See* Method signatures
Signing applets, 131
Silverman, Brian, 3
Simlink
configuring, 260–261
declarations, 264–269
description, 240, 258
floor plans, 262–269
future design tools, 280–281
geometry argument, 266

getting started, 258–260

installing, 260

placements, 266–267

Rossum meters, 280

running, 261–262

simulating a robot body, 269–277

Simple robot design, 277–280

Simple Steering Drive Robot (Roverbot), 88, 93

SimpleRobot.java class, 278–279

SimpleWriteRead.java, 112, 119

Simulating a robot body, 269–277

Simulator for LEGO Java Operating System (leJOS), 258–281

Sleeping threads, 306

Smart brick. *See* Robotics Command Explorer (RCX)

Sniffing, 60

Sockets, 124, 132–139

Software for RIS, replacing, 11–14

Solaris

    access to native ports, 43

    Java Communications Extension API (JCE API), 32

    javax.comm.properties configuration file, 37, 47–49

    native library, 46–47

Solorzano, Jose, 15, 170, 176–177

Solutions, third-party. *See* LEGO Java Operating System (leJOS); legOS replacement firmware; pbForth language

Solutions Fast Tracks

    communication, RCXJava API, 165–166

    Introduction, 26–27

    Java Communications Extension API (JCE API), 77–78

    Jini, 394–395

    LEGO Java Operating System (leJOS) internals, 328–329

    LEGO Java Operating System (leJOS) introduction, 200–201

    LEGO Java Operating System (leJOS) programming, 241–242

LEGO Java Operating System (leJOS) tools, 285–286

    RCXPort Java API, 106–108

Sound class, 181–182

Sounds, used in debugging, 236–237

Source code of leJOS, 311–312

srec format, 304

Stacks

    frames, 310

    memory location, 308

    object references, 177

    size, changing, 324

    threads, 305–306, 310

    usage, finding, 315–316, 319–321

StackTest.java, 320–321

Started threads, 305

stateChanged() method, 186

States of threads, 305–306

Static field record, 303

Static state, 303

Steering

    control of, 222–223

    LineFollowBehavior.java, 228–229

    never-ending turn, 228

    restricted, 223–225

    subsumption architecture, 225–226

    Turner.java, 224–225

    TurnResolve.java, 232–236

Stop bits, 45

Streams, interchanging between serial ports, 62–64

String objects, manipulating, 206–210

StringBufferTest, 207–208

StringTest.java, 206

Structure of RCX

    logical, 9–11

    physical, 7–9

Stub objects, 353–355

Stuber, Jürgen, 15, 170, 177

Subsumption architecture, 204, 225–226

Sun Solaris

access to native ports, 43
javax.comm.properties configuration file, 37, 47–49
native library, 46–47
Sunny days, 173
switch statement, 174–175, 330
Switches, command-line, 246
Switch_thread_hook(), 307
Syngress Web site, 5
System sounds, by aCode, 182
System.out.println(), 378

T

TCP sockets, 124, 132
TCP-to-RCX proxy server, 136–139
TECHNIC series, 3, 24
TestEnumeration.java, 35–37
TestEnumeration.java code, 35
Testing programs, 238–240
TestOwnership.java, 38–41
TestOwnership.java code, 38
TestUSB.java, 73–74
Text programming, 12
TextLCD class, 180–181
Third-party solutions. *See* LEGO Java Operating System (leJOS); legOS replacement firmware; pbForth language
Threads
  stacks, 310
  states, 305–306
tick_hook(), 307
Timing, 306–307
TinyVM, 15, 176, 300
Tips and tricks, 281, 323–326
Tools, GNU, 313
Touch sensors, 4
Tower drivers, 65
Towers
  emulating, 145–147
  multiple, 72
  serial, 6–7, 28

sunny days, 173
Universal Serial Bus (USB), 6–7, 28, 64–65, 84
See also Infrared (IR) towers
Transmitter, infrared (IR), 4
Tricks and tips, 281, 323–326
Troubleshooting with RCXPort API, 96–97
TSK. *See* Jini, Technology Starter Kit (TSK)
Turn, never-ending, 228
Turner.java, 215–216, 224–225
TurnResolve.java, 232–236

U

Ultimate Accessory Set, 24
Ultimate Builders Set, 24
Universal resource locators (URLs). *See* Web sites
Universal Serial Bus (USB)
  Java Communications Extension API (JCE API), 66–75
  javax.usb extension API, 67
  LEGO Java Operating System (leJOS), 202
  leJOS Visual Interface (lVI), 287
  Linux LEGO USB driver, 250
  ports, 64, 68–75, 124
  RCXJava API, 124
  RCXPort incompatibility, 84
  RCXTools program, 287
  tower drivers, 64–65
  towers, 6–7, 28, 64–65, 84
  Windows, 64–65, 120
  See also rcx.comm.* subpackage
UploadRam command, 21
URLs. *See* Web sites
USB. *See* Universal Serial Bus (USB)

V

Van Dam, Bert, 151
Verbose output, 239, 249, 301
Version compatibility, 5, 17
Video camera compatibility, 14, 25

Virtual machine, RCX, 20–21, 90, 298

Visible Light Link (VLL), 4

Visual Command add-on, 25

Visual NQC integrated development environment (IDE), 13

Visual programming interfaces

  leJOS Visual Interface (lVI), 16, 253–258

  Not Quite C (NQC), 13

  RCS Code language, 18–19

  versus text (command-line), 12, 246

Vlissides, John, 221

VLL. *See* Visible Light Link (VLL)

VM. *See* Virtual machine, RCX

VMStatistics.java class, 315–316

W

Waiting threads, 306

Web sites

  barcode software, 23

  blocking light sensors, 185

  commands in RCX opcodes, 12, 83, 112, 304

  Forte for Java, 251

  GCC-3.0 cross-compiler for leJOS, 313

  Hitachi H8 microprocessor manual, 299

  Jad debugger, 281

  Java Communications Extension API (JCE API), 32

  Jini BuildTool, 389

  Jini community, 334

  Jini information, 397

  Jini Technology Starter Kit (TSK), 337

  Jlint debugger, 281

  LEGO educational branch, 6

  LEGO Java Operating System (leJOS) debuggers, 281

  LEGO Java Operating System (leJOS) downloading, 170

  LEGO Java Operating System (leJOS) source code, 312

librcx library, 313

MINDSTORMS SDK 2.0 download, 17

neural networks code, 151, 162

NQC language, 93, 96

RCXPort API source code, 82

Rossum Playhouse, 260

sensors, 24, 184

Simlink, 260

subsumption architecture, 204

Syngress, 5

win32com.dll native library, 46, 49, 112–113

Win32Driver, 66

win32usb.dll native library, 112–113

Windows

  access to native ports, 43

  CygWin, 177

  Cygwin system, 313

  Java Communications Extension API (JCE API), 32

  Java extensions location, 48

  Java runtime *(jview)*, 49

  javax.comm.properties configuration file, 37, 47–49

  LEGO Java Operating System (leJOS) environment, 171

  native library, 46–47

  ports, identifying, 71

  RCXPort and USB, 86

  Universal Serial Bus (USB) port, 120

  Universal Serial Bus (USB) tower driver, 64–65

  USB support in leJOS, 250

  win32com.dll native library, 46, 49, 112–113

  Win32Driver, 66

  win32usb.dll native library, 112–113

Writing to serial ports, 54–56

X

XON/XOFF, 45

SYNGRESS PUBLISHING LICENSE AGREEMENT